Introducing government

Introducing government

A reader

Edited by
Ralph Young, Chris Binns, Martin Burch,
Douglas Jaenicke *and* Michael Moran

Manchester University Press
Manchester and New York
Distributed exclusively in the USA and Canada by St. Martin's Press

Copyright selection and editorial material © Ralph Young, Chris Binns, Martin Burch, Douglas Jaenicke and Michael Moran 1993.

While copyright in the selection and editorial material is vested in the editors, copyright in individual chapters belongs to their respective authors, and no chapter may be reproduced wholly or in part without the express permission in writing of both author and publisher.

Published by Manchester University Press
Oxford Road, Manchester M13 9PL, UK
and Room 400, 175 Fifth Avenue,
New York, NY 10010, USA

Distributed exclusively in the USA and Canada
by St. Martin's Press, Inc.,
175 Fifth Avenue, New York, NY 10010, USA

British Library Cataloguing-in-Publication Data
A catalogue record for this book is available from the British Library

Library of Congress Cataloging-in-Publication Data
Introducing government : a reader / edited by Ralph Young ... [et al.].
    p.   cm.
    ISBN 0-7190-3980-0. – ISBN 0-7190-3981-9 (pbk.)
    1. Comparative government.   2. Great Britain – Politics and government.   3. United States – Politics and government.   4. Soviet Union – Politics and government.   I. Young, Ralph (C. Ralph)
JF51.I575   1993   93–19688
320.3 – dc20   CIP

ISBN 0 7190 3980 0 *hardback*
ISBN 0 7190 3981 9 *paperback*

Typeset in Hong Kong
by Best-set Typesetter Ltd.

Printed in Great Britain
by Redwood Books, Trowbridge

Lyf

Contents

Preface

Introducing Government has acquired a design that is both ambitious and modest. As the field of political science has evolved over the past two generations, it has developed a diversity and breadth which would be difficult for an introductory reader like ours to fully reflect. We have therefore had to set ourselves a more limited set of objectives in assembling a collection of materials that would provide an appropriate accompaniment to a foundation course in the study of politics. Yet within these limits, we have sought to apply rigorous criteria of quality and relevance in selecting readings that would assist students in gaining an appreciation of the nature of contemporary political analysis.

The concerns which have guided our choice of contents for the *Reader* have been shaped by our own experience at the University of Manchester with the teaching of Government I, an introductory course in comparative politics that has undergone considerable rethinking and adaptation in recent years – not least in response to a rapidly expanding student enrollment, which has climbed to a level exceeding 700.

We have thus recognized the benefits to be derived for students from a *comparative* approach by directing attention to three divergent types of political system – the parliamentary system which has evolved in Britain, the presidential system found in the United States, and the socialist 'democracy' of the former Soviet Union. The emphasis on political systems to which a 'democratic' label can be attached provides us, in turn, with a unifying thematic focus. Our introductory section includes several contributions which illuminate the complex character of the democratic polity by subjecting it to a varying set of analytical lenses – here, those used respectively by the pluralist, elitist, and Marxist approaches. The following case-studies of Britain and the United States offer examples of stable liberal democracies whose historical development has diverged substantially and whose modern political systems provide contrasting models of democratic practice. The inclusion of the Soviet

Union underlines the conflicting intepretations to which 'democracy' can give rise in practice. The emergence of the Soviet state from the revolutionary turbulence of 1917 and its subsequent evolution (and spectacular collapse in 1991) also enable us to explore the inherent tensions between democratic and non-democratic structures in twentieth-century societies undergoing rapid social and economic modernization.

In our selections, we have sought to place stress not simply on supplying information concerning the institutional frameworks distinguishing our three cases but on how these institutions operate in practice, that is, on the *dynamics* of contemporary political systems. This should enable students to acquire an understanding of the manner in which the character of political institutions is shaped by the political and social forces which act through them as well as by the formal constitutional, legal or organizational blueprints that define their functions and powers.

If the current *Reader* is a by-product of our experience of introducing students to the study of comparative politics at Manchester, it is also a lineal descendant of a prior collection, *Three Political Systems* (Manchester, 1985); two of the current editorial team, Martin Burch and Doug Jaenicke, served as co-editors of the earlier work (with our late colleague John Gardner). There is continuity between these two volumes in the countries which have been selected for extended treatment and also in some of the contributions used; of the forty individual selections that form the contents of *Introducing Government*, nine have been held over from the earlier volume because of their continuing usefulness. On the other hand, we have added an introductory section on the study of politics and the nature of the democratic state as well as a substantial body of fresh material reflecting shifts in the focus of our own concerns, current developments in scholarship, or recent changes in the political systems we have selected for study.

Inevitably in an enterprise of this nature, difficult choices have had to be made both as to what to include and what to omit. Considerations of length and cost, and ultimately of the need to ensure the volume's accessibility for an undergraduate audience, have prevented the coverage of certain topics which we would otherwise have included; federalism and the Supreme Court in the American case and local government in the British are examples readily at hand. The text and footnotes of our selections have undergone extensive editing to ensure a sufficiently austere average length per contribution to permit the breadth of coverage we felt essential to our overall objectives. Because the original length of several of our contributions pointed to the likelihood that they would require considerable trimming, we resolved, as an editorial strategy, to avoid the use of dots (. . .)* to indicate individual deletions; in this case, the claims of scholarly precision seemed clearly out-

* In article 1.4, dots have been included at the request of the publisher.

weighed by the need to maximise clarity and continuity in the presentation of the materials.

Ralph Young
Chris Binns
Martin Burch
Doug Jaenicke
Michael Moran

February 1993

Part One
Theories of politics

Introduction

Politics is an everyday activity and almost everyone has some political views. The study of politics involves the analysis of those views, and the collection and analysis of evidence bearing on political activity. Like any other academic discipline, political science develops its own specialized language – terms which have acquired particular meanings, and which can be used by those who study the discipline to communicate with each other. This opening section is about some of the most important terms that we have to use in the study of politics, and about the debates to which those terms have given rise.

At the heart of political inquiry lie two central concepts: the concept of politics itself; and the concept of power – its meaning, its distribution and its justification. Any introduction to politics has to begin with a clarification of the nature of the activity under study. The boundaries of that activity are not immediately clear. In its widest sense, we instinctively recognize politics as an activity which involves the exercise of power in the taking of decisions, which involves one individual or group of individuals arriving at a decision, often at the expense of others. Viewed thus, 'politics' is a universal activity which takes place in all sorts of social settings: decisions are made in churches, families, even in tennis clubs. But the discipline of politics has been concerned with politics with a capital 'P': with politics in institutions known variously as states and governments. This concentration is partly a matter of expediency and partly a matter of intellectual principle. If we tried to study politics everywhere – in any institution where decisions are taken – our field of study would become impossibly large. But we also have positive reasons for concentrating on governments and states, for it is in these institutions that we find the greatest concentrations of power in the modern world.

A focus on government and the state, however, begs an important question: how do we distinguish the nature of government and the state from other important institutions in society, and what exactly is the difference between 'state' and 'government'? These questions are vital in defining the boundary of political study, and in identifying the nature of the institutions at the heart of the discipline. Our first extract, from Robert Dahl's famous introduction to political analysis, *Modern Political Analysis*, explores the nature of these questions, and in particular the features that distinguish particular *governments* from those creations called *states*.

The most important questions to be answered about any system of government concern the second key concept of political science, power. They are: who controls the system of government; and what arguments exist to justify different systems of control? In our time, perhaps the most important answers to those questions have come from theorists of *democracy*. Until comparatively recently in the history of political thought democracy was a dubious notion. From the time of the great political philosopher of ancient Greece, Aristotle (384–322 BC), to that of the great nineteenth-century English political philosopher John Stuart Mill (1806–73), it was viewed with hostility or, at best, suspicion. In the twentieth century, however, the notion that democracy was the best system of government became widely accepted, especially in the rich and powerful states of North America and Western Europe. But the widespread acceptance of democracy as a principle which could guide and justify how power in government should be distributed has not stilled debates. It is in these debates that we can follow, not only arguments about democracy itself, but about the nature of power in a modern state.

The first and most obvious debate concerns the meaning of the term democracy. The word has Greek roots, denoting rule by the people. This in turn raises a wide range of questions: what does an entitlement to popular rule mean in practice, and who, exactly, are 'the people'? Reading 1.2, from Barry Holden's *Understanding Liberal Democracy*, examines precisely these issues, and sketches the Greek origins of the term. The Greek origins of democratic government are important historically, but of course democracy in our time is practised under very different conditions from those existing in ancient Greece. One of the most important differences concerns the scale of systems of government. Greek democracy, insofar as it was practised, was conducted in small communities. That form of democracy is largely unknown in today's world, and is completely unknown in the government of the modern nation state, where the people are usually numbered in their tens or even hundreds of millions. That change in scale has transformed democratic politics. The origins of the transformation lie in the development of the theory of representative government. In the theory of representative government the direct rule of the people is displaced by rule through a small group 'representing' the wider community, for instance in a parliament. The theory of representative government, as it first developed, had little to do with achieving democracy. Indeed, representative government was a barrier against democratic politics, a device for putting power into the hands of a small group of politicians who would channel, and suppress, the demands coming from the wider society.

But since the middle of the nineteenth century the right to vote in elections that choose representatives has in many nations been extended to the whole adult population. Thus representative government has formally become democratic. This historical shift from direct democracy on the model of communities in ancient Greece to representative democracy is identified by Robert Dahl as one of the 'great transformations' in political history. Reading 1.3, from his study of *Democracy and Its Critics*, explores the implications of this shift. Is it possible for the people at large really to exercise power when they do not directly participate in government, but instead elect the governors? Dahl has labelled such a system 'polyarchy'. The word has Greek roots, and signifies a system of rule by small groups, called elites. But the need to win elections in which the whole adult population takes part means that these elites have to compete for the support of the people, and thus are compelled to act in a way responsive to their wishes. Polyarchy is therefore a system of rule by competing elites who have to be responsive to the popular will.

Advocacy of democratic government was once confined to radicals and revolutionaries. Nowadays support for its principles comes from right across the political spectrum. When traditional conservatives and supporters of Marxism all claim, sincerely, to be democrats, can we say that there exists any set of core values which may be described as distinctive to democracy, and, if so, what is the relationship of these values to the historical legacy of democratic theory? These are the questions raised in reading 1.4, which is taken from David Held's book, *Models of Democracy*.

Democracy, once a marginal and dangerously radical theory of government, is now conventionally accepted across a wide range of states, and across the gamut of political creeds. But it has not carried all before it, even at the level of theory. During the closing decades of the nineteenth century and the early decades of the twentieth century there emerged, chiefly on the continent of Europe, a group of trenchant critics of democracy. They denied both the possibility that it could be practised, and the desirability of so doing. These critics are often called the 'classical elitists', because they asserted that elitism – rule by a few – was a better and more realistic theory of government than anything provided by democracy. They remain important in contemporary debates about power because they raised awkward, still relevant questions: how is it possible to have popular control when most people seem to have neither the inclination nor the skill to practise government; how can the people at large exercise influence when government is a web of big, complex organisations in which only a small minority of the population can participate? Reading 1.5, from Geraint Parry's book *Political Elites*, surveys the core ideas developed by the classical elite theorists.

The elitist critique is developed from a position of hostility to democratic theory or practice. But there is another influential body of criticism whose attitude to democracy is less unsympathetic. This work draws on Marxism, the body of work associated with the writings of the German revolutionary social theorist Karl Marx (1818–83). Marx argued that control of economic resources determined control of political power; that the chief social groups – classes – were defined by whether or not they controlled the major economic resources in a society; and that in capitalist societies a small class of capitalists owned and controlled the most important economic resources, and thus ultimately also dominated government. In the modern world the most important democracies – notably the United States of America – also have capitalist economies. Modern observers sympathetic to Marxism therefore argue that it is impossible for such systems to be truly democratic: because economic resources are controlled by a minority of capitalists it follows that, whatever the formal rules, power will ultimately rest with that minority, whose interests in turn conflict with those of the mass of non-capitalists. That is the essence of the critical account of American democracy offered in reading 1.6, which is extracted from a larger analysis by Joshua Cohen and Joel Rogers. As that extract shows, however, analyses of democratic politics influenced by the Marxist tradition are far from being unremittingly hostile. There are two reasons for this. First, both Marxism and democratic theory share a common historical identity. Democratic theory, like Marxism, emerged as a radical and critical body of ideas. Marxists appeal to this tradition of radical democracy, rather than rejecting the appeal of democracy in general. Second, as Cohen and Rogers make plain, modern Marxist theory does not reject the relevance of democratic procedures, such as competitive elections and universal suffrage. It argues, however, that such procedures, while they modify the workings of a capitalist society, must always struggle against the fundamental inequalities of capitalism.

Michael Moran

1.1 Government and the state

Robert A. Dahl

In every society, people tend to develop more or less standard expectations about social behavior in various situations. One learns how to behave as a host or a guest, a parent or grandparent, a 'good loser,' a soldier, a bank clerk, a prosecutor, a judge, and so on. Patterns like these, in which a number of people share roughly similar expectations about behaviour in particular situations, are called *roles*. We all play various roles and frequently shift from one role to another rapidly.

Whenever a political system is complex and stable, political roles develop. Perhaps the most obvious political roles are played by persons who create, interpret, and enforce rules that are binding on members of the political system. These roles are *offices*, and the collection of offices in a political system constitutes the government of that system. At any given moment, of course, these offices, or roles, are (aside from vacancies) filled by particular individuals, concrete persons – Senator Foghorn, Judge Cranky, Mayor Twimbly. But in many systems the roles remain much the same even when they are played by a succession of individuals. To be sure, different actors may – and usually do – interpret the role of Hamlet or Othello in different ways, sometimes in radically different ways. So, too, with political roles. Jefferson, Jackson, Lincoln, Theodore Roosevelt, Wilson, and Franklin Roosevelt, for example, each enlarged the role of president beyond what he had inherited from his predecessors by building new expectations in people's minds about what a president should or legitimately could do in office. 'There are as many different ways of being President,' Nelson Polsby asserts, 'as there are men willing to fill the office.'[1] Yet expectations as to the proper role of the president also limit the extent to which they can make it what they wish – a fact dramatized by President Johnson's decision in 1968 not to seek re-election because, in effect, he could no longer play the presidential role in the way that he believed the office required.

But – a reader might ask – in defining *government* as we have just done, don't we create a new problem for ourselves? If there is a great variety of political systems – from trade unions and universities to countries and international organizations – what about *the* Government? After all, in the United States, as in most other countries, when you speak of *the* Government everyone seems to know what you mean. Of all the governments in the various associations of a particular territory, generally one is in some way recognized as *the* Government. How does *the* Government differ from other governments? Consider three possible answers:

(1) *The* Government pursues 'higher' and 'nobler' purposes than other governments. There are least three difficulties with this proposal. First, because people disagree about what the 'higher' or 'nobler' purposes are, and even whether a given purpose is or is not being pursued at any given moment, this criterion might not be very helpful in trying to decide whether this or that government is *the* Government. Second, despite the fact that people often disagree over how to rank purposes or values and may even hold that *the* Government is pursuing evil ends, they still agree on what is and what is not *the* Government. An anarchist does not doubt that he is being oppressed by *the* Government. Third, what about bad Governments? For example, do democratic and totalitarian governments *both* pursue noble purposes? That point seems logically absurd.

Our first proposed answer, then, confuses the problem of defining Government with the more difficult and more important task of deciding on the criteria for a 'good' or 'just' Government. Before we can decide what the *best* Government is, we must know first what *the* Government is.

(2) Aristotle suggested another possibility: *The* Government is distinguished by the character of the association to which it pertains – namely, a political association that is self-sufficient, in the sense that it possesses all the qualities and resources necessary for a good life. This definition suffers from some of the same difficulties as the first. Moreover, if it were strictly applied, we should have to conclude that no Governments exist! Aristotle's idealized interpretation of the city-state was very far from reality even in his day. Athens was not self-sufficient culturally, economically, or militarily. In fact, it was quite unable to guarantee its own peace or independence; without allies, it could not even maintain the freedom of its own citizens. What was true of the Greek city-states is of course equally true today.

(3) *The* Government is any government that successfully upholds a claim to the exclusive regulation of the legitimate use of physical force in enforcing its rules within a given territorial area.[2] The political system made up of the residents of that territorial area and the Government of the area is a *State*.[3]

This definition immediately suggests three questions:

(1) Can't individuals who aren't Government officials ever legitimately use force? What about parents who spank their children? The answer is, of course, that the Government of a State does not necessarily *monopolize* the use of force, but it has the exclusive authority to set the limits within which force may legitimately be used. The Governments of most States permit private individuals to use force in some circumstances. For example, although many Governments forbid cruel or excessive punishment of children, most permit parents to spank their own offspring. Boxing is permitted in many countries.

(2) What about criminals who go uncaught? After all, no country is free of assault, murder, rape, and other forms of violence, and criminals sometimes escape the law. The point is, however, that the claim of the Government of

the State to regulate violence and force is successfully upheld, in the sense that few people would seriously contest the exclusive right of the State to punish criminals. Although criminal violence exists, it is not legitimate.

(3) What about circumstances of truly widespread violence and force, such as civil war or revolution? In this case no single answer will suffice. During some periods, no State may exist at all, since no government is capable of upholding its claim to the exclusive regulation of the legitimate use of physical force. Several governments may contest for the privilege over the same territory as was the case in Lebanon following the outbreak of religious wars in 1975. Or what was formerly a territory ruled by the Government of one State may now be divided and ruled by the Governments of two or more States, with gray stateless areas where they meet.

We can be reasonably sure of one thing: when large numbers of people in a particular territory begin to doubt or deny the claim of the Government to regulate force, then the existing State is in peril of dissolution.

Abridged from Robert A. Dahl (1991), *Modern Political Analysis*, 5th edition, pp. 9–11. Reprinted by permission of Prentice Hall, Englewood Cliffs, NJ.

Notes

1 See N. Polsby (1976), *Congress and the Presidency*, 3rd edn., Prentice-Hall, Englewood Cliffs, NJ. Polsby compares the presidents from Franklin Roosevelt to Gerald Ford. See also James David Barber (1972), *The Presidential Character: Predicting Performance in the White House*, Prentice-Hall, Englewood Cliffs, NJ.
2 Adapted from Max Weber (1947), *The Theory of Social and Economic Organization*, trans. A. M. Henderson and Talcott Parsons, Oxford University Press, New York, p. 154, by substituting 'exclusive regulation' for 'monopoly' and 'rules' for 'its order'.
3 Capitalized here to avoid confusion with constituent states in federal systems.

1.2 Defining democracy

Barry Holden

The word 'democracy' was first used in the fifth century BC by the Greek historian Herodotus; it combined the Greek words *demos*, meaning 'the people', and *kratein*, meaning 'to rule'. Abraham Lincoln's famous definition of 'democracy' was 'government of the people, by the people, for the people'. Phrases such as 'government by the people' and 'rule by the people' occur very commonly as definitions of 'democracy'. The definition can be made more precise – or more illuminating – by elaborating on the relevant notion of government or rule and assuming that a crucial element in such a notion is the idea of making and implementing decisions. One can also 'cover' certain ambiguities and difficulties by 'escape clauses'. In this way the following definition can be proposed: a democracy is a political system in which the whole people, positively or negatively, make, and are entitled to make, the basic determining decisions on important matters of public policy. We shall end this section by commenting on this definition and on some of the issues it raises (for a fuller discussion see Holden (1974)).

The first comment concerns the specification of 'entitlement' ('the people ... make, *and are entitled to make*, the basic ... decisions ...'). It is this entitlement to, as well as the actuality of, decision making by the people that distinguishes a democracy from, say, a weak or ailing dictatorship. A system in which the ruler gives way to the people's wishes, because of the threat of riot, insurrection or whatever, is one in which the people are making the basic determining decisions. But such a system is not a democracy because the people are not *entitled* to make these decisions. The entitlement referred to comes from a constitution, or other system of basic norms, which *authorises* the making of the basic determining decision by the people. It may not always be obvious what the constitution lays down. It might be argued that in Britain the 'constitution' – if such it can be called – does not of itself authorise decision making by the people. Nonetheless such authorisation is given by widely and strongly held beliefs about the proper functioning of the political system, and these are sustained by, and reflected in, key conventions of the constitution – such as the convention that a government resigns if its party is beaten at a general election.

The converse is equally important. Entitlement alone is not enough: in order to qualify as a democracy the people must *actually* make, as well as being entitled to make, the basic political decisions. It must be recognised that it is possible to ask whether the people actually do make the basic decisions in political systems, such as the British and American, in which there is no doubt that they are entitled to do so, and hence whether they really are democracies. Systems with the forms of democracy are not necessarily democracies.

A second comment concerns the notion of 'basic determining decisions on important matters of public policy'. The phrase 'basic determining decisions' is more or less self-explanatory. The reference is to basic decisions which actually determine courses of events and from which subsidiary decisions and actions flow. To take an example from personal life, a decision to go on holiday which results in a holiday – that is, which results in the actual occurrence of the complex of decisions, actions and events that make up a holiday – could be referred to as a basic determining decision. 'Basic determining decisions on important matters of public policy' are basic political decisions; the significance of the term 'important' will be taken up in a moment. A body which makes such decisions holds supreme political power.

Such bodies are often referred to as being sovereign, or as possessing sovereignty. Democracy, indeed, is often characterised as a political system in which the people are sovereign, or in which there is popular sovereignty. There are difficulties with the concept of sovereignty.[1] Not the least of these are the distinctions and overlaps between the ideas of supreme *power* and supreme *authority*[2] which concern the relationship, just discussed, between actually making, and being entitled to make, basic political decisions. Because of these difficulties some have suggested doing away with the concept of sovereignty. But its use is surely too widespread for this to be feasible; certainly the notion of popular sovereignty is very deeply embedded in democratic thought.

The third comment to be made about the proposed definition of 'democracy' relates to the 'escape clauses' used to 'cover' variations of meaning. Thus the phrase 'decisions on *important* matters of public policy' covers a gradation of views about the proper role of popular decision making. At one extreme are conceptions of democracy in which the people make the basic determining decisions on a few salient matters only – essentially on the appointment of governors and the broadest, and only the broadest, of outlines of the policies they are to follow. At the other extreme are conceptions in which – with the aid, perhaps, of devices such as referenda – the people make the basic decisions on all but the most routine of matters. Similarly the phrase 'whether positively or negatively' is used to cover differing notions about the origination of policy. On the one hand there is the 'positive' conception that policy should originate with the people: the notion that the people initiate policy proposals. On the other hand the 'negative' conception sees the people merely responding to policy proposals. Here the idea is that they choose among proposals that are put to them by those who would be their governors: the people then do not initiate policy, they consent to policies that are initiated elsewhere.

The meaning of 'the people'

The final comment to be made about our proposed definition of 'democracy' concerns 'the people'. This is, of course, a crucial concept. But it is also one which incorporates notions that co-exist only uneasily and which sometimes are in opposition to one another. This gives rise to differing ideas, loosely, though significantly, related together within the concept of the people. Here we need to indicate another difference of interpretation, which gives rise to differences of conception which cut across the individualist-corporate distinction. This difference concerns the proportion of a relevant society that is held to be included within the meaning of 'the people', the 'relevant society' in any particular case being the one which is subject to, and delimited by, the state whose democratic nature is being assessed.[3] It might be assumed that all the current members of the relevant society must be included within the people.

But straight away the qualification 'all _adult_ members' would usually be agreed. In fact the meaning of 'the people' has varied quite widely, and has not always included all adult members. In ancient Athens, often regarded as the original and archetypal democracy, only a minority of the society was included: aliens, slaves and women were excluded. Women – constituting a good 50 percent of any relevant society – were given the vote only relatively recently in modern democracies: in 1920 in America, in 1918 (but only in 1928 with the same age qualification as men) in Britain, and as recently as 1971 in Swiss national elections. Again, from Aristotle onwards the term 'the people' has had a sense in which it means 'the poor' or 'the poor people' (in Aristotle's case 'those of the poor who are not aliens, slaves or women'!) This meaning is echoed in those Marxist-Leninist notions where democracy is equated with the dictatorship of the proletariat. It is also reflected in anti-democratic thought, where the people have often been characterised as the mob. By way of contrast, 'the people' sometimes meant the middle classes rather than the poor – the term then being used to refer to those who had a stake in society and were thereby properly members of it, i.e. property owners.[4]

What is the upshot of this variation in meaning? Are political systems with widely differing proportions of society having a share in political power all to be counted as democracies, because different meanings are given to 'the people'? According to Schumpeter, for example, it would seem that more or less any kind of political system in which governmental power depends on winning competitive elections could be counted as a democracy (Schumpeter 1976). Even where there is clearly rule by a minority Schumpeter maintains that is a democracy provided those who hold political power *consider themselves* to constitute 'the people': even South Africa could count as a democracy! This sort of view is surely unacceptable. And yet it would appear difficult to deny that the meaning of 'the people' is an arbitrary matter if one accepts any exclusions. We have already mentioned that the exclusion of non-adults is very commonly accepted. Is this not as arbitrary as counting out any other category – be it women, the rich, the poor, slaves, those with a certain colour of skin, or whatever? The answer to this, it can be argued, is provided by three considerations.

First, there has been a historical change of meaning. The development of democratic theory was tied in with the growth of the demand for universal suffrage. Whatever used to be the case, in democratic thought today 'the people' almost invariably means virtually the whole adult population (and even the democratic status of ancient Athens itself tends to be queried because of its 'undemocratic' conception of 'the people').

Second, there are good reasons for this change – for this enlargement – of meaning. They are reasons which overlap with the arguments for democracy itself. In essence they are the grounds for the view that as large a proportion as possible of the members of a society should take part in the making of basic political decisions. Essentially, democrats hold that all those who are not obviously unfit to do so should take part in political decision making. Now although Schumpeter, for example, argues that such fitness 'is a matter of opinion and degree' (Schumpeter 1976), the point is that democrats can and do reach some kind of objectively based agreement on this matter. This is reflected in those limits to membership of the people that *are* commonly prescribed, even by democrats: it is generally accepted that there are compelling reasons for not giving the vote to children, the insane and – less certainly – criminals. There are two points to note. The first is that these exclusions reflect very general agreement about what makes some people unfit for political decision making: that they are incapable of the relevant thought processes (criminals are sometimes held to have excluded themselves from the community, but here the agreement is less widespread). Moreover – and this is the crucial point – although there might be some individuals whom all would agree are unfit for political decision making, children and the insane (and possibly criminals) are the only *categories* of individuals about which there is this type of agreement. The second point to note is that a dispute about the precise *location* of the boundary of a category does not imply dispute about it as a category of individuals to be excluded. Disagreement about how much 'irrationality' constitutes insanity, and what age marks the beginning of adulthood – 18, 21 or whatever – does not call into question agreement about the exclusion of the insane and children from political decision making. No one would give the vote to three-year-olds.

The third consideration behind the view that the democratic conception of 'the people' is non-arbitrary and legitimate is more complex. But let us put the matter as simply as possible. In liberal democratic theory conceptions of 'the people' are generally 'individualist'. We shall be discussing this later, but the key point is that according to such conceptions 'the people' means simply a collection of individuals, and this is all it can mean. The question then arises: which individuals? And some are excluded – as we have just seen. However, 'corporate' conceptions of the people also exist. Here the people is a corporate entity equivalent to, having the same 'boundaries' as, the relevant society. As such the people is a body consisting not only of the individual members of a society at a particular moment in time, but also of the past and future members; as well as the institutions, structures and culture within which such individuals find themselves. Just as, say, a regiment consists of more than the individuals who happen to be serving in it at any particular time: its past and future membership and its history, traditions, customs and so on are crucial features of its existence. Indeed, how else could you distinguish it *as* a regiment or as a particular regiment? Now, since such corporate conceptions of the people embrace the whole of society, all individuals within a society at any particular time tend automatically to be included. These conceptions occur outside liberal democratic theory. Non-liberal democratic theory contains such conceptions and they also occur within non- or anti-democratic theory. But the point is that they can be combined with the idea that supreme authority resides in the people. In contrast to the liberal democratic idea, however, it is not then held that this supreme authority entitles the people to make policy decisions. Rather the people's authority confers legitimacy on those who do make decisions. Decision-makers symbolically represent[5] the people perhaps – as in some medieval conceptions of kingship. Since there is no question of decisions being made by the people, the question of fitness for decision making does not arise and all individuals can quite happily be included within the conception of 'the people'. Here, then, is a concept of 'the people' as possessing supreme authority and quite clearly including all individuals within its meaning. True, this concept is not part of democratic or, at any rate, liberal democratic theory; but, because of the shared idea of supreme authority, it influences concepts within democratic theory. And it tends to legitimise the most inclusive notions of the proportion of individuals that are to be counted as an integral part of 'the people'.

  The dominant meaning of 'the people', then, in the definition of 'democracy' includes all – or virtually all – the adult population. But we should recognise that there is also a secondary meaning. The notion of 'the people' meaning 'the poor people' has been referred to already. It has been so persistent, however, that this idea of 'the common people' must be regarded as a meaning – albeit a subsidiary one – in its own right, as in the expression 'a man of the people'.

Abridged from Barry Holden (1988), *Understanding Liberal Democracy*, Philip Allan, Oxford, pp. 5–10. Reprinted by permission of Harvester Wheatsheaf.

Notes

1 On the notion of sovereignty see, for example, Stankiewicz (1969) and Hinsley (1986).
2 See, for example, Holden (1974), pp. 10–11.
3 This statement, in fact, brushes over some quite troublesome difficulties – see, for example, Dahl and Tufte (1973) and Whelan (1983) – quite apart from the question of whether democracy is necessarily a form of state.
4 See, for example, Spearman (1957).
5 On 'symbolic representation' see, for example, Birch (1972).

References

Birch, A. H. (1972), *Representation*, Macmillan, London.
Dahl, R. A. and E. Tufte (1973), *Size and Democracy*, Stanford University Press, Stanford, CA.
Hinsley, F. H. (1986), *Sovereignty*, 2nd edn, Cambridge University Press, Cambridge.
Holden, B. (1974), *The Nature of Democracy*, Nelson, London.
Schumpeter, J. (1976), *Capitalism, Socialism and Democracy*, Allen and Unwin, London.
Spearman, D. (1957), *Democracy in England*, Rockliff, London.

Stankiewicz, M. J., ed. (1976), *In Defence of Sovereignty*, Oxford University Press, New York.

Whelan, F. G. (1983), 'Prologue: democratic theory and the boundary problem' in J. R. Pennock and J. W. Chapman, eds., *Liberal Democracy*, Nomos XXV, New York University Press, New York.

1.3   Democracy and polyarchy

Robert A. Dahl

Modern democratic ideas and practices are a product of two major trans-formations in political life. The first swept into ancient Greece and Rome in the fifth century BC, and receded from the Mediterranean world before the beginning of the Christian era. A thousand years later some of the city-states of medieval Italy were also transformed into popular governments, which however receded during the Renaissance. In both cases, the locus of demo-cratic and republican ideas and practices was the city-state. In both cases, popular governments were ultimately submerged in imperial or oligarchic rule.

The second major transformation, to which we are the heirs, began with the gradual shift of the idea of democracy away from its historic locus in the city-state to the vaster domain of the nation, country, or national state. As a politi-cal movement and sometimes as an achievement – not merely an idea – in the nineteenth century this second transformation acquired great momentum in Europe and the English-speaking world. During the twentieth century the idea of democracy ceased to be, as it had been heretofore, a parochial doctrine embraced only in the West by a small proportion of the world's people and actualized for a few centuries at most over a tiny portion of the earth. Though it is far from a worldwide achievement, in the last half-century democracy in the modern sense has gained almost universal force as a political idea, an aspiration, and an ideology.

This second great movement of democratic ideas and practices has, how-ever, profoundly transformed the way in which the notion of a democratic process has been, or can be, achieved. The most powerful, though not the only, cause of this transformation is the shift in its locus from the city-state to the national state. Beyond the national state now lies the possibility of even larger and more inclusive supranational political associations.

For over two thousand years – from classical Greece to the eighteenth century – it had been a dominant assumption of Western political thought that in democratic and republican states the size of the citizen body and of the ter-ritory of the state must both be small, indeed by modern standards minuscule.

The idea and the ideals of the polis, the small unitary city-state of kinfolk and friends, lived on well after city-states themselves had all but disappeared as a historical phenomenon.

As a result of the rise of national states, from about the seventeenth century onward the idea of democracy would have had no feasible future if its locus had not been transferred from the city-state to the national state. In the *Social Contract* (1762), Rousseau still clung to the older vision of a people wielding final control over the government of a state that was small enough in population and territory to enable all the citizens to gather together in order to exercise their sovereignty in a single popular assembly. Yet less than a century later the belief that the nation or the country was the 'natural' unit of sovereign government was so completely taken for granted that in his *Considerations on Representative Government* [1861] John Stuart Mill, stating in a single sentence what to him and his readers could be taken as a self-evident truth, dismissed the conventional wisdom of over two thousand years by rejecting the assumption that self-government necessarily required a unit small enough for the whole body of citizens to assemble.

Even Mill, however, failed to see fully how radically the great increase in scale would necessarily transform the institutions and practices of democracy. At least eight important consequences have followed from that epochal change in the locus of democracy. Taken together they set the modern democratic state in sharp contrast to the older ideals and practices of democratic and republican governments.

Representation

The most obvious change, of course, is that representatives have largely displaced the citizen's assembly of ancient democracy. Representation, in origins a non-democratic institution, [has come] to be adopted as an essential element of modern democracy .

The first successful efforts to democratize the national state typically occurred in countries with existing legislative bodies that were intended to represent certain fairly distinctive social interests: aristocrats, commoners, the landed interest, the commercial interest, and the like. As movements toward greater democratization gained force, the design for a 'representative' legislature did not have to be spun from gossamer fibers of abstract democratic ideas; concrete legislatures and representatives, undemocratic though they were, already existed. As a consequence, the advocates of reform sought to make existing legislatures more 'representative' by broadening the franchise, adopting an electoral system that would make members more representative of the electorate, and ensuring that elections were free and fairly conducted. In addition, they sought to ensure that the highest executive officer (whether president, prime minister, cabinet, or governor) would be chosen by a majority of the legislature or by the electorate at large.

Although this brief description of a general path to democratization cannot do justice to the many important variations in each country, something roughly along these lines took place in the first national states to be democratized. It took place, for example, in the American colonies prior to the revolution – a hundred-and-fifty-year period of pre-democratic development the importance of which is often underestimated – and, after independence, in the thirteen American states. To be sure, in designing the Articles of Confederation after independence, American leaders had to create a national congress virtually from scratch; and shortly thereafter the US Congress was cast in its more lasting form at the Constitutional Convention of 1787. Yet in designing the Constitution the delegates to the convention always assumed as a starting point the specific features of the British constitutional system – notably king, bicameral parliament, prime minister, and cabinet – even as they altered the British model to fit the novel conditions of a country formed from thirteen sovereign states and lacking both a monarch to serve as head of state and the hereditary peers needed for a house of lords.

In Britain, where the prime minister had already come to be dependent on the confidence of parliamentary majorities by the end of the eighteenth century, a major goal of democratizing movements from 1832 onward was to broaden the right to vote for members of Parliament and to ensure that parliamentary elections were fair and free. In the Scandinavian countries, where as in England legislative bodies had existed since the Middle Ages, the task was both to make the prime minister dependent on parliament (rather than the king), and to expand the suffrage for parliamentary elections. So too in Holland and Belgium. Although from the revolution in 1789 to the Third Republic in 1871 France followed a somewhat different path, what democratic movements demanded was not dissimilar to what was taking place elsewhere.

It would be a mistake, however, to interpret the democratization of existing legislative bodies as nothing more than ad hoc adaptations of existing institutions. Once the locus of democracy shifted to the national state, the logic of political equality, now applied to countries enormously greater than the city-state, clearly implied that most legislation would have to be enacted not by the assembled citizens but by their elected representatives. For it was as obvious then as now that, as the number of citizens increases beyond a rather small if imprecise limit, the proportion of citizens who can assemble together (or, even if they can, have an opportunity to participate by anything more than voting) must necessarily grow smaller and smaller. That observation was made repeatedly until, as with Mill, it could be utterly taken for granted. Yet, as Rousseau rightly foresaw in the *Social Contract*, representation was bound to alter the nature of citizenship and the democratic process. As we shall see, large-scale democracy lacks some of the potentialities of small-scale democracy.

Unlimited extension
Once representation was accepted as a solution, the barriers to the size of a democratic unit set by the limits of an assembly in a city-state were eliminated. In principle, no country could be too extensive, no population too vast for a

representative government. In 1787, the United States had a population of about four million, already gigantic by the standards of the ideal Greek polis. Some delegates to the Constitutional Convention daringly forecast a future United States with a hundred million or more inhabitants, a figure finally surpassed by 1915. In 1950, when India established its republican parliamentary system, its inhabitants numbered around 350 million. So far it has been impossible to specify a theoretical upper limit.

Limits on participatory democracy
As a direct consequence of greater size, however, some forms of political participation are *inherently* more limited in polyarchies than they were in city-states. I do not mean to say that participation in democratic or republican city-states actually achieved anything like the limits of its potentialities for participation. But theoretical possibilities existed in many ancient and medieval city-states that do not exist in a democratic country, even a relatively small country, because of the sheer magnitude of its citizen body and (of less importance) its territory. The theoretical limit of effective political participation, even with modern electronic means of communication, rapidly diminishes with scale.

Diversity
Although the relation between scale and diversity is not linear, the larger and more inclusive a political unit, the more its inhabitants tend to exhibit greater diversity in ways relevant to political life: in local and regional loyalties, ethnic and racial identities, religion, political beliefs and ideologies, occupations, lifestyles, and so on. The relatively homogeneous population of citizens united by common attachments to city, language, race, history, myth, gods, and religion, which was so conspicuous a part of the ancient city-state vision of democracy, now became for all practical purposes impossible.

Conflict
As a consequence of diversity, however, political cleavages are multiplied, political conflict is an inevitable aspect of political life, and political thought and practices tend to accept conflict as a normal and not aberrant feature of politics.

A striking symbol of the change is James Madison, who at the American Constitutional Convention in 1787, and later in his defense of it in *The Federalist*, met head-on the historical view, which was still reflected in anti-Federalist objections to the absurdity and iniquity of the attempt to form a democratic republic on such a grotesque scale as a federal union of the thirteen states would create. In a brilliant polemic, Madison contended that, because conflicts of interest were in the nature of man and society, and the expression of these conflicts could not be suppressed without suppressing freedom, the best cure for the mischiefs of faction was to enlarge the scale.

In contradiction to the classical vision, then, in which a more homogeneous body of citizens could be expected to share rather similar beliefs about the common good, and to act on those beliefs, the notion of the common good is stretched much more thinly in order to encompass the heterogeneous attachments, loyalties, and beliefs formed among a body of diverse citizens with a multiplicity of cleavages and conflicts. It is stretched so thinly, in fact, that we are compelled to ask whether a concept of the common good can now be much more than a poignant reminder of an ancient vision that irreversible change has made irrelevant to the conditions of modern political life.

Polyarchy

The change of scale and its consequences – representative government, greater diversity, the increase in cleavages and conflicts – helped to bring about the development of a set of political institutions that, taken together, distinguish modern representative democracy from all other political systems, whether non-democratic regimes or earlier democratic systems. This kind of political system has been called *polyarchy*.

Polyarchy can be understood in several ways: as a historical outcome of efforts to democratize and liberalize the political institutions of nation states; as a distinctive type of political order or regime different in important ways not only from non-democratic systems of all kinds but also from earlier small-scale democracies; as a system (à la Schumpeter) of political control in which the highest officials in the government of the state are induced to modify their conduct so as to win elections in political competition with other candidates, parties, and groups; as a system of political rights; or as a set of institutions necessary to the democratic process on a large scale. Though these ways of interpreting polyarchy are different in interesting and important ways, they are not inconsistent. They simply emphasize different aspects or consequences of the institutions that serve to distinguish polyarchal from non-polyarchal political orders.

Social and organizational pluralism

A further concomitant of the greater size of the political order and the consequences so far described – diversity, conflict, and polyarchy – is the existence in polyarchies of a significant number of social groups and organizations that are relatively autonomous with respect to one another and to the government itself: what has come to be called *pluralism* or, more specifically, social and organizational pluralism.

The expansion of individual rights

Although less directly related to the change in scale, one of the most striking differences between polyarchy and all earlier democratic and republican systems is the astounding expansion of individual rights that has occurred in countries with polyarchal governments.

In classical Greece, freedom was an attribute of membership in a particular city, within which a citizen was free by virtue of the rule of law and the right to participate in the decisions of the assembly. Arguably, in a small and relatively homogeneous group of citizens bound by ties of kinship, friendship, neighborhood, market, and civic identity, participating with one's fellow citizens in all the decisions affecting their common life is so fundamental and comprehensive a freedom that other rights and liberties lose much of their importance. Yet to offset this idealization it needs to be added that small communities are generally less renowned for their freedom than for their oppressiveness, particularly to nonconformists. Even Athens found itself unwilling to tolerate Socrates.

In countries with polyarchal governments the number and variety of individual rights that are legally specified and effectively enforced have increased with the passage of time. In addition, because citizenship in polyarchies has been expanded to include almost the entire adult population, virtually all adults are entitled to primary political rights; the slaves, metics, and women excluded from full citizenship in the Greek democracies have all gained the rights of citizenship in modern democratic countries.

The greater scale of society has undoubtedly made some contribution to the expansion of individual rights. For one thing, democracy on a large scale requires the institutions of polyarchy, and as we have seen these institutions necessarily include primary political rights that go well beyond those that citizens were entitled to in earlier democratic and republican orders. Moreover, the greater scale probably stimulates a concern for rights as alternatives to participation in collective decisions. For, as the social scale increases, each person necessarily knows and is known by an ever smaller proportion of all the people. Social ties and personal acquaintance among citizens give way to social distance and anonymity. In these circumstances, personal rights attached to citizenship – or simply to personhood – can ensure a sphere of personal freedom that participation in collective decisions cannot. Further, as diversity and political cleavages grow, individual rights may be seen as a substitute for political consensus. If conflicts of interests are normal and the outcomes of decisions are highly uncertain, personal rights provide a way of ensuring for everyone some free space that cannot be easily violated by ordinary political decisions.

Polyarchy

Polyarchy is a political order distinguished at the most general level by two broad characteristics: citizenship is extended to a relatively high proportion of adults, and the rights of citizenship include the opportunity to oppose and vote out the highest officials in the government. The first characteristic distinguishes polyarchy from more exclusive systems of rule in which, though opposition is permitted, governments and their legal oppositions are restricted to a small group, as was the case in Britain, Belgium, Italy, and other

countries before mass suffrage. The second characteristic distinguishes polyarchy from regimes in which citizenship does not include the right to oppose
and vote out the government, as in modern authoritarian regimes. More
specifically, polyarchy is a political order distinguished by the presence of
seven institutions, all of which must exist for a government to be classified as a
polyarchy.

1 *Elected officials.* Control over government decisions about policy is constitutionally vested in elected officials.
2 *Free and fair elections.* Elected officials are chosen in frequent and fairly
   conducted elections in which coercion is comparatively uncommon.
3 *Inclusive suffrage.* Practically all adults have the right to vote in the
   election of officials.
4 *Right to run for office.* Practically all adults have the right to run for
   elective offices in the government, though age limits may be higher for
   holding office than for the suffrage.
5 *Freedom of expression.* Citizens have a right to express themselves on

Table 1.3(1) *Polyarchy and the democratic process*

The following institutions...	*are necessary to satisfy the following criteria*
1 Elected officials 2 Free and fair elections	I. Voting equality
1 Elected officials 3 Inclusive suffrage 4 Right to run for office 5 Freedom of expression 6 Alternative information 7 Associational autonomy	II. Effective participation
5 Freedom of expression 6 Alternative information 7 Associational autonomy	III. Enlightened understanding
1 Elected officials 2 Free and fair elections 3 Inclusive suffrage 4 Right to run for office 5 Freedom of expression 6 Alternative information 7 Associational autonomy	IV. Control of the agenda
3 Inclusive suffrage 4 Right to run for office 5 Freedom of expression 6 Alternative information 7 Associational autonomy	V. Inclusion

political matters broadly defined, including criticism of officials, the government, the regime, the socioeconomic order, and the prevailing ideology.

6 *Alternative information.* Citizens have a right to seek out alternative sources of information. Moreover, alternative sources of information exist and are protected by laws.

7 *Associational autonomy.* To achieve their various rights, including those listed above, citizens also have a right to form relatively independent associations or organizations, including independent political parties and interest groups.

The relation between polyarchy and the requirements of the democratic process are set out in Table 1.3(1).

Appraising polyarchy
Typical of democrats who live in countries governed by authoritarian regimes is a fervent hope that their country will one day reach the threshold of polyarchy. Typical of democrats who live in countries long governed by polyarchy is a belief that polyarchy is insufficiently democratic and should be made more so. While intellectuals in democratic countries where polyarchy has existed without interruption for several generations or more often grow jaded with its institutions and contemptous of their shortcomings, it is not hard to understand why democrats deprived of these institutions find them highly desirable, warts and all. For polyarchy provides a broad array of human rights and liberties that no actually existing real world alternative to it can match. Integral to polyarchy itself is a generous zone of freedom and control that cannot be deeply or persistently invaded without destroying polyarchy itself. And because people in democratic countries have a liking for other rights, liberties, and empowerments, that essential zone is enlarged even more. Although the institutions of polyarchy do not guarantee the ease and vigor of citizen participation that could exist, in principle, in a small city-state, nor ensure that governments are closely controlled by the citizens or that policies invariably correspond with the desires of a majority of citizens, they make it unlikely in the extreme that a government will long pursue policies that deeply offend a majority of citizens. If citizen control over collective decisions is more anaemic than the robust control they would exercise if the dream of participatory democracy were ever realized, the capacity of citizens to exercise a veto over the re-election and policies of elected officials is a powerful and frequently exercised means for preventing officials from imposing policies objectionable to many citizens.

Compared then with its alternatives, historical and actual, polyarchy is one of the most extraordinary of all human artifacts. Yet it unquestionably falls well short of achieving the democratic process. From a democratic point of view, many questions can be raised about the institutions of large-scale democracy in the national state as they exist today. The most important of these are, in my view, the following:

1 In the conditions of the modern and postmodern world how, if at all, can we realize the possibilities of political participation that were theoretically present, though often not fully achieved in practice, in small-scale democracies and republics?
2 Does polyarchy presuppose conditions that most countries lack and will continue to lack? Are most countries therefore unsuitable for polyarchy and prone instead to democratic breakdown or authoritarian rule?
3 Is large-scale *democracy* possible at all, in fact, or do tendencies toward bureaucratization and oligarchy necessarily rob it of its essential meaning and justification?
4 Does the pluralism inherent in large-scale democracy lethally enfeeble the prospects for achieving the common good? In fact, does a *common* good really exist to any significant degree?
5 Finally, would it be possible to move beyond the historic threshold of polyarchy to a more completed attainment of the democratic process? In short, given the limits and possibilities of our world, is a third transformation a realistic possibility?

Abridged from Robert A. Dahl (1989), *Democracy and Its Critics*, pp. 213–24. Reprinted by permission of Yale University Press, New Haven.

1.4 Contemporary models of democracy

David Held

The dispute over the contemporary meaning of democracy has generated an extraordinary diversity of democratic models: from technocratic visions of government to conceptions of social life marked by extensive political participation. . . .

New Right thinkers have in general tied the goals of liberty and equality to individualist political, economic and ethical doctrines. The individual is, in essence, sacrosanct, and is free and equal only to the extent that he or she can pursue and attempt to realize self-chosen ends and personal interests. Equal justice can be sustained between individuals if, above all, individuals' entitlement to certain rights or liberties is respected and all citizens are treated equally before the law. In this account, the modern state should provide the necessary conditions to enable citizens to pursue their own interests; it should uphold the rule of law in order to protect and nurture individuals' liberty, a state of affairs in which no one is entitled to impose their vision of the 'good life' upon others. This has been, of course, a central tenet of liberalism since Locke: the state exists to safeguard the rights and liberties of citizens who are ultimately the best judge of their own interests . . .

By contrast, New Left thinkers have defended the desirability of certain social or collective means and goals. For them, to take equality and liberty seriously is to challenge the view that these values can be realized by individuals left, in practice, to their own devices in a 'free-market' economy and a minimal state. Equality, liberty and justice . . . cannot be achieved in a world dominated by private ownership of property and the capitalist economy. These ideals . . . . can be realized only through struggles to ensure that society, as well as the state, is democratized, i.e. subject to procedures that ensure maximum accountability. Only the latter can ultimately guarantee the reduction of all forms of coercive power so that human beings can develop as 'free and equal'. While New Left thinkers differ in many respects from traditional Marxist writers, they share a concern to uncover the conditions whereby the 'free development of each' is compatible with the 'free development of all'. . . .

The views of the New Right and New Left are, of course, radically different. The key elements of their theories are fundamentally at odds. It is therefore somewhat paradoxical to note that they share a vision of reducing arbitrary power and regulatory capacity to its lowest possible extent. Both the New Right and the New Left fear the extension of networks of intrusive power into society, 'choking', to borrow a phrase from Marx, 'all its pores'. They both have ways of criticizing the bureaucratic, inequitable and often repressive character of much state action. In addition, they are both concerned with the political, social and economic conditions for the development of people's capacities, desires and interests. Put in this general and very abstract manner, there appears to be a convergence of emphasis on ascertaining the circumstances under which people can develop as 'free and equal'.

The concept of 'autonomy' or 'independence' links together these aspirations and helps explain why they have been shared so widely. 'Autonomy' connotes the capacity of human beings to reason self-consciously, to be self-reflective and to be self-determining. It involves the ability to deliberate, judge, choose and act upon different possible courses of action in private as well as public life. Clearly, the idea of an 'autonomous' person could not develop while political rights, obligations and duties were closely tied, as they were in the medieval worldview, to property rights and religious tradition . . .

Liberalism advanced the challenging view that individuals were 'free and equal', capable of determining and justifying their own actions, capable of entering into self-chosen obligations. . . . The development of autonomous spheres of action, in social, political and economic affairs, became a (if not *the*) central mark of what it was to enjoy freedom and equality. While liberals failed frequently to explore the actual circumstances in which individuals lived . . . they none the less generated the strong belief that a defensible political order must be one in which people are able to develop their nature and interests free from the arbitrary use of political authority and coercive power. And although many liberals stopped far short of proclaiming that for individuals to be 'free and equal' they must themselves be sovereign, their work was preoccupied with, and affirmed the overwhelming importance of, uncovering the conditions under which individuals can determine and regulate the structure of their own association . . .

Liberals have always argued that 'the liberty of the strong' must be restrained, although they have not, of course, always agreed about who constitutes 'the strong'. For some 'the strong' has included those with special access to certain kinds of resources (political, material and cultural), but for others 'the strong' has been elements of the *demos* itself. But whatever the precise conception of the proper nature and scope of individual liberty, liberals have been committed to a conception of the individual as 'free and equal' and to the necessity of creating institutional arrangements to protect their position, i.e. they have been committed to a version of the principle of autonomy.

Could Marxists (orthodox or otherwise) and the New Left theorists subscribe to the principle of autonomy? There is a fundamental sense . . . in which the answer to this question is 'no'. They have not thought it necessary to establish a theory of the 'frontiers of freedom' which 'nobody should be permitted to cross' in a post-capitalist political order. . . . This is precisely the sense in which the left does not have an adequate account of the state and, in particular, of democratic government as it exists and as it might be. Its dominant view of the future has always been that its 'music' could not and should not be composed in advance. . . . However, matters ought not to be left here; for there is another sense in which this position is misleading. Marx's attempt to unpack the broad conditions of a non-exploitative society – an order arranged 'according to need' which maximises 'freedom for all' – presupposes that such a society will be able to protect itself rigorously against all those who would seek to subject productive property and the power to make decisions once again to private appropriation. In the account offered by New Left thinkers, a similar presupposition is also clearly crucial. . . . But [these] ideas . . . remain, unfortunately, undeveloped. Participatory democracy requires a detailed theory of the 'frontiers of freedom', and a detailed account of the institutional arrangements necessary to protect them, if it is to be defended adequately. . . .

The specification of a principle's 'conditions of enactment' is a vital matter; for if a theory of the most desirable form of democracy is to be at all plausible, it must be concerned with both theoretical and practical issues. . . . A consideration of principles, without an examination of the conditions for their realization, may preserve a sense of virtue, but it will leave the actual meaning of such principles barely spelt out at all. . . .

A starting point for reflection is provided by Table 1.4(1), which sums up (albeit in rather stark form) some of the central positions of liberalism and Marxism.... There are good grounds for taking seriously some of the central arguments and, thus, some of the central prescriptions of *both* liberalism and Marxism. The principle of autonomy can only be conceived adequately if we adopt this ... approach. It is important to appreciate, above all, the complementarity of liberalism's scepticism about political power and Marxism's scepticism about economic power....

Liberalism's thrust to create a sovereign democratic state, a diversity of power centres and a world marked by openness, controversy and plurality is radically compromised by the reality of the so-called 'free market', the structure and imperatives of the system of private capital accumulation. If liberalism's central failure is to see markets as 'powerless' mechanisms of co-ordination and, thus, to neglect ... the distorting nature of economic power in relation to democracy, Marxism's central failure is the reduction of political power to economic power and, thus, to neglect ... the dangers of centralized political power and the problems of political accountability. Marxism's embodiment in East European societies today is marked by the growth of the centralized bureaucratic state; its claim to represent the forces of progressive politics is tarnished by socialism's relation in practice, in the East and also in the West, with bureaucracy, surveillance, hierarchy and state control. Accordingly, liberalism's account of the nature of markets and economic power must be rejected while Marxism's account of the nature of democracy must be severely questioned.

It is important to take note, furthermore, of some of the limitations shared by liberalism and Marxism. Generally, these two political traditions have failed to explore the impediments to full participation in democratic life other than those imposed, however important these may be, by state and economic power. The roots of the difficulty lie in narrow conceptions of 'the political'. In the liberal tradition the political is equated with the world of government or governments alone. Where this equation is made and where politics is regarded as a sphere apart from economy or culture, that is, as governmental activity and institutions, a vast domain of politics is excluded from view: above all, the spheres of productive and reproductive relations. The Marxist conception of politics raises related matters. Although the Marxist critique of liberalism is of great significance, its value is ultimately limited because of the direct connection it postulates ... between the political and the economic. By reducing political to economic and class power, and by championing 'the end of politics', Marxism itself tends to marginalize or exclude certain types of issue from politics....

The narrow conception of 'the political' in both liberalism and Marxism has meant that key conditions for the realization of the principle of autonomy have been eclipsed from view: conditions concerning, for example, the necessary limits on private possession of the means of production, if democratic outcomes are not to be skewed systematically to the advantage of the economically powerful (insufficiently examined by liberalism); and the necessary changes in the organisation of the household and childrearing, among other things, if women are to enjoy 'free and equal' conditions (insufficiently examined by both liberalism and Marxism).... In order to grasp the diverse conditions necessary for the adequate institutionalization of the principle of autonomy, we require a broader conception of 'the political' than is found in either of these traditions.

In my view, politics is about power; that is, it is about the *capacity* of social agents, agencies and institutions to maintain or transform their environment, social or physical. It is about the resources that underpin this capacity and about the forces that shape and influence its exercise ... Accordingly, politics is a phenomenon found in and between all groups, institutions ... and societies, cutting across public and private life. It is expressed in all the activities of cooperation, negotiation and struggle over the use and distribution of resources. It is involved in all the relations, institutions and structures which are implicated in the activities of production and reproduction in the life of societies. Politics creates and conditions all aspects of our lives.... If politics is conceived in this way, then the specification of the conditions of enactment of the principle of autonomy amounts to the specification of the conditions for the participation of citizens in decisions about issues which are important to them (i.e. us). Thus, it is necessary to strive towards a state of affairs in which political life – democratically organized – is, in principle, a central part of all people's lives. Can this state of affairs be specified more precisely? How can 'the state' and 'civil society' be combined to promote the principle of autonomy?

The heritage of classic and contemporary democratic theory

If the force of the above argument is accepted ... for the principle of autonomy to be realized ... would require the creation of a system of collective decision-making which allowed extensive involvement of citizens in public affairs. A powerful case can be made ... that such a system ... would have to meet the following criteria:

1 Equal votes: The rule for determining outcomes ... must take into account, and take equally into account, the expressed preferences of each citizen as to the outcome; that is, votes must be allocated equally among citizens.
2 Effective participation: Throughout the process of making ... collective decisions, each citizen must have an adequate and equal opportunity for expressing a preference as to the final outcome.
3 Enlightened understanding: In order to express preferences accurately, each citizen must have adequate and equal opportunities ... for discovering and validating his or her preferences on the matter to be decided.

Table 1.4(1) *Justified prescriptions of liberalism and Marxism*

Liberalism	Marxism
1 Hostility to and scepticism about state power, and emphasis on the import-ance of a diversity of power centres	1 Hostility to and scepticism about con-centration of economic power in private ownership of the means of production
2 Separation of state from civil society as an essential prerequisite of a democratic order	2 Restructuring of civil society, i.e. transformation of capitalist relations of production, as a pre-requisite of a flourishing democracy
3 The desirable form of the state is an impersonal (legally circumscribed) structure of power	3 The 'impersonality' or 'neutrality' of the state can only be achieved when its autonomy is no longer compromised by capitalism
4 Centrality of constitutionalism to guarantee formal equality (before the law) and formal freedom (from arbitrary treatment) in the form of civil and political liberties or rights essential to representative democracy: above all, those of free speech, expression, association, belief and (for liberal democrats) one-person-one-vote and party pluralism	4 The transformation of the rigid social and technical division of labour is essential if people are to develop their capacities and involve themselves fully in the democratic regulation of political as well as economic and social life
5 Protected space enshrined in law for individual autonomy and initiative	5 The equally legitimate claims of all citizens to autonomy are the foundation of any freedom that is worth the name
6 Importance of markets as mechanisms for coordinating diverse activities of producers and consumers	6 Unless there is public planning of investment, production will remain geared to profit, not to need in general

4 Final control of the agenda by the demos: The demos must have the exclusive opportunity to make decisions that determine what matters are and are not to be decided by processes that satisfy the first three criteria.
5 Inclusiveness: The demos must include all adult members except trans-ients and persons proved to be mentally defective. (Dahl, 1985, pp. 59–60)

If the right to 'equal votes' is not established, then there will be no mechanism that can take equally into account, and provide a decision pro-cedure to resolve differences among, the views and preferences of citizens ... If citizens are unable to enjoy the conditions for 'effective participation' and 'enlightened understanding', then it is unlikely that the marginalization of large categories of citizens in the democratic process will ever be overcome, nor that the vicious circles of limited or non-participation will be broken. If the 'final control' of the 'political agenda' is out of the hands of citizens, then 'rule by the people' will exist largely in name only ... If the *demos* does not include all adults ... then it will clearly fail to create the conditions for 'equal involvement'. It is hard to see how persons could be politically equal if any of these criteria were violated. ...

Among the many questions that remain are: under what conditions might it be possible for citizens to be in a position to enjoy equal political status and effective opportunities for participation? If the principle of autonomy is to be realized, how is it to be institutionalized in a way that might guarantee collective decision-making? Answers to these questions are, unfortunately, by no means straightforward. ...

The classical Athenian model, which developed in a tightly knit community, cannot be adapted to 'stretch' across space and time. Its emergence in the context of city-states and under conditions of 'social exclusivity' was an integral part of its successful development. In circumstances that are socially, economically and politically highly differentiated, it is very hard to envisage how a democracy of this type could succeed. ... Unless we believe in the plausibility of a world in which not only are Wittgenstein, Freud, Sid Vicious and members of our local community agreed on a common vision of life, but where the social basis of all group and class conflicts is eliminated as well, direct democracy is not a good gamble. A system to promote discussion, debate and competition among often divergent views – a system encompassing the formation of movements, pressure groups and/or political parties with leaderships to help press their cases – seems unavoidable.

In addition, while the evidence certainly indicates that we learn to participate by participating, and that participation does help foster ... an active and knowledgeable citizenry, the evidence is by no means conclusive that increased participation *per se* will trigger a new renaissance in human development. It would be unwise to count on people generally becoming more democratic, co-operative and dedicated to the 'common good'. It would probably be wiser to presuppose – especially for the purpose of assessing the contemporary relevance of competing democratic models – that people will not, as one commentator aptly put it, 'perform substantially better either morally or intellectually than they do at present'. ... Moreover, it is at least questionable whether participation *per se* leads to consistent and desirable political outcomes; an array of possible tensions can exist between individual liberty, distributional questions (social justice) and democratic decisions. ... Enhanced political participation must take place within a legal framework that protects and nurtures the enactment of the principle of autonomy. The principle of autonomy must have priority over any objective of creating unlimited or uncircumscribed participation.

One cannot escape . . . the necessity of recognizing the importance of a number of fundamental liberal tenets: concerning the centrality, in principle, of an 'impersonal' structure of public power, of a constitution to help guarantee and protect rights, of a diversity of power centres within and outside the state, of mechanisms to promote competition and debate between alternative political platforms. What this amounts to, among other things, is confirmation of the fundamental liberal notion that the 'separation' of the state from civil society must be a central feature of any democratic political order. . . .

Within the history of liberalism the concept of 'civil society' has, of course, been interpreted in a variety of different ways. . . . There is a profound sense, moreover, in which civil society can never be 'separate' from the state; the latter, by providing the overall legal framework of society, to a significant degree constitutes the former. None the less, it is not unreasonable to claim that civil society retains a distinctive character to the extent that it is made up of areas of social life – the domestic world, the economic sphere, cultural activities and political interaction – which are organized by private or voluntary arrangements between individuals and groups outside the *direct* control of the state. . . . It is in this sense that the notion is used here. Thus understood, the terms of the argument can be restated as follows: centralized state institutions . . . must be viewed as necessary devices for, among other things, enacting legislation, enforcing rights, promulgating new policies and containing inevitable conflicts between particular interests. Representative electoral institutions, including parliament and the competitive party system, are an inescapable element for authorizing and co-ordinating these activities.

However, to make these points is not to affirm any one liberal democratic model as it stands. It is one thing to accept the arguments concerning the necessary protective, conflict-mediating and redistributive functions of the democratic state, quite another to accept these as prescribed in the models of liberal democracy from Bentham to Schumpeter. . . . There are profound difficulties . . . with each of the major models of liberal democracy. . . . Accordingly, in order for state institutions to become effective, accessible and accountable regulators of public life, they have to be rethought and, indeed, transformed in many respects.

Advocates of liberal democracy have tended to be concerned, above all else, with the proper principles and procedures of democratic government. By focusing on 'government', they have attracted attention away from a thorough examination of the relation between: formal rights and actual rights; commitments to treat citizens as free and equal and practices which do neither sufficiently; conceptions of the state as, in principle, an independent authority and involvements of the state in the reproduction of the inequalities of everyday life; notions of political parties as appropriate structures for bridging the gap between state and society and the array of power centres which such parties and their leaders cannot reach; conceptions of politics as governmental affairs and systems of power which negate this concept. None of the models of liberal democracy is able to specify adequately the conditions for the possibility of political participation by all citizens, on the one hand, and the set of governing institutions capable of regulating the forces which actually shape everyday life, on the other. The conditions of democratic participation, the form of democratic control, the scope of democratic decision-making – all these matters are insufficiently questioned in the liberal democratic tradition. The problems are, in sum, twofold: the structure of civil society (including private ownership of productive property, vast sexual and racial inequalities) ... does not create conditions for equal votes, effective participation, proper political understanding and equal control of the political agenda, while the structure of the liberal democratic state (including large, frequently unaccountable bureaucratic apparatuses, institutional dependence on the process of capital accumulation, political representatives pre-occupied with their own re-election) does not create an organizational force which can adequately regulate 'civil' power centres.

Democracy: a double-sided process

The implications of these points are profound: for democracy to flourish today it has to be reconceived as a double-sided phenomenon: concerned, on the one hand, with the *re*-form of state power and, on the other hand, with the restructuring of civil society.... The principle of autonomy can only be enacted by recognizing the indispensability of a process of 'double democratization': the interdependent transformation of both state and civil society. Such a process must be premised by the acceptance of both the principle that the division between state and civil society must be a central feature of democratic life and the notion that the power to make decisions must be free of the inequalities and constraints imposed by the private appropriation of capital....

The enactment of the principle of autonomy requires us to re-think the forms and limits of state action and the forms and limits of civil society. The questions arise: how, and in what ways, might state policy be made more accountable? How, and in what ways, might 'non-state' activities be democratically re-ordered? ... [It] is clearly important to add some institutional detail to the argument presented so far, if the conditions of enactment of the principle of autonomy are to be envisaged at all. What follows, however, is nothing other than the briefest of sketches: an agenda for further thought.

In the West the need to democratize political institutions has mostly been confined to questions of reforming the process whereby party leaders are selected and changing electoral rules. Other issues which are occasionally raised include public funding of elections for all parties meeting a minimum level of support; genuine access to, and more equitable distribution of, media time, freedom of information ... deconcentration of the civil service to the regions along with its decentralization; the defence and enhancement of local government powers against rigid, centralized state decisions; and experiments to make government institutions more accountable and amenable to their 'consumers'. All these are important issues, which must be developed further if adequate strategies are to be found for democratizing state institutions. But none of them will make a decisive contribution to making the polity more democratic unless a further difficult problem is confronted: can the requirements of democratic public life . . . be reconciled with those institutions of state . . . which thrive on secrecy and control of the means of coercion and which develop their own momentum and interests. . . . This . . . problem . . . can only be confronted by exploring ways in which the sovereignty of parliament can be established over the state, and the sovereignty of society – of all citizens – over parliament. How might this be done?

In many countries, West and East, the limits of 'government' are explicitly defined in constitutions and bills of rights which are subject to public scrutiny, parliamentary review and judicial process. This idea is . . . fundamental to the principle of autonomy. However, the principle of autonomy requires these limits on 'public power' to be reassessed in relation to a far broader range of issues than has been hitherto commonly presupposed. If people are to be free and equal in the determination of the conditions of their own lives . . . they must be in a position to enjoy a range of rights not only in principle, but also in practice. The rights of citizens must be both formal and concrete. This entails the specification of a far broader range of rights, with a far more profound 'cutting edge', than is allowed typically. Such a 'system of rights' would both constrain and enable collective activities across a broad domain.

What would be included in such a system? A constitution and bill of rights which enshrined the principle of autonomy would specify equal rights with respect to the processes that determine state outcomes. This would involve not only equal rights to cast a vote, but also equal rights to enjoy the conditions for effective participation, enlightened understanding and the setting of the political agenda. Such broad 'state' rights would, in turn, entail a broad bundle of social rights linked to reproduction, childcare, health and education, as well as economic rights to ensure adequate economic and financial resources for democratic autonomy. Without tough social and economic rights, rights with respect to the state could not be fully enjoyed; and without state rights new forms of inequality of power, wealth and status could systematically disrupt the implementation of social and economic liberties. . . .

Accordingly, in this scheme of things, a right to equal justice would entail not only the responsibility of the state to ensure formal equality before the law, but also that citizens would have the actual capacity . . . to take advantage of opportunities before them. Such a constitution and bill of rights would radically enhance the ability of citizens to take action against the state to redress unreasonable encroachment on liberties. It would help tip the balance from state to parliament and from parliament to citizens. It would be an 'empowering' legal system. Of course, 'empowerment' would not thereby be guaranteed; no legal system alone is able to offer such guarantees. But it would specify rights which could be fought for by individuals, groups and movements . . . and which could be tested in, among other places, open court.

The implications for civil society are in part clear. To the extent that its anatomy comprises elements that undermine the possibility of effective collective decision-making, they would have to be progressively transformed. A democratic state and civil society is incompatible with powerful sets of social relations and organizations which can . . . distort democratic outcomes. At issue here is, among other things, the curtailment of the power of corporations to constrain and influence the political agenda, the restriction of the activities of powerful interest groups . . . to pursue unchecked their own interests, and the erosion of the systematic privileges enjoyed by some social groups . . . at the expense of others. The state and civil society must, then, become the condition for each other's democratic development.

Under such conditions, strategies would have to be adopted to break up old patterns of power in civil society and, in addition, to create new circumstances which allowed citizens to enjoy greater control of their own projects. . . . If individuals are to be free and equal in the determination of the conditions of their own existence, there must be a multiplicity of social spheres – for example, socially owned enterprises, independent communications media and health centres – which allow their members control of the resources at their disposal without direct interference from the state, political agencies or other third parties. . . . Many of the 'units' of civil society might approximate to, or come to share, the conditions under which direct democracy could flourish. But an experimental view of such organizational structures would have to be taken. The state of democratic theory and the knowledge we have of radical democratic experiments does not allow wholly confident predictions about the most suitable strategies for organizational change. In this particular sense, the 'music of the future' can only be composed in practice. The nature and form of different types of democracy and their pertinence to different social and political conditions needs very careful further examination.

Abridged from David Held (1987), *Models of Democracy*, pp. 267–87. Reprinted by permission of Polity Press, Cambridge.

References

Dahl, Robert A. (1985), *A Preface to Economic Democracy*, Polity Press, Cambridge.

1.5 Elite theory and democracy

Geraint Parry

The 'classic' texts of elitist thought are undoubtedly Vilfredo Pareto's *The Mind and Society*, Gaetano Mosca's *The Ruling Class* and Robert Michels's *Political Parties*. To these might be added James Burnham's *The Managerial Revolution* and C. Wright Mills's *The Power Elite*.[1] The core of the elitist doctrine is that there may exist in any society a minority of the population which takes the major decisions in the society. Because these decisions are of such wide scope, affecting the most general aspects of the society, they are usually regarded as *political* decisions even where the minority taking them are not 'politicians' in the usual sense of members of a government or legislature. Thus Mosca's 'political class' includes the wider circle of those who influence governmental decisions as well as those who formally 'decide' policies. According to the classical elitist thesis the minority gains its dominant position by means beyond ordinary election. Thus the elite may be powerful as a result of the revolutionary overthrow of the previously dominant group as in the case of the early Bolshevik leadership in the Soviet Union. The elite may owe its position to conquest – the Norman rulers of Saxon England after 1066. It may be powerful because of its monopoly of the crucial productive resources of a society, or its influence may be due to its embodying in fact or in appearance certain social or religious values widely shared in a tradition-bound society. But even where, as is normally the case in modern societies, the dominant minority at the very least includes some who have been elected to positions of leadership the elitists claim that electoral victory is not gained entirely by open democratic means. The appearance of democratic majority control over the minority is deceptive. The minority is in a position to manipulate the electoral process to its own ends by means of a range of measures from sheer coercion of voters, through bribery or the skilled use of propaganda to the selection of the candidates. The sovereign electorate will 'choose' its leaders from those acceptable to the elite.

In such ways the dominant minority escapes the control of the majority. The elitist thesis does not merely assert that in a society the minority makes decisions and the majority obeys. This is an obvious truism with no power to explain political relationships. That fewer people issue laws, orders and instructions than receive and obey them is a fact scarcely worth commenting upon. The elitist argument is a much stronger one. It is that the dominant minority cannot be controlled by the majority, whatever democratic mechanisms are used. No mechanism for ensuring the accountability of the leaders to the public, no ideology which enshrines the principle of majority will can prevent the elite from imposing its supremacy over the rest of society.

Because of their power, their organization, their political skill or their personal qualities, the members of the elite are always potentially capable of exploiting their positions so as to preserve the elite's domination. An implication of this is that the supposed elite constitutes a coherent, united and self-conscious group – and these qualities appear in nearly all definitions. Indeed, what James Meisel calls the 'three Cs' – group consciousness, coherence and conspiracy (the last term meaning a 'common will to action' rather than 'secret machinations') – are clearly necessary features of the concept of an elite.[2] To be of any relevance to a study of political influence the group must act together as a group, with some shared purposes. If the group does not act as a unified body it is less an elite than a category of 'top persons' in the particular sphere in question – the category of the 'most wealthy men' in the USA or the category of 'public school products' in Britain. The unity of the elite is sometimes seen as the outcome of the elite's social background and sometimes the product of the very organization of the elite itself – an *esprit de corps* arising from their common situation and interest, and joint action of the group. In every case the cohesiveness of the elite is seen as one of its chief strengths.

These qualities of self-consciousness, coherence and unity are held to reinforce the advantageous position of the elite in its relations with other groups in the society. The elitists regard power as cumulative. Power is a means to obtain other social goods – wealth, economic influence, social status, educational advantages for their children. In turn these become themselves powers - wealth makes for greater wealth and for access to political power, a group's social prestige adds weight to its political activities. Both wealth and educational opportunities will tend to maintain the elite's domination in subsequent generations, converting it into a hereditary caste. These advantages of *positions déjà prises*, as Mosca termed them, serve to increase the distance between the elite and other groups. They emphasize the exclusiveness of the elite and the difficulty of obtaining entry into it on any other than the elite's own terms. The strength of the elite is in many respects indicated by its ability to lay down the terms for admission to the circle of the politically influential, terms which may include conformity to standards of wealth, social background, educational attainment and commitment to the elite's interests and ideology. On the other hand the elite's survival may, as we shall see, depend on its capacity to adjust to pressures from outside itself and even to admit elements from other social interests into the elite.

The size of the elite envisaged by elitists depends on where they draw the line between the politically influential and the less influential. Several elitists distinguish between two levels or strata within the elite. Such a distinction appears in Mosca, Pareto and Mills. Though each of these writers draws the distinction between the upper and lower levels of the elite in a somewhat different way, this common pattern is significant. It represents an attempt by the elitists to take into account differences both in the degree and the type of influence which the various members of the elite may possess. In some cases the lower stratum of the elite is a bridge between the core of decision-makers and the rest of society. It mediates between the rulers and the ruled by transmitting information in either direction and by providing explanations and justifications for elite policy. It may also be the source from which the higher elite is recruited as well as the level at which outsiders first enter elite circles from below.

Mosca, for example, holds that the key to the stability of any political system lies more in the quality of the lower level of the elite than in the 'few dozen persons who control the state machine'. He draws an analogy with the relative importance to an army of its generals and its officer corps. If all the generals were to be lost it would be a severe blow to the army, but if the officers were lost the army would disintegrate. In the same way the cohesion of a society depends on the lower stratum of the elite which provides the leadership material for the society as well as the essential linkage with those who are led. The simple fact that those who take the 'decisions' in a society do not comprise all those who have 'influence' gives rise to the similar distinction between elite levels in the theory of C. Wright Mills. Mills distinguishes between an 'inner core' and the 'outer fringes' of the 'power elite'. The inner core is made up of the men who are 'in' on the major decisions, whilst the outer members are 'those who count', whose views and interests have to be considered and conciliated by the inner core even where they do not actively participate in a given decision.

Pareto's suggested division of the elite is on a different basis. The 'governing elite' is composed of all political influentials, whether they exercise this influence directly or indirectly. It could include members of the government and of an opposition party as well as industrialists, labour leaders, military personnel or any others in the society, to the extent that they made an impact on political decision-making. The 'non-governing elite' consists of the leaders in any of the many and varied activities which do not affect political issues.

With the exception of Mills, all those referred to here as the 'classical elitists' held that the existence of a ruling elite was a necessary feature of all societies. Only Mills confined his observations to one society at one period – the USA in the 1950s – explicitly recognizing that other societies and, indeed, the same society at other periods might differ radically in their power structure. For Mosca and Pareto the necessary existence of ruling elites was one of the laws of politics which social science had uncovered. Nature, including human social nature, was uniform. Men were moved by the same passions and interests in the present as they had been in the past. As a consequence, patterns of social and political conduct were, in essentials, repetitive. The entire records of history stood as a storehouse of evidence as to man's political experience. The assumption of the uniformity of nature permitted the elitists to predict the futility of egalitarian attempts, such as those of the Marxists, to establish a classless society. Elites were not merely features of all hitherto existing societies but of every society that might conceivably exist in the future.

Within the general thesis of elitism the 'classical elitists' displayed important differences. The most crucial of these differences was as to the qualities and social opportunities a group needed to possess if it were to gain an elite position. Four broad positions may be discerned. Firstly, there were those who, like Mosca and his disciple Michels, held that an elite owed its power predominantly to its organizational abilities. Pareto and his followers, by contrast, traced the elite's position to the psychological make-up of both elite and non-elite, this being in turn explicable in terms of certain constancies in human nature. James Burnham, attempting a marriage between elitism and Marxism, saw the power of the elite as a consequence of its control of economic resources. C. Wright Mills similarly explained the elite's dominance not as a product of the personal qualities of its members but of the positions they held in a number of key institutions within the society.[3]

Mosca and Michels: an organizational approach

Mosca gave, in a famous passage, the most concise statement of the general elitist position:

Among the constant facts and tendencies that are to be found in all political organisms, one is so obvious that it is apparent to the most casual eye. In all societies ... two classes of people appear – a class that rules and a class that is ruled. The first class, always the less numerous, performs all political functions, monopolizes power and enjoys the advantages that power brings, whereas the second, the more numerous class, is directed and controlled by the first, in a manner that is now more or less legal, now more or less arbitrary and violent, and supplies the first, in appearance at least, with material means of subsistence and with the instrumentalities that are essential to the vitality of the political organism.[4]

Neither one man nor the mass of the people can rule. The single ruler needs the backing of advisers and administrators, propagandists and police. On the other side 'the people' can only act politically under the direction of a small group of leaders.

The key to elite control lay for Mosca in a minority's capacity for organization. Elite *position* comes as a result of its members possessing, either in fact or in the estimation of others in the society, some attribute which is valued in the society. The attribute may be wealth, a concern for the public good, military prowess or status in a religious hierarchy. Elite *control*, however, depends on the minority's capacity to weld itself into a cohesive force presenting a common front to the other forces in society. A minority, Mosca believes, has advantages simply because it is a minority.

A small group is more readily organized than a large one. Its internal channels of communication and information are much simpler. Its members

can be contacted more speedily. As a result, a small minority can formulate
policies rapidly, can agree on the presentation of the policies and give the
appearance of complete solidarity in its public statements and actions. The
consequence is that despite the apparent superiority of a majority over a
minority, in any concrete situation it will be the minority that will be the
stronger. The unorganized majority will be merely a large aggregation of
individuals without a common purpose or any generally acknowledged system
of communicating information or co-ordinating policy.

As we have seen Mosca's elite or ruling class was subdivided into a higher
and a lower stratum. Influenced by the growing power in his day of the party
machine Mosca regarded the innermost core of the elite as comprising the
party 'bosses' who directed the party's electoral campaigns and thereby controlled the parliament. These 'grand electors', as Mosca terms them, not only
deliver the vote in the electoral area where their power is based but, most
importantly, they pick the candidates. They determine the range from which
the electorate must make its supposedly 'free choice'. Such party bosses,
existing, as they did, behind the scenes and having no constitutional or legal
standing, were in no way accountable to the electorate. The representatives
are the mere tools of the bosses.

Although Mosca holds that every society will be dominated by a ruling class
this does not imply that there are no substantial differences between political
systems. They differ in two main respects – the direction of the flow of
authority and the source of recruitment to the ruling class. Mosca discerned
two 'principles' according to which authority flowed and two 'tendencies'
according to which elite membership was recruited. Authority in any political
organization either flows downward – the 'autocratic principle' – or upward –
the 'liberal principle'. In an autocracy officials are appointed and granted
authority by some higher official. In a liberal system the rulers are authorized
by those ruled – usually by means of election. 'Autocracy' and 'liberal' are
'ideal types' of systems of authority to which any given society will conform to
a greater or lesser degree. Many will be mixtures of these principles.

Recruitment of the ruling class will, Mosca suggests, display either an
'aristocratic' or a 'democratic' tendency. The tendency is aristocratic when
new members of the ruling class are recruited from the descendants of
the existing ruling class – a disposition which all ruling classes share. The
democratic tendency is displayed where the ruling class is renewed from the
lower class of those ruled. Both these tendencies are ever present in political
systems but vary in intensity from time to time and place to place with the
aristocratic tendency sometimes prevailing and at other times the democratic.
In its extreme form each tendency has its dangers. A society which is overwhelmingly aristocratic will tend ultimately to stultify with its ruling class
losing contact with the needs and interests of the society. The opposite
extreme – where the democratic tendency is completely dominant – logically
designates a revolutionary situation. A ruling class scarcely exists since it is in

the process of replacement from below. Clearly, on Mosca's analysis, this
position would rapidly stabilize itself since the revolutionary lower classes are
always led by a minority which inevitably converts itself into a new ruling
class. Normally the democratic tendency is more moderate – a process of very
gradual infiltration of the ruling class by individuals from the lower class.
Such a moderated democratic tendency may even be interpreted as a conservative force. It permits the ruling class to be renewed and rejuvenated by
being brought into contact with the interests and aspirations of the ruled. By
this means the ablest amongst those ruled are recruited for the ruling class,
thus preventing a decline in the quality of leadership it provides.

In the main work of Mosca's disciple, Robert Michels, the central theme is
once again that elite control depends upon organization. Michels extends this
to mean not merely that organizational ability grants power but that the very
structure of any organized society gives rise inevitably to an elite. In Michels'
celebrated formulation: 'Who says organization, says oligarchy'.

Michels' method of investigation was, perhaps, the most rigidly 'scientific'
of any of the 'classical' elitists. He proposed a hypothetical law governing all
social organizations – the celebrated 'iron law of oligarchy' – and then proceeded to test the hypothesis by examining the organizations which *prima facie*
seemed to constitute the outstanding counter-examples to the law. The
organizations studied were the socialist parties of Europe in the years before
the war and in particular the German socialist party. These parties were
dedicated to preserving equality and democracy in their internal organization.
They regarded their leaders as mere agents of the mass party. Sovereignty
within the party lay with the conference of the party composed of elected
delegates. The parties devised machinery such as frequent elections, to ensure
that 'the party leads and the leaders follow'. Leadership was constantly dis-
trusted, particularly middle-class intellectual leadership in what were basically
proletarian parties. It is, however, Michels's contention that even such organizations, devoted to the negation of any tendency towards elite control,
nevertheless display the 'iron law of oligarchy'.

Michels never offered a precise formulation of the law of oligarchy but its
meaning is clear. In any organization of any size leadership becomes necessary
to its success and survival. The nature of organization is such that it gives
power and advantages to the group of leaders who cannot then be checked or
held accountable by their followers. This is true despite the fact that where
the leadership is elected the leaders are supposedly the agents of those
electing them. There are two sets of factors which cause this result – organizational factors and psychological. Of these the organizational factors are by far
the most significant.

Michels argues that as soon as human co-operative activities attain the size
and complexity which warrant the term 'organization', technical expertise is
required if the enterprise is not to founder. Like Max Weber before him,
Michels insists that attempts at control of an organization by the mass of its

members involves an amateurishness totally self-defeating in an age of large-scale organization. A political party campaigning to gain power needs to organize its vote, canvass supporters, supply information for speakers, raise contributions, attend to the party's financial structure and its legal standing. It needs to establish a co-ordinated policy line for the sake of consistency and solidarity. All these activities require expertise which the mass of members may not have the aptitude to develop and for which they certainly lack the leisure. Mass control conflicts with efficiency and is replaced by professional direction both in policy-making and in technical administration. The result of this 'technical indispensability of leadership' is that control of the party passes into the hands of its leading politicians and its bureaucracy.

Michels then demonstrates that power breeds power – a central tenet of elitism. The leadership controls the party funds and the party's channels of information – notably its newspaper – it attempts to select parliamentary candidates, it dispenses patronage. Its activities are news, publicized even by the opposition press. An important feature in Michels' analysis is his recognition of the impact that the party's role in the whole political system of the society has on the internal power structure of the party. Power for the party necessitates electoral success. Electoral success, however, requires the support of voters who are not necessarily party members – people who are less committed to party principle, who are on the 'margin' of the party. To gain their allegiance the party must moderate its dogma, must provide continuity of leadership to give an assurance of stability, must devote itself to organizing its vote rather than maintaining the purity of its doctrine.

Ultimately the party is forced to adopt a hierarchy which mirrors the hierarchical power structure in the political system as a whole with 'shadow' ministers supported by an efficient bureaucracy. Mass control is discovered to be incompatible with political power and so oligarchy triumphs, with the leadership proven to be 'stable and irremovable'. Even the attempts to maintain a proletarian leadership for the proletarian parties and thus prevent the estrangement between leader and led is, Michels insists, foredoomed to failure. Instead a 'proletarian elite' emerges which ceases to be proletarian in anything but origin as it exchanges manual for desk work and wages for salary. The leaders are 'bourgeoisified', strangers to their class, and the party hierarchy becomes an established career offering a rise in social status as well as in income.

Though Michels confines his particular analysis to political parties the law of oligarchy is intended to have general application to all organization including the organization of the state as such. The majority will never rule despite the formal apparatus of universal suffrage and the myths of majority will. Democracy in the sense of the rule of the whole people or of the majority is impossible. In any democracy the major decisions will be taken by a powerful oligarchy. But Michels comes round to a limited defence of democracy. It allows the emergence of a number of rival parties – each led by an oligarchy –

whose competition ensures a certain amount of indirect influence to the people whose support they must cultivate. The democratic tendency restrains but cannot prevent the oligarchical. As with Mosca elitism makes a compromise with pluralism when democracy is defined in terms of the competition between oligarchies.

The counterpart of the elite in all these theories is the 'mass'. There is much less disagreement amongst elitists as to the nature of the mass than there is as to the character of the elite. The mass is, typically, 'atomized'. Its members are not organized for concerted political action. Instead each person tends to live his own private life, concentrating on his own interests both in work and leisure. His contacts with others in the mass tend to be limited to the members of his family, neighbours and his immediate work associates. The narrow confines of such a life limit the individual's view of public affairs. In contrast to the elite he lacks the vantage point from which to see the whole of the social system – its movements and interactions. Only the elite is able to transcend the milieu in which it finds itself and create a new environment. Only the elite in the command posts of the society gains an overall view. The perception of the mass is fragmented. It is unable to see even the purpose of its own activities since it does not see what part they play in the total structure.

The mass is able to act as a single unit only when it is integrated from outside by the elite. Leadership can transform the mass from an aggregation of isolated units into a solid, unified group. But this unity is entirely artificial. It does not arise spontaneously from within the mass. Lenin, the elitist amongst theorists of working class revolution, demanded that the spontaneous uprisings of the workers should be consciously resisted since the workers themselves never transcend their mileux to see the distinction between bread riots and total revolution. Instead the revolution should be directed by an elite of trained, professional revolutionaries able, from their central positions in the movement, to co-ordinate its activities. In this way otherwise meaningless isolated uprisings by the mass gained revolutionary significance. The impact and involvement of the mass was paradoxically greater as a result of the direction given by an elite of possibly a mere dozen men. Lenin indeed presses the contrast between elite and mass to its extreme limit by suggesting that without leadership there is no such coherent thing as a 'people' – there is merely a mass.

Lenin's extreme version of the dependence of mass action upon elite leadership was occasioned by the need for disciplined, secret revolutionary organization in an autocratic police-state. Other elitists present a version of the theory for more democratic societies which is milder but not different in kind from that of Lenin. For Mosca and Michels the mass in a representative democracy was politically incompetent, apathetic and inert. Far from being politically ambitious the individuals in the mass were glad to have the responsibility of decision-making taken off their shoulders. The mass displays a psychological need for guidance and direction. Even the working class movements aiming to promote mass interests collapsed without the leadership of a bourgeois oligarchy. Political initiative became the responsibility of the elite as a result, in large part, of the indifference of the mass. The elite cultivates its coherence and consciousness whilst adopting towards the mass a policy of 'divide and rule'. Horizontal contacts between members of the society break down and are replaced by vertical contacts between atomized individuals and the elite. Modern totalitarian regimes using techniques of terror have been interpreted as acting in this manner to ensure the complete atomization of the mass and to force each individual to display allegiance only to the centre.

Ideology and social control

No elitist claims that the elite maintains its domination over the other classes merely by the exercise of coercion. In fact the study of the coercive powers of the elite plays a very small part in elitist analysis. The elitists wish to make the far more significant point that elite rule comes to be accepted by the rest of the society. Accordingly the elitists deal extensively with the process by which an elite gains the support of the rest of society. The elitists in this respect studied, prophesied and promoted not so much an age of violence as an age of propaganda. Any group aspiring to power will, the elitists suggest, attempt to justify its potential activities. To do this successfully it must state its aims not in self-interested terms but in ways which will gain the acceptance of all other classes and groups in the society. It will, therefore, appeal to some set of general moral and political principles which the society at large will be prepared to acknowledge as having universal validity – as being principles which any person or group might properly follow in political dealings. Despite their appearance of universality, however, such principles promotes the particular interests of the group advocating them. What purports to be a philosophy establishing general truths is in fact an ideology protecting partial interests. It assists in binding the group together with a set of shared values. Such an ideology is not necessarily the conscious conspiratorial construction of the elite. Its members may be entirely convinced of the truth of the principles they enunciate. In fact it is a mark of the success of an ideology that it is accepted as part of the received opinion of the whole of the society, looked upon as being as normal as any feature of the natural landscape.

To the extent that the elite does consciously construct and propagate its ideological defence it is aided, the elitists argue, by its control of the communications media. The elitists accept Marx's assertion that 'the ideas of the ruling class are, in every age, the ruling ideas'. The dominant political class is at the same time the dominant intellectual class. Education, newspapers and the other mass media may all come under the control of the elite. Through these media the elite may spread the values and principles which implicitly legitimize the elite's position. In this the elite is aided, Wright Mills suggests, by the 'mass' character of the mass media. A single message is transmitted to millions of individuals in the mass, each of whom receives the message in isolation from the others. There is no scope for any response from the person in the mass. He cannot discuss or answer back. The flow of propaganda – possibly disguised as information – is one-way, from elite to mass. The members of the mass are receivers, not transmitters.

By such techniques an elite can cultivate a legitimacy it might otherwise lack. According to Mosca and Pareto the mass is by no means averse to such social control. The mass, Mosca suggests, desires to be governed. But the mass does not like to think of itself, or to be thought of, as succumbing to force. This would be an affront to human dignity. Political ideologies thus permit the mass to consider itself ruled according to some great moral principles. Pareto detects a certain idealism amongst the masses, who are more likely to follow some grand principle such as nationalism than a calculation of self-interest which may be a more intricate matter to follow. Ideology satisfies the masses at the same time as controlling them.

The perpetuation and replacement of elites

Given the great accumulation of powers in the hands of an elite, it may seem, at first sight, surprising that any elitist can speak of an elite as losing its dominant position. Yet just as Marx spoke of history as the history of class struggles, so Pareto spoke of it as the 'graveyard of aristocracies'.

Elitists suggest two broad sets of factors to explain the downfall and replacement of elites – 'structural' factors and 'socio-psychological' factors. In the first case structural changes in the society bring about changes in the dominant minority in the society. The displacement of the elite occurs independently of the character and motivation of the elite. In the second case the elite is displaced as a result of some change in the attitudes or abilities of the elite.

The Marxist has, by his own rights at least, a convincing explanation for social changes. According to Marx class change occurs as a consequence of a major change in the economic system which is itself caused by the introduction of new productive techniques to meet economic demands. As the new mode of production displaces the old economic forms so the class which is associated with the new means of production rises to dislodge the existing ruling class, whose power is dependent on its ownership of the now outmoded productive forces. There is in Marx's view nothing of any substance that the existing ruling class can do to prevent the economic developments which result in its own overthrow. This incapacity to alter the course of history in an intended direction represents a very significant limitation to the power of Marx's ruling class. Marx repeatedly makes clear that these structural changes occur 'independently of the will' of the dominant class which by its own actions unconsciously digs its own grave. No amount of good resolutions or moral or political reform can alter the outcome.

Mosca, by contrast, is less deterministic. There is, admittedly, something Marxian about the way in which Mosca relates changes in elite domination to the rise of new interests or 'social forces' in a society. Where new economic interests develop or a new intellectual discovery is exploited or a new ideological movement wins allegiance the dominance of the elite is affected. The composition of the elite will reflect the balance of social forces within the society. No ruling class can govern for long if it sets its face against the developments occurring in the society and the economy. Mosca's ruling class is not a veto group which can expect on all occasions to deny the implementation of policies for which all other groups in the society are pressing. Rather the survival of the elite depends on its ability to adjust its own policies to meet the demands of the various interest groups. The elite aims, it appears, at a compromise which will satisfy the interests and yet leave the elite in its position of power.

Mosca's position differs fundamentally from that of Marx in two ways. Firstly, of course, the social forces which influence changes in the elite are much wider than the economic factors of Marx's analysis. Secondly, the ruling class is not helpless in the face of developments 'independent of its will'. Depending on its political skill and flexibility the elite may be able to ride out the storm and reemerge in its dominant position. It may adapt its policies to meet the new pressures upon it but retain its original composition. More frequently, Mosca suggests, the ruling class will open its ranks – particularly the lower stratum – to the newer elements in society and so modify the composition of the class and the interests it represents. This would not, however, be equivalent to a total class revolution. Rather, the new elements would be assimilated into the old ruling class. The established elite would be renewed and invigorated by the ablest representatives of the new forces in the new society. At the same time the new elements in turn become imbued with certain of the values of the elite. There is a fusion of elements rather than a total revolution. This process need not, moreover, be cataclysmic. The normal pattern of social mobility is for one group and then another, one able individual and then another to enter the lower stratum of the elite in a continuous process of 'molecular rejuvenation'. Cataclysmic change occurs as a result of the ruling class being closed to recruitment from below. Such a closed elite results in a condition of 'class isolation' in which the rulers cease to be aware of fundamental currents of change in society and hence lack the flexibility and skill to accommodate the new social forces.

Pareto, as ever, is less easy to categorize. On the one hand the displacement of one elite by another is as inevitable as any Marxian historical process. On the other hand the change is explained in terms of the psychological make-up of the elite and the non-elite rather than, as in Marx, in terms of some independent factor to which the elite necessarily reacts. The process of replacement occurs in two ways – by a gradual process of infiltration similar to that described by Mosca and termed by Pareto the 'circulation of elites', or by a violent revolution involving the total replacement of one elite by another.

The classical elitists' accounts of elite renewal, elite circulation or elite replacement were intended to illuminate what all thought to be the all-important underlying constancy – the existence in all social situations of a ruling minority and a ruled majority. The elitists see their accounts of social change as the very proof of their theories. The critic, however, might with equal justification conclude that these accounts are an attempt to save the consistency of the thesis of inevitable elite control in the face of the obvious social phenomenon of changes of rule.

> Abridged from Geraint Parry (1969), *Political Elites*, George Allen & Unwin, London, pp. 30–5, 54–63. Reprinted by permission of Routledge, London.

Notes

1 See V. Pareto (1935), *The Mind and Society*, Harcourt-Brace, New York; G. Mosca (1939), *The Ruling Class* (ed. Livingston), McGraw-Hill, New York; R. Michels (1958), *Political Parties*, Free Press, Glencoe, IL.; J. Burnham (1942), *The Managerial Revolution*, Putnam, New York; and C. Wright Mills (1956), *The Power Elite*, Oxford University Press.
2 James H. Meisel (1958), *The Myth of the Ruling Class: Gaetano Mosca and the Elite*, University of Michigan Press, Ann Arbor, MI.
3 The contributions of Mosca and Michels are of particular interest here, and are discussed in the following section. For further analysis of the work of Pareto, Burnham and Mills, see G. Parry (1969), *Political Elites*, George Allen and Unwin, London, pp. 45–54. (Ed.)
4 Mosca, *The Ruling Class*, Ch. II, p. 1.

1.6   The class bias of capitalist democracies

Joshua Cohen and Joel Rogers

To describe the American system as a capitalist democracy is in part to indicate the presence within a single social order of private property, labor markets, and private control of investment decisions on the one hand, and such formal organizations of political expression as political parties and regular elections on the other.

Capitalist democracy is different from plain capitalism, since workers possess political rights. Along with rights of speech and association, they can vote, join or form political parties, and engage in a number of other actions in the political arena which can influence the behavior of capital by influencing state policies. By using their vote, for example, workers can promote politicians committed to maintaining higher levels of employment, or punish those who are not so committed. The legality of such political action reduces its cost and thereby increases its likelihood. But the presence of political rights can also enhance the ability of workers to engage in forms of opposition outside the arenas of formal politics. It can, for example, enhance their ability to form trade unions or other secondary organizations from which to press further political demands. Capitalist democracy's provision of political rights creates more favorable conditions for the material gain of workers than do other kinds of capitalist regimes, such as fascism or bureaucratic authoritarianism.

But if capitalist democracy is not just capitalism, still less is it just democracy. In a capitalist democracy the exercise of political rights is constrained in two important ways. In the first place, the political rights granted to all citizens, workers among others, are formal or procedural, and not substantive. They do not take into account the inequalities in the distribution of resources, characteristic of capitalism, which decisively affect the exercise of political rights and importantly limit their power of expression. Both an unemployed worker and a millionaire owner of a major television station enjoy the same formal right of free speech, but their power to express and give substance to that right are radically different.

But before considering in detail the role played by the resource constraint in the normal course of politics, a second constraint needs to be introduced. Capitalist democracy does not only rest on the material inequalities that limit the effective expression of the formal rights it guarantees. Capitalist democracy also tends to direct the exercise of political rights toward the satisfaction of certain interests. This structuring of political demand, the 'demand constraint,' is crucial to the process of consent. The problem highlighted by the demand constraint might be put this way. It is clear that within capitalist democracies there are profound underlying structural inequalities that shape the normal course of politics. How is it that politics in a capitalist democracy can proceed at all without the underlying inequalities themselves becoming a central object of political conflict? Why do people consent?

Two answers to the question of consent are familiar. According to the first sort of account, determined opposition to capitalist democracy is stifled by force or fear in anticipation of the use of force. The second sort of account relies upon some kind of mass delusion as the explanation of consent.

The central thesis is that capitalist democracy is in some measure capable of satisfying the interests encouraged by capitalist democracy itself, namely, interests in short-term material gain. Capitalist democracy is capable of satisfying the standards of rational calculation encouraged by its structure.

Capitalist democracy rewards and thereby promotes certain sorts of interests and patterns of behavior based on those interests, and given those interests and patterns of behavior it is capable of providing satisfaction. Though fear and delusion no doubt play a role, consent is based on narrowly defined calculations of private advantage, calculations which together comprise a norm of 'economic rationality.'

To say that economic rationality is especially important within capitalist democracy is merely to claim that calculation of economic interest has a special importance in capitalist democracy because it is especially encouraged by the system, and its pursuit tends to reproduce that system over time.

Capitalism is a form of economic organization in which profit provides the motive for investment and investment decisions are preeminently the decisions of competing units of capital. Capitalists earn profits by, among other things, hiring labor at wages that permit the extraction of profit. Those whom they hire typically have no other assets than their ability to work.

As a result of their control of investment, the satisfaction of the interests of capitalists is a necessary condition for the satisfaction of all other interests within the system. Failing to satisfy the interests of capitalists means failing to secure them adequate profits. But if profits are insufficient, there will be no investment. If there is no investment, then there is no production or employment. If there is no production or employment, then workers whose principal resource is their capacity to produce starve to death. It might be objected that modern capitalist democracies protect workers against such a fate through the provision of unemployment insurance and other assistance programs. But such welfare measures are themselves dependent upon tax revenues. The requirement of profitable accumulation is not eliminated by the 'welfare state.'

Under capitalism, therefore, the welfare of workers remains structurally secondary to the welfare of capitalists, and the well-being of workers depends directly on the decisions of capitalists. The interests of capitalists appear as general interests of the society as a whole, the interests of everyone else appear as merely particular, or 'special.'

In fact, the dependence of workers on capitalists runs even deeper. While present profits are a necessary condition for future well-being, they are not a sufficient condition. Material uncertainty remains in the society, since investment decisions remain out of the reach of social control. Profits can be consumed, used for financial speculation, diverted to rare coins, racehorses and antique cars, or used for productive investment outside the economy from which they were extracted. And even if profits are reinvested in the domestic economy, profits made in Factory A can be diverted to a new Factory B within the same economy, but employing different workers. Or profits made in Factory A can be used to automate Factory A completely, throwing workers out of work.

There is then a characteristic economic rationality to the actions of workers specifically encouraged by capitalism. In the face of material uncertainties arising from continued dependence on the labor market under conditions of the private control of investment, it makes sense for workers to struggle to increase their wages.

In a capitalist democracy, workers' struggles to improve their material position are aided by the existence of political rights. Given the potential material benefit deriving from the exercise of such rights, and given the pervasive material uncertainty for workers characteristic of capitalism, it makes sense that workers' use of political rights be directed toward the achievement of material ends. The structure of capitalist democracy thus effectively encourages the reduction of politics to striving over material gain. Workers can vote for social programs such as Social Security, unemployment insurance, or Medicaid and Medicare to protect themselves from poverty and the extremities of unemployment. They can rally around more ambitious programs of economic stabilization, such as full employment acts, or they can press for the passage of laws easing the constraint on their own organization. What a capitalist democracy provides are specifically political means whereby workers can try to reduce their material uncertainty. But material uncertainty remains. For future uncertainty to be eliminated (leaving aside the uncertainly of nature), workers would have to control investment themselves. Such control violates the very definition of capitalism as a form of economic organization in which investment decisions are pre-eminently the decisions of competing capitals.

It might be objected that workers might use their political rights to contest the basic structure of capitalist democracy. Workers might exercise their rights of association and suffrage by forming political parties and voting for programs that call for the transformation of the entire social order. Given the structure of capitalist democracy, it may be economically rational to use political rights for short-term material gain. But in what sense is it rational to consent to that basic structure itself, and not pursue transformative struggle?

Capitalist democracy encourages economic calculation through the generation of conditions of material uncertainty. But economic calculation leads rationally to a rejection of more radical longer-term struggles against capitalism itself. Short-term material improvement is the preferred aim of materially based conflict within a capitalist democracy because of the different requirements and competing logics of short-term pursuits and longer-term struggles, and the rational pursuit of material advantage within capitalist democracy thus leads to a less radical and less global pursuit of short-term material gain.

Short-term struggles are relatively easy to co-ordinate. One can even engage in them all by oneself. One can try to get a raise or a promotion by flattering the boss, or working late in the evening. Short-term struggles are often recognized and licensed by the state, as in enabling legislation for the formation of trade unions as bargaining representatives for workers, or penalties imposed on employers for failing to bargain with those representatives. In addition to relative ease of co-ordination and potential for official recognition, short-term struggles always have the advantage of relative clarity of aims. While there might be debate and sharp disagreement about *how much* to demand, there is not the same problem of determining *what sorts* of demands to make, as is commonly the case in longer-term struggles. This is true even for militant short-term struggles to alter the conditions under which material benefits are bargained for within a capitalist democracy, as in struggles to organize unions or to form a party of labor. Even in these cases, the relative clarity of purpose facilitates the struggle.

Where successful, the cumulative effect of short-term struggles can be materially very satisfying. Capitalism can improve workers' material well-being. Often individual workers do better than they have done in the past. And this can be the case even if not all workers are better off. Even during times of recession, some people get raises. Even if wages overall are dropping, it may be the case that a strong union can get better wages for its members. Having encouraged the reduction of political conflict to struggle over material interest, capitalist democracy provides many avenues to and examples of short-term satisfaction of those interests. In so doing, capitalist democracy more specifically encourages the reduction of politics to striving for *short-term* material gain.

It might still be argued that while it is rational for individual workers to try to improve their position within capitalist democracy, the only way for all workers to improve their material position steadily would be by struggling together to overthrow capitalism. This may indeed be true, but at almost any given point it is also true that it would be economically irrational for individual workers to engage in such a struggle. In contemplating the costs of such a long-term fight, individual workers face a familiar problem of collective action.

In considering social struggle, individual workers lack information about how other workers will behave. Other workers or groups of workers may choose not to join the struggle, or they may abandon it at a later point. Undertaking a long-term battle against capitalism under such conditions of uncertainty means that individual workers do not know how great their personal burden of the costs of that struggle will be. It therefore makes sense for individuals to try to get as much as they can for themselves in the short run before even contemplating co-operation with others in the longer term. But the achievement of short-run material satisfaction often makes it irrational to engage in more radical struggle, since that struggle is by definition directed against those institutions which provide one's current gain.

Thus the situation in which workers make their decisions leads them rationally, on the basis of material interest, to choose not to struggle against capitalism. The long-term production of consent within capitalist democracy is based on just such short-term decisions to consent to capitalist production. The system can provide workers with short-term material satisfaction, and workers participate in the system to assure that satisfaction. And even when capitalism is failing to deliver material benefits, rational calculation does not mandate a longer-term transformative conflict. Individual workers may hope that the burdens of decline will not fall on them. They may calculate that protecting existing gains from further erosion is more likely to deliver benefits than engaging in a costly and in any case uncertain long-term effort.

Let us assume for the sake of argument that all workers solved their problems of information and co-ordination and came together to radically contest the system. Assuming that such contestation was motivated exclusively by interests in short-term material gain, no transition to a more materially satisfying social order could be completed under democratic conditions.

Fighting for total system transformation carries many costs. People often get killed. Internal resistance from capitalists is substantial. External pressures are often exerted by international lending agencies or hostile states.

But assume that there is no violence, or internal subversion, or external subversion. Even in such a scenario, one cost that always accompanies a transition out of capitalist democracy is economic crisis. As workers try to change the basis of economic institutions from profit to something else, capitalists withdraw their capital. It makes sense for them to withdraw, since they can no longer be assured of making profits, and even if the state offers them guarantees, their future position is uncertain. But if investment stops, chaos results.

Economic crisis means that short-term material interests suffer. But if support for the project of transition is motivated by short-term material interests, then at the point of economic crisis, support will begin to vanish.

The integrity and relative stability of capitalist democracy indicated by the demand constraint permits and encourages a more normal course of operation based on compromise between workers and capitalists. Workers must 'agree' not to enforce wage demands that preclude profits. Capitalists must 'agree' to invest a sufficient share of profits to provide for future well-being. An important asymmetry remains between the concessions of the two classes. Workers are agreeing to something they are doing now, namely, restraining wages. Capitalists are agreeing to do something in the future, namely, invest a sufficient share of profits. Uncertainty and conflict are never fully eliminated, and any compromise therefore remains an unstable one.

Within the boundaries just described, there is a range of possible outcomes pertaining to both the shares of product distributed between capitalists and workers and to the direction of profit to productive investment. Both Sweden and the United States are capitalist democracies, for example, but Sweden is much more a 'welfare state' than the United States. The range of possible outcomes within the boundary conditions of capitalist democracy provides yet another source of uncertainty and possible conflict within the system. At any given point, the outcome achieved along this range is importantly determined by the relative power of workers and capitalists, including their degree and forms of organization and their willingness to engage in conflict at all. In determining this balance, the first constraint on the exercise of political rights, the 'resource constraint', figures prominently.

The ability to take advantage of the formally equal political rights characteristic of capitalist democracy is not only a function of an individual's own resources. It also depends upon the ability of large numbers of individuals who share common interests to co-ordinate their actions in pursuit of those interests. The ability to co-ordinate, however, requires more than shared enthusiasm or convergent interests. Successful co-ordination commonly requires the expenditure of material resources and the availability of strategic information. Everything else being equal, co-ordination is easier to achieve for small groups than for larger ones, and the likelihood of its occurrence varies directly with the probability of its success.

On each of these dimensions, capitalists have advantages over workers. They have enormous fixed and liquid assets. They already know a great deal about their own operations, the conditions in their industry, and the economic situation more generally, all of which is information essential to their own economic performance, and all of which makes them relatively better informed and hence more efficient political actors. They operate as a relatively limited number of units, often of colossal size. Their importance to the economy guarantees their access to key decision-makers, including public officials and other capitalists, and together importance and access increase the likelihood that they will get what they want.

These advantages of assets, structurally based information, limited numbers, and access to key decision-makers are cumulative in their effect. The presence of accumulated reserves lowers the costs of political action. Good information makes the target of political action more clearly visible. Together, information and assets reduce both the need for and the relative cost of acquiring further resources. From this position of initial strength, co-ordination is further facilitated, made less costly, by the relatively limited number of actors involved. Importance to the economy and access to other decision-makers finally ensures that action will be given due regard.

Let us begin with an accurate assumption of initial gross inequalities in resource distribution. Let us assume, too, on the basis of our discussion of the demand constraint, that actors within the political arena behave in economically rational ways. In deciding how to act they must consider not only the potential benefits of a course of action, but also both the likelihood of success and costs of the action, including the cost of foregoing *other* courses of action. Economic rationality dictates that an action should be undertaken if and only if the expected value of the benefits of the action exceeds the expected value of the full range of costs.

Two problems will be examined here. The first is a problem of information; the second, of bargaining and co-ordination. Rational economic motivation applied to questions of information acquisition dictates that information should be acquired only if the marginal cost of that information is exceeded by the marginal benefits gained by action on that information. For most citizens, there is virtually no costly acquisition of political information that satisfies this condition. Policy choices rarely present the average citizen with opportunities for great personal gain, and the average citizen is in any case almost powerless to affect any policy choice alone. The small expected benefit, discounted by the ineffectiveness of personal action, is virtually always outweighed by the costs of acquiring relevant information. Citizens therefore choose, rationally, to limit their acquisition of information to that information which can be obtained at zero cost. They choose a strategy of 'rational ignorance.' Virtually the only information that satisfies the conditions of zero cost is that which is supplied 'free' by advertisers, lobbyists, and the like. This information, however, is by no means objective. Its very supply derives from the interest private decision-makers with a large stake in the outcome of a particular decision have in trying to influence that decision in a direction beneficial to themselves.

The constraints voters place on their own acquisition of information, and the special interest that motivates the supply of 'free' information by producer groups, result in distortions in the consideration of issues of public policy. It makes sense, for example, for the private individuals who will benefit from a taxpayer subsidy of a $37 billion Alaska natural gas pipeline to spend hundreds of thousands of dollars lobbying and advertising to influence that decision, but it makes no sense for any individual taxpayer to spend any amount of time or money acquiring the information needed to make a correct decision about the pipeline. In the same way, it makes sense for sugar growers to spend money lobbying for import restrictions on sugar, because for sugar growers that decision is of monumental importance, but it makes no sense for individual consumers of sugar to spend time or money acquiring information or organizing around the import question. If, on the other hand, there is another producer group with a very large stake in the price of sugar, for example the manufacturers of soft drinks, who purchase tons and tons of sugar each week, such information acquisition and organization does make sense. Because of the many divisions among producers, such situations are common. Often different producer groups take turns bombarding the public with misleading information. This is called 'national debate.'

In a system of formal political equality, the information problem thus compounds economic inequality by guaranteeing a systematic bias in the information upon which public decisions are made. The bias is systematic in the sense that it is always weighted toward producers and against consumers, toward capitalists and against workers, and correspondingly affects the resulting decisions. Such a bias is generated within this system *because* all the important actors – producer lobbyists and advertisers, politicians and voters – are behaving in economically rational ways. The information problem thus helps to generate further inequalities even without the additional impetus produced by the tremendous direct payoffs, bribes, campaign contributions, and backdoor pledges that place the stamp of private dominance on the American public arena.

The second major aspect of the resource constraint concerns the process of group mobilization and bargaining. The bargaining of groups within the political system further compounds economic and political inequality because of the persistence of so-called free-rider problems. The free-rider problem is a problem of collective action. It arises from the existence of 'public' or 'collective' goods whose provision benefits all members of a group, and whose 'consumption' by any member of the group does not preclude consumption by any other. There is however a difficulty in providing for such collective goods, since individuals who are economically motivated have little or no incentive to contribute voluntarily to their provision. This is true even when the individuals would derive benefits from the goods. Not contributing ensures zero costs, but does not exclude receipt of the benefits that may be achieved through the contributions of others. One's own contribution, on the other hand, does not guarantee that the good will be made available. It thus ensures the presence of costs but not the receipt of benefits. Given a free choice, it makes sense to take a 'free ride' on the backs of others.

Free-rider problems are important because collective goods are commonly the object of bargaining or struggle in the political system. The sugar import restrictions mentioned earlier provide one example of such group benefits. If import restrictions are imposed, they benefit all domestic sugar growers. Another example would be clean air. If clean air standards are enacted and enforced, everyone breathes easier. National defense, street lights, public parks, and public education are all similar goods in that consumption of the good by one person does not preclude consumption by another.

The examples indicate that collective goods comprise many of the most familiar objects of political concern, but they also underscore the fact that where collective goods are provided they are usually provided through the state. In the political arena, the free-rider problem most commonly and directly arises as a problem of mobilizing people to make demands upon the state for the provision of some particular collective good. While the free-rider problem confronts all attempts to mobilize in pursuit of collective goods, the force of the problem depends on the size of the group, the resources available to those who wish to organize, the relative improvement brought about by the benefits struggled for, and the certainty of achieving those benefits through concerted action. If the group is small, it is easier to co-ordinate. If the benefits are large, there is more initial incentive to join in their pursuit. If the benefits are certain, the cost of achieving them can be allocated more rationally. If initial resources are high, then potential free riders can be coerced into joining the struggle or rewarded by others for not disrupting it. While any mobilization offers opportunities for participation, the participation of the rational economic actor may follow on receiving 'an offer he couldn't refuse'. In all these respects, capitalists have advantages over workers. They can more easily solve their free-rider problems.

If the information problem thus tends to distort public debate, the free-rider problem tends to bias the pattern of public expenditures and benefits. More specific benefits applicable to small groups of powerful actors are easier to organize for and extract from the state than benefits which will accrue to much larger groups in the political system. Getting a tax write-off for the ten largest oil companies is easier to organize and achieve than getting clean air for everyone, getting preferential trade treatment for the steel industry is easier than getting safe working conditions for the workers in that industry.

This bias toward more specific expenditures and benefits has a differentiated impact on workers and capitalists. This is not only because capitalists can more readily solve their free-rider problems in the pursuit of more particular collective benefits, but because their greater initial resources enable them to compensate for the failure of the political system to provide adequate public goods. A rich person is less critically affected by the absence of decent public schools, or effective police protection, or attractive public recreational facilities than a poor person. Rich people can afford to send their children to private schools, or can hire bodyguards or private security forces, or purchase a private beach house or ski condo, all with a relatively small impact on overall resources. The poor person cannot. This difference in impact of the free-rider problem upon capitalists and upon workers compounds the structural inequality with which we began our discussion of the resource constraint.

Abridged from Joshua Cohen and Joel Rogers (1983), *On Democracy: Toward a Transformation of American Society*, Penguin, Harmondsworth, pp. 49–66. Reprinted by permission of Viking Penguin, a division of Penguin USA Inc.

Part Two
The British political system

Introduction

Britain's democracy has ancient foundations and many of its practices are based on principles and conventions which have developed piecemeal over time. The concept of the liberty of the individual was established in Britain prior to the arrival of what would normally be recognized as the characteristic features of representative government, such as universal suffrage and a mass party system. Moreover, Britain is almost unique amongst modern democratic states in not having a written and codified constitution, and consequently there is no system of superior constitutional law and no entrenched concept of citizen rights. In fact the constitutional framework is ambiguous. It is usually regarded as consisting of certain major statutes, conventions of government and administration (such as the individual responsibility of ministers to Parliament for the work of their departments), and fundamental principles like the rule of law, which holds that all are to be treated equally under the law regardless of circumstances or status.

So far as the individual is concerned, the essential idea is that of the liberty of the subject rather than the rights of the citizen. In theory Britons are at liberty to do whatever they choose to do so long as it is not specifically forbidden by the authorities. Traditionally the authorities have allowed a wide degree of liberty, and this has been enshrined in the development of the common law, which recognizes a number of basic freedoms, such as those of assembly, speech and movement. The important point to note is that these are accepted and not constitutionally guaranteed freedoms. Underpinning the system is the central doctrine of the 'Sovereignty of Parliament', which holds that all law-making finally resides in Parliament and that no Parliament can bind its successor. Consequently the concept of a superior law above the everyday activity of Parliament is alien to the British tradition.

This lack of a clear and binding constitutional framework has ensured that British democracy has been both flexible and adaptable to changing circumstances. Such features are often seen as the chief merits of the system. Set against these, however, is the danger that without an entrenched constitution and bill of rights the liberties of the subject and the principles of the constitution may be eroded over time. In effect there are no final means to either clarify or enforce limits on state action. It is considerations of this nature plus the example of what takes place elsewhere, as well as the influence of critical judgements by the European Court, that have led to an increasingly vigorous discussion of the constitutional basis of British politics.

It is appropriate, therefore, to begin with the extract by Anthony Lester (2.1). He reviews the lack of constitutional guarantees and positive rights in the United Kingdom. He notes the piecemeal way in which legislation on, for example, discrimination on grounds of race, religious belief and sex is applicable in different parts of the country. He raises serious questions about accepted principles such as the rule of law and points out that state agencies are, in some instances, exempt from the provisions of the law. He argues that this places the state in Britain in a more privileged position than is the case in those countries which have a written constitution and an enforceable bill of rights. He also examines the weakness of Parliament when it comes to effectively scrutinizing the work of the executive, especially in the judicial field.

One view as to why the structure and operation of British politics has not changed fundamentally over the years is that the population is both deferential and acquiescent, and thus that Britain provides a classic example of an 'allegiant democracy', in which citizens are highly supportive of the structure and operation of the state and citizen involvement is limited and takes place through established channels. The extract by Geraint Parry and George Moyser (2.2) examines the extent and nature of political participation in Britain. Basing their findings on a large-scale national survey they conclude that serious protest activity is rare and that most people limit their participation in politics to relatively infrequent and established activities such as voting, signing petitions and, more occasionally, contacting their representatives. They also review who participates and show how this is related to personal resources, notably education and wealth, group affiliation and age and gender. The picture that emerges is of a population which participates only to a limited degree.

In addition to voting in elections, there are two other well established channels through which the participation of citizens takes place: pressure groups and political parties. Paul Whiteley and Steve Winyard (2.3) analyse one set of pressure groups – the poverty lobby. They analyse the composition of this lobby, the strategies and tactics employed by the various groups involved and their effectiveness in influencing public policy. Contrary to accepted wisdom, they show that the most influential groups tend to be those which work through Parliament, the media and political parties rather than those which mainly pursue an 'insider' approach by exploiting direct contacts with civil servants and ministers.

The nature of the British party system is considered in the piece by Stephen Ingle (2.4). He examines seven major assumptions which are often made about British political parties, and shows that these need to be either qualified or even dismissed. His analysis amounts to a critique of the two-party system, which in recent years has tended to break down at the electoral level, while within Parliament and central government one party has become dominant: the Conservatives.

British representative democracy is centred upon Parliament, and, as previously noted, the concept of parliamentary sovereignty places Parliament at the centre of the constitutional framework. Indeed this doctrine leads to one of the central questions that has to be posed about the nature of the British system – who or what controls Parliament? In essence the key element is party, and through party discipline, the party leadership or ministerial team in government. In this context Gavin Drewry's (2.5) outline of the legislative process should be read alongside Richard Rose's (2.6) analysis of the emerging patterns of dissent in the House of Commons. Reviewing evidence which suggests a more assertive role for Parliament, Rose concludes that change has in fact been marginal and that the subordinate relationship of Parliament to the executive, through the governing party, still remains the norm.

Because of the centralized nature of the British state, at least in a purely formal sense, the operations of the executive arm of government are bound to be of considerable importance. Anthony King (2.7) examines the office of the prime minister and outlines seven main tasks which incumbents are expected to perform. He notes that much depends on how each particular prime minister chooses to use the powers and resources granted to him or her, while at the same time emphasizing that there are important constraints upon the exercise of this power. The most important of these – a limited scope for independent decision-making and the uncertain tenure of the prime minister as party leader – are in fact built in to the nature of the governmental and party systems. At the same time, as Martin Burch (2.8) points out, the procedures and the manner of handling business in the central executive have been changing in response to both individual and more long-term factors concerning the volume and complexity of business. He highlights the growing use of an informal structure of 'decision shaping' underlying the more formalized structure of Cabinet and its committees. Though this pattern was a prominent feature of Margaret Thatcher's premiership, it was already emerging before her period in office.

One major constraint on the prime minister and ministers alike is the existence of a permanent civil service. This is examined in the piece by Shirley Williams (2.9), who writes with the experience of one who has been a senior cabinet minister. She shows that the orthodox constitutional doctrine that ministers are responsible to Parliament for what happens in their department is seriously flawed on grounds of both administrative logic and actual practice. Moreover the growth in recent years of a more vigorous Parliament, mass media and public have made it even more difficult to sustain this doctrine. Her contribution reveals the opportunities available to civil servants to shape the content of policy decisions.

The role of institutions and the particular personnel who occupy them in determining policy outcomes need to be set alongside the impact of deeper factors embedded in the nature of the political system itself. This is clearly brought out in the piece by Arnold Heidenheimer, Hugh Heclo and Carolyn Adams (2.10). This compares policy patterns in Britain, France and Sweden and emphasizes the extent to which there are characteristic national 'styles' of policy making and the manner in which these, in turn, vary across policy sectors such as health and education. They go on to consider the evidence that institutional and constitutional patterns can have a significant effect on the successful outcome of policies. In essence their argument is that the day-to-day operation of political forces has to be set within the context of a range of wider factors which serve to shape and channel them.

Martin Burch

2.1 Problems of the 'constitution'

Anthony Lester

The system under stress

Equality in parts

It follows from the fact that, unlike most other countries, the United Kingdom does not enunciate civil rights and freedoms in positive terms that there is no common core of national civil rights which are guaranteed irrespective of the particular part of the country in which the individual happens to be. Indeed, there is no 'national law' of any kind except to the extent that Acts of Parliament have been applied to the whole of the United Kingdom. Even in the rare instances in which positive rights have been conferred by Parliament (rather than being derived negatively from the absence of any legal prohibition), they have not been conferred upon a national basis.

For example, Parliament has legislated extensively in one area to which most other democracies accord special constitutional protection – namely, equality of treatment without unfair discrimination. However, because British legislation is characteristically specific, pragmatic, and piecemeal, there is no coherence about the guarantees of non-discrimination in this country. In Britain it is unlawful to discriminate on racial grounds,[1] but racial discrimination is not unlawful in Northern Ireland. It is unlawful in Northern Ireland to discriminate on grounds of religious belief or political opinions,[2] but such discrimination is not unlawful in Britain.[3] It is unlawful throughout the United Kingdom to discriminate on the grounds of sex;[4] but the protection of the law is divided by the Irish Sea, so that the Equal Opportunities Commission and the Equal Opportunities Commission for Nothern Ireland are forbidden to share information about their investigations into suspected unlawful sex discrimination,[5] and the employment provisions are confined only to employment at establishments in Britain or in Northern Ireland.[6] The concepts of discrimination also differ radically as between the British sex- and race-discrimination and the Northern Ireland religious-discrimination statutes, the former covering direct and indirect discrimination, the latter covering only direct discrimination.

Devolution in a vacuum

The absence of a national corpus of enforceable constitutional rights was a serious problem during the abortive attempt in the mid-1970s to devolve legislative and executive powers to Scotland (and executive powers to Wales). The preparatory work on proposals for the devolution of power to Scotland and to Wales was undertaken by the (Kilbrandon) Royal Commission on the Constitution. The Kilbrandon Report recommended the transfer of substantial powers to a Scottish Assembly, but it rejected a federal solution, including a justiciable Bill of Rights.[7] The Report, like so many previous British commentaries, did not comprehend the strongly unifying character of a federal system in maintaining a national framework for a plural society.

Unfortunately, the government accepted the Kilbrandon Report's view.[8] It is characteristic of the pervasive influence of the doctrine of Parliamentary sovereignty and of English dislike of justiciable constitutional rights that the government originally found it necessary to leave open[9] the question whether there should be any judicial review at all of the exercise of the legislative powers of the proposed Scottish Assembly. Eventually the government decided in favour of judicial review,[10] but there were no existing enforceable constitutional criteria for determining whether the legislative actions of the Scottish Assembly were compatible with the economic and political unity of the United Kingdom and the rights and liberties of its citizens.

The 'Scottish Problem' – that is, the problem of how to concede home rule to Scotland without destroying the unity of the Kingdom – may well return to perplex Whitehall and Westminster. So may the problem of devolving power from the over-centralized centre to English and Welsh Regional Assemblies and executives. It is therefore still worth while to consider the consequences of the absence of enforceable constitutional criteria in this context.

Let us suppose that the Scottish Assembly had been established, and that it had been dominated by members of the Scottish National Party seeking to secede from the Union and therefore eager to provoke conflicts about matters of policy between the Assembly in Edinburgh and the central government in London. Suppose also that the Scottish Assembly had passed an enabling measure in a field such as commerce expressly devolved to them by the Westminster Parliament. On its face the Scottish measure might come within the powers devolved to the Scottish Assembly, but in practice the measure might be able to be applied so as to discriminate against persons not born in or resident in Scotland.

In the absence of constitutional criteria, judicial review would be confined, at any rate according to the traditional approach, to a textual analysis of the language of the Devolution Act and the Scottish measure to determine the 'pith and substance' of the Scottish measure. There being no constitutional guarantee of freedom of commerce throughout the country or of equal protection of national law, our courts would not consider the consequences of the operation of the Scottish measure for 'inter-state' commerce and equality of citizenship. Provided that the subject was within an expressly devolved area, our courts would be likely to declare that the Scottish measure and its application were lawful. The hypothetical Scottish measure would therefore have received judicial blessing even though it was discriminatory in effect and threatened to 'Balkanize' the United Kingdom. If the central government were able and willing to intervene by relying upon the sovereignty of the Westminster Parliament to exercise overriding powers, it would thereby risk arousing resentment and strengthening the forces of separatism in Scotland. If the central government were unable or unwilling to intervene, the fundamental unity and freedom of commerce of the United Kingdom would be impaired, and citizens of the United Kingdom would be denied equal protection of the laws.

Fortunately, the United Kingdom belongs to the European Community and it is bound by the European Convention on Human Rights. If the Scotland Act 1978 had come into force after the referendum, our courts would have had the duty to ensure that Assembly measures complied with the directly effective provisions of Community law. In this way Community principles would have served as a substitute for some of the elements of a coherent national constitutional framework. For example, our courts could have held that an Assembly Act operated in breach of the Community guarantees of the free movement of goods, services, and labour, and the right of establishment, without discrimination based on nationality.

But what our courts could not have done was to rule upon the compatibility of an Assembly Act with the European Convention on Human Rights. Because the Convention has not been incorporated into our legal system it has no legal force and does not bind ministers, civil servants, or a Scottish Assembly. Furthermore, although section 19 of the Scotland Act would have required the Secretary of State to refer questions about the Assembly's legislative powers to the Judicial Committee of the Privy Council for decision, it confined to the Secretary of State, rather than to the Judicial Committee, the question whether an Assembly Bill was 'compatible with Community obligations or any other international obligations of the United Kingdom'. In a crucial area in which the Judicial Committee might have been able to apply the Convention as a substitute for a United Kingdom Bill of Rights, the 1978 Act ineptly reserved the matter for the opinion of the Minister. And if the Secretary of State had failed to uphold the fundamental rights of the Convention against an offending Assembly measure, then under our bizarre arrangements the only judicial remedies would have been those of the European Commission and Court of Human Rights.

The absence of constitutional guarantees also means that the institutions of regional and local government and their electors have no enforceable protection against legislative usurpation by the central government in Parliament. Our omnipotent Parliament may abridge the taxing powers of local government; it may abolish local government elections; it may abolish local government itself, including the Greater London Council and the metropolitan county councils. The government in Parliament may do so from whim or prejudice or political disagreement with the policies of the elected local authorities. It may do so without obtaining a special majority and without having recourse to a referendum. The central government could not, of course, use its legislative majority to act in this way in some other modern democratic countries.

Government immunities and the rule of law

According to Dicey,[11] one particular virtue of our system, compared with less favoured nations elsewhere, is that 'here every man, whatever be his rank or condition, is subject to the ordinary law of the realm and amenable to the jurisdiction of the ordinary tribunals'. The reality is rather different. Despite the Crown Proceedings Act 1947, the government and public authorities continue to enjoy special immunities from ordinary legal process. For example, neither the Ministry of Defence nor a member of the armed forces is liable in tort for causing the death or personal injury to another member of the armed forces while on duty, even in time of peace. Police officers and prison officers are not entitled to bring a claim for unfair dismissal before an industrial tribunal. There are very wide powers enabling the government to exclude Crown employment from the rights and remedies conferred by the employment protection legislation and the Sex Discrimination and Race Relations Acts. These exemptions from liability cannot be challenged before our courts, but their application may well be contrary to the Convention. In cases involving sex discrimination they are subject to Community law.

A series of cases brought by prisoners against the United Kingdom under the European Convention illustrate the tenacity of governments in clinging to their self-interested theory of the English rule of law. They arose at a time when the English courts gave little hope of redress to prisoners for violations of their civil rights.[12] In October 1980 the Commission upheld the complaints of seven applicants. The Commission's report revealed the extent of the subterranean restrictions on prisoners' correspondence. With effect from December 1981 the Home Office made major reforms of these practices, which the Court subsequently held[13] to have been in breach of the Convention.

At every stage successive governments had resisted any encroachment upon their power to decide whether and to what extent prisoners should be able to complain to lawyers, MPs, and public authorities, and to bring legal proceedings against the Home Office. In countries with enforceable constitutional guarantees of fundamental rights, this pattern of abuse of power could have been speedily remedied by national courts. In the United Kingdom the only effective remedies were those of the European Convention.

Public authorities as private persons

The still remaining governmental immunities from legal process are happily rare and exceptional. What are of much greater practical significance are the unjustifiable advantages enjoyed by public authorities because of the absence of a comprehensive system of public law which guarantees positive rights and freedoms for the citizen and which imposes correlative duties upon the State and its agents.

Since 1950 our courts have developed important principles of administrative law and statutory interpretation, so as to ensure that public authorities act fairly and in accordance with the law; and with the introduction of a modern procedure of judicial review of administrative action the courts increasingly seek to distinguish between 'public law' and 'private law'. The adverse consequences for the citizen are procedural and substantive. The doctrine of exclusivity of judicial review under RSC Order 53, propounded by the House of Lords in *O'Reilly's case*,[14] imposes procedural disadvantages upon applicants suing *public* bodies which do not impede access to remedies against powerful *private* institutions. Moreover, under our incomplete system of public law, unlike 'more developed legal systems',[15] those injured by illegal acts of the administration cannot be compensated unless those acts are tortious. In this respect public authorities are in a more privileged position in this country than in Commonwealth countries with written constitutions and enforceable Bills of Rights.[16]

The absence of a code of positive principles of public law means that public officers are sometimes able to act as though they were private individuals without special public duties. For example, it follows from the absence of a general right of privacy in the English law of tort, still less of a constitutional guarantee in 'public law', that a police officer is as much entitled to tap a telephone as is any private person.[17] Given the incomplete nature of our public law, it is necessary to have recourse to the European Commission to establish a breach of Article 8 of the Convention.

The most dramatic and increasingly frequent cases in which public authorities have been able to take advantage of the theory of legal equality, which treats them as if they were private persons, have arisen in relation to the balance between free expression and personal privacy. Subject to the exception provided by section 10 of the Contempt of Court Act 1981, public authorities (which enjoy public-interest immunity against the disclosure of some categories of their own documents) have been able to rely upon private law rights of property and confidentiality in order to protect official secrets against disclosure to the public. Because public authorities are not under a duty imposed by public law to respect the right to freedom of expression, the issues have been decided within the framework of private law, as though a government department or a public corporation were a private person enforcing private rights.

The English approach is fundamentally different from the approach under the European Convention or its equivalent in national Bills of Rights. Article 10 of the Convention guarantees the right to free expression subject to certain specific and limited exceptions. Where a public authority interferes with the right to freedom of expression, the burden is upon the State and its agents to show that the interference is not only for a legitimate purpose but also that it is 'necessary' to achieve that purpose in serving a 'pressing social need'.[18] Whether under the Convention or under an enforceable Bill of Rights, the starting points is the right to free expression. In our legal system the right to free expression has no enforceable constitutional protection. The starting point is the right to property of the State or its agents and the burden is upon the individual to persuade the court that proprietary rights should exceptionally be displaced or overridden.

Even if our courts had been required by Act of Parliament to have regard to the rights guaranteed by Article 10 of the Convention, the results of these cases might well have been the same. But the judicial method and the burden of proof would have been entirely different. The argument would have begun with the individual's right to free expression and the necessary exceptions to that right, rather than with the proprietary rights of public authorities.[19] The 'Spycatcher' litigation has changed all of this. Influenced by the case law of the European Court (as well as by the Crossman Diaries case) the English Courts have rejected the Crown's argument that it is to be equated with a private individual invoking private law. Instead, they have weighed the competing *public* interests using a European approach.[20]

Antiquated machinery of government

Parliament is and must remain at the centre of our system of government. But Parliament is less well equipped today to exercise independent control of the executive than it was in 1900. There has been little expansion in House of Commons staff to match the growth of government during the century. Nor does the Commons sit for much longer than before the First World War. An MP who sat in the Commons in 1900 would find little in the present framework of operation to surprise him (including the overwhelmingly male composition of the Commons).

He would, however, be bewildered by the vast increase in the scale and nature of the work of the Commons. There are now fourteen House of Commons Departmental Select Committees, where in the 1960s there was only the Select Committee on Nationalised Industries. The annual length of the statute-book doubled between 1945 and 1965, and since 1965 it has further grown from about 1,800 pages to 2,800 in 1980. There has been a similar increase in the volume of delegated legislation. In the twenty years from 1951 to 1970, over 43,000 statutory instruments were made, an average of over 2,000 a year, or nearly double the number at the beginning of the century. A growing amount of subordinate legislation consists of regulations and directives made under the Treaty of Rome. Not surprisingly, large chunks of complex and technical Acts of Parliament and subordinate instruments are turned into law without parliamentary scrutiny or debate, their contents understood by only a handful of expert administrators. These examples illustrate the strains which are being imposed not only Parliament but also upon ministers and their civil servants.

A few more facts and figures will illustrate the scale of the problem of systemic overload.[21] The total number of parliamentary questions tabled to all government departments in 1964–65 was about 20,000. In 1981–82 it had increased to over 35,000. In 1964–65, 1,173 parliamentary questions were asked of the Home Secretary. In 1981–82 their total had more than doubled to 2,596. In 1967 about 9,400 letters were sent to the Home Office which required a considered ministerial reply. Ten years later the total had more than doubled, and in 1982 it was 24,255.

Many of these parliamentary questions and letters raised important issues about individual rights and freedoms. It is essential in a democracy that they should be raised and that they should be properly answered; just as it is essential that the legislation passed by Parliament should be properly scrutinized and debated. The strains imposed by these changes in the quantity of legislative and executive business are immense.

Despite its size, the House of Commons cannot carry the weight of its responsibilities as the clearing-house for all legislation and the airing of all grievances. The unreformed House of Lords cannot share the burden adequately. Nor is the burden shared, as it is in many other democratic countries, by regional assemblies and executives. On the contrary, the present tendency is towards undemocratic centralism. More and more *ad hoc* regional organizations are nominated instead of elected; their day-to-day work is outside effective parliamentary control. Numerous private organizations, including multinational companies, professional and trade associations, and trade unions, exercise such great power in our modern industrial state that they are 'private governments' within their own domain.

Our machinery of government is nowhere more antiquated than in the area of law and justice. Unlike other Commonwealth countries and Western European countries, only the functions of a Ministry of the Interior are co-ordinated by a single department of state – the Home Office. All the other functions, mainly of a Ministry of Justice, are fragmented among other different governmental agencies, with inadequate ministerial supervision and responsibility and therefore inadequate parliamentary accountability.

One consequence of these archaic arrangements is that governments do not receive adequate legal advice. The Lord Chancellor invariably sits in the Cabinet. But he has no formal responsibility for giving legal advice to the government. Whether he does so, perhaps at a Cabinet meeting, is a matter of chance; and his office has neither the responsibility nor the resources for giving comprehensive and systematic legal advice. Formally, the responsibility for legal advice to government lies with the Attorney-General,[22] who is not usually in the Cabinet and not at the centre of government policy-planning.

Government bills are drafted in the Office of Parliamentary Counsel, but subordinate legislation is not. Formally, Parliamentary Counsel are responsible to the Prime Minister: in practice, they are almost totally autonomous and show every intention of remaining so. There is a standing Cabinet Committee on Legislation, usually chaired by the Lord Chancellor, and responsible in theory for ensuring that draft bills give effect to government policy and are otherwise fit to be presented to Parliament. But, unlike the French Council of

State, that Committee is not equipped to scrutinize government bills for compliance with the fundamental (if unwritten) principles of the constitution. Nor does it have the resources to scrutinize the mass of subordinate legislation drafted by government departments themselves. The current state of our statute-book is a monument to the defects of our present system of preparing intelligible and consistent legislation.

The Office of Parliamentary Counsel is not alone in its lack of accountability to Parliament. Because of their judicial functions, the Lord Chancellor's Department and the Law Officers' Department are not subject to the scrutiny of the Commons Select Committee on Home Affairs or any other select committee. For reasons lost in the mists of antiquity, the Treasury Solicitor's Department answers to the Chancellor of the Exchequer.

Examples of the inertia of the system are legion. Despite the repeated recommendations of the Lord Chancellor's Advisory Committee on Legal Aid,[23] there is still no unified approach to legal services, and no coherent public policy on the funding of law centres. Our Parliamentary commissioner is more fettered in his powers than ombudsmen in the rest of the world.[24] Our Law Commissions deal with a narrower and more technical agenda than other Law Commissions in the Commonwealth. The Law Commission has recommended[25] that an inquiry into the existing state of administrative law should be carried out by a Royal Commission or committee of comparable status. Successive governments have refused to authorize such an inquiry.

Our failure as a nation to reform and to renew our constitutional and legal system cannot be explained wholly or even mainly by the antiquated machinery for governing law and justice in this country. But the inadequate nature of the machinery makes it peculiarly difficult to launch comprehensive and coherent proposals for change; the governing of justice is fragmented between the Lord Chancellor's Department, the Law Officers' Department, and the Home Office; the Lord Chancellor is inhibited by his judicial responsibilities and lack of political strength equal to the Home Secretary's; and the Home Office is afflicted by departmental schizophrenia, torn between its functions as a Ministry of Justice and as a Ministry of the Interior, with the Ministry of the Interior naturally tending to prevail.

The end of isolation

Since the middle of the century the United Kingdom has become more and more isolated in its constitutional arrangements. We are almost alone in the Commonwealth in lacking a written constitution. We are also in a minority in having no enforceable Bill of Rights. By approving independence constitutions for the new Commonwealth, the Parliament of Westminster has exported the fundamental rights and freedoms of the European Convention (which are incorporated into those constitutions) on a scale without parallel in the rest of the world. In those Commonwealth countries which have preserved their democracies since independence, judges habitually review the constitutionality of legislation and administrative action against standards directly derived from the Convention. But the Westminster Parliament has failed to use its sovereign powers to secure the rights and freedoms of the Convention for the people of this country by incorporating the Convention into our law.[26] We are also isolated from the twenty other member countries of the Council of Europe which have written constitutions and an enforceable Bill of Rights. A century after the publication of Dicey's prejudiced comparative constitutional study, we can see the great virtues of the French and West German systems. And the inadequacy of our own system is highlighted by our membership of the European Community, whose framework and working methods are derived from civil-law countries with written constitutions, fundamental rights, and comprehensive systems of public law.

The peculiar genius of the British constitution is supposed to consist in its flexibility and capacity for evolutionary change. But the most striking characteristic of our constitution has been its failure to adapt to the changed needs of the nation. Every recent attempt at major reform has been blocked or mismanaged: incorporation of the European Convention; the electoral system; the House of Lords; devolution; regional and local government; citizenship; public access to official information; administrative law.

> Abridged from Anthony Lester, 'The constitution: decline and renewal' in Jeffrey Jowell and Dawn Oliver, eds. (1989), *The Changing Constitution*, 2nd edition, Clarendon Press, Oxford, pp. 352–69. Reprinted by permission of Oxford University Press, Oxford.

Notes

1 Race Relations Act 1976.
2 Fair Employment (Northern Ireland) Act 1976.
3 Unless religious discrimination is also contrary to the Race Relations Act 1976, as in *Mandla v. Dowell Lee* [1983] ICR 385 (HL); or contrary to the common law; see *Cumings v. Birkenhead Corporation* [1972] Ch. 12 (CA).
4 Sex Discrimination Act 1975; Sex Discrimination (Northern Ireland) Order 1976, 1976 No. 1042 (NI 15); Equal Pay Act 1970; Equal Pay (Northern Ireland) Order 1970.
5 Sex Discrimination Act 1975, s. 61, and Sex Discrimination (Northern Ireland) Order 1976, Article 61. Each Commission is a separate legal entity for the purposes of the restrictions on the disclosure of information to 'any other person'.
6 Sections 6 and 10 of the 1975 Act and Articles 8 and 13 of the 1976 Order. It follows that a woman could be discriminated against in Northern Ireland by a large employer based in Britain if the Northern Ireland 'establishment' by which she was employed came within the 'small employer' exception in Article 8(3)(b) of the 1976 Order. However, the 'small employer' exception has been held by the European

Court of Justice to be contrary to Community law because of its overbreadth; see *Commission of the European Communities v. United Kingdom* [1984] 1 All ER 353, 363.

7 Report of the Royal Commission on the Constitution 1969–1973 (1973), Cmnd. 5460, paras. 538–9, 746–55.

8 *Democracy and Devolution: Proposals for Scotland and Wales* (1974), Cmnd. 5732, para. 2.

9 *Our Changing Democracy: Devolution to Scotland and Wales* (1975), Cmnd. 6348, paras. 62–5.

10 *Devolution to Scotland and Wales: Supplementary Statement* (1976), Cmnd. 6585, para. 14.

11 A. V. Dicey (1959), *Introduction to the Study of Law and of the Constitution*, 10th edn, Macmillan, London, p. 193.

12 See *Becker v. Home Office* [1972] IQB 407 (CA); *Arbon v. Anderson* [1943] IKB. 252; *Silverman v. Prison Commissioners* (1955) Crim. LR 116; *Williams v. Home Office* (No. 2) [1981] 1 All ER 1211.

13 *Silver and Others v. United Kingdom*, Judgement of 25 March, 1983, Series A, No. 61, 5 EHRR 347.

14 *O'Reilly v. Mackman* [1983] AC 237 (HL).

15 *Hoffmann-La Roche v. Secretary of State* [1975] AC 295 (HL), p. 539 *per* Lord Wilberforce.

16 Compensation is also recoverable for breaches of the European Convention on Human Rights under Article 50.

17 See *Malone v. Metropolitan Police Commissioner* [1979] Ch. 344. But see now the Interception of Communications Act 1985.

18 *The Sunday Times* Case, Judgement of 26 April 1976, Series A, No. 30, para. 59.

19 Compare the dissenting speeches by Lord Scarman and Lord Simon of Glaisdale, relying upon Article 10, with the majority in *Home Office v. Harman* [1983] AC 1 (HL), which regarded the case as having nothing to do with the right to free expression.

20 The interlocutory proceedings are reported in [1987] 1 WLR 1248. The merits are reported in [1988] 2 WLR 805, and the House of Lords' final decision is in [1988] 3 WLR 776.

21 I am grateful to the Home Office for providing this information so as to enable me to bring up to date the figures contained in a speech made by the Home Secretary, Mr Roy Jenkins, in March 1976 on 'Human rights and constitutional change', *Human Rights Review*, 1, 1976, pp. 193–4, from which this section draws heavily.

22 For the sake of brevity this account ignores the arrangements for Scotland and for Northern Ireland.

23 See the Thirty-third Annual Report of the Lord Chancellor's Advisory Committee on Legal Aid (1983) HC 137, para. 170.

24 See Parliamentary Commissioner for Administration, *Annual Report*, London, 1983, Introduction, paras. 7 and 8.

25 Law Commission Working Paper No. 40, Remedies in *Administrative Law* (1969), Cmnd. 4059; Report (1976), Cmnd. 6407.

26 See A. Lester, 'Fundamental rights: the United Kingdom isolated?', *Public Law*, 46, 1984, pp. 56–7.

2.2 Political participation in Britain

Geraint Parry and George Moyser

Wherever one takes a position in the great debate between representative and participatory democrats it is clear that no democracy can function without the involvement of its citizens. What is at issue is the extent and nature of the citizen participation which is thought to be required if a democracy is to be worthy of its name. Whilst this is a fundamentally normative issue, the protagonists on both sides regularly cite evidence as to actual levels of participation and draw inferences from that evidence in support of their contentions.

On the one side are those who assert that in Britain 'some of the spectators have begun to descend on to the field'; on the other are those who say that 'the "grass roots" of politics seem shrivelled and starved of the nourishment of participation by the citizens'.[1] For this reason, as Jane Mansbridge has said, 'field studies of what happens to various ideals when people try to live by them could prove useful in clarifying a wide range of normative questions'.[2]

Accordingly, our aim has been to map political participation in Britain, examine its underlying structure and, finally, to draw some conclusions about the prospects for the kind of democracy which the country may become.[3]

How much participation?

In Table 2.2(1) we present the percentages of the total national sample reporting having performed each of twenty-three political actions at least once in the last five years. It will be seen that the activity in which most people have been engaged is voting. In this respect voting is exceptional. It is subject to intensive mobilization by the parties and the political class in general. But it is apparent that there is far more to participation than voting. Quite substantial minorities have contacted representatives and officials. Smaller numbers have worked either with organized groups or in a more informal manner with friends and neighbours to deal with an issue or problem. Party compaigning involves still fewer people. Canvassing is a demanding form of political activity requiring a substantial degree of commitment. This is registered in the fact that only 3.5 percent have done it, although it has to be recognised that opportunities for many such campaigning activities occur only at periodic elections.

Implicit in much of the concern in recent years about the changing and less 'civic' quality of the British culture has been the belief that protest is on the increase. Firm evidence as to such trends is notoriously difficult to discover. However, from the figures in Table 2.2(1) it is apparent that, with one notable

Table 2.2(1)   *How much participation is there in Britain?*

	Percentage Yes/at least once in last five years
A: Voting	
1 voted in every/most local elections	68.8
2 voted general election 1983	82.5
3 voted European election 1984	47.3
B: Party Campaigning	
4 fund raising	5.2
5 canvassed	3.5
6 clerical work	3.5
7 attended rally	8.6
C: Group Activity	
8 informal group	13.8
9 organized group	11.2
10 raised a political issue in group	4.7
D: Contacting	
11 member of parliament	9.7
12 civil servant	7.3
13 councillor	20.7
14 town hall	17.4
15 media	3.8
E: Protesting	
16 attended protest meeting	14.6
17 organised petition	8.0
18 signed petition	63.3
19 blocked traffic	1.1
20 protest march	5.2
21 'political' strike	6.5
22 political boycott	4.3
23 used physical force	0.2

(N = c. 1570)

exception, protest activity is quite rare – although no rarer, it might be noted, than campaigning for a party. The exception is signing a petition, which is the only activity to rival voting, and one which requires little more effort. The more radical types of direct action are performed by quite small proportions and the 'use of physical force against political opponents' was so rare as not to be analysable through this type of sample survey.

Another way of considering the profile of participation is to ask how far it is concentrated amongst a small number of activists or spread in a relatively egalitarian manner evenly amongst the population at large. In Britain, relative to a notional maximum of twenty-three actions, the overall rate of participation is rather low. The average person has performed only just over four of these actions (4.2) in the five-year period. Only a very small minority (4 percent) have done nothing whatsoever. However, a truer test of activism might be to discount the four 'easy' acts of voting and signing a petition. In this case the average citizen has undertaken only about one and a half of the more demanding activities. Indeed nearly half (45.8 percent) had done nothing beyond those four 'easy' activities. By this measure, the spectators in the stands outnumber the players (those who have done six of the demanding actions) by about eight to one.

Who participates?

The British population ranges, it has been seen, from the inert to the highly active. To the degree that participation has some effect in getting issues on to the agenda and, generally, ensuring that people are heard, it becomes relevant to know whether certain sectors of the population are more prominent than others. Is there a 'bias' to participation?

There are many ways in which the population can be categorized – by class, wealth, education, gender, age, race and area of residence amongst others. Within the compass of a summary such as this it is not possible to analyse all these factors.[4] It is therefore essential to concentrate on a few, those crucial to the analysis or of particular social and political interest.

(a) *Resources.* In common with some earlier studies we have employed a resource model as the baseline for this part of the analysis. By 'resources' we mean material wealth, educationally based skills, and membership of organizations such as political parties, trades unions and voluntary groups. Collectively, these are resources which place persons in a better position to promote their interests by some form of political action. A lack of resources increases the odds against political success.[5]

Resources may be divided into those of an individual nature (wealth and education) and those based on groups (ties to organizations). Education was measured by possession of formal qualifications. Wealth was measured by an index constructed from stated income, ownership of a house, car and stocks and shares. As is commonly found, wealth and education are strongly associated but not to the extent, for example, that lack of education entirely excluded persons from being at the highest level of the wealth scale.

Education has frequently been found to have a positive association with participation.[6] This 'law' generally holds true for Britain. Graduates are amongst the top 12 percent on the overall participation scale whilst the 46.6 percent of the sample with no qualifications are clustered towards the bottom of the ladder. Those without formal education have, on average, performed about one political action beyond voting and petitioning, whereas graduates have done 3½, which, by British standards, makes them highly participatory. This relationship between education and participation holds, if in slightly moderated form, if we control for the possession of wealth and organizational resources. Education, in short, provides its own impulse to participation.

The same relationship holds true for most of the distinct modes of action. The only exception is voting where, puzzlingly, graduates vote less than average. But they do more contacting, campaigning, collective action and, significantly, direct action. Protest is associated with the well-educated, rather than with the educationally less advantaged (although it has to be recalled that the latter are far greater in number).

Wealth also has a generally positive association with overall participation. The 'haves' participate more than the 'have nots'. Those in the wealthiest 5 percent of the population perform on average three actions. But, unlike education, controlling for the possession of other resources reduces the effect of wealth as an independent factor to such a marked extent that it ceases to be significant. This is also true, although less completely so, of the connection between wealth and the several modes of participation. These do, however, show some interesting variations. The wealthier one is the more likely one is to vote. There is no sudden dip in turnout as there was with graduates. In all but one of the modes they also participate more, although only slightly so after adjusting for other resources. The exception is, not unexpectedly, direct action. It is the poor who protest, not the wealthy.

Education and wealth here seem at odds with one another despite the generally positive association of the two sets of resources. Closer examination mitigates the discrepancy. There appear to be two major sources of direct action. The first is amongst the poor who do, however, have at least some educational qualifications, at least up to 'O' level. Materially disadvantaged, their education may have encouraged them to perceive a political element in their lack of rewards. This group includes some of the unemployed. The second source is amongst the very well-educated whose material rewards are only in the intermediate range and not at the wealthiest level. Whether they were socialized at university and polytechnic into post-materialist values[7] or are simply concerned with their material advantage, they are more sympathetic to the less conventional spheres of political action.

Group-based resources have been measured by a person's adherence to formal organizations, in particular to political parties, trades unions and other voluntary associations. These may range from major interest groups and causes to leisure groups with little or no political involvement. (It should be noted, however, that mere membership, even of a political party is not in itself taken to be participatory *activity*.) Around two-thirds of the population belong to one formal organization but the average is less than two. At the same time, these group resources tend to be cumulative: party members and trades unionists are more prone to be tied also to other voluntary groups. By and large it is also the case that those with greater individual resources (wealth and education) also possess more group resources. Thus collective resources in Britain are not, on the whole, a way in which less economically advantaged individuals can fully compensate politically by solidaristic action.[8] This is not to say that the poor and less educated are not organized but that they tend to be out-organized by the better-off.

Group affiliation is amongst the most powerful predictors of participation – the strength of the linkage being twice that for education and many times stronger than for wealth. To belong to a network of organizations is strongly associated with activism in general and in a variety of directions. Those who lack ties are well below the average level of participation. One tie brings a person up to the average. The participatory threshold is firmly crossed by those with three ties, which applies to only 10 percent of the sample. They have performed on average nearly three actions over and above voting and signing a petition. Those with four ties rise to an average of 4.5 actions, which makes them more than twice as participatory as the wealthiest 5 percent of the population and almost twice as active as graduates.

The number of a person's ties does not greatly affect direct action or party compaigning. However, contacting and, especially but not surprisingly, collective action are strongly associated with group affiliation. The *kind* of groups one is involved in also makes a difference to one's propensity to participate. The more one's groups are themselves organizations in which political issues are raised or discussed the more likely one is to be politically active. The same is true, moreover, of those who say they are active within their groups. Activity is thus self-reinforcing.

Two kinds of organization deserve particular mention for their proximity to political action – trades unions and political parties. Union membership gives some boost to participation but the surprise, perhaps, is that it is not greater. Once we control for other individual and group resources it is fairly modest. However, it is greater than the boost given by membership of only one voluntary group. Moreover, even if the impact is, on average, not very considerable, the base of union membership is extremely broad. Furthermore, those few who are highly active within the union movement are also amongst the most participatory in the population.

Membership of a political party, although not a form of participation by our definition, is undeniably closely connected to political activity, if only because members are clearly open to mobilization for campaigning purposes. But there are plenty of party members who do nothing in the way of further action. Nevertheless, party members are indeed highly participatory although their numbers (7.4 percent of the sample) are such that their overall impact is not necessarily greater than that of trade unionists. Members of all parties, and especially Labour adherents, are, on average, very active both overall and in nearly every mode of participation, even after controlling for the possession of other resources. Conservatives, not surprisingly, are the only party members who are well below average in direct action. They compensate, however, by voting more regularly than their main rivals.

For all the variations in the type of impact upon participation made by groups it remains the case that, taken together, organizational ties count for a great deal. Nevertheless, important as they are, it is necessary to take account of other possible influences. Two personal factors in particular have attracted considerable attention in this context – age and gender.[9]

(b) *Age and gender.* There are two major ways in which age and participation may be related. There may be a 'life-cycle effect', according to which 'participation rises in early years, peaks in middle age, and falls in later years'.[10] Secondly, there could be a 'generational effect' whereby, for example, the young adopt a stance towards participation quite different from that of their elders.[11] Deciding between these two explanations on the basis of evidence drawn from a single survey is not easy. The data are capable of alternative interpretations and, strictly speaking, the generational view would require a repeated panel study.

The evidence does, on the whole, support the view that participation displays a rising and falling pattern with age. The reason appears to be the change in resources, a good deal of which seems to be due to the life-cycle. Nevertheless, we can expect future older generations to be more wealthy by virtue of expanded house-ownership and, perhaps, to have associated interests to defend by political activity. The gradually rising levels of educational qualifications may also make a long-term impact on participation.

There is one significant difference in participatory patterns which does seem to be the effect of the changing generations. In one respect only are the young (aged 18 to 29) more active: they are more prone to direct action. This still holds true when resources are taken into account, along with such possible life-cycle factors as length of residence and marital or parental status. The young are also moderately active (although still below average) in collective action which, it will be recalled, also includes milder forms of protest. There may here be some sign of a generational shift away from conventional activities towards the unconventional. Only time will tell whether this was a passing feature of 'Thatcher's Britain' or something which will be sustained as this younger generation gets older.[12]

Recent years have seen a long overdue interest in the involvement of women in politics. A standard finding has been that there is a gender gap in citizen participation in favour of men.[13] The evidence of the present survey is that this view must be revised, since the participatory gap in favour of men is now very slight indeed in Britain.[14] Overall, on the scale of nineteen actions (beyond voting and signing petitions), men have undertaken 1.60 and women 1.41 – a difference of less than a fifth of one action. Moreover the relationship between gender and participation is very weak.

A closer analysis does reveal more divergences which, however, do not all point in the same direction. The general pattern of slight 'under-participation' by women turns out to be true of nearly all the modes of participation. The suggestion, which has sometimes been advanced, that women might be relatively more involved in direct action or collective action does not appear to be true for our sample. However, the gender gap disappears almost entirely in the case of party campaigning. When it comes to voting, the female respondents out-participate men.[15] If we then control for resources along with other personal factors, such as age, the gender gap actually reverses itself for overall participation and women are seen to be more active, relatively, than men in party campaigning and collective action as well as voting.

When, in addition, one probes the personal factors which might influence participation one finds that there are some which would appear to de-activate women relative to men. Thus, married women with children are, compared with their male counterparts, less politically involved. By contrast, the single woman is more active than the single man and most active, in relative terms, are female single parents. This may suggest that the feminist agenda can surmount lack of resources. There is, finally, one small group of women who are intensely participatory – members of feminist groups. They are very few in numbers in our sample and, therefore, due care should be exercised in interpreting the results. However, they were in the top 6 percent of participants and were particularly involved in collective and direct action rather than voting or contacting. It is premature to consider such active feminists as heralding a new era in women's participation – they are atypical in being very well-educated and integrated into a network of other groups. But they do indicate one way in which political consciousness may overcome structural and cultural barriers to female participation.

Abridged from Geraint Parry and George Moyser (1990), 'A map of political participation in Britain', *Government and Opposition*, XXV, pp. 147–9, 154–60. Reprinted by permission of *Government and Opposition*.

Notes

1 D. Marquand (1988), *The Unprincipled Society: New Demands and Old Politics*, Fontana, London, p. 237; S. Barnes, M. Kaase *et al.* (1979), *Political Action: Mass Participation in Five Western Democracies*, Sage, Beverly Hills, p. 84.

2 Jane Mansbridge (1980), *Beyond Adversary Democracy*, Basic Books, New York, p. xii.

3 The study is based on a sample survey conducted in 1984–85 of around 1,600 citizens in Britain (excluding Northern Ireland), coupled with a survey of a further 1,600 citizens and some 300 leaders in six contrasting localities. It is a survey of actual participation over the five-year period and not of willingness to act (potential participation). The study was funded mainly by the Economic and Social Research Council (UK). Further details can be found in G. Parry and G. Moyser (1984), 'Political participation in Britain: a research agenda for a new study', *Government*

and *Opposition*, XIX, pp. 68–92. The full report appears in G. Parry, G. Moyser and N. Day (1992), *Participation and Democracy*, Cambridge University Press, Cambridge.

4 Fuller treatment can be found in Parry, Moyser and Day, *Participation and Democracy*.

5 Resources are closely related to social class but, in our view, a resource-based analysis is, for these purposes at least, more fine-grained than one based on class. See G. Moyser and G. Parry (1987), 'Class, sector and political participation in Britain', Manchester Papers in Politics, Department of Government, University of Manchester.

6 See L. Milbrath and M. Goel (1977), *Political Participation: How and Why Do People Get Involved in Politics?*, Rand McNally, Chicago, pp. 98–102.

7 See R. Inglehart (1977), *The Silent Revolution: Changing Values and Political Styles among Western Publics*, Princeton University Press, Princeton, NJ.

8 See A. Pizzorno (1970), 'An introduction to the theory of political participation', *Social Science Information*, 9, pp. 29–61.

9 See Milbrath and Goel, *Political Participation*, pp. 114–18.

10 N. Nie, S. Verba and J.-O. Kim (1974), 'Political participation and the life-cycle', *Comparative Politics*, 6, pp. 319–40.

11 See Barnes, Kaase *et al.*, *Political Action*.

12 Compare M. Kent Jennings (1987), 'Residues of a movement: the ageing of the American protest generation', *American Political Science Review*, 81, pp. 367–82.

13 Milbrath and Goel, *Political Participation*, p. 116.

14 For a discussion of the patterns in other Western democracies see J. Lovenduski (1986), *Women and European Politics: Contemporary Feminism and Public Policy*, Wheatsheaf, Brighton; C. Christy (1987), *Sex Differences in Political Participation: Processes of Change in Fourteen Nations*, Praeger, New York; R. Dalton (1988), *Citizen Politics in Western Democracies*, Chatham House, Chatham, NJ.

15 Compare I. Crewe, T. Fox and J. Alt, 'Non-voting in British general elections 1966–1974', in C. Crouch (ed.) (1976), *British Political Sociology Yearbook*, III: *Participation in Politics*, Croom Helm, London, pp. 38–109.

2.3   Interest groups: the poverty lobby

Paul Whiteley and Steve Winyard

The purpose of this article is to describe the main characteristics of the poverty lobby in Britain, and to discuss the strategies and effectiveness of the groups within it. We begin by briefly describing the framework of social security policy-making within which groups operate. This leads into a discussion of the characteristics of the poverty lobby as a whole, a lobby which is generally larger than has been recognized in the existing literature. After that we examine the strategies and tactics of lobbying by considering examples of particular groups, and this is followed by a discussion of group effectiveness.[1]

Together with a number of tax allowances, benefits and family benefits constitute a system of income maintenance which aims to assist in particular the pensioners, the disabled, one-parent families, the unemployed, and families with children. Social security is the largest single item of government expenditure and in 1982–83 accounted for $31 bn., over one third of total public spending.[2] The Beveridge Report on which the post-war social security system was based envisaged that insurance benefits would be the main source of income support, with means-tested social assistance (National Assistance/ Supplementary Benefit) playing a residual and declining role. However, due to the failure of successive governments to provide adequate insurance benefits, together with adverse social, economic and demographic trends, the numbers receiving NA/SB has increased threefold since 1948.

The growing number dependent on means-tested benefits, together with other deficiencies in the income maintenance system, meant that poverty has grown over time. However, it was only recognised as a significant problem in the mid-1960s when it 'quickly became the leading social issue of the decade, confronting the Labour Government with one of its most difficult social policy decisions'.[3] The re-emergence of the poverty issue was also accompanied by a growth of pressure group activity. New organisations such as CPAG (Child Poverty Action Group) were set up while other long-established organisations such as the National Council for One Parent Families (NCOPF) increased their efforts to influence the income maintenance policies of Government. These groups became known as the 'poverty lobby', although they do not constitute an organised, centrally co-ordinated lobby.

The poverty lobby

Despite the fact that the term is used very frequently, the 'poverty lobby' has never been clearly defined in the literature. Some writers discuss this lobby without offering any explicit definition of its membership and characteristics. Others define it but in rather limited terms which we will argue are inadequate for understanding its true nature and functions.

One of the main reasons for this failure to recognize the full extent of the lobby is that many writers do not take into account sporadic intervention by groups in the policy process. Some groups only get themselves involved in campaigns occasionally, yet this can be quite important in terms of outcomes. Other better known groups are involved on a continuous basis. Also there are some groups that are thought of by informed opinion as welfare and service provision agencies but do in fact in their own way undertake a significant amount of lobbying.

We would define the poverty lobby as those voluntary organisations which regularly or sporadically attempt to influence the income maintenance policies of government in favour of the poor. Using a variety of sources,[4] we built up a list of 31 organisations that were clearly undertaking this type of work.

Following a filter questionnaire which we sent to a further 60 organisations, we included another 11 groups, giving 42 in all. We interviewed leading activists in these groups, in most cases the director or general secretary. We adopted a focused interview approach, taking up a series of themes with them, probing in depth at each stage about the structure, resources, strategies and impacts of their organization. In addition we interviewed MPs, ministers, and senior civil servants, thus building up a more comprehensive picture of the work of such groups.

A primary aim was to assess the lobbying input of each group: that is the amount of time, resources and personnel devoted to influencing income maintenance policy. In the table we list the 42 groups, categorised by the amount of lobbying activity they undertook in the late 1970s. In this table a high level of activity refers to groups which are continuously involved in interest representation, usually with staff involved on a full-time basis. A medium level of lobbying activity covers groups that were sporadically but fairly regularly undertaking work of this kind. Low refers to groups which were only occasionally involved, either on their own behalf or in conjunction with others, in lobbying activities.

The Child Poverty Action Group is a clear example of a group categorised as high on the lobbying scale. Two members of staff were engaged virtually full-time on this type of work, and the group mounted a number of major campaigns in the 1970s, for example to secure the introduction of Child Benefits and the abolition of the wage stop rule.

CPAG was establised in 1965 following a series of meetings arranged by the Quakers. Its founders were mainly Society of Friends members or academics involved in poverty research, including Brian Abel-Smith and Peter Townsend. It rapidly developed its own distinctive approach to lobbying which involved extensive use of the press, the production of high quality research papers on the problems of the poor, and the development of a network of sympathetic opinion leaders in politics and the media. Our research showed that activists in other groups admired the CPAG 'house style' and in some cases sought to emulate it.

An example of a group in the medium category was the National Council for the Single Woman and her Dependants (NCSWD). It would only intervene sporadically in the policy-making process when issues affecting its membership were being discussed. Its style was also very different from that of CPAG, being described by the chairman of the Supplementary Benefits Commission as 'genteel and most unstrident'.[5] It was nevertheless highly successful, playing a crucial part in the introduction of new benefits for the disabled and in particular the Invalid Care Allowance (ICA). In one of our interviews a senior civil servant in the DHSS said that the ICA 'derived almost completely from their activities'.

An example of a group in the low category was the British Association for the Hard of Hearing. It arose as a national co-ordinating agency for social clubs for the partially deaf and is still primarily concerned with promoting social activities and services. But it does occasionally act at the national level to promote the interests of hard of hearing as opposed to the totally deaf.

Another area of interest is the distinction between promotional groups that attempt to speak *for* a particular interest and representational groups that claim a membership made up *of* a particular client group. There is, however, significant variation within these categories: in the former case the groups differ in the extent to which they successfully promote an interest, and in the latter case in the scope and range of interests they represent. Whilst we have divided the groups into categories in the table, it should be stressed that there is in fact a continuum. At the one end there are groups like Gingerbread and the National Federation of the Blind which are strongly representational, with membership made up exclusively of single parents and the blind, whilst at the other are groups such as Youthaid and the Campaign for the Mentally Handicapped that are clearly promotional.

Those groups that have attracted the most attention in the media were established in the 1960s and 1970s and can be described as the 'new poverty lobby'. They contrast with long-established groups such as the Royal National Institute for the Blind and the Family Welfare Association which appear to play a less obvious role in income maintenance lobbying. We can see in the table that there is some reason for this belief since out of 16 groups in the high category, 10 were set up after 1960 and are part of this 'new poverty lobby'.

LOBBYING INPUT OF GROUPS WITH DATE ESTABLISHED AND WHETHER PROMOTIONAL (P) OR REPRESENTATIONAL (R)

High

Royal Association for Disability and Rehabilitation, 1977	(R)
Disablement Income Group, 1965	(P)
Disability Alliance, 1974	(R)
MIND, 1946	(P)
Spastics Society, 1957	(P)
Child Poverty Action Group, 1965	(P)
National Council for One Parent Families, 1918	(P)
Campaign for the Homeless and Rootless, 1973	(R)
Gingerbread, 1970	(R)
Age Concern, 1940	(R)
Help the Aged, 1962	(R)
National Federation of Old Age Pensioner Associations, 1938	(R)
Low Pay Unit, 1974	(P)
Youthaid, 1977	(P)
Shelter, 1966	(P)
National Council for Voluntary Organisations, 1919	(R)

Medium

Royal National Institute for the Deaf, 1911	(R)
Royal National Institute for the Blind, 1868	(R)
National Federation of the Blind, 1947	(R)
National Society for the Mentally Handicapped, 1946	(P)
Campaign for the Mentally Handicapped, 1971	(P)
National League of the Blind, 1954	(R)
Family Welfare Association, 1860	(R)
National Association for the Care and Resettlement of Offenders, 1966	(P)
British Union of Family Organisations, 1949	(P)
CRUSE (National Association for Widows), 1959	(R)
National Association of Widows, 1969	(P)
National Association for the Single Woman and her Dependents, 1965	(R)
National Federation of Women's Institutes, 1917	(R)
Shelter Housing Aid Centre, 1969	(P)

Low

British Association for the Hard of Hearing, 1947	(R)
British Polio Fellowship, 1930	(R)
Psychiatric Rehabilitation Association, 1959	(P)
Union of Catholic Mothers, 1913	(R)
British Association of Settlements, 1926	(R)
Family Services Unit, 1947	(P)
National Womens Aid Federation, 1975	(R)
Womens Liberation Campaign for Financial and Legal Independence, 1977	(R)
National Federation of Claimants Union, 1968	(R)
Prisoners Wives and Families Society, 1973	(R)
Prisoners Wives Service, 1965	(P)
Catholic Housing Aid Society, 1954	(P)

Strategies and tactics: what does the poverty lobby do?

When attempting to influence income maintenance policy, the poverty lobby has a number of possible targets. The most obvious is Whitehall, which includes ministers and civil servants, and specifically the Department of Health and Social Security, the Treasury and to a lesser extent the Social Security Advisory Committee (SSAC), whose role is largely advisory and which replaced the Supplimentary Benefits Commission (SBC). A second target is Parliament, particularly backbenchers and committees, although some groups regard the House of Lords as important [sic] as the Commons. A rather less important focus for group activity is the political parties. In this case most groups do not have regular contact and those that do will often tend to focus on the party in power. Finally, most groups seek to influence informed public opinion through the media. This means primarily seeking coverage in quality newspapers and journals as well as the radio and television.

We can illustrate the sorts of strategies that groups adopted by some examples. To do this we will look at Age Concern, the Disablement Income Group, National Council for One Parent Families, and the Low Pay Unit.

Age Concern

In 1940 the National Council of Social Service (NCSS) set up the National Old People's Welfare Council (NOPWC) to co-ordinate the work of local groups helping old people who were badly affected by evacuation. This work expanded after the war, with groups meeting needs through the provision of day centres, clubs, meals on wheels, transport and other services. By 1970 there were over 700 local groups and it was decided that the NOPWC should become independent from the NCSS and be known as Age Concern England (ACE). The Director argued that this marked a sharp change of direction, 'from an organisation based on middle-class philanthropy to one that would listen to the elderly and provide for their needs'.

Age Concern has a governing body of approximately 150 representatives from local groups, local authorities and central government departments which oversees the national campaigns. In 1982 it had an expenditure of over £870,000. The Director plays a major part in these campaigns but in addition ACE has a full-time parliamentary lobbyist who works with the All Party Pensioner Group as well as with individual backbenchers. For example, she provides briefings for debates on the elderly and help with Early Day Motions and Parliamentary Questions. ACE is not simply reactive but tries to initiate discussion of certain issues, and in 1978 published a document containing 127 specific policy recommendations, a number of which were on income maintenance issues. The Director said 'We have a love-hate relationship with government ... because we are in partnership as regards service delivery but we are a critic in the policy area'. They have regular contact with officials, ministers and backbenchers over a wide variety of issues, for example the adequacy of death grants, the value of the retirement pension, and housing provision for the elderly.

An example of successful lobbying was Age Concern's intervention over the new State Pension Scheme introduced in 1978. One of the anomalies of the original scheme was that people due to retire in 1978–79 would have paid contributions but received no benefits. After an active campaign, its Director claimed to have got the then government to change its mind. The organisation issues regular press releases which aim to maximise impact with both policy-makers through the quality press and the general public through the popular press.

Disablement Income Group

The Disablement Income Group (DIG) was started by a letter in the *Guardian* in 1965 written by two housewives with multiple sclerosis. This sparked off a large correspondence and an organisation was quickly formed with the aim of securing a national disability income scheme covering all disabled people and based on consistent and equitable principles. DIG has a National Executive Committee elected by the membership which oversees the work of the full-time staff. In 1982 its total expenditure was £126,600.

DIG has a particularly effective parliamentary spokesman, Peter Large. In his view parliamentary lobbying is important, but it is also essential to get officials within the DHSS to support particular proposals. He also believes that it is necessary to get public support which creates the right 'groundswell of opinion'. Thus he identifies Whitehall as the main target but feels that it is not possible to ignore Parliament and informed public opinion. However, close contact with officials does not mean that DIG always seeks consensus. For example, it claimed to have arranged a defeat of the Labour government in the House of Lords on the issue of the earnings rule for invalidity pensions. This was done against the advice of senior civil servants who were afraid that the change would 'open the floodgates'. Peter Large stated that 'if you can engineer a defeat, it really concentrates the mind of the government'. In his view, 'consistency and accuracy get home but they need to be backed by public support'. For example, DIG has held a number of 'rolling lobbies' which involved large numbers of disabled people meeting their MPs in the central lobby of the House of Commons. This secured extensive coverage in the media and effectively focused the attention of MPs on the needs of disabled people.

The National Council for One Parent Families

The National Council for One Parent Families (NCOPF) was set up in 1918 by a philanthropist, Lettice Fisher, who was concerned about the high rate of infant mortality amongst the children of single-parent families. Today it is run by a Committee of Management of 18 which is elected by the 360 members of Council. The Council is made up of some individual members, who are invited to become members since NCOPF does not have a mass membership with voting rights; representatives of local authorities; voluntary organisations and housing bodies. In 1982–83 it had 33 staff and a budget of £354,000. Most of the staff were involved with running the advice and information services, with only the Director and Deputy Director spending a significant amount of time on campaigns.

The NCOPF aims to draw attention to the needs of single-parent families and to influence policy on a wide range of issues. In 1981, for example, it campaigned on the value of benefits, the problem of take-up of the One

Parent Benefit, Supplementary Benefit regulations, divorce law, family taxation, the rate support grant, the Nationality Bill, social work services, homelessness and perinatal mortality. Its main lobbying orientation is toward Whitehall, although it does also work closely with MPs when this is felt necessary in order to secure changes. The NCOPF's relationship with the DHSS is particularly interesting in that senior civil servants use it to get detailed feedback on how policies operate. The DHSS has an observer on the Committee of Management and in addition send officials to NCOPF conferences. The Director of NCOPF noted an amateur/professional distinction in the Whitehall machine between civil servants, 'many of whom are absolutely superb on social policy', and ministers who did not get a chance to build up such expertise.

The NCOPF claimed a number of successes in its campaigning activities. In 1978 it persuaded the Labour Secretary of State to reduce the maximum hours of work allowed for single-parent families before they were eligible for Family Income Supplement. In Sir Geoffrey Howe's first budget of June 1979 Child Benefit was increased by 50 pence, partly as a result of lobbying by the NCOPF, according to its Deputy Director, Paul Lewis. Finally, it claimed to have influenced the decision to allow one-parent families to qualify for the higher long-term Supplementary Benefits rate after one year instead of two years.

Low Pay Unit

The Low Pay Unit was set up in 1974 by Frank Field, who at the time was Director of CPAG. He realised that low pay was one of the primary causes of family poverty, but it could not be tackled directly by campaigning on benefits. The main objective of the LPU is to draw attention to, and campaign for improvements in, the position of the low paid. Whilst the primary focus has been those workers covered by wages councils, it has also produced reports on homeworkers, taxation and the low paid, public sector employees and the disabled. The Unit has a small advisory committee to oversee its work, some affiliated organisations, but no voting membership. In 1982–83 it had a staff of seven workers and a budget of £57,000.

Given that the Unit's first Director was Frank Field, its campaigning style was, not surprisingly, similar to that of CPAG. The main orientation was towards Parliament and the media, although there was some contact with officials at the Department of Employment and ministers. An example of successful lobbying was the Unit's campaign to improve enforcement of the Wages Council statutory minimum rates. This was started in 1976 with the publication of *Policing Low Wages*[6] and lead to an increase in the number of Wages Inspectors employed by the Department and to the adoption of a new 'blitz' strategy (i.e. blanket searches for underpayment cases in particular towns). One important element of the campaign was joint action with the

Society of Civil Servants, the union that represents the Wages Inspectors. Also of significance was the support of a number of backbench Labour MPs who took up the issue and secured an adjournment debate in 1976. Since 1979 the Department of Employment has been far less receptive to the Unit's work and, as a result, the focus of its campaign has shifted somewhat. More work has been undertaken with trade unions, for example the National Union of Public Employees, and this culminated in the adoption of a statutory national minimum wage as TUC and Labour Party policy. In addition, the Unit has attempted to make use of international treaties such as the European Social Charter and International Labour Organisation Conventions to bring pressure to bear on the UK government.

Joint action

Looking at the poverty lobby as a whole, most of the time the organisations involved work separately and indeed are sometimes in competition. However, there has been an increasing amount of joint action in recent years and this is worth looking at as a separate issue.

Joint action takes a number of different forms and can best be examined in terms of the degree of permanence of the alliance. There is firstly joint action which takes place for a strictly limited purpose such as the publication of a joint report. For example, following the arrests in 1982 of 283 claimants at a fake Oxford unemployment benefit office, five organisations published *Poor Law*.[7] This was highly critical of the police and DHSS operation and made a number of recommendations to improve the housing position of single people. At a second level there is the temporary alliance formed for the purpose of a joint campaign. 'Dignity in Death', for example, was a campaign involving some 40 organisations, initiated by Age Concern in 1979, to secure an improvement in the value of the death grant. Similar, although with a far broader remit, is the Unemployment Alliance, an informal working party of some eight organisations serviced by the National Council of Voluntary Organisations. Launched in May 1981, it aims 'to increase public concern and understanding of the social and economic costs of unemployment, and to promote constructive measures to combat it'.[8] On a rather more permanent level there are long-term alliances between groups with most lobbying being undertaken jointly. For example, the main organisations for the blind act together as 'the Joint Deputation', and the four main organisations for the deaf come together as 'the Panel of Four' in order to make representations to Whitehall. Finally there are 'umbrella bodies' with an organisation and finances of their own, whose membership consists of other groups. A good example of this is the Royal Association for Disability and Rehabilitation (RADAR), which was established in 1977 with strong encouragement from the then Minister for the Disabled, Alf Morris. Approximately 300 organ-isations are members both at the national and local levels. For example,

DIG and the British Polio Fellowship are affiliated as national organisations and the Bristol Council for the Disabled as a local organisation. In addition, approximately 45 County Councils, most London Boroughs and some Metropolitan Boroughs are members.

Another form of joint action involves links with producer interests, particularly trade unions. The best example of this was the co-operation between the main pensioner organisations and the TGWU and TUC during the 1974–79 Labour government to secure significant improvements in the retirement pension. These links were formalised with the establishment of the Pensioners Convention in 1979. The success of this joint action has prompted other groups to seek similar links. The CPAG had some success on the Child Benefits issue, but other groups have experienced difficulties in dealing with trade unions, which tend to be slow-moving and relatively conservative on social policy questions. The Deputy Director of NCOPF remarked rather ruefully, 'If only we could get a union to sponsor one parent families like Jack Jones sponsored the elderly'.

The effectiveness of the poverty lobby

These examples give an indication of the variety of activities undertaken by groups in the poverty lobby. But how effective have these efforts been in changing outcomes? We examine this next.

One of the most difficult tasks in the analysis of pressure groups is to evaluate their effectiveness. Policy making is a complex, multi-faceted process involving many different actors, and decision-makers rarely change policies in response to pressure from a single group. Generally, groups influence outcomes in conjunction with other actors such as backbench MPs, civil servants and other groups. For this and other reasons the question of interest group effectiveness is probably the least adequately researched aspect of the study of pressure groups.

Our research showed that groups in the poverty lobby can exercise both influence and power. The distinction between these two is not precise, but the former generally refers to the use of persuasion to change outcomes and the latter usually to the use of sanctions to ensure compliance. The poverty lobby does not, of course, exercise sanctions, but it can exert power in the sense of changing political agendas. This is the 'second face of power' discussed by Bachrach and Baratz.[9]

We explored the question of group effectiveness in two ways. Firstly, we asked groups to give concrete examples of decisions by government which they felt they had played an important role influencing. Some of these have already been referred to. In addition, respondents were asked to discuss, in general terms, the factors which they felt helped to make a particular group effective. In this way we aimed to get general opinions about group influence as well as specific illustrations on how influence is exercised.

The second approach was to ask senior civil servants and key backbench MPs the same kinds of questions, inviting them to comment in both general and specific terms. By examining the opinions of 'insiders' as well as group activists we hoped to build up a picture of the impact and significance of group lobbying.

To consider concrete policy outcomes first, just under half of the groups could cite one or more examples of influence over policy. These varied from specific changes in regulations such as amendments to the Chronically Sick and Disabled Persons Act of 1970, cited by the Royal National Institute for the Deaf, to a much more general change such as a contribution to the doubling of family allowances during the 1970s, cited by CPAG. Some groups cited small changes which followed almost from their service provision activities; others cited larger changes which they saw as being part of a 'grand' strategy.

Overall though, groups which had a 'grand' strategy failed to achieve the really big policy changes which they sought. For example, a number of the disability groups wanted a comprehensive disability allowance to be introduced, but this was never achieved. Instead, piecemeal gains were obtained which brought particular benefits to particular categories of the disabled.

In view of this, why then do we suggest that groups can exercise power? This interpretation emerged from the discussion of the general determinants of group effectiveness. Group activists and insiders such as senior civil servants and backbenchers agreed that a small number of groups had succeeded in helping to place poverty back on the political agenda during the 1960s and early 1970s. Prior to this poverty had been largely a non-issue because it was thought by many people no longer to exist. Thus it is in the specific sense of changing political agendas that groups can, on occasions, exercise power. A similar point might be made about the role of a group like Shelter in placing the issue of homelessness on the agenda in the late 1960s. As Bachrach and Baratz argue, influencing agendas is an important aspect of power, even if it does not involve the use of sanctions.

Turning next to perceptions of the types of activities which make for effectiveness, a wide variety of answers were given by the respondents to this question. For some factors there was a wide consensus about what promoted effectiveness, for others there was rather less consensus. The single most widely held belief about effectiveness was that groups require accurate and detailed information about the needs of their clients and the impact of the social security system on them. This information was seen as a valuable resource in dealing with policy-makers and in building a constructive long-term relationship with officials. Some groups also recognized that good research could attract grant money from trusts, which play an important role in aiding fledgling groups.

A second widely held belief was that contacts with the media and 'responsible' publicity promoted effectiveness. Many respondents distinguished between responsible publicity, which meant coverage in the quality press about group activities, and irresponsible publicity, which meant attacks on the character and motives of ministers and officials or illegal demonstrations such as sit-ins in Supplementary Benefits offices. This was seen as counter-productive.

A third factor which a number of respondents mentioned was the importance of having clear, politically realistic aims. Some groups, for example Gingerbread, have a highly decentralised structure which emphasizes local group autonomy. This may be good for democracy but it inhibits the group's effectiveness because it was perceived to produce incoherence in spelling out the group's objectives.

A more controversial view was that a group needed 'insider' status or, as one respondent put it, 'powerful friends' to be effective. This was implying something more than the generally accepted view that good contacts with officials and ministers pay off. Rather, it was the view that a quiet process of lobbying in the corridors of power pays dividends. This argument has respectable support from academic research on producer groups by Beer and Eckstein.[10] Their work suggested that narrowly focused lobbying, which concentrated on Whitehall, ignored Parliament and avoided the media, would be most successful.

However, our own findings suggested that this view is not valid. Firstly, it appears that groups which pursued a broad strategy aimed at Parliament, the media and political parties while working together with other groups were more likely to be successful than groups pursuing an unobtrusive 'insider' strategy aimed only at Whitehall. A related point is that the sample contained examples of groups which had been sponsored by the government (e.g. RADAR) and which therefore might be thought to have easy insider access. However, such groups did not appear to be more effective than others; on the contrary, there was even evidence to suggest that close insider status can inhibit the impact of a group, reducing rather than increasing its effectiveness.

Most officials and MPs accepted that groups required support from the public and Parliament, and therefore lobbying should be targeted at a wider audience than just officials and ministers in Whitehall. One senior civil servant in the DHSS argued that effectiveness depended on the ability to 'strike a chord with public opinion'; he went on, 'groups may harness the tide, but there must be a tide running for them to be effective'.

An example of the importance of publicity concerns the Supplementary Benefits Commission 'A' code which was a detailed set of regulations governing the payment of benefits to particular categories of claimant. A senior official in the Supplementary Benefits Commission conceded that the code had been amended in response to pressure from groups, part of which involved publicity over anomalies in the regulations.

As well as group strategies, we found that group effectiveness also depends upon the environment within which social security policy is formulated; one of the key determinants of the environment is the state of the economy. A number of respondents argued that it had become harder to achieve improvements in social security provision as the 1970s went on. This was a reflection of economic crisis, low growth and, of course, the political priorities of the Thatcher administration since 1979. Another important environmental factor is public opinion. A number of surveys have demonstrated general support for welfare spending in Britain. However, levels of support for increased spending on Child Benefit, unemployment benefit or income support for the low paid are significantly lower than public support for pensions or the disabled. The public distinguish between a 'deserving' and an 'undeserving' poor. This, coupled with economic adversity which makes people feel less generous, puts a real constraint on redistribution in favour of the poor.

A third important environmental factor is the structure of central government, the milieu in which policy making takes place. Our interviews suggested that it had become rather segmented into competing issue communities. Central government increasingly resembles an imperfectly linked network of policy communities rather than a coherent, hierarchical organisation. Policy appears to be increasingly fragmented into these issue communities. However, changes in the structure of central administration may have adversely affected the position of groups within the social security issue community in the 1980s. In 1980 the Supplementary Benefits Commission was abolished and its administrative functions merged into the DHSS. The SBC was seen by some groups as an 'in house' pressure group pressing for extensions of income support programmes. Under its last chairman, David Donnison, the Commission maintained a certain independence from government, publishing an annual report which by the late 1970s argued forcefully for extensions of income support. Poverty groups clearly lost an influential friend when Donnison left and the reorganisation was carried out.

Group resources were the third important factor in explaining group effectiveness in addition to group strategies and the political environment. This refers primarily to political rather than financial resources and consists of a number of different things. Firstly, there is the political attractiveness of the client group. It is easier to arouse public concern for the elderly than for, say, offenders or the low paid. Thus an attractive clientele is a real asset.

A second major political resource is the quality of the information the group can provide. We have already referred to the importance of this in the discussion of group strategies. But it can be regarded as a resource because decision-makers valued feedback on the operation of the social security system, which they very often did not get from ministry sources. Such information helped groups to build a long-term relationship with decision-makers. As the Director of NCOPF said: 'Influence in Whitehall is strongly linked to the accuracy of the information provided'.

A third important resource is the ability to co-operate with producer and other groups in the pursuit of particular campaigns. One of the most successful campaigns was the Child Benefits Now campaign which brought together some eighteen organisations to press the Labour government to implement plans for the tax-free Child Benefit. Disablement, by contrast, is an issue area which had remained fragmented, with a number of umbrella groups seeking to speak for the disabled. Considerable rivalry between the Disablement Income Group, the Disability Alliance and RADAR has reduced the effectiveness of disability groups overall in the perception of decision-makers. This implies that whilst joint action will not necessarily ensure success, the failure of groups in an issue area to work together may seriously weaken their effectiveness.

Conclusions

The poverty lobby is a large and important actor in the policy-making process, in an area with the largest budget of any governmental programme. Groups in this area represent consumer rather than producer interests, but that has not prevented them from exercising influence and on occasion power over policy outcomes.

Groups in the poverty lobby vary in terms of the strategies and tactics they pursue and in the resources they bring to the process of lobbying. It seems clear than an unobtrusive insider strategy is less likely to be effective than a broad open strategy which emphasizes contacts with Whitehall, Parliament, the media and the political parties.

However, group effectiveness is also influenced by the environment within which groups operate and the resources they bring to lobbying activity. While the political and economic environment has grown more adverse in recent years, the role of groups has become more important because of the increasing numbers in poverty. Thus pressure group work on behalf of the poor is likely to grow in significance in the future.

> Abridged from Paul Whiteley and Steve Winyard (1988), 'The poverty lobby in British politics', *Parliamentary Affairs*, XLI, pp. 195–208. Reprinted by permission of Oxford University Press, Oxford.

Notes

1 The research in this paper is discussed more fully in P. Whiteley and S. Winyard (1987), *Pressure for the Poor*, Metheun, London.
2 HM Treasury (1983), *The Government's Expenditure Plans 1983–4 to 1985–6*, HMSO, London.
3 K. Banting (1979), *Poverty, Politics and Policy*, Macmillan, London, p. 66.
4 E.g., National Council for Voluntary Organisations (1979), *Voluntary Social Services*, Bedford Square Press, London; P. Shipley, ed. (1976), *The Guardian Directory of Pressure Groups and Organisations*, Wilton House. See also the list of organisations

submitting evidence to the Finer Committee and the Royal Commission on the Distribution of Income and Wealth.

5 D. Donnison (1982), *The Politics of Poverty*, Martin Robertson, Oxford, p. 128.

6 S. Winyard (1976), *Policing Low Wages*, Low Pay Unit, London.

7 R. Francy (1972), *Poor Law*, Campaign for Homeless and Rootless.

8 R. MacLachlan (1982), 'Charities unite to protect the unemployed', *Voluntary Action*, Spring.

9 P. Bachrach and M. S. Baratz (1970), *Power and Poverty*, Oxford University Press, New York.

10 See S. Beer (1956), 'Pressure groups and parties in Britain', *American Political Science Review*, 50, pp. 1–23; and H. Eckstein (1960), *Pressure Group Politics: The Case of the British Medical Association*, Allen and Unwin, London.

2.4   British political parties

Stephen Ingle

To begin, we can agree that most commentators during the past two decades would accept the following as the guiding assumptions concerning the operations of the British party system:

1 Britain has a predominantly two-party system in which the major parties represent competing ideologies which distinguish each from the other and unite the adherents of each against the other.

2 This two-party system makes voters' choice possible by canalising policies into two broad alternatives, thus allowing for the popular endorsement of one alternative which takes the form of a mandate to the victorious party.

3 The defeated party makes the government accountable by scrutinising policy and performance through a range of parliamentary procedures which were designed with this objective in mind.

4 In a two-party system the need to win support from the uncommitted voters in the centre of the spectrum presses both parties towards consensus politics, thus restricting partisanship (or adversarianism) to rhetoric and encouraging continuity of policy.

5 Over a period of time both major parties will share power more or less equally.

6 The victorious party in a general election will *usually* represent the majority of voters (not always: that would be too much to expect).

7 As a consequence of the operation of these principles Britain has, during the last twenty years or so, possessed a party system which, despite

its acknowledged deficiencies (such as the under-representation of minorities), allows for strong, efficient and legitimate government.

Perhaps. In any event we shall be in a better position to judge after we have examined each of the assumptions. First, then, we will examine assumptions concerning the two-party system and competing ideologies.

Two competing parties

Even a cursory study of party history will indicate that British politics have not traditionally been dominated by two parties. Only for comparatively brief periods in British history have two national parties, organised and disciplined especially for that end, dominated the Houses of Parliament. This is not a matter of judgement but of easily verified fact and it is thus all the stranger that most recent writers on the party system have operated on the assumption of a two-party norm. Robert McKenzie's *British Political Parties*, published in 1955, perhaps the major contribution to the literature, devoted only two of its 597 pages to the Liberal Party (and those in the appendix), and none at all to any other minor party. No doubt this made sense in the 1950s when the Liberal Party in the House of Commons had been reduced to a rump of six and over 90 percent of voters were supporting the two major parties.

The limitations of the two-party model were exposed, though, as early as 1958 by a Liberal by-electoral victory at Torrington and although one chance victory could be written off, the subsequent victory in suburban Orpington in 1962, with a swing to the Liberals from the Conservatives of over 20 percent, and a total Liberal vote of over 3 million in the 1964 general election could not be. Nevertheless, the two-party model managed to incorporate this apparently irreconcilable development without much difficulty. Research indicated that much of the Liberal vote was a protest – against the malfunctioning of the two-party system. If it were to function properly, then, the protest would go away. Moreover, it was discovered that for others the Liberal Party was a half-way house, a brief refuge on a once-in-a-lifetime journey from left to right, or vice versa. So rather than challenging the two-party model the Liberals actually confirmed it, operating as a necessary safety valve. The intermittent success of the Scottish National Party (SNP) and Plaid Cymru in the late 1960s and 1970s clearly represented a different phenomenon and yet they were treated in much the same manner, as being vehicles of protest concerning very specific failures of the two-party system.

Politicians and political commentators who subscribed to the two-party model had always assumed that protest votes were primarily by-electoral indulgences and that, come the general election, the model would reassert itself. It failed to do so in February of 1974 when there were major successes for the nationalists and over 5 million voted Liberal. The result was a slender Labour victory, so slender that eight months later Prime Minister Wilson gave the electorate another opportunity to come to its senses. The result, however, was much the same, and it became obvious that, in the medium term at least, the two-party model, for all its convenience, would have to be shelved. Quite suddenly British political commentators began to write about multi-party politics and to ask questions about the party system which some continental commentators had been asking a decade before.

By the 1980s the Liberals had established a regular support of between 15 and 25 percent and when, in 1981, they formed an alliance with the newly emerged social-democratic defectors from the increasingly left-wing Labour Party, the Social Democratic Party (SDP), they enjoyed public support in the opinion polls of over 40 percent for more than six months. Clearly no commentator could dismiss this as simply a safety valve.

In the general election of 1983 the Alliance came desperately close to gaining more votes nationally than the Labour Party, though it failed to make any impact in terms of representation, gaining only 23 MPs from its 7 million votes. A less successful result in the 1987 general election led to the merging of the Liberals and the majority of the SDP to form (eventually) the Liberal Democrats. A substantial minority of the SDP strove to retain its independence under the leadership of Dr David Owen, but Owen disbanded the party in 1990. The merged Liberal Democrats went through two trying years of internal disputes, a leadership contest, intense financial difficulties, and a fierce struggle for the centre vote with the rump SDP in a background dominated by a Labour Party successfully attempting to re-establish itself as a force for moderate left-of-centre politics. In the European elections of 1989 the Liberal Democrats' lacklustre campaign led to their securing a substantially smaller proportion of votes than the Green Party and most commentators were speaking of a return to two-party politics. By 1990 however, Liberal Democrat finances were in better order, the new leader Paddy Ashdown had begun to establish himself as a national figure, and the SDP had vanished; an unexpected by-electoral victory at Eastbourne set the seal on the party's (re?)emergence as a national force.

What this review of recent party history indicates is that the two-party model is not only inappropriate for analysing British politics historically but, apart from a brief period in the 1960s and 1970s, it is by no means wholly appropriate even to the modern era.

Two competing ideologies

If the picture of two parties completely dominating British politics is seen to be somewhat inappropriate, the picture of two associated dominant ideologies must fall *ipso facto*. It is possible to take the argument further though and to examine the extent to which, irrespective of their lack of dominance, the two major parties have, in the past two decades, possessed ideologies which actually do distinguish them from their opponents and unite their supporters. Investigation of the policy commitments of both the Conservative and Labour Parties reveals what might euphemistically be called some interesting anomalies. ⟨

Anthony Quinton speaks of three chief principles of Conservatism: traditionalism, which he describes as a strong emotional attachment to existing procedures, faith in a fixed constitution and a strong belief in the rule of law; organicism, which compares society to a natural living body comprising an ecology of mutually beneficial relationships, implying, in political terms, a hierarchy built on duties and privileges (Disraeli's 'one nation'); finally scepticism, frequently associated with the Christian concept of original sin, which emphasises the limitations of human endeavour, and finds political form in a strong belief in limited government.[1] For O'Sullivan this last is the lynchpin of Conservatism, its major distinguishing feature.[2] We might add pragmatism to this list, since Conservatives have traditionally claimed to be prepared, unlike socialists, to put 'reality' before ideology. In the nineteenth century, however, the Conservative Party was opposed by *laissez-faire* Liberalism and became the party of intervention, in its attempt presumably to act 'organically' and secure the interests of all citizens. In the twentieth century too, under leaders like Neville Chamberlain and Harold Macmillan, the party supported substantial government intervention in the economy, afterwards earning the opprobrium of neoliberals in the party like Lord Joseph. Later, Edward Heath's neocorporatist policies showed scant regard for limited government.

More recently, under the leadership of Margaret Thatcher, a Conservative government embarked on an enterprise nothing less grand than to reshape society – precisely the kind of task Conservatives would traditionally have considered to be both inappropriate and indeed obnoxious. The 1988 Education Reform Act, for example, conferred no fewer than 240 new powers upon the Secretary of State, over sixty of which were the direct result of government-backed amendments. It would be no exaggeration to say that the sweeping reforms of the Thatcher era exhibited a distaste for tradition, a complete rejection of the ethos of organicism – indeed Thatcher argued that there was no such thing as society – and a willingness to strengthen the powers of the central government in so profound a way as to change the shape of the constitution (*vis-à-vis* local government for example). As for pragmatism, whilst it is clear that nearly all governments will trim their policies in the light of 'reality', Thatcher made a fetish of conviction politics and in pursuing single-mindedly the establishment of the community charge against all good advice, she actually came to epitomise the very antithesis of pragmatism. Thus the Conservative government under Margaret Thatcher represented the polar opposite of the chief Conservative virtues. To put it simply, the policies of the Thatcher government strongly reinforced the message of history, that in office Conservative governments show little more than a random or at most a symbolic relationship with Conservative ideology.

As for the Labour Party, it has been demonstrably riven by ideological disputes since its inception.[3] Has its role been to establish socialism or to pursue the interests of the working class? If it were to be argued that these are two sides of the same coin, then how should the party react to the fact that the working class does not seem to perceive this unity? For the Fabians, socialism required the establishment of an elite which would run society in the interests of all, but for others socialism implied a diffusion of power, giving people some control over their own lives. In office Labour governments tended to increase state control via nationalisation, but such a policy became increasingly unpopular with the working class who, faced with great bureaucratic administrative structures, felt no sense of ownership of the state's industries and services, but rather a sense of alienation towards them. By the late 1950s, following the party's third successive electoral defeat, strenuous efforts were made to 'liberate' the party from its commitment to nationalisaton, but Labour Conferences saw this as treachery and resisted.

The Wilson government of 1966 was the only post-1950 Labour government with a strong majority. Its trumpeted commitment, though, was not so much to socialism as to the 'white heat of the technological revolution'; that is, to spreading greater wealth and to improving services through transforming industrial performance rather than transforming the structure of power within society. This policy, which anyway was not successful, earned the displeasure of many backbenchers, one of whom declared that he had not struggled so hard to replace a middle-class Conservative government with a working-class Conservative government. When Wilson's government attempted, through its bill *In Place Of Strife* to reform the trade-union movement, this sense of betrayal became greater. When Wilson returned to office in 1974 and when, after his retirement, James Callaghan became Prime Minister, a knife-edged majority and a pact with the Liberal Party made a full-blooded redistributive socialist policy impossible. Yet it was quite plain that no such policy had been envisaged by the party and one is forced to conclude that, with the exception of the 1945–50 government, when a centralised command economy already existed as a legacy of the war, Labour governments have not conspicuously advanced the cause of socialism. When, from 1979 onwards, the left wing of the party sought to wrench power from the right, this was partly a response to a double failure: the deeper failure of not having advanced socialism but also the more present failure of having lost electoral support through general ineptitude. By 1983 the left had secured some notable victories: the programme of compulsory re-selection for MPs, the electoral college for choosing the party leader, greater party involvement (through the National Executive Committee) in drawing up the manifesto and the election to leader of that doughty champion of the left, Michael Foot. If Labour had been elected in 1983 the country could have expected its most radical government since 1945; in the event Labour was humiliated. Ex-Labour Cabinet minister Peter Shore referred to the party's manifesto as 'the longest suicide note in history'.

By 1987 Labour's radicalism was already being undermined. Neil Kinnock urged the electorate to vote not for socialism, nor even for Labour, but for Kinnock. After a good but unsuccessful campaign Kinnock and his allies set about a review of all aspects of Labour's policies and structure. The consequences of this review could hardly have been greater.

The voter might legitimately express some bewilderment about what the Labour Party has stood for over the years. Bound by its 1918 constitution to bring the means of production and exchange into social ownership – to a socialist economy – it has signally failed to do so despite internal pressure. Currently the party has made it plain that it has no such commitment and yet the most recent and most detailed study of the party membership[4] indicates that the party rank-and-file remain strongly in favour of extending nationalisation, pro-nuclear disarmament, strongly pro-trade union (wishing to see the restoration of the right to secondary picketing, for example) and strongly in favour of increasing taxation to improve services.

In short Labour Party history presents a pendulum swing back and forth from socialism to social democracy, with the swing to the latter normally synchronising with (admittedly rare) periods of government. This division is substantially the one which confronted the party at its inception and the subsequent failure to resolve it means that the party presents no ideological consistency to the voter. Smith's Labour Party in the 1990s is as different from the party of Callaghan and Foot as Thatcher's Conservative party was from the party of Macmillan and Heath. The idea of two competing ideologies which are consistent and which distinguish each from the other and unite the adherents of each against each other is not simply borne out in reality.

Two competing policy programmes?

Having established this lack of consistency concerning party ideology – and not just over the past twenty years – it becomes difficult to take too seriously the idea of the major parties canalising policy into two broadly understood alternatives for popular choice and endorsement. Irrespective of ideological inconsistency, however, it is clear that during the modern period party identification has become much less pronounced amongst the electorate than was once the case. A study by Rose and McAllister, for example, using a factor analysis of voter preference amongst Conservative, Labour and Alliance supporters, indicated a substantial measure of agreement in the three key policy areas of welfare, morality and racialism.[5] Indeed, only fifteen of forty-five policy issues elicited any measure of disagreement among supporters of the three major parties. The authors concluded that only socialism excited real disagreement but the split was not along party lines: attitudes to socialism divided both Labour and the Alliance and united (in hostility) only the Conservative voters.[6] Moreover, Labour voters were in disagreement over twenty-six out of forty-five issues, Alliance voters on twenty-five and Conservatives on nineteen. There is no evidence that Margaret Thatcher's electoral victories owed anything to public support for her policies; indeed the Conservative vote actually fell in 1983. On the basis of their analysis the authors were able to suggest two conclusions: that disagreement is commonly within and not between parties and that how a person thinks about issues is a poor guide to how he/she votes. If these conclusions were out of line with other findings we might have cause to question them but they are not; they make it clear that a claim made on behalf of any party which secured an electoral victory that it has a mandate from the people to enact its policies is always likely to be dubious. If, as is almost invariably the case, the victorious party represents only a minority of the electorate, the claim must be meaningless. The mandate claimed by the present government, for example, is based upon the support of a minority of a minority of a majority. And, as Pimlott pointed out, that original minority (constituting the Conservative vote in 1987) represented the 'smallest proportion of the popular vote of any Tory administration since 1922'.[7]

Two-party accountability

The third generalisation to be considered concerns government accountability through vigilant opposition, made the more important because, in a two-party system, the opposition is also the alternative government. Parliamentary procedures ensure that government policy is scrutinised by the opposition, which is able to focus public attention upon policies it considers harmful. It is quite obvious that any government during the past twenty years with a working majority, if it had the support of its own backbenchers, need have no fear that its policies would be defeated. Norton has shown that, since the Heath ministry, government backbenchers have acted with a measure of independence and have been able to influence their own party leaders.[8] What he cannot show is any measure important to a government with a working majority being defeated in the House, nor can he show the opposition having any noticeable direct influence. It would be a nonsense to suggest that debate in the House of Commons is a charade simply because, when a government has a working majority, the result is always predictable. Nevertheless, it is fair to question the extent to which accountability may be said to exist in a parliamentary system which allows a government to put on the statute book a law as widely reviled by politicians and people of all political persuasions as the community charge. It is also fair to question the effectiveness of Question Time, especially Prime Minister's Questions, if government ministers set their minds to self-advertisement rather than answering questions. During Margaret Thatcher's prime ministership the average number of questions 'answered' fell from around nine per session to around five.[9]

Indeed, it can be argued that far from ensuring government accountability the British two-party system actually hinders the process. Since information is seldom neutral it tends to be a commodity which governments hoard; consequently British government is arguably the most secretive of the Western democracies. The present government has sought to prevent the select committee system, for example, from attaining anything like the influence of its American counterpart by placing strictures on the kind of information that civil servants may make available. State security is a goal for which it is worth making sacrifices of openness; government embarrassment is not.

Even when it is readily available, however, the nature of information has changed. As policy has come to cover areas of increasing complexity so it has become more technical and indeed technological. It has, as a direct consequence, become less amenable to adversarial scrutiny. Yet the procedures which Parliament uses for purposes of scrutiny remain largely unchanged. Even where they have changed, as in the system of select committees established after 1979, the partisan-ideological confrontation of the two major parties places strict limits on their capacity to effect change as well, as mentioned, as on their freedom of enquiry. What this means is that the opposition will tend to engage the government on aspects of its policy which are amenable to adversarial presentation rather than its more important aspects. A detailed study of health politics between 1970 and 1975 examplified the consequences of this quite clearly.[10] The hugely expensive structural changes envisaged by the National Health Reorganization Act were less effectively discussed than the decision not to provide birth control free on prescription. Although only £3 million of public funds were involved, this issue proved very suitable for adversarial debate, with the traditional rallying cries of equality, responsibility, welfare and bureaucracy punctuating debate regularly. One- or two-tier administrative structures, co-terminosity with local government and the role of family practitioner committees did not fire the blood. Nor is it simply the manner in which such matters are debated; as policy becomes more complex and technical so the inputs come 'increasingly not from parties but from experts within the executive. The procedures for assessing these policies, however, continue to operate as if they *were* partisan– ideological and so remain basically adversarial.'[11]

Two-party consensus

The next generalisation concerns the alleged centripetal tendency of British politics: the need to win votes in 'the middle ground' draws both parties towards consensual politics. This is an argument especially associated with Richard Rose's *Do Parties Make A Difference?*[12] In crucial areas of the economy, says Rose, major developments are not much influenced by change of government; whether we examine inputs (matters within the government's control, such as setting the minimum lending rate, the level of public-sector borrowing and of public expenditure) or economic outcomes only partly under government control (such as inflation, unemployment and economic growth), it is 'long-term secular trends independent of party which influence the direction of the economy, not party policy'.[13] Moreover, his studies led him to conclude that party politics were consensual and not adversarian in character for three reasons: the electorate tends to agree on major issues; parties in government moderate their ideological preferences for fear of what their opponents might do when they come to power; finally, new governments face old problems with old advice and the same kinds of restraint. Adversarianism, then, he concludes, is largely rhetorical and not real.

On the other hand, it can be argued that rhetoric is very much a part of reality. In S. H. Beer's words, rhetoric establishes 'the framework of public thinking about policy'[14] and Labour's comments about what it intends to do when in government will only be ignored if it is quite certain either that Labour will not be able even to try to do what it promises or that it is not at all likely to gain power. As to the argument that parties are prisoners of economic trends, this is at most only partly true; there is no justification, for example, for assuming that Labour would have responded to the economic problems of the 1980s by a policy of privatisation. Outside economic policy there are probably even greater differences of party, none more so than in education, for example: Labour's ideology in the 1960s and Conservative ideology in the 1980s have had profound and profoundly different effects upon Britain's education system. Their combined impact can only have been harmful.

Two-party power sharing

The fifth generalisation suggests that the two major parties would, over a period of time, share power more or less equally. In fact this is far from the truth. Parties of the left have been in government with a good working majority on only three occasions in this century: 1906, 1945 and 1966. Their total number of years in office with good majorities this century amounts to thirteen. The Conservatives have done as well since 1979! By contrast, if we include coalitions which they dominated, the Conservatives have been in power with good majorities for some fifty-eight years. On average then, the Conservatives are more than four times as likely to be in power than Labour. The last twenty years have been typical, with the Conservatives in office with a good working majority for [eighteen] years, Labour enjoying five years with a tiny and disappearing majority.

The sixth generalisation suggested that, by and large, victorious parties represent the majority of the electorate. In fact on only three occasions in the last century has an incoming government represented a majority of the electorate: in the first, 1900, the victorious Conservatives were in alliance with Liberal Unionists; in the second and third, 1931 and 1935, they were the dominant partner in coalitions. Only in 1931 when the coalition secured the support of 67 percent of those who voted could a British government genuinely be said to represent a clear majority of the voters: only once in hundred years. No surprise, then, that no government in the past two decades has represented a majority of the voters because not once in the last *century* has a major party fighting on its own won a majority, which casts an intriguing reflection on the notion of legitimacy.

Two-party efficiency

The final generalisation declares that the operation of the British two-party system provided for a government which, if not fair to minorities, was at least efficient, legitimate and strong. Perhaps having turned the spotlight on the system, its efficiency and legitimacy appear substantially more flawed and ambiguous than we thought. As for its strength, two final thoughts. If a government is single-minded enough, against all opposition, to pass a particular measure only for it to be reversed later by another government when it proves unworkable, is that an indication of strength on the part of both governments although the net consequence is nothing? Second, if the British two-party system produces strong government, why is it that, in times of national emergency, when it is almost universally agreed that strong government is needed, it is to coalitions that Britain tends to turn?

In addition to these deep-seated anomalies and ambiguities, the spotlight also reveals, finally, that since 1979 the Conservative Party has, to all intents and purposes, provided not only the country's government but, through its backbenches, the chief opposition. With the departure of Thatcher it unseated the government and provided a change in government. In all this the official opposition parties, and indeed the electorate, were merely observers.

> Abridged from Stephen Ingle, 'All you never wanted to know about British political parties' in Bill Jones and Lynton Robins, eds. (1992), *Two Decades in British Politics*, pp. 23–36. Reprinted by permission of Manchester University Press, Manchester.

Notes

1 Anthony Quinton (1978), *The Politics of Imperfection*, Blackwell, Oxford, p. 24.
2 N. K. O'Sullivan (1976), *Conservatism*, Dent, London, p. 24.
3 For a full account of the origin and nature of these disputes see R. N. Berki (1975), *Socialism*, Dent, London.
4 Patrick Seyd, Paul Whiteley and David Broughton, 'Labour reorganisation down at the grassroots,' paper presented to PSA Specialist Group on Parties and Elections, 1990.
5 R. Rose and I. McAllister (1986), *Voters Begin to Choose*, Sage, London.
6 *Ibid.*, p. 143.
7 *Sunday Times*, 20 November 1988.
8 Philip Norton (1986), 'Independence, scrutiny and rationalization: a decade of change in the House of Commons,' *Teaching Politics*, 15, pp. 69–97.
9 Ian Aitken, *Guardian*, 12 December 1990.

10 Stephen Ingle and Philip Tether (1981), *Parliament and Health Policy: The Role of MPs 1970–75*, Gower, Farnborough, 1981.
11 *Ibid.*, p. 155.
12 Richard Rose (1984), *Do Parties Make a Difference?* 2nd edn, Macmillan, London.
13 *Ibid.*, p. xxix.
14 S. H. Beer (1965), *Modern British Politics*, Faber & Faber, London, p. 347.

2.5   Parliament and legislation

Gavin Drewry

Parliament and legislation

The House of Commons spends at least half its time talking about legislation and a considerable amount in addition talking about matters which may give rise to legislation and matters arising, directly or indirectly, from past legislation. Yet it is a commonplace that Parliament is not a law-making body, save in the important but strictly formal senses recognised by the courts and by constitutional theory. As Walkland succinctly puts it:

The legislative process in Britain is now complex: it comprises deliberative, Parliamentary and administrative stages over all of which executive influence is predominant. Legislation is now an almost exclusive executive function modified, sometimes heavily, by practices of group and Parliamentary consultations.[1]

And:

In so far as there is a 'deliberative' stage in the legislative process, this is now found much earlier than the Parliamentary stages, in the interplay between political parties, pressure groups, Departments and the Cabinet, which together form a complex decision-making structure, involving a variety of social and political forces.[2]

Thus today's conventional wisdom is that the parliamentary stages of the legislative process are, for purposes of getting policies converted into laws, the least creative ones; that Parliament has relinquished any capacity for legislative initiative it may once have possessed to the executive in its midst; that Parliament 'legitimates' but does not 'legislate'. Such views, expressed thus crudely, conceal a large number of value judgements and begged questions and cannot fairly be used as slogans to justify a dismissive attack upon parliamentary government; it is arguable that 'legitimation' is an essential function in any ordered society, and that a facility for public ventilation of policy issues cannot be brushed aside merely because it falls short – even a long way short – of a Utopian view of what representation and democracy are all about.

But in this instance conventional wisdom does accord with the facts of life. On the principle that one picture is better than a thousand words, the legislative process can usefully be portrayed diagrammatically as involving four interlocking and overlapping functions (see Figure 2.5(1)): 1. Inspiration; 2. Deliberation and Formulation; 3. Legitimation; 4. Application – plus a capacity for 'feedback', or learning by experience. If one accepts this as broadly accurate then it can be seen that the role of Parliament (in so far as the latter is separable from the executive which sits in it) impinges hardly at all on 1 or 4. It has slightly more of a part to play in 2, both overtly in so far as limited facilities exist for debates on White Papers, etc., and more covertly in the day-to-day interaction of MPs and Ministers, for example in party committees and in tea-rooms and bars. And the Finance bill is an important exception, the secrecy of its preparation giving peculiar importance to its parliamentary stages, during which substantial changes are often made following pressure group representations which, in the case of other bills, are normally taken into account much earlier; the norm is for formulation and legitimation to be kept apart. Parliament's key role in legitimation derives, as has already been hinted, more from widely believed theories of representative government than from any realistic assessment of its impact upon legislation.

Private Members' bills are a somewhat aberrant departure from the picture of the legislative process sketched above; and it is arguable, in any event, that the minority of backbench bills which actually reach the statute book (and many that fail are propaganda exercises rather than law-making ones) do so only with government approval and can thus be regarded as a peculiar species of government bill.

Before leaving this matter a note of caution must be sounded. Although it may be accepted that Parliament's role in the legislative process is preeminently a passive one, in which Parliamentarians sit back and eat what is given to them, there are significant exceptions where the menu is changed as a result of complaints, or where the waiter is forced to take away an unpalatable dish.

But the most important caveat lies in the nature of parliamentary 'influence'. As Bachrach and Baratz pointed out in a famous article, power is something with two faces; it is necessary to look not only at decisions, but also at non-decisions, at why some issues never emerge into the public political arena at all.[3] The number of concessions forced from Ministers in the form of bills abandoned or amendments carried may not amount to very much, but we do not know how often an idea fails to get beyond the 'inspiration' stage or through its 'formative and deliberative' stages because of the daunting prospect of having ultimately to justify an unpopular policy in public.

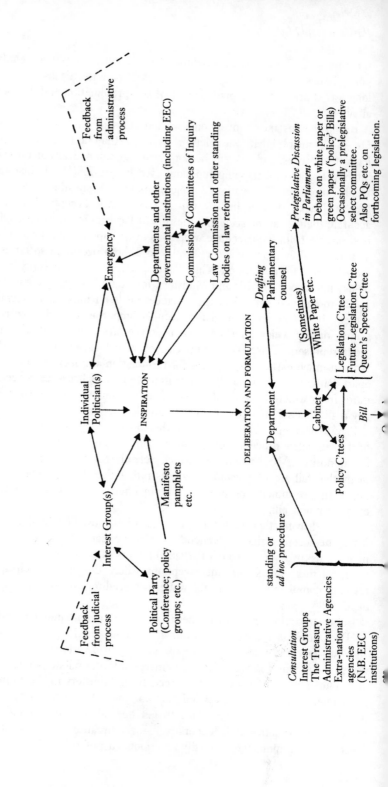

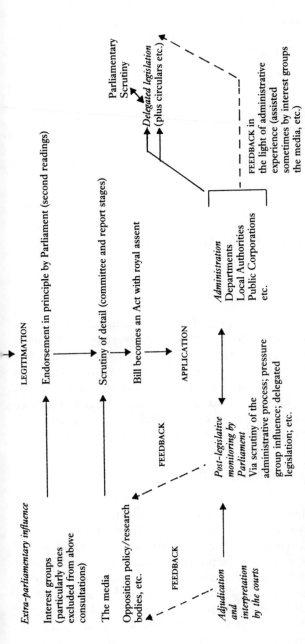

Extra-parliamentary influence

Interest groups
(particularly ones
excluded from above
consultations)

The media

Opposition policy/research
bodies, etc.

LEGITIMATION

Endorsement in principle by Parliament (second readings)

Scrutiny of detail (committee and report stages)

Bill becomes an Act with royal assent

APPLICATION

Administration
Departments
Local Authorities
Public Corporations
etc.

Parliamentary
Scrutiny

Delegated legislation
(plus circulars etc.)

FEEDBACK in
the light of administrative
experience (assisted
sometimes by interest groups
the media, etc.)

FEEDBACK

*Post-legislative
monitoring by
Parliament*
Via scrutiny of the
administrative process; pressure
group influence; delegated
legislation; etc.

FEEDBACK

*Adjudication
and
interpretation
by the courts*

Figure 2.5(1) *Government legislation*

Abridged from Gavin Drewry, 'Legislation', in Stuart A. Walkland and Michael T. Ryle, eds. (1981), *The Commons Today*, Fontana, London, pp. 91–4. Reprinted by permission of Fontana, an imprint of HarperCollins Publishers Ltd., London.

Notes

1 S. A. Walkland (1968), *The Legislative Process in Great Britain*, Allen and Unwin, London, p. 20.
2 *Ibid.*, p. 71.
3 P. Bachrach and M. S. Baratz (1966), 'Two Faces of Power', *American Political Science Review*, 56, pp. 947–52.

2.6   Parliament, party and dissent

Richard Rose

Party, not Parliament, determines control of British government. Events of the past decade appear to challenge [this] norm of party government. Dissent by individual MPs has increased and has been given increasing attention. The 1974–79 Parliament witnessed a period of minority party government and ended with the defeat of the governing party on a vote of confidence. The 1979–83 Parliament has witnessed the creation of a new party and an Alliance with the proclaimed intention of 'breaking the mould' of party government. Hence, it is necessary to ask whether this is still the era of party government.

The iron cage of party government in Britain

When Bagehot wrote *The English Constitution* in 1867, Parliament could be considered an elective chamber in which shifting combinations of MPs sustained a ministry. Individual MPs could and did act as individuals; party discipline was weak and in decline. Whereas in 1836 more than nine-tenths of Conservative MPs voted together in 56 percent of divisions, as did 40 percent of Liberals, by 1860 such cohesion was shown by Conservatives in only 31 percent of divisions and by Liberals in 25 percent. Whereas in 1836 74 percent of all divisions found one or both parties voting in a cohesive manner, by 1860 this occurred in only 51 percent of divisions. Disciplined voting fell, even though the frequency of the governing party putting on the whips rose.

   Organised partisan elections and organised party voting came with the expansion of the franchise. Before the 1867 Reform Act, MPs could see themselves as unfettered representatives (and sometimes as owners) of their constituencies. After the broadening of the franchise, by 1885 MPs became representatives of disciplined parties. The number of divisions in which Conservatives voted cohesively (that is, nine-tenths of MPs in a party voting together) rose from 31 percent in 1860 to 91 percent in 1899, and the proportion of cohesive divisions among Liberals rose from 25 percent in 1860 to 76 percent in 1899. Whereas in 1860 both parties failed to vote cohesively in half the divisions in the Commons, by 1899 this occurred in only 2 percent of all divisions.[1]

Party cohesion is a means to an end; it ensures the parliamentary endorsement of government measures. Whereas the total number of divisions in the House of Commons has tended to increase through the decades, the number of defeats for the government of the day has dropped greatly from an average of 10 defeats a session in the decade 1857–66 to less than five by 1877, and to less than one a session by the turn of the twentieth century. At the height of disciplined parliamentary parties in the period 1947–63, the government was on average defeated in a vote on the floor of the Commons only once every three years. Moreover, only twice in this century, once in 1924 and once in 1977, has the government of the day been defeated in a second reading vote on the principle of a bill.[2]

Party discipline gives authority to party government. From 1945 to 1978, a government could expect to see nearly 97 percent of all the bills it introduced enacted into law during a session of Parliament. The chief reason for a government bill not passing was that the government ran out of time. Usually, a government ran out of time because it called a general election in the middle of a parliamentary session, causing all pending legislation to lapse. Very occasionally a government bill was stopped by a filibuster by a group of opponents. While a successful filibuster makes an interesting case study, it remains a *deviant* case (Table 2.6(1)).

The complement of success by the governing party is failure by the Opposition, however well it criticises proposals by the government of the day. The Opposition party is condemned to being on the losing side in the Commons for up to five years because it has less than half the votes. The scale of Opposition weakness is indicated by the fate of its amendments to government legislation, the simplest and least way in which an Opposition may hope to modify the government's legislative policy. In three sample sessions between 1967 and 1971, ministers in the governing party moved a total of 1,772 amendments; 99.9 percent were approved by the Commons. By contrast, of the Opposition's 3,673 amendments only 4.4 percent were approved by the Commons. Backbench MPs in the governing party fared almost as badly; only 9.5 percent of their amendments were approved.

To speak of the government controlling votes in the Commons is only half correct; the correct description is to say that the governing party controls the Commons. Party government in Britain starts from the assumption that the first-past-the-post electoral system will give one party an absolute majority in

Table 2.6(1)   *Proportions of government bills approved by Parliament*

		Introduced	Approved	Approved (%)
1945–50	(Labour)	310	307	99.0
1950–51	(Labour)	99	97	98.0
1951–54(a)	(Conservative)	167	158	94.6
1955–59	(Conservative)	229	223	97.4
1959–64	(Conservative)	251	244	97.2
1964–65(a)	(Labour)	66	65	98.5
1966–69(a)	(Labour)	215	210	97.7
1970–73	(Conservative)	192	189	98.4
1974–78(a)	(Labour)	260	236	90.7
Totals		1,789	1,729	96.6

Note:
(a) Omits final session of Parliament, interrupted by government calling a general election, voiding all pending bills.
Sources: 1945–69: Calculated from V. Herman (1974), 'What governments say and what governments do: an analysis of post-war Queen's Speeches', *Parliamentary Affairs*, 28, Table 1. 1970–76: Calculated from G. Drewry, 'Legislation', in S. A. Walkland and M. Ryle (eds. 1981), *The Commons Today*, Fontana, London, pp. 66, 113.

the House of Commons. Since 1931, this assumption has been true for all but three years. The governing party must be disaggregated into two distinct components of unequal size: frontbench MPs (i.e. ministers) and backbench MPs. Backbench MPs outnumber frontbench MPs by a ratio of about three to one. In 1950, government ministers holding paid appointments were 22 percent of the number needed to ensure a Commons majority; in 1960 ministers numbered 21 percent of a notional majority; in 1970 and again in 1979 ministers were 27 percent of a notional majority.[3] Moreover, when the votes of several dozen unpaid but bound-by-discipline parliamentary private secretaries are added, then the government itself constitutes up to 36 percent of the votes required for a parliamentary majority.

The question thus arises: why do a majority of MPs in the governing party accept discipline from the minority who are government ministers? Party is the answer; it is the tie that binds frontbench and backbench MPs together to control British government. All members of the governing party share some collective goals, both ideological and instrumental. Much as they may differ among themselves, almost all are united in wishing to maintain their party in government, and to secure their own and their party's victory at the next general election. For this reason, sharp disagreements are likely to be differences about means. The end is common: electoral victory.

The votes of backbench MPs are a weak resource. Yet because the expectation of party loyalty is so strong, any deviation therefrom appears disproportionately important: abstention or a vote against the government by half a dozen or by a dozen MPs in the governing party can make headline news, and backbenchers can sometimes use the threat of public rebellion to secure ministerial modification of a policy. Debate within the governing party in private meeting rooms in the Palace of Westminster is tending to replace inter-party debate between government and Opposition as the chief mechanism for influencing the government of the day. But there remain strict limits on the extent to which backbench MPs can criticise their leaders in government. Ministers can accept criticism from their own extremists, whose ideological principles will differentiate them from the Opposition even more than from their own party leaders. To defeat a government measure, backbenchers in the governing party must be prepared to combine with the whole of the Opposition to secure a majority of votes. In the 1974–79 Parliament, the minority Labour government benefited because the votes of at least four different Opposition parties were required to form a majority against it.

Is the House of Commons becoming less disciplined?

It is sometimes suggested that the changing social character of individual MPs makes party less and less the determining factor in relationships between Cabinet and Commons. The line of reasoning is as follows. MPs are increasingly treating their position as a full-time rather than a part-time job, because of the demands of contemporary politics. The average MP is now more committed to Parliament as a profession, and on average better educated too.

Confident, successful people who find themselves in a full-time job will start looking for things to do. Articulate and energetic full-time MPs are less likely to be content to be lobby-fodder loyalists.

When there is not an opportunity for effectively influencing policy as ministers or shadow ministers, backbench MPs wanting to make an impact in the Commons can try to influence events by asserting themselves *against* party discipline. MPs who put their views on policy before their party's position can show their disagreement by votes on the floor of the House of Commons.

To determine whether the House of Commons as a whole is changing, we must determine two things: whether or not individual dissent is increasing, and also, whether or not party discipline is collectively losing effect.

In the post-war era there has been a definite increase in the number of MPs who will bark, that is, express disagreement with their own front bench by voting against the party whips. A majority of MPs express disagreement by voting against the party whip on the floor of the House of Commons one or more times during the life of a Parliament. In the 1970–74 Conservative government, 61 percent of backbench Conservative MPs voted against the government whip at least once. In the 1974–79 Labour government, 81 percent of all Labour MPs voted against a party whip at least once, and 89

Table 2.6(2)   *Frequency of MPs voting against party whips, 1970–79*

	1970–74 Parliament (a)			1974–79 Parliament (a)		
	Con (b) N	Cum've %	Lab N	Cum've %	Con N	Cum've %
None	108	41	62	19	31	11
Only once	53	61	32	28	17	16
2–9 times	58	83	90	56	144	66
10–19 times	4	84	37	67	74	91
20–29 times	1	84	32	77	11	95
30+ times	41(b)	100	77	100	15	100

Notes:

(a) Because sources differ in their base. 1970–74 Conservative figures refer to back-benchers only and 1974–79 data to all MPs, both front and backbenchers.

(b) The EEC bill, with 85 divisions, was the cause of most dissent in this Parliament. If EEC dissenters are disregarded, then 71 percent of Conservative MPs voted against whips no more than once, and 98 percent less than ten times (See Norton (1978). *op. cit.* Tables 3.1, 3.4).

Sources: Compiled from P. Norton (1978), *Conservative Dissidents*, Temple Smith, London, Tables 3.1, 3.4, and P. Norton (1980). *Dissension in the House of Commons, 1974–1979*, Clarendon Press, Oxford, Table 4, p. 435.

percent of all Opposition MPs (Table 2.6(2)). Frontbench party leaders and whips must recognise that there is now a point at which a backbencher will not vote with the party, and a further point at which abstentions will be turned into dissent by voting against the party in the Commons.

One bite in the leg of the party whips does not make a dog dangerous. The suggestion that the House of Commons is now filled with rebel MPs, who roam the jungle freely rather than being caged, is grossly misleading. The number of times an MP votes against the party whips in a Parliament is very few. In the 1970 Parliament the median Conservative MP voted against government whips only once, and four-fifths less than ten times (Table 2.6(2)). In the 1974–79 Parliament, the median MP voted half a dozen times against his party whips.

Given that there are more than one thousand divisions in the course of a Parliament, an MP can bark a number of times yet still be voting with the party on 99 percent or more of all divisions. A half a dozen dissents implies very occasional disagreement by MPs with their keepers in the iron cage of party discipline. In the 1970–74 Parliament, there were 1,101 divisions; hence, the median Conservative did not flout party discipline in 99.91 percent of all divisions. In the 1974–79 Parliament, there were 1,505 divisions. If the median Labour MP voted against the whip seven times, the MP was with the whip on 99.5 percent of all divisions. If the median Conservative voted against

Table 2.6(3) *Unanimity in party voting in the House of Commons, 1945–79*

	Unanimity	Dissent by one or more MPs
	(% of divisions)	
1945–50	93	7
1950–51	97.5	2.5
1951–55	97	3
1955–59	98	2
1959–64	86.5	13.5
1964–66	99.5	0.5
1966–70	90.5	9.5
1970–74	80	20
1974	77	23
1974–79	72	28
Average per Parliament	89	11

Source: Norton, *Dissension in the House of Commons, 1974–79*, Table 1, p. 428.

the whip six times, the average Conservative MP was with the whip on 99.6 percent of all divisions. In the 1974–79 Parliament, the most dissenting Labour MP, Dennis Skinner, voted against party whips in 156 divisions – yet this also meant that Skinner went along with the government in 90 percent of all divisions. On the Conservative side, the most dissenting MP, Nicholas Winterton, voted against the party whip on 92 occasions – but went along with it on 94 percent of all occasions.[4]

While MPs are inclined to bark against the government more often today than in the recent past, 100 percent agreement remains the norm in party votes in the House of Commons. Since 1945, 89 percent of whipped votes have produced a totally disciplined response by MPs in both parties without a single MP voting against the party whip (Table 2.6(3)). The height of disciplined voting was in the period from 1945 to 1959, when more than 95 percent of all divisions witnessed complete unanimity by both major parliamentary parties. From 1959 to 1970 the level of unanimity was about 90 percent. Since 1970 the number of divisions in which both parties have been unanimous has fallen to 'only' 75 percent, but to record that three-quarters of all divisions in a decade of unusually fractious politics have no dissenting vote on either side of the House is to emphasise the persisting strength of party discipline.

Abstentions cannot be considered here because the records of the House of Commons do not distinguish voluntary from involuntary abstentions. When no whip is on, 400, 500 or more MPs may not bother to vote, thus giving tacit support to the bill. When a three-line whip is on, the total number of abstentions will be relatively few and most of those not voting will usually be absent on non-political grounds. It is very unusual for a government to be defeated by the abstention of supporters motivated by political opposition to the measure at hand.

To have a collective impact upon party government, individual MPs must combine to express their dissent. One MP's vote is only $\frac{1}{318}$th of what is needed for a majority in the Commons. The conventional measure of the absence of party discipline, developed by A.L. Lowell, is that at least 10 percent of MPs should vote against the party majority. Lowell regarded party discipline as having become strict because the proportion of cohesive votes rose from less than half in the mid-nineteenth century to 91 percent among Conservative MPs in the 1890s, and to more than three-quarters among Liberal MPs. But by the standards of the post-1945 House of Commons, parties were far less cohesive at the height of late nineteenth-century party

Table 2.6(4)   *Party cohesion in House of Commons divisions 1830–1979*

	Conservatives		Liberals	
	% cohesive	% (N) dissent	% cohesive	% (N) dissent
1836	56	44	40	60
1850	45	55	37	63
1860	31	69	25	75
1871	61	39	55	45
1881	72	29	66	34
1894	91	9	81	19
1899	91	9	76	24
			Labour	
1945–50	99.7	0.3 (4)	99.6	0.4 (5)
1950	100	0 (0)	99.6	0.4 (1)
1951–55	100	0 (0)	99.3	0.7 (6)
1955–59	100	0 (0)	99.8	0.2 (2)
1959–64	99.9	0 (1)	99.8	0.1 (2)
1964–66	99.8	0 (1)	100	0 (0)
1966–70	99.3	0.7 (9)	98.9	1.2 (14)
1970–74	99.9	0.1 (1)	99.1	0.9 (10)
1974	98.2	1.8 (2)	95.5	4.5 (5)
1974–79	98.3	1.7 (25)	94.4	5.6 (84)

Sources: 1836–1899: A. L. Lowell (1908), *Government of England*, Macmillan New York, II, p. 81. 1945–79: Compiled from Norton, *Dissension in the House of Commons, 1974–79* (Labour), Table 6, p. 439; Norton, *Conservative Dissidents* (Conservatives), Table 8.7; and Norton, *Dissension in the House of Commons, 1974–79*, Table 1, p. 428; supplemented by Norton's files.

discipline than they are today (Table 2.6(4)). In the 1970s the extent of party cohesion has fallen from virtual completeness, but this is not to say it constitutes evidence of frequent organised dissent.

Dissent among backbench MPs occurs, but it is usually a 'lone wolf' phenomenon. Individual MPs are more likely than heretofore to carry their disagreement with party whips to the point of a vote against the party line, but dissenting MPs do not hunt in a pack, that is, they do not band together to bring collective pressure on their frontbench leadership. In an average post-war Parliament, 10 percent of Conservative MPs have banded together to vote against their party whip in only one division in every 500, that is, about once in two years. On the Labour side, 10 percent of MPs have banded together to vote against the party whip in only one division in every 200, that is, about once a year.

When backbench MPs dissent from their frontbench leadership, it is usually in the name of greater partisanship and not in rejection of partisanship. Dissent has usually reflected differences within a party about what party principles imply in a given situation; it does not normally represent agreement with the Opposition. This is particularly true in the Labour Party [where] MPs nearly always vote the official Labour line or, if they disagree with their front bench, assert an alternative Labour line rather than deviate toward their opponents. Complementary behaviour is shown by Conservative MPs.

A defeat of the government in a vote in the House of Commons is something very different from facing intra-party dissent in a division that the governing party nonetheless wins. Whereas the governing party can ignore or ride down a dissenting vote, a defeat is a signal that it cannot ignore. How often is dissent carried to the ultimate, a bite as well as a bark of protest?

In the period from 1900 to 1970, the governing party was defeated on average about once every two years in the House of Commons, usually on amendments to legislation. The governing party's dominance of the House of Commons was virtually complete. In the 1970s, individual MPs sometimes slipped from the iron cage of party government, but defeats by group defection remained very much the exception. In the 1970–74 Conservative government, there were 1,101 divisions, but in only six was the government defeated as the result of intra-party dissent. In the 1970–79 Parliament, the Labour government was involved in 1,505 divisions; the government was only defeated as a result of intra-party dissent 23 times, 1.5 percent of all divisions. In addition, the Labour government suffered 19 defeats in consequence of lacking an absolute majority and having several Opposition parties ganging up against it.[5]

Whilst the number of defeats suffered by government has risen by post-1945 standards, the control of the governing party in the Commons remains very great.[6] In the 1970s, the government on average suffered defeat three times a session from intra-party dissent, less than in any decade in the period 1847 to 1886 inclusive, and from 1974 to 1979 it was defeated an average of seven times a session by intra-party dissent. Overall, from 1970–79 the governing party was defeated seven times a session, less than the average for the decade from 1847 to 1856 or from 1857 to 1866.

Overall, the evidence of the post-war era shows that individual MPs' behaviour is changing, but its collective effect upon the House of Commons is slight. The small scale of change must be emphasised. Otherwise, any departure from 100 percent unanimity, both the norm and the actuality at recent points in British parliamentary history, can be misinterpreted as a breakdown of the iron cage of party discipline. Moreover, misinterpretation is encouraged by specific facts of the 1974–79 Parliament. Because the Labour government lacked an overall majority, it was ready to tolerate defeat in the Commons by its opponents, and therefore to tolerate defeat by its own dissenters as well. By parliamentary standards of the past half-century, the 1974–79 period was an aberration.

By comparison with the mid-nineteenth century House of Commons, the iron cage of party discipline is far stronger today than in the past. The same is true in comparisons between Britain and many other legislatures in the Western world. The proportion of government bills approved by the British Parliament is as high or higher than in other Western legislatures for which data has been complied by the Inter-Parliamentary Union. In Britain, 93 percent of government bills were enacted. By comparison, in British-style parliaments in Australia, New Zealand and Canada, a government is less certain of carrying out its wishes – and the same is true in Continental parliaments with a variety of party systems. British MPs may increasingly bark, but they rarely bite the hand that leads them by comparison with MPs in other Western nations.

Given the mid-nineteenth century evidence that disciplined parties are not a necessary condition of British government, and the 1970s evidence that party discipline is contingent, not inevitable, the question that should be asked is: what kind of changes in the political system might break, or at least bend, the bars enough to alter the cage of party government?

Disappointment with the achievements of successive Labour and Conservative governments is the fundamental cause of increasing dissent by MPs. Dissent is a negative gesture, a sign of disliking what has happened. The inability of party leaders in office to meet the expectations they have raised in opposition has been cumulative for two decades. The1959 general election, when Harold Macmillan campaigned on the theme of prosperity, was the last general election in which a party in office won a vote of confidence from its supporters after a full term. One does not need to believe that British government has 'failed', whatever that term may mean, in order to recognise that the successes of governing parties have been fewer than disappointments in the past two decades.

MPs faced with a government that does not inspire confidence in its record may still remain within the iron cage of party politics. But they will do so with less and less confidence that their leaders are in control of the situation or know what they are doing; this lack of confidence may spill over into dissent. To disappoint MPs who have been whipped to support a party line that is not justified in the event can invite greater trouble subsequently. Hence, the governing party is asking for fewer votes of confidence. The government of the day has always had the power to decide whether or not it regards a bill on which it may be defeated as a vote of confidence. The minority status of the 1974–79 Labour government made it very anxious to avoid votes of confidence. The idea that all votes in the Commons are *de facto* votes of confidence in the government of the day is now a constitutional myth.

History shows that change in Parliament is recurring. The roles of MPs were not fixed once for all at the founding of Parliament in the thirteenth century. MPs were much more independent of party a century and a half ago than they are today. The variability of the role in British government over the centuries is a caution against assuming the fixity of the *status quo*. The slow pace of change and the very limited deviations from collective party discipline are a caution against using the bark of dissent as evidence of a break in the bars of the iron cage of party government.

> Abridged from Richard Rose (1983), 'Still the era of party government', *Parliamentary Affairs*, XXXVI, pp. 282–99. Reprinted with permission of Oxford University Press, Oxford.

Notes

1 A. L. Lowell (1908), *The Government of England*, Macmillan, New York, II, pp. 77, 81.
2 P. Norton (1981), *The Commons in Perspective*, Martin Robertson, Oxford, p. 86.
3 See D. E. Butler and A. Sloman (1980), *British Political Facts, 1900–1979*, Macmillan, London, p. 78.
4 P. Norton (1980), *Dissension in the House of Commons, 1974–1979*, Clarendon Press, Oxford, p. 435.
5 See Lowell, *Government of England*, p. 80; and P. Norton, 'Government defeats in the House of Commons: myth and reality,' *Public Law*, 1978, p. 361.
6 See Norton, *Commons in Perspective*, p. 227ff.

2.7 The British prime minister

Anthony King

The requirements of the job

The person who walks for the first time through the door of Number 10 as prime minister does not create or re-create the prime ministership: the job, to a considerable extent, already exists. There are certain tasks that any prime minister is expected to perform. If he or she did not perform them, everyone would be surprised; no one would know who else should perform them, and the system would cease to function in anything like its present form.

Seven such tasks stand out. All of them are now mandatory in the sense that a prime minister who did not perform them or who delegated them to others would be thought to be shirking his or her responsibilities.

1 The appointment and dismissal of ministers has been the prime minister's task ever since the monarch ceased to appoint cabinet ministers (except in a purely formal way) in the eighteenth century. The prime minister's duty in this regard has gradually been extended to include non-cabinet ministers as well.[1] The prime minister decides which government offices will exist, whom to appoint to those offices, whom to dismiss from them.

One major qualification, needs, however, to be made to this last statement. In 1981 the parliamentary Labour Party voted to change its Standing Orders to restrict the range of choice of cabinet ministers available to an incoming Labour prime minister. Standing Order E of the parliamentary Labour Party now reads:

When the Party is in Office, the Cabinet shall continue to be appointed by the Prime Minister. On taking Office as Prime Minister, the Leader shall appoint as members of his Cabinet those who were elected as members of Parliamentary Committee at the Dissolution and have retained their seats in the new Parliament.

Since the parliamentary committee or shadow cabinet now contains 21 members of the House of Commons apart from the leader, the 1981 change means that any incoming Labour prime minister will in the future have almost no say in the membership of his or her cabinet, though he or she will still control the disposition of offices.[2]

2 The prime minister is responsible for all appointments to the top two rungs of the home civil service – permanent secretary and deputy secretary – and for major appointments in the foreign service, including (in practice if not in theory) important ambassadorships abroad. For domestic posts, the prime minister is advised by the head of the home civil service, who in turn is advised by a small body of senior officials called the Senior Appointments Selection Committee. For foreign posts, the prime minister's advisers are the Foreign Secretary, the permanent secretary at the Foreign Office and, at one remove, the Foreign Office Senior Selection Board. The prime minister usually accepts official advice, but may reject a particular name and may occasionally ask that additional names be considered.[3]

3 The prime minister – any prime minister – is expected to chair meetings of the cabinet and important cabinet committees, to be responsible for determining which items will appear on the agendas of such meetings

and, at the end of the discussion of each agenda item, to 'sum up' the cabinet's or the committee's conclusions. The British prime minister differs from many other heads of government in being expected to interpret the results of cabinet discussions rather than taking formal votes.[4]

4 The prime minister has to attend the House of Commons twice each week while Parliament is sitting in order to answer 'prime minister's questions'. This responsibility, like the responsibility to chair cabinet meetings, may be delegated, but only when the prime minister is ill or out of the country on official business. Apart from answering questions twice a week and voting from time to time, the British prime minister (contrary to widespread belief) has virtually no other parliamentary responsibilities. Prime ministers were once expected to speak in major debates and to make major policy statements on behalf of the government. Not any longer. Recent research has shown that most recent prime ministers have been exceedingly sparing in their parliamentary appearances. Thatcher, in particular, almost never intervened in debates.[5] It is striking that, before the publication of the research, few had noticed this dereliction from what would once have been regarded as one of the prime minister's chief responsibilities.

5 The prime minister's fifth mandatory task is a relatively new one, the product of the past two decades. Before the Second World War, meetings between or among heads of government were rare. Even in the 1950s and 1960s, summit meetings were relatively rare. Since the early 1970s, however, Britain's prime minister has been expected to attend the six-monthly summit of European Community heads of government and also the annual summit of the Group of Seven industrial countries. The biennial summit of Commonwealth heads of government is also on the prime minister's permanent agenda. The prime minister is enmeshed , as a central part of his or her working life, in a network of relationships extending far beyond Britain's shores.

6 The prime minister's sixth responsibility is the one about which least is known – at any rate in detail – to the outside world. The British prime minister is, in effect, 'the minister for the security services'. Although the lines of authority affecting the British secret services are almost as secret as the services themselves, there can be little doubt that, formally as well as informally, all of the main ones, for both budget and operations, converge on the prime minister.[6] In addition, the prime minister has been statutorily responsible since 1989 for the appointment of a commissioner to oversee the security services and, in particular, the home secretary's issuing of search warrants and warrants authorising telephone tapping.

7 During the First World War the prime minister acquired, almost by accident, responsibility for determining, within the limits of the law, the date on which a general election is to be held. Before 1914, the timing of

elections was a matter for the cabinet collectively. Since 1918, it has been a matter for the prime minister personally.[7] The task is onerous and in no way strengthens the prime minister's hand *vis-à-vis* the other members of his or her government: if the prime minister gets the timing right and the governing party wins, the prime minister benefits, but so does the rest of the government; if he or she gets the timing wrong and the party loses, the prime minister is uniquely to blame. Prime ministers sometimes probably wish they could revert to the pre-1914 convention; but to do so in the circumstances of the 1990s would smack of cowardice.

These are the seven main tasks that the prime minister is expected to perform: the principal 'expectations of the role'. But it is worth drawing attention to one omission from this list – one, as it were, non-expectation of the role. The Basic Law of the German Federal Republic states in Article 65 that 'the Federal Chancellor shall determine, and be responsible for, the general policy guidelines', and the whole weight of German history supports the idea that the country's head of government is responsible for providing policy leadership. Similarly in France the Constitution of the Fifth Republic states in Article 20 that 'the Government determines and directs the policy of the nation' and in Article 21 that 'the Premier directs the activity of the Government', the implication being that the premier has a central policy-making role to play.

There is, however, no such presumption in Britain. A prime minister may choose to give his or her government policy guidance or leadership, but there is no expectation that he or she will do so. The job does not have policy leadership as one of its positive requirements. Prime ministers are, of course, expected to give their government a certain style or tone (they could hardly fail to do so); they are expected to referee political fights among ministers; they are expected to be the managers of the government's political business. But they are not expected as a matter of routine to be their government's policy leader. Some prime ministers (Attlee, Wilson, Callaghan) have seen their role largely as political management. Others (Churchill, Macmillan, Heath) have sought to make an impact in specific areas of policy (frequently foreign policy). But only a very few, of whom Thatcher was the extreme example, have sought to make all their government's policies their own. Moreover, there is every reason to think that her successor, John Major, is already reverting to the pre-Thatcher norm.

The possibilities of the job

The prime ministership in Britain is remarkably malleable. Harold Wilson was a highly activist prime minister during his first term (1964–70); he was much more passive during his second term (1974–76). Sir Alec Douglas-Home was a minimalist prime minister in almost every sense; Margaret Thatcher was a maximalist in almost every sense. There is scarcely a dimension of the job along which different prime ministers have not varied.

One factor contributing to this variation is the absence in Britain of anything approaching a written constitution. Britain's political arrangements are largely governed, not by written rules but by what trade unionists call 'custom and practice'; and few of Britain's customs and practices are at all precisely specified. Any prime minister is therefore in a position to arrogate to himself new tasks or functions, knowing that the charge of 'unconstitutional behaviour' can almost never be made to stick, and knowing, too, that any minister seeking to make the charge stick and thus to limit the prime minister's power is thereby involved in a direct challenge to the prime minister's authority, thus putting his or her own political career at risk. Prime ministers are inhibited, when they are, by a sense of constitutional propriety and/or by a personal preference for a more collegial, less prime minister-centred style of government and/or by a feeling that they are politically vulnerable and that any attempt to extend their authority will only make them more vulnerable. Most prime ministers in British history have been influenced by one or more of these factors most of the time; the distinguishing feature of Margaret Thatcher's premiership was how seldom she was influenced by any of them.[8]

'Constitutional propriety' includes the belief – constantly reinforced by politicians' and civil servants' behaviour, seldom, if ever, openly challenged – that the 'best', the most authoritative, indeed the only authoritative policy decisions in the British governmental system are collective cabinet decisions or decisions taken on the cabinet's behalf and in its name. The cabinet as a body has a universally acknowledged right of decision and veto. A would-be powerful prime minister therefore can, on the one hand, take advantage of the British constitution's porousness and informality but, on the other, must reckon at all times with the cabinet's undoubted constitutional superiority. No one can ever know in advance just how strong the fetters on a given prime minister are; but they are always there. In effect the power of the prime minister is what a prime minister wants, and is able, to get away with.

Against that background, what are the actual and potential sources of the power of a prime minister? What are the possibilities of the office as distinct from its requirements?

To begin with, a prime minister who wishes to assert his or her authority benefits from having, precisely, 'authority' in the most generalised sense of that term: the authority that arises out of mere possession of the office, as distinct from any special skills or qualities that an individual brings to it. The prime minister has an invisible but discernible aura. A request to another minister from the prime minister is more than just a request: it smacks of command. In acting as prime minister, it helps simply to *be* prime minister.

The requirement to chair the cabinet and major cabinet committees is also useful. The chairman of any committee is often in a position to dominate it or at least to have a disproportionate amount of influence over its proceedings. The reasons are obvious: the chairman controls the agenda; he is likely to see the papers in advance of everyone else; he can speak at will from the chair; he decides who else will speak and in what order; he can, in all kinds of subtle ways, influence the tone and flow of the debate; in the absence of formal voting, he sums up the debate at the end; not least, he is likely to be able to influence the contents of the minutes. These powers can seldom be used to flout what is clearly the collective will of the majority; but they can always be used, including by a British prime minister, to nudge – sometimes even to steer – collective decisions in a desired direction.

That the prime minister as chairman of the cabinet 'is likely to see the papers in advance of everyone else' relates to another attribute of the premiership that can be to the advantage of a prime minister, especially an ambitious one: the prime minister is the only member of the government who is in a position to take – indeed can hardly avoid taking – an interest in almost everything that the government is currently doing. More than any other minister, the prime minister is involved in a flow of business, of meetings, paper and telephone calls, that encompasses the full range of the government's activities. He or she is therefore in a position to intervene in the business of any and every other minister and also to see the connections among aspects of the government's work that are widely dispersed and may not seem, to others, to be related. The prime minister, in short, is likely to be the only minister who sees 'the big picture'.

He or she is also the only minister with a strong personal incentive to see and also to grasp the big picture, in its political as well as its policy aspects. In the British system the prime minister is held responsible for everything that goes wrong in everyone's office. Since everyone knows in advance that the prime minister will be blamed, the prime minister is tacitly accorded an open licence to enquire, to intervene, to goad, to check, to prod, to remonstrate, even to dominate. Other ministers are only 'ministerially responsible'; it is the prime minister who is politically responsible.[9]

This ultimate political responsibility manifests itself in another way, one that distinguishes Britain from many (most?) other democratic countries. In many (most?) countries, the structure of the government is determined by law. Thus, if the head of government or the government collectively wants to establish, say, a new department of energy or a new department of the environment, an enabling statute must be passed in due form by the national legislature. In Britain, by contrast, the prime minister determines, not merely who will be in the cabinet and what positions they will hold, and not merely which cabinet committees will exist and who will sit on them, but also, and most remarkably, which administrative departments of state will exist and which functions of state will be assigned to them.

In practice, this control over administrative structures, as well as persons, considerably enhances a prime minister's potential power. In 1970 Edward

Heath created the Central Policy Review Staff to suit his purposes as prime minister; in 1983 Margaret Thatcher abolished it to suit hers.[10] In 1988 Thatcher was dissatisfied with the performance of John Moore, the minister in charge of the Department of Health and Social Security; she therefore, by administrative fiat, split the department into two, assigning to Moore the lesser of the two halves from her point of view, Social Security.

The fact that a modern prime minister's job has an international – or, better, a transnational – dimension probably also enhances his or her power (just as it probably does that of heads of government in other countries). When real decisions are to be taken at summit meetings, such as the European Community's, then collective bodies like cabinets have little alternative but to grant some powers of agency to their national representatives.

A prime minister's ability to command the attention of the media (television and the press) is sometimes cited as a factor tending to increase prime ministerial power; and it is undoubtedly true that sometimes a prime minister's power *vis-à-vis* other ministers may be augmented by his or her capacity to influence the flow of government publicity and, more specifically, by a well-judged television interview or perhaps by the ability to win and retain the support of important newspaper editors and proprietors. But it must be evident that from a prime minister's point of view television and the press are two-edged swords. Prime ministers sometimes seek positively to command the attention of the media; but sometimes they undoubtedly wish the media would go away.

Finally, the prime minister, subject to the proviso mentioned earlier about incoming Labour prime ministers, has, as we have seen, the power to appoint, dismiss and reassign cabinet and other ministers. And here we come to the nub of the matter. It is impossible to doubt that, of all the prime minister's powers, the one that gives by far the greatest leverage over his or her government is the power (as the Americans say) to 'hire, fire and relocate'. The British prime ministership, shorn, for example, of its power to appoint senior civil servants or of its responsibility for the security services, would still be recognisably the same office; but, shorn of its power over ministerial appointments, it would no longer be the prime ministership in anything like the form that it has been known in since the eighteenth century. The appointment power is crucial.

The reason is simple – and has gained in force over recent generations. The great majority of British politicians are career politicians. They eat, breathe and sleep politics. Most of them passionately want to be ministers; or, if they are already ministers, they want to be promoted in the ministerial hierarchy, and they certainly do not want to be demoted, shunted sideways or dismissed.[11] It follows that the prime minister of the day is in an exceedingly powerful position. He or she is the monopoly supplier of a good, ministerial office, which is in very short supply and for which there is an enormous demand. He or she can exploit this monopoly position to influence the behaviour of backbenchers who want to be ministers and of ministers who want to be promoted and not to be dismissed.

Needless to say, the prime minister's power of appointment is not, in the real world, unfettered. Ministers must come mainly from the House of Commons. In the Labour Party, the ministers in an incoming government are now, in effect, elected by the parliamentary party. And there will be many occasions when the political costs of sacking a given minister, or of not appointing him or her in the first place, will outweigh any political benefits to be gained. Nevertheless, when all the necessary qualifications have been made, it is the prime minister's power of appointment and dismissal that, above all else, sets him or her apart from all other ministers.

The limitations on the office

A discussion like the foregoing of the sources of a prime minister's power and influence needs to be complemented by a discussion of the limitations on that power and influence. Several have been referred to, at least implicitly, in what has been said already.

The principal limitation on a prime minister's power lies in the fact that in the British system he or she has only very limited scope for independent decision-taking. The range of matters about which the prime minister can say 'Do this' or 'Do that' and be confident that it will be done is very restricted. The British constitution assigns the prime minister no substantial powers beyond the ones already referred to; the prime minister does not normally hold any governmental office other than the prime ministership;[12] and in Britain there are very few statutes that the prime minister administers on his or her own personal authority (the Security Service Act being one of only a handful). The result is that, if the prime minister wishes to act, he or she must normally act through others: either the responsible minister, if the matter falls within the purview of a single government department, or the cabinet or a cabinet committee if the matter affects several departments. The prime minister can exert considerable, sometimes enormous, influence over these other individuals and collectivities; but ultimately the decisions are theirs, not his or hers.

The prime minister's power is also limited, in subtle as well as obvious ways, by the fact, also referred to above, that the prime minister holds power by virtue of being leader of the ruling party and that there is always the possibility, however remote, that he or she can be deposed as party leader. This threat need never become a reality to have real effects. Except in the immediate aftermath of election victories or when for some other reason their political stock is especially high, most prime ministers most of the time are probably conscious, if with only a small particle of their minds, that they are, after all, politically mortal and that there are large numbers of people, including many of their closest colleagues, who would like nothing better than to replace them.

These constraints are the two main limits on prime-ministerial power; but any head of government is also, of course, limited by a variety of more mundane considerations: lack of time, lack of energy (even Thatcher's energy was not limitless), lack of expertise, the normal human inability to focus on everything at once. In addition, the British prime minister is handicapped to some degree, in comparison with some other heads of government, by having only a very small personal staff.

Staff services

The size of a modern prime minister's staff can be illustrated in the case of Thatcher. Her personal staff – the people, apart from secretaries and telephonists, who worked for *her* – consisted of five private secretaries (civil servants on secondment from line departments, who kept the prime minister company, kept her papers flowing, kept notes of her meetings other than cabinet and cabinet committee meetings and acted as her liaison with ministers, departments and the outside world generally), a personal assistant (who helped her with her wardrobe and more personal arrangements), a secretary for appointments (a civil servant who, despite his splendid title, deals with non-political appointments and other relatively minor matters), a foreign affairs adviser (an ex-Foreign Office official who kept an eye on the Foreign Office, of which she was suspicious, on her behalf), a political secretary (who was her day-to-day liaison with the Conservative Party and with people in her constituency), an eight-strong Policy Unit (whose members, a mixture of career civil servants and outsiders, gave her free-wheeling advice on both the political and the substantive aspects of future and current policy), two press secretaries (the chief press secretary is usually, but not always, a highly political civil servant), a parliamentary private secretary (a backbench MP who provides relatively informal liaison with other backbench MPs), a parliamentary clerk (a civil servant, who organises the purely parliamentary side of the prime minister's working life) and the more or less free-standing Efficiency Unit (a small group of civil servants, headed by an outsider, which sought to respond to the former prime minister's personal concern for governmental efficiency). In her various roles as chairman of the cabinet, minister for the civil service and minister for the security services, Thatcher was also served by the cabinet secretary.[13]

The total prime-ministerial staff comes to between two dozen and about thirty people, of whom perhaps seventeen or eighteen are intimately concerned with policy and the politics (and presentation) of policy. This group is very small by the standards of many other countries, including many countries with governmental machines smaller than Britain's.

Conclusions

It should be evident by now that anyone studying the British prime ministership is, or should be, studying dynamics and variety, not just statics and
uniformity. The outlines of the job remain roughly the same and change only
slowly through time, but the way in which the job is done varies enormously.
Think of any pair of post-war prime ministers, one of whom succeeded the
other, and the point is made.

Variety comes in two forms. First, there is variety *between* and *among*
different prime ministers. Different people bring different personalities to the
job; they have different goals; they adopt different styles, and they find themselves operating in different political environments. Second, there is variety
within the lifetime of a single premiership. This variety can be deliberate on
the part of the prime minister (Thatcher's governing style became more
dominant as she became increasingly confident and determined); or, more
commonly, it can be dictated from outside by changed circumstances, as a
prime minister's personal standing, electoral prospects and professional repu-
tation change through time. In other words, the student of the subject needs
to study, not *the* prime minister but prime minister*ships*.

One important general point can, however, be made. The British system of
government contains checks and balances (we have referred to several), but it
contains fewer checks and balances than can be found in almost any other
country calling itself a democracy. In Britain there is no system of judicial
review (except of the details of statutes); there are no coalitions and therefore
no coalition partners in the government to check one another; there are no
significant sub-national units of government; there is no independent legislative assembly – and the British tradition of strict party discipline means that
the government of the day can almost invariably count on the backing of its
supporters (note the word) in the division lobbies in the House of Commons.

It follows that, especially in the age of the career politician, the British
prime minister is probably able to be more powerful inside his or her own
government than any other head of government anywhere else in the democratic world. Britain may no longer be powerful as a country, but the power of
the prime minister within the British state, if he or she chooses to exercise it,
is immense.

> Abridged from Anthony King (1991), 'The British prime minister-
> ship in the age of the career politician,' *West European Politics*, XIV,
> pp. 31–47. Reprinted by permission of Frank Cass & Company
> Ltd., London.

Notes

1 The gradual extension of the prime minister's power of appointment seems never
  to have been traced. It seems that cabinet ministers once appointed junior ministers

on their own. Then they began to consult the prime minister before making junior ministerial appointments, which nevertheless were still their own to make. Now prime ministers make all ministerial appointments, junior as well as senior, on their own, though they may on occasion, if they choose, consult their cabinet colleagues. See Kevin Theakston (1987), *Junior Ministers in British Government*, Basil Blackwell, Oxford, Ch. 1.

2 The Parliamentary Labour Party's standing orders, like the Conservative Party's leadership procedures, appear not to have been published and to be available only from the PLP. The 1981 change seems to have been a result of the desire of right-wing MPs, who dominated the parliamentary party, to offset the growing left-wing domination of the Labour Party in the country. If the left was going to dominate the choice of leader, then the right was determined to dominate his choice of cabinet colleagues.

3 See the accounts of Peter Hennessy (1989), *Whitehall*, Secker and Warburg, London, pp. 630–34, and in *Top Jobs in Whitehall: Appointments and Promotions in the Senior Civil Service*, Report of a Royal Institute of Public Administration Working Group, London, 1987. The upper ranks of the British Civil Service are not politicised in the way they are in some other West European countries. The men and women whom the prime minister appoints are career civil servants and will remain in post even if the prime minister or the party in power changes. Most prime ministers have intervened only occasionally in the choice of senior officials, in the sense of playing an active part in the process.

4 Little has been written about the process of coming to collective decisions – in the British case, the prime minister's 'summing up' – but see Jürg Steiner and Robert H. Dorff (1980), 'Decision by interpretation: a new concept for an often overlooked decision mode', *British Journal of Political Science*, 10, pp. 1–13.

5 The research is reported in Patrick Dunleavy, G. W. Jones and Brendan O'Leary (1990), 'Prime ministers and the Commons: patterns of behaviour, 1868 to 1987', *Public Administration*, 68, pp. 123–40.

6 On the prime minister's involvement in 'Secret Departments', see Hennessy, *Whitehall*, pp. 471–4.

7 An account of what brought about the change – it certainly had the quality of an accident about it – is given by Geoffrey Marshall in *Constitutional Conventions: The Rules and Forms of Political Accountability*, Clarendon Press, Oxford, 1984, Ch. 3.

8 The only factor that appears to have inhibited her more or less continuously was the need to preserve the outward, and some of the inward, norms of cabinet government. Thatcher did not want to be seen to be bringing about a radical change in the British system of government. She saw no need to do so in order to achieve her objectives, and constitutional reform was not one of the items on her personal agenda. Her successor has inherited an office that, formally, has changed scarcely at all. On Thatcher's approach to the prime ministership and the conduct of government, see Hugo Young (1989), *One of Us: A Biography of Margaret Thatcher*, Macmillan, London; Peter Jenkins (1987), *Mrs. Thatcher's Revolution: The Ending of the Socialist Era*, Jonathan Cape, London; Anthony King, 'Margaret Thatcher: the style of a prime minister' in Anthony King, ed. (1985), *The British Prime Minister*, 2nd edn, Macmillan, London, Ch. 4; and Anthony King, 'Margaret

Thatcher as a political leader' in Robert Skidelsky (ed.) (1988), *Thatcherism*, Chatto and Windus, London, Ch. 2.

9 'Ministerial responsibility' is a concept with almost mystic status in the British system. The curious should consult Geoffrey Marshall (ed.) (1989), *Ministerial Responsibility*, Oxford University Press, Oxford.

10 Tessa Blackstone and William Plowden recount the often turbulent history of the Central Policy Review Staff in *Inside the Think Tank: Advising the Cabinet 1971–1983*, Heinemann, London, 1988.

11 See Anthony King (1981), 'The rise of the career politician in Britain – and its consequences', *British Journal of Political Science*, 11, pp. 249–85.

12 The contrast can be drawn with France, where the prime minister has often also been defence minister. The last prime minister to hold a major office of state apart from his own was Churchill, who was his own defence minister for a few months in 1951–52.

13 The authority on the staffing of the prime ministership is G. W. Jones. See 'The prime minister's aides', in King, *British Prime Minister*, Ch. 3, and his paper, 'The prime minister's office since 1979: the United Kingdom' (mimeo, 1990). A few of the many who have served on prime ministers' staffs have written personal accounts of their experiences. See in particular Lord Egremont (1968), *Wyndham and Children First*, Macmillan, London; Douglas Hurd (1979), *An End to Promises: Sketch of a Government 1970–74*, Collins, London; Marcia Williams (1972), *Inside Number 10*, Weidenfeld & Nicolson, London; Joe Haines (1977), *The Politics of Power*, Jonathan Cape, London; and Bernard Donoughue (1987), *Prime Minister: The Conduct of Policy under Harold Wilson and James Callaghan*, Jonathan Cape, London.

2.8   The cabinet under Mrs Thatcher

Martin Burch

The issues surrounding the resignation of Mr Lawson as Chancellor of the Exchequer in October 1989 raised once again the question as to whether under Mrs Thatcher's premiership collective Cabinet government still operates. It has been noted that since 1979 Cabinet meets less often and that the number of committees and cabinet papers has fallen (Hennessy 1986, page 99). One view is that Cabinet has ceased to be an important forum for discussion and decision, and it generally serves to ratify decisions that have been reached elsewhere. A more charitable view holds that Cabinet has become a residual institution in that it is left with the task of determining the residue of issues that it has proved impossible to settle at a lower level (Burch 1988). Both views suggest a downgrading in the centrality of Cabinet and its further decline as a major forum for the handling of government business.

Now if the business of government is not so frequently handled in Cabinet, where is it being shaped and determined? Before answering that question we need to note two preliminary points. First, in order to understand the contemporary significance of Cabinet it is essential to set it within the wider systems of organisations which immediately surround it. For the 21 members of Cabinet meeting together once a week for two to three hours constitute only one small part of a series of relationships that operate above and beyond particular government departments. It is through these relationships that policy within the Cabinet system is shaped and determined and they operate as follows.

1 Through the 'formal structure' of Cabinet and Cabinet committees (both those consisting of ministers and those involving civil servants) which are administered and serviced by the Cabinet secretariat.
2 Through the 'informal structure' of personal contacts between those who engage in or are connected with the activities which take place within the formal structure. Such informal contacts range from the casual 'chat' in the corridor, to encounters in more organised meetings – the key point is that they all take place within the Cabinet system, *but* outside the formal structure.

The second preliminary point is that, while the formal elements of Cabinet, its secretariat and its committees have remained constant features of the Cabinet system throughout the post-war period, the exact composition and scope of these elements and the informal aspects of their operation have varied enormously. The operation of the Cabinet system is very much affected by the characters, opinions and prejudices of the people involved: it is a highly personalised set of institutions. It is also quite compact and self-contained: usually only a small number of people (between 20 and 50) are actively engaged in handling each particular policy issue and their activities are shrouded in secrecy. There are patterns and there have been significant changes in the way in which business is handled. So let us return to our question – if not in Cabinet, where are matters being determined?

Use of cabinet committees

Let us start with the formal system. Under Mrs Thatcher a large proportion of overall business is determined in Cabinet committee. There is nothing novel or improper about settling matters at this level. It is laid down in the rules of procedure which cover the handling of business and the practice has been widespread throughout the postwar period. In a survey I have undertaken of 42 past Cabinet ministers with experience of Cabinets over the years 1970–1989, all accepted that much business was determined at committee level and that this practice is necessary in order to ensure that Cabinet is not over-burdened with business (see also Hailsham 1987, page 7). The point is that the practice of determining matters in committee has been extended both in terms of the proportion of business coming into the formal Cabinet system which is dealt with at that level, and the significance of the items that are so handled. Consequently many major items of business have largely been dealt with in committee including banning trade unions at GCHQ, abolition of the Metropolitan Counties, introduction of the community charge (poll tax), sale of British Telecom and other state industries, reform of the National Health Service and the formulation of the means by which to effect the transfer of Hong Kong to the Chinese authorities. Some of these matters were subsequently reported to Cabinet, but all were really shaped and determined below Cabinet level.

So far as there has been a pattern in the use of committees the tendency has been to settle many matters in one of three main policy committees dealing with economic, overseas and defence, and home affairs. While these often consider proposals that have effectively been determined elsewhere, it is certainly the case that more discussion and deliberation on specific policy matters takes place in these committees than in Cabinet. Again this practice is not new. The consequence has been that the formal structure of the Cabinet system has operated in a rather compartmentalised way in that policy development has tended to be contained amongst fairly distinct groupings of ministers and civil servants in each of the general spheres of policy denoted by these three main committees. One result is that co-ordination takes place either above cabinet or at a sub-cabinet level and this can raise problems about the coherence of the government's programme. It also serves to further dilute the role of cabinet in co-ordinating the overall development of the government's policy programme.

Routine matters are kept out

Many routine matters are not brought within the Cabinet system and, whenever possible, the tendency has been for matters to be settled in or between departments. Many issues involve more than one department and these are usually dealt with through either a Cabinet committee or interdepartmental committee (a working group operating outside the confines of the cabinet system) or ministerial correspondence. In interviews, those with experience of Cabinet government since 1979 mentioned the extensive use of ministerial correspondence as a means of clarifying and settling minor issues involving two or three ministries. In general the approach is to transact business on paper rather than through formal meetings which are costly in terms of both time and effort.

This technique of reaching decisions through correspondence is also applied at the level of a Cabinet committee in that two or more ministers may be asked to settle an item outside the committee and to then inform its members through correspondence of their decision. This practice of conducting business within the scope but outside the confines of the committee is well established. The consequence of the application of these and other techniques has been to limit the amount of business going into the system. Interestingly this is one instance in which departments may have been strengthened as against any centralising trend usually regarded as characteristic of the Thatcher administrations.

Matters arrive in a more refined state

Business is substantially refined before being brought into the formal Cabinet system. This reflects the more onerous conditions which are required to be settled if an item is to be taken up, conditions which are in part a result of the heightened priority given to the Treasury's attempts to constrain and control spending. A development which can be traced back at least to the early 1970s but which was given extra emphasis with the coming to power of a Conservative government in 1979 pledged to cutting the size of the public sector and to achieving 'value for money' in public spending. So that no item involving extra spending, staffing, and/or accommodation or which has implications for financial policy can be brought into the formal Cabinet system unless it can be shown that consultations have taken place and, in many instances, agreements have been reached with the Treasury. These restrictions are not new (indeed the point about extra spending can be traced back to 1869) but they have been applied more stringently since 1979. In addition, since 1983, following the adoption of an efficiency programme across all departments (the Financial Management Initiative), a new policy proposal requiring consideration in the formal Cabinet system must be supported with a statement about what it is likely to cost, is meant to achieve and how its achievement will be evaluated. These conditions have meant that more details of policy have to be worked out prior to issues entering the Cabinet system.

In addition the sources of policy initiatives have altered. In particular the Prime Minister and the Prime Minister's Policy Unit have played a more substantial role. Ideas from this small unit of eight to nine full-timers, once they attract the Prime Minister's interest, have often gone on to be developed in the departments (Willets 1987). The change is significant, for previously more initiative lay in the hands of departments and less was exercised from No. 10. One consequence is that an issue may already have gathered some momentum and support within the informal Cabinet system before it is worked upon by the department prior to it entering the formal system. And, if the proposal survives departmental scrutiny, given its origins in No. 10, it is likely to be dealt with quite speedily.

Matters are more pre-determined

The most significant change in the operation of the Cabinet system under Mrs Thatcher is the extent to which the informal structure has been enhanced and the formal one downgraded. In some instances the function of Cabinet and its committees has been reduced to ratifying or marginally developing proposals that have been extensively worked out in the informal system. To use a phrase popular amongst administrators, policy is more extensively 'pre-cooked' before it arrives in the kitchen. This pre-cooking has taken place in a wide range of types of informal groupings, usually centred on the Prime Minister (see Seldon 1990, page 115). They include what might be seen as the most structured of informal groups such as committees chaired by the Prime Minister which are not listed as Cabinet committees, are not necessarily serviced by members of the Cabinet secretariat, and produce memorandum for action from the Prime Minister's office rather than official minutes from the Cabinet secretariat. Alternative examples are the meetings which take place *à deux* between the Prime Minister and her staff and one other minister and his staff, or the informal lunches at No. 10 to which Cabinet ministers currently in favour are invited.

An effect of the more extensive preparation of materials in the informal Cabinet system is to further shift policy initiatives on certain key issues away from departments to the Prime Minister's office. So the informal structure has become both more significant and more centred upon the Prime Minister and business flows, not only through the Cabinet secretariat but also, and more extensively, through the Prime Minister's office. A second consequence is that issues arrive in the formal machine at a fairly late stage in their development, they already have a body of opinion behind them, are worked out in some detail, and are placed before ministers (and officials) not previously involved who have limited information and opportunities to organise an alternative view or to press for substantial amendment. By the time such issues get into the machine they are difficult to stop or alter.

In sum, the changes examined above suggest two important consequences for the way in which cabinet government operates today. On the one hand there is less business going through the formal system and it is handled more speedily. On the other, the formal system is increasingly used as a means of clarifying and endorsing matters largely pre-determined elsewhere and is used less than was previously the case as a mechanism for actually formulating policy and achieving consensus across departments.

Why have these changes taken place?

In part they reflect long-term trends which pre-date the coming to power of the Thatcher governments, so that her premiership has simply seen the development of practices which were already established. In part, also, some innovations reflect the administrative styles of particular ministers, especially the Prime Minister, as well as their attempts to overcome the tactical difficulties involved in carrying through significant policy changes.

Important amongst the deeper seated factors has been the sheer volume and complexity of business of a cross-departmental nature facing all governments in the post-war period. 'Big government' covers a multiplicity of tasks, often of a highly specialised nature, and the small number of ministers and officials at the centre of government are in continual danger of being overwhelmed by the demands placed upon them. Hence it has been necessary to find ways of limiting the amount of material going into the system. Indeed the general rule so far as the handling of business is concerned is that matters should be settled at as low a level as possible and only those matters which cannot be so settled or are considered to require collective agreement should be brought to Cabinet and even its committees.

Where there has been a change in established practice is in the range of matters which have been considered to require collective agreement at Cabinet level. While this has varied across different Cabinets, in general since 1974 there has been a tendency to cut back on the number of Cabinet meetings. Consequently, the amount of business that can be fully transacted in Cabinet has inevitably fallen. Cabinet meetings are presently down to about 45 a year compared to more than twice that number in the 1940s, 1950s, 1960s and early 1970s (Hennessy 1986, page 99). But the pattern is complicated, for on top of this general trend over time, there is some variation according to the party composition of Cabinets. Former Labour Cabinet ministers interviewed were less happy about (and less supportive of) the extension of activity at sub-Cabinet level than were Conservative ones. Also the practice of allowing Cabinet committees to decide matters without reference to Cabinet itself has been gradually expanded. These developments can be seen as logically following on from the need to avoid overburdening busy ministers in an age of large-scale government.

Other factors are peculiar to the style and practice of policy making developed by successive Thatcher governments. Of some importance has been the perception of the Prime Minister – and those supporting her – that the basic purpose of Cabinet government is not so much the formulation and widescale discussion of policy, but its application (for a contrasting view, see Jones 1990). After all, according to this view, the thrust and general tenor of policy has been settled in the election manifesto, and it is the business of ministers to work on the details and to see them carried out. Mrs Thatcher made this clear before taking office in 1979 when she said, 'We've got to go in a clear and agreed direction. As Prime Minister I couldn't waste time having any internal arguments.' (Harris 1988, page 79). Such an action approach is greatly assisted by confining decision-making to those who are likely to be involved in the development and application of an issue, whereas spreading the net more widely, an essential prerequisite of a more deliberative and collective approach, is likely to slow things down and complicate matters.

The way in which cabinet machinery has been managed under Mrs Thatcher is also a response to the tactical problem of bringing about innovations in policy in the face of hostility from within government. Certainly the Prime Minister and those in the administration who have supported her have seen themselves as engaged in pushing through some significant and fundamental policy changes in the face of opposition from sections of the government's own members and supporters as well as from within the bureaucracy. Moreover members of this 'prime ministerial' group tend to regard the formal Cabinet system as functioning in such a way as to generally produce a consensus across departments and, thus, to blunt whatever radical edge a policy may have. From their perspective the tactical situation facing the Thatcher governments is perhaps best summarised as one of radical Conservatism versus a conservative establishment and the image which is conjured-up is that of a prime ministerial group at the centre of government battling against opposition from both outside and within (see Young 1989, page 242; Jenkins 1989, pages 183–4).

This 'bunker' mentality helps to explain the tendency to pre-cook policy; for a policy is more likely to survive if it is introduced into the system at a late stage in its development. Additionally the need to overcome opposition in Cabinet and amongst certain ministers meant it was tactically sensible to avoid Cabinet, some committees or, indeed, any forums where recalcitrant ministers were likely to be in a majority or were afforded enough time and information with which to un-pick a proposal. Such circumstances of internal opposition have not applied throughout Mrs Thatcher's tenure. They applied initially and have applied on occasions thereafter. However, it seems that having discovered the utility of by-passing various groups and forums the tendency has been to continue the practice. It is, after all, not only a way of minimising opposition, it also ensures a more speedy flow of business.

Depending on one's point of view, these may be seen as advantages, but the drawbacks of this very informal style of management for the nature of policy making in the Cabinet system are at least two-fold. First, there is the risk that the operation of the central machinery of government is not subject to clear lines of control and, therefore, when something goes amiss, blame is difficult to apportion. It has been a hallmark of the Thatcher governments that when an internal crisis arises and breaks through the wall of official secrecy there is always much confusion about who was supposed to have been doing what. Consequently, responsibility is obscured and accountability rendered ineffectual. The obvious implications for both responsible and responsive government need not be laboured. Secondly, the standards and thoroughness of policy-making may be compromised. One potential pitfall of by-passing or marginalising the formal machinery of Cabinet government is that some important details and forseeable consequences of a policy proposal may be overlooked with the result, as a one-time Cabinet minister put it, that policy emerges 'half-baked'. Then it either has to be substantially amended by ministers in the course of its being legislated (a characteristic feature of much important legislation under the Thatcher governments) or it is likely to have an unexpected, and possibly unwelcome, impact on the electorate once the policy is actually applied.

Table 2.8(1)   *Cabinet Committees*

STANDING MINISTERIAL

1 *Major Established Committees*

(a) Policy – meet regularly, often once a week, during the Parliamentary session

EDP	OPD	EDH
Economic Affairs	Overseas & Defence	Home Affairs incl. social
Chair: PM	(incl. Northern Ireland)	education, housing, health
13 core[1] ministers	Chair: PM	Chair: Home Secretary or
	6 core ministers	other senior minister
		17 core ministers

(b) Business Management

LG	FLG
Legislation scrutinises bills	Draft of Queen's Speech
prior to submission to	and planning of future
Parliament	legislative timetable. Meets
Chair: Leader of the House	frequently between May and
of Commons	September
8 core ministers plus	Chair: Leader of the House
Chief Whip and Law	of Commons
Officers	5 core ministers plus
	Chief Whip and Law
	Officers

2 About 20 *other ministerial standing committees* are usually in operation. Not all of these meet on a regular basis. These, as in the case of '*ad hoc*' committees, may involve junior ministers.

AD HOC MINISTERIAL

These are established from time to time to deal with a specific issue and then in most cases cease to function. They are given a number and designated either GEN or MISC interchangeably with different Prime Ministers. Mrs Thatcher's were designated MISCS, John Major's GENS.

CIVIL SERVICE COMMITTEES – standing and '*ad hoc*' – these often mirror ministerial committees.

Note: [1] 'core' refers to the number of Cabinet ministers who are usually regular members of the committee. Others may be called in on particular items of business.

Of course a valid response to these criticisms is that the style of managing cabinet machinery developed since 1979 is the necessary cost involved in any attempt to introduce radical policy innovations into an inert and resistant system. In particular to rely substantially on the formal machinery would only lead to policy based on compromises between the interests within government and minimise the chances of fundamental changes being made in the activities of the state. An observation which suggests that the proper solution to the problem of bringing about radical change within government would be to strengthen the leadership capacity of the Cabinet system – either at the level of the Cabinet *or* the Prime Minister. Yet in order to avoid an over-concentration of power at this core-executive level, an essential corollary of such a reform would need to be some measure to ensure that the operations of the Cabinet system are both more accountable to Parliament and more subject to public scrutiny. We need an executive system that is both effective and responsible. The danger is that nowadays we may end up with neither.

> Abridged from Martin Burch (1990), 'Cabinet government,' *Contemporary Record*, IV, pp. 5–8. Reprinted by permission of Frank Cass & Company Ltd., London.

References

Burch, M. (1988), 'The British Cabinet: a residual executive', *Parliamentary Affairs*, 41, pp. 34–48.
Hailsham, Lord (1987), *Will Cabinet Government Survive?* Granada Guildhall Lecture, Granada Group, London.
Harris, K. (1988), *Thatcher*, Weidenfeld & Nicolson, London.
Hennessy, P. (1986), *Cabinet*, Basil Blackwell, Oxford.
Jenkins, P. (1989), *Mrs.Thatcher's Revolution*, Pan Books, London.
Jones, G. (1990), 'Mrs. Thatcher and the power of the prime minister', *Contemporary Record*, 3, pp. 2–6.
Seldon, A. (1990), 'The Cabinet Office and co-ordination, 1979–87', *Public Administration*, 68, pp. 103–21.
Willets, D. (1987), 'The role of the prime minister's Policy Unit', *Public Administration*, 65, pp. 443–54.
Young, H. (1989), *One of Us*, Macmillan, London.

2.9   Ministers and civil servants

Shirley Williams

Where does power in Britain actually reside? Does it reside with Ministers, in turn responsible to an elected Parliament, as constitutional doctrine decrees? Does it reside with the civil service, which sees Ministers come and go, but itself goes on for ever? Or is it to be found somewhere different from either of these?

The orthodox constitutional doctrine is clear. It is that Ministers are responsible to Parliament, and through Parliament's elected representatives, to the people, for everything that happens in their department. Second, Ministers share collective responsibility for the actions of the government, whether or not those actions relate to the Minister's own department. These doctrines are the core of Cabinet government. It is the collective responsibility of the Cabinet to Parliament that determines the role of the Prime Minister as *primus inter pares* – neither a president, a chief nor a king. Without the support of his Cabinet, the Prime Minister cannot in practice continue to govern; without the support of Parliament, he is constitutionally unable to do so.

One has only to state the first proposition, that Ministers are responsible to Parliament for everything that happens in their departments, to perceive that it cannot actually be the case. It is a doctrine which by its very nature cannot coincide with reality. If it ever did so coincide, it may have done so in some of the nineteenth century administrations that followed the two later reform bills – those of Derby and Disraeli or of Gladstone. In the past century, government has grown enormously, in the range of matters it concerns itself with, in the amount of money it spends, and in the volume of its communications with the public at large and with special interest groups in particular.

It is simply impossible to believe that a Minister can oversee two or three thousand letters and communications going to and coming from the world outside each day, or that he or she could personally take the dozens of individual decisions that make up much of a department's work. For instance, the Home Office deals with hundreds of cases involving the granting of parole, or the placing of offenders in open rather than closed prisons every year. The Department of Health looks into complaints by patients about their treatment by a particular hospital. The Minister will see the most difficult of these cases, where a tricky decision is involved, perhaps calling into question the administration of a health authority or a local education authority, or involving strongly held public views. He or she will also be expected to answer Parliamentary Questions on any of these individual cases, should an MP decide to raise it.

In the light of the growing responsibilities of government, the doctrine of individual ministerial responsibility is becoming less and less credible anyway, but three recent developments undermine it further. The first of these is that the press, radio and television have become much more aware of the internal workings of government departments, of their internal and external relations, and of the influence of individual civil servants upon departmental policy than was the case a decade ago. Journalists frequently meet and entertain senior civil servants and may establish close relations with them.

Furthermore, newspapers in recent years have published government docments, confidential memoranda, committee papers classified as restricted, and even private correspondence on public issues, some of which were almost certainly obtained from civil servants. Indeed the determined struggle to uphold the secrecy of British government and administration, a struggle waged by senior civil servants and supported by many Ministers, is doomed as much by the media's existing access to much classified material as by parliamentary pressures for open government.

The second important area where the pressures are growing is within Parliament itself. Parliament, partly because the quality of backbenchers has improved, and partly because more parliamentarians are full-time than used to be, is much more anxious to pursue what it regards as things that have gone wrong and is much more anxious to get select committees looking into government departments.

I once fought a Member of Parliament, a most distinguished gentleman who had been re-elected through four different elections and whose only known recorded comment in the House of Commons was to ask if the windows might be closed. I do not believe that today an MP would escape censure by his constituency association or his constituency party if that was his sole contribution to Parliament. The number of written questions put down, the number of weekly oral questions put down, the requests for Private Members' time, the number of people seeking to get debates after 10 o'clock, all have multiplied over the last fifteen years and there is no sign that they are likely to decrease.

Third, but not least important: we clearly have, partly as a result of mass secondary education, a very much less resigned public than we used to have. It is quite interesting to look at the difference in the amount of constituency post that Members of Parliament get, depending upon what sort of con-stituency they represent. Generally speaking, if an MP represents a new town or suburb for example, his or her constituency correspondence will be of the order of two to four hundred letters a week. If he or she represents either a safe old-shire constituency as a Conservative or a safe north-eastern industrial seat as a Labour Member of Parliament, constituency correspondence is likely to be about one-quarter, maybe fifty or a hundred letters a week. Now the difference is not just the traditional difference between a fairly resigned part of the country, a part of the country that isn't used to things changing much or happening much. It is also a generational difference. Younger constituents are much more likely to make demands.

Let me simply take the fifteen years I was a Member of Parliament. I think in that time my constituency correspondence increased something like three times over, to the point of becoming virtually insupportable in terms of my ability to answer it on the basis of only one full-time secretary. Now very many are the signs of this: the number of requests for public inquiries, the ways in which those public inquiries attract all sorts of local groups and special interest groups, often very well-informed people, the amount of money that is put into resisting the coming of motorways, or new housing developments, the way in which requests to override local authority decisions have increased very sharply, for instance in my old Ministry, the Department of Education. There is all sorts of evidence to show that we have a much more keen, much more enthusiastic, much more activist, much less easily satisfied public than we used to have. So, there is more press attention, more parliamentary pressure, and a less resigned public. And all that is good. But these things multiply the work of departments and multiply the areas for which the Minister is theoretically responsible. And so I am going to sum up the orthodox constitutional doctrine by saying that I myself believe it is reaching the end of its ability to be sustained as a constitutional fiction. It is a convenient constitutional fiction.

Now the alternative thesis is that bureaucracy rules. Let me dismiss the constitutional fiction about ministerial responsibility and take the opposite paradigm. There is a strong section of opinion in the major political parties that believes the civil service in a tactful, delicate, largely hidden way runs the country. One can sum it up in terms of a cartoon that was carried in *The Guardian*, illustrating a slashing attack on the civil service by my erstwhile colleague Mr Michael Meacher: there was a drawing of a very large car, which was filled with pinstriped senior civil servants (presumably most of them Permanent Secretaries) and in front, sitting on the bonnet clutching a toy steering wheel, was the Minister, who was being driven about by the gentlemen inside the car. He clearly was under the happy illusion that he was driving the car, rather in the way that small children of two can be persuaded that that stick-on steering wheel is actually in control. The view that bureaucracy rules is the view that Ministers are essentially an elected figleaf, and that there is a complicated conspiracy to do them down and to destroy their policies.

The first argument is that the civil service manipulates individual Ministers and it does so by the simple process of flattering them. Now it is perfectly true that the minute you become a Minister you normally cease to have a name, and you certainly cease to have a christian name, and you begin to be called by a title. Ergo, you are known as Parliamentary Secretary or sometimes briefly as 'puss', when you first start your ministerial career. That doesn't addle the brain too much because it's a rather contemptuous term and you know it perfectly well if you are a 'puss' or a Parliamentary Under-Secretary, the lowest form of ministerial life. There again the fiction – and this really is fiction – is that Parliamentary Secretaries and Permanent Secretaries are on an equal level of power, and that a locked argument between them can only be broken by somebody who is a Minister of State or a Secretary of State.

Then you move up, and are called Minister of State or even Secretary of State. This always seems to me to be an extremely cumbrous title. Sentences of the form 'ABC comma Secretary of State comma ABC' become very long. It is important that one does not get addicted to being called Secretary of State, to being treated with deference, and to being treated with great politeness. It is perfectly true that Ministers can be flattered, not least by these impressive appellations, but if so, the blame lies with the Minister, not with the civil service.

A second argument is that Ministers are isolated, that they are far less part of the network than the civil service is, and that therefore they can be pushed and persuaded into not adopting policies the department is not happy with or into adopting policies the department wants them to adopt, because they are lonely people and they are assailed from all sides by very strong and powerful arguments. It is true that Ministers are almost, though not quite, alone in their department, and that senior Ministers often have to take the most difficult decisions by themselves. But it is open to senior Ministers to discuss policies and tactics with their junior colleagues. All departments have at least one junior Minister, and most have three or more. These are party colleagues, concerned about the success of the government because they are seen as sharing responsibility for its achievements and its failures. Since Harold Wilson's first administration, Ministers can also employ a maximum of two advisers, men and women personally close to them, selected by the Minister, and almost invariably of his own political outlook. These advisers have been valuable eyes and ears for the Minister, and also create a useful network of communication between the Minister and the department, and between the Minister and the party, in Parliament and outside. Ministers also spend about half their lives in the House of Commons which often, ludicrously, means that they sit up half the night; there is nothing to stop them walking down corridors in a beehive which consists entirely of their colleagues who are also Ministers or MPs. So Ministers do not need to be isolated; if they are isolated it is either because they have decided to be isolated, or because the colossally heavy load of departmental papers on which decisions have to be made each night simply precludes them from taking time off for consultation and conversation.

One way of breaking down this sense of isolation is to create a large number of ministerial committees. Towards the end of the last Government, I think I was serving on about twenty separate Cabinet Committees of one kind or another, in which I constantly met the same fellow Ministers. If I had not been able to get to know their thinking pretty well and they to know mine, I would have been spending my time in an extremely unconstructive way. Now a lot of ministerial committees tends to create a circle of Ministers which parallels the official committees' circle of officials, and so you get two balancing systems in effect where everybody meets everybody else in a familiar circle. If you reduce the number of ministerial committees, as I believe Mrs Thatcher did, you may get a balance in which the official committees become more important and become the hub of government, rather than the ministerial committees. Alternatively, you may get a strong inner-Cabinet structure in which the Prime Minister and a few chosen people around him or her become, in effect, the major decision-makers.

The striking thing about British government is that the Cabinet is a very flexible concept. Almost anything is possible, from the rather presidential style of government which Mr Heath adopted at one stage in his administration, to a highly collective form of government, in which the Cabinet really does make the big decisions. I would not, however, so characterize the administrations in which I served on the Cabinet. They, I think, were characterized by an informal inner Cabinet, of perhaps three or four people gathered around the Prime Minister. The individuals might be different according to the issue under discussion, but for most of the major decisions they would be the same.

Typically, as I have said, Cabinet Committees in Britain consist of Ministers, with a civil servant as secretary, and the official committees which underpin them consist of civil servants. Mixed committees of Ministers and civil servants are rare, though they do exist. I served on one in the 1960s which concerned itself with science and technology. Such mixed committees have the great advantage of demonstrating to Ministers that there are differences of view between officials and between departments; and inability to agree is not a genetic trait of the ministerial breed.

A third argument is that Whitehall can be mobilized against what an individual Minister may want to do by manipulating the inter-departmental framework. I believe there is some truth in that. Obviously an inter-departmental framework of committees, both ministerial and official, cannot be dispensed with. Most Cabinet decisions, and many departmental ones, have repercussions that go far beyond one department. The inter-departmental framework is very powerful; it does mean that a Minister in a particular department can be effectively blocked or constrained by the reactions of other departments. I myself have seen quite a lot of memoranda from other departments which say, 'you should come down against Mr or Mrs So-and-So's proposals, because they would mean A, that your budget is cut because they are going to be expensive, or B, they are going to create considerable administrative strains, or C, they're not going to interest you anyway because it's not your department'. So a very enterprising or very bold Minister can be stopped through the inter-departmental framework. But the Minister will certainly overcome any such obstruction if he or she has the backing and confidence of the Prime Minister and the Cabinet. Civil servants are after all human, and if they believe their Minister has embarked upon a foolish or unwise policy, and if they further believe it will not command Cabinet or prime ministerial support when it becomes known, they cannot really be blamed for not putting a great deal of effort into it.

However, the inter-departmental framework itself has considerable strains within it. It is not by any means the case that Whitehall, any more than Westminster, presents – except to the most undiscriminating eye – a solid front. For example, the strain between the Treasury and spending departments is always there. It can become very acute, especially at times of public expenditure cuts. That is a strain which any department that knows its way around recognizes, a ripple in the smooth inter-departmental surface. Again there are always ripples in the inter-departmental surface because departments traditionally adopt rather different attitudes about particular aspects of policy. To take one instance of this: protectionism versus free trade. There are almost automatically different attitudes between the Department of Trade, which has traditionally been a free trade department and still is to a very great extent, and the Department of Industry or the Department of Employment, which have a considerable tendency towards protectionism because of the nature of their clients and because of what they can see happening to the clients in certain situations where trade is totally unconstrained and where their clients are losing out in consequence.

So the inter-departmental framework is by no means as smooth a surface as Ministers sometimes believe it to be, especially in their first few years. For example, if a policy that is particularly cherished by a department is threatened by opposition from another department or by the Treasury, the department will do everything in its power, in support of its Minister, to defend the policy or to fight for it; and in my experience that alliance will hold through both official committees, ministerial committees and the Cabinet itself, though it may not prevail. Departments judge Ministers by how hard they fight, not so much with, as for, the department. One measure of their determination is of course success – in getting the policy through or the expenditure cuts averted or reduced. But it is not the sole measure; Whitehall has a remarkable bush telegraph system, and word soon gets back to a department about how its Minister has acquitted himself on the battlefield. Furthermore, Ministers and departments may find common cause against another department, either because it is muscling in on their territory (what Americans call 'turf disputes') or because of traditional differences of the kind mentioned above. Departments can create informal alliances; and so can Ministers. If the Ministers and the Permanent Secretaries all work closely together, a good deal can be achieved.

A fourth argument concerns civil servants restricting and controlling relevant information. This seems to me a very crude way of trying to gain control over a Minister. In my view any Minister worth his or her salt ought not to put up with it. It is a question of remembering to keep asking for the same information and when you have asked three times and had nothing, hitting the roof in a structured sort of way. Hitting the roof in a structured sort of way is something that Ministers should only do occasionally, and they should always do it as a form of dramatic acting and not because they have actually lost their temper (which will almost invariably mean they lose out).

A more subtle form of obstruction is to take the Minister's instructions and then simply to do nothing. Ministers rarely have time to progress-chase their smaller decisions. Unless the matter is bound to come up again, a Minister's decision may just get itself lost. If the Minister does recall his decision, administrative error or clerical misfiling provide handy excuses. One of the main benefits of having political advisers is that they can act as progress-chasers for the Minister and prevent decisions losing themselves.

While I would want to qualify what the critics have said on these points, on two arguments I find myself in agreement. It depends very much what department you are in whether advice tends to take a monolithic form or tends to take a collegiate form. Let me explain what I mean. Advice that tends to take a monolithic form – and, for example, I found that when I was in the Home Office advice tended to take a monolithic form – is advice which grows like a tree. People contribute to the brief as it goes up towards the Minister, but dissenting opinions are gradually knocked out so that in the last two or three stages from Assistant Secretary, Under Secretary to Deputy Secretary – or if it is an extremely important policy, from Under Secretary, Deputy Secretary to Permanent Secretary – all dissenting views disappear from the files and what you are left with finally is the official view.

Now, if you are a Minister the monolithic structure of advice (it has been, I think, characteristic of the British civil service that the structures have been mainly monolithic) is extremely irritating. What it says to you is, 'Minister, you either accept or reject this advice, but if you reject this advice you are on your own. You're going to be doing so without any structure of thought, without any structure of fact, without any structure of advice. But of course if you want to do it, Minister, you may do it – more fool you.' Now, generally speaking, in a monolithic advice pattern the only basis upon which the Minister can reject the advice that he has received is by saying: 'There are political considerations here which override'. It is not untypical of the relationship between Ministers and the civil service that some civil servants feel the only proper basis for a Minister to disagree with official advice is by pleading political reasons or – dare I say – political dogma. Speaking as a Minister, I find that extremely unattractive. I do not believe that Ministers should overrule only on grounds of political dogma. I believe they should overrule because what they have seen of society or the world outside leads them to reach different conclusions, which may not be necessarily coloured by political partisanship, about the advice that they are offered.

The collegiate structure has been typical in recent years of the Foreign Office, and is increasingly being accepted by domestic departments as well. Ministers get a number of policies put before them – options, if you like – each of them argued forcibly by different civil servants, where the Minister can call a meeting in which people are free to express different views upon which would be the best policy to answer the problem, and in which the Permanent Secretary or the Deputy Secretary will not delicately indicate his disapproval of a point of view different from his own. If the Minister is going to consider also parliamentary pressures and public concern, and balance out the different pressures on the department, then collegiate advice is a much more democratic kind of structure and generally speaking leads to better conclusions.

Agendas for Cabinet or Cabinet Committee meetings can be a further instrument of control. Here again the problem is one both for Ministers and for the civil service, except for those very particular civil servants who become Secretaries to the Cabinet or members of the Cabinet Office. It is of course true that control of a Cabinet or Cabinet Committee agenda effectively gives one much closer control over the policy structures than would be the case if the Cabinet agenda were rather more flexible than it is. There is no 'any other business' on a Cabinet agenda, amazingly, and therefore no room to take on board last-minute crises. Admittedly the forty-eight hour rule, that is to say

that all papers are supposed to have forty-eight hours' notice given to them, is quite often broken; but the discretion to do so is that of the Cabinet Secretary. Therefore considerable power rests with the Prime Minister and the Secretary of the Cabinet, and sometimes with what I described earlier as the inner Cabinet. Whether it is necessary to control agendas to that extent, I would beg leave to doubt.

I do not myself believe in either the traditional constitutional doctrine about ministerial responsibility nor in the more modern opposed doctrine that bureaucracy rules. After a good deal of thought, I have come to the conclusion that power consists of intersecting rings; it resides in the areas where people are able to come together between the civil service, Ministers, and to some extent a third group, pressure groups.

> Abridged from Shirley Williams, 'The decision makers', in Royal Institute of Public Administration (1980), *Policy and Practice: The Experience of Government*, RIPA, London, pp. 81–92, 103. Reprinted by permission of the Royal Institute of Public Administration.

Biographical note

The Rt. Hon. Shirley Williams was MP for Hitchin from 1964–74 and for Hertford and Stevenage from 1974–79. Her first ministerial post was in the Ministry of Labour. She served as Paymaster General and Minister of State in the Department of Education and Science (1967–69) and the Home Office (1969–70). In 1974 she became Secretary of State for Prices and Consumer Protection and in 1976 Secretary of State for Education and Science.

2.10   Patterns of public policy

Arnold J. Heidenheimer, Hugh Heclo and Carolyn Teich Adams

Policy patterns – national, sectoral, and temporal

The affluence and temper of an era have potent impact on policy development. One writer predicted in the early 1970s that the welfare state 'rides the wave of the future,' and that apart from some 'marginal' American groups, there were 'no signs of dispositions to curb it' (Girvetz, p. 520). A decade later the picture was quite different, but the impact of the expenditure crunch had varied greatly in the policy areas. Education and housing had been cut back much more than health; there are many more unemployed teachers than physicians. At the same time, the distribution of resources among sectors and subsectors varied considerably from nation to nation. How, therefore, can we analyze the impact of time periods, national settings, and policy sector characteristics on the content of policies? To answer this question, we must examine how they interact in good *and* bad economic climates.

Let us approach this broad subject by drawing on studies which have examined the shaping influences of national system variables, on the one hand, and policy sector variables, on the other. We have identified many discrete differences among nations' handling of various challenges; but to what extent can these habits and experiences be subsumed under consistent national models of policy-making? Are these models applied similarly in most policy areas, or do the various sectors develop their own policy-making characteristics? If national institutions help shape national 'styles', do the styles remain constant as long as the institutions don't change? To what extent can national policy styles explain why some countries might be more successful in some policy areas than in others?

Some political scientists thus have directly characterized national styles. The British style has been identified with a tendency toward extensive consultation, an avoidance of radical policy changes, and a disposition against actions which would challenge well-entrenched interests. The French style, by contrast, is said to exhibit a greater willingness to enforce radical policy change even against the resistance of strong sectional interests. The Swedish style has also been noted to have a capacity for radical policy innovation, but with widespread consultation and great efforts to wear down and convert opposing interests (Gustafsson and Richardson).

Building on such characterizations, another political scientist developed the extended typology shown in Table 2.10(1). He ranked three countries on six dimensions. Sweden ranked highest on four of the dimensions. Its policy-making was the most consultative and also the most open. Its policy processes were most deliberative but most radical in their proclivities toward sweeping change. The British were ranked lowest on all but two of these dimensions. The French ranked lowest on consultation and highest on centralism and level of conflict. This general policy model was then applied to the area of higher education policies to see if the pattern would hold.

The author found a 'high degree of fit' between the generalized national policy style models and the particular case of higher education. In eight of the eighteen cells of the table, the rankings were in full consonance; in four of the cells, the rankings were reversed; and in six cases, the fit was indeterminate or arguable (Premfors). But one could also interpret the data to show that the policy area characteristics probably produced the significant deviations that the author noted.

Analysts of health politics have also examined whether national political systems or policy sector characteristics have had stronger effect on policy-making. An influential early study of British medical interest groups concluded that the major determinants of policy in the health sector were functions of the national political system (Eckstein). Other authors argued that the crucial

Table 2.10(1) *Policy styles in Britain, France, and Sweden*

	Britain	France	Sweden
Policy Change	Non-radical (3)	Occasionally radical (2)	Radical (1)
Centralism	Less centralized (3)	Highly centralized (1)	Centralized (2)
Consultation	Quite extensive consultation (2)	Limited consultation (3)	Extensive consultation (1)
Openness	Secretive (3)	Quite secretive (2)	Open (1)
Conflict Level	Quite low (2)	High (1)	Low (3)
Deliberation	Not very deliberative (3)	Quite deliberative (2)	Very deliberative (1)

Source: Rune Premfors (1981), 'National policy styles and higher education in France, Sweden and the United Kingdom', *European Journal of Education*, XVI, pp. 253–62. Reprinted by permission of Carfax Publishing Co., Abingdon, Oxon.

nature of their services gives physicians in all Western countries overwhelming political resources and that national contexts are comparatively insignificant as determinants of political influence (Marmor and Thomas). A subsequent study of German health politics concluded, more in line with the first study, that 'much of the political power of physicians can be accounted for by characteristics of the political system and by political decisions, rather than by the technical nature of medical care or by ideological beliefs and values about health care' (Stone, p. 18).

Another political scientist has examined rule-making in the area of occupational safety and health, considering American and Swedish practices to see how institutions embedded in dissimilar political systems handled almost identical problems. For example, how did administrative agencies set tolerance levels for noise, chemical pollution, and construction industry standards? By and large the contents of these regulations turned out to be 'surprisingly similar' (Kelman, pp. 51 and 81), even though the legislative processes varied enormously and the values of the bureaucrats were very different in the two national settings. In this instance the characteristics of the policy sector, when combined to some extent with the reform ethos of the period in which the rules were made or changed, outweighed the differences of the national settings.

The findings were quite different when the same political scientist examined the implementation processes of the same rules in the same countries. The enforcement methods applied by health and safety inspectors in similar industrial settings displayed striking differences of style, with much heavier reliance on fines and other punitive methods in the United States. These national characteristics are attributed to the greater reliance in the United States on adversarial relationships and institutions in both the political and judicial systems. Although differences of national style might have been expected to affect *both* rule-making and rule implementation, they left a much sharper imprint on the latter (Kelman, Chapter Five).

The fact that subnational differences in political cultures may affect policy implementation as strongly as cross-national ones has been illustrated epigrammatically and empirically in a study of nursing-home regulation in England, New York, and Virginia. The researchers had come across the following epigram:

Question: How many Virginians, New Yorkers, and Englishmen does it take to change a light bulb?
Answer for Virginia: Three. One to change the bulb, two to talk about how good the old one was.
Answer for New York: Thirty-seven. One to change the bulb, and a 36-member law firm to sue for damages under the product liability laws.
Answer for England: Only one. But he won't do it because the bulb has always worked in the past.

They proceeded to see whether empirical research would bear out the epigrammatic model.

The size of each regulatory staff assigned to check on nursing-home standards began to supply an answer. New York had more than twice as many regulators as England and Virginia put together. The story of New York's 'exceptionalism' was based on a long history of nursing-home scandals, which caused the industry to be treated with aggressive suspicion, leading to complex regulations and close supervision of the inspectors, to conform to a 'no-nonsense deterrence' model linked to threats of litigation and punishment. In both England and Virginia, by contrast, they found compliance models based on a 'deliberate emphasis on building up trust relationships with the facilities, with no apparent sense that this may risk regulatory capture by the industry' (Day and Klein, p. 328). The great contrast in regulatory styles for the same industry between the two American states calls into question the role played by a national style, and stresses the need to better understand why the actors in the two American states interacted so differently from each other.

One might also compare the relative fit of sectoral patterns to generalized national models. One would scarcely expect to find many situations in which the strength of the national policy style is completely overwhelmed or reversed by the factors peculiar to any one policy sector. After all, many of the key actors, from parliamentarians, to finance ministry officials, to government auditors, serve to extend homogeneity among the policy sectors. However distinct some policy subsystems are – due to the privileges of a dominant profession as in health or due to the varying autonomy of regional governments or such institutions as central banks – most characteristics of national policy style are likely to be strongly reflected in the individual policy areas.

Up to now there have been very few systematic attempts to compare functionally different policy areas cross-nationally. One could seek to determine, for instance, whether policy processes in housing conform more to general national policy styles than do those in economic management. One difficulty here would be agreeing how to select and measure the relevant indicators. Another would involve the fact that national policy styles change over time. Thus, when many new groups entered into the policy process in Sweden in the late 1970s, some of the differences between Swedish and British policy-making that had been clear-cut a decade or two earlier were diminished (Gustafsson and Richardson, p. 33).

Another comparative approach identifies policy experiences as either very successful or very unsuccessful, and then asks whether this was because of, or in spite of, the national policy style. Such an inquiry into the recent failures of British economic policy noted that Britain failed to replicate both the links between public and private sectors and the bargaining machinery that weighed social benefits against inflationary debits (instruments used, for example, in France and Germany). These shortcomings were said to reflect some yet more general attributes 'embedded in institutional and constitutional rigidities that serve politicians well, but serve the country poorly' (Ashford, p. 121).

Recent attempts to harmonize national policies in such larger supranational political entities as the EC have added more interest to the question of how 'nations matter'. Is it more through their historically determined set of institutions or by the cultural orientations of their elites and mass publics? Or do both translate equally into national styles, serving as the 'missing link' between institutional and cultural preconditions and policy outputs (Feick and Jann)? What role does the long-time rule of one dominant party and its past policy performance in countries like Sweden or Japan play in determining present national variances (Pempel, 1988)? In other words, do past policy successes or failures through a political learning process shape the ideas and values of the elites and mass publics about future policy choices, bringing about some 'dominant rule system' in a nation (Verba *et al.*, Heclo and Madsen)?

Abridged from Arnold J. Heidenheimer, Hugh Heclo and Carolyn Teich Adams (1990), *Comparative Public Policy*, 3rd edition, pp. 349–54. Reprinted by permission of St. Martin's Press, New York.

References

Ashforld, Douglas (1980), *Politics and Policy in Britain*, Temple University Press, Philadelphia.
Day, Patricia and Rudolf Klein (1987), 'The regulation of nursing homes: a comparative perspective', *Milbank Memorial Quarterly*, 65, pp. 303–47.
Eckstein, Harry (1960), *Pressure Group Politics*, Stanford University Press, Standford.
Feick, J. and W. Jann (1988), 'Nations matter: vom eklektismus zur integration in der vergleichenden policy forschung' in M. G. Schmidt (ed.), *Staatstätigkeit: International and Historisch Vergleichende Analyses*, Westdeutscher Verlag, Opladen.
Girvetz, Harry K. (1968), 'Welfare State' in David L. Sills (ed.), *International Encyclopedia of the Social Sciences*, Macmillan and the Free Press, New York, 16, pp. 512–21.
Gustafsson, Gunnel and Jeremy Richardson (1980), 'Post industrial changes in policy style', *Scandinavian Political Studies*, 3, pp. 21–37.
Heclo, H. and H. Madsen (1987), *Politics and Policy in Sweden*, Temple University Press, Philadelphia.
Kelman, Steven (1981), *Regulating America, Regulating Sweden: A Comparative Study of Occupational Safety and Health Legislation Policy*, MIT Press, Cambridge, MA.
Marmor, Theodore and David Thomas (1971), 'Doctors, politics and pay disputes: "pressure group politics" revisited', *British Journal of Political Science*, 2, pp. 412–42.
Pempel, T. J. (1988), 'Japan and Sweden: Polarities of "Responsible Capitalism"', paper given at Comparative Politics conference, City University of New York, September.
Premfors, Rune (1981), 'National policy styles and higher education in France, Sweden and the United Kingdom', *European Journal of Education*, 16, pp. 253–62.
Stone, Deborah A. (1980), *The Limits to Professional Power: National Health Care in Federal Republic of Germany*, University of Chicago Press, Chicago.
Verba, Sidney *et al.* (1987), *Elites and the Idea of Equality: A Comparison of Japan, Sweden and the United States*, University of California Press, Berkeley.

Part Three
The American political system

Introduction

Introductory textbooks frequently describe United States government and politics as a pluralist political system characterized by social heterogeneity and 'separated institutions sharing power', The selections in this section underline that while these general characterizations possess some validity they do not tell the entire story.

Numbers 10 and 51 of *The Federalist Papers* provide the first contribution on United States politics. Written in 1787–88 by James Madison under the pseudonym of 'Publius' as a defence of the proposed United States constitution, these two essays could easily have been placed in the *Reader*'s theoretical section. Addressing the problem of majority tyranny which he identifies as the principal political problem confronting the United States, Madison develops a pluralist solution – 'extensive political rights, free elections, social heterogeneity, institutional complexity, and a procedural consensus.

While pluralist accounts emphasize the formal equality of political rights of United States citizens, the second and third selections explore the actual dynamics of interest group politics. Racial segregation enforced by government coercion challenges any benign pluralist interpretation of United States politics and questions whether the United States constitution achieved its minimal aim of preventing a majority faction from using governmental power to tyrannize over a minority. Departing from conventional patterns of interest group politics, the black-led, bi-racial civil rights movement employed disruptive protest in the streets to compel the national government to protect civil rights and eventually to prohibit legal segregation. Yet, as the analysis by Frances Fox Piven and Richard Cloward (3.2) makes clear, direct action protest was only a necessary, not a sufficient, condition, since other factors contributed to the success of the direct action campaign.

Furthermore, the violent repression directed at the civil rights movement also disclosed the exceptional difficulties which at least some new, previously excluded groups must overcome when they seek entry into the political system. Hence, while a pluralist interpretation emphasizes how open the United States political system is to new groups because of extensive formal political rights and numerous loci of governmental power, this case study raises the question of how permeable the United States political system actually is.

The contribution by Kay Lehman Schlozman (3.3) provides empirical support for the theoretical argument by Cohen and Rogers (in 1.6) that business has a structural advantage in interest group formation and maintenance. Or, to put it another way, Cohen and Rogers' account of the resource constraint explains what Schlozman describes. Investigating what interests are actually represented by organized groups in the Washington pressure group system, Schlozman concludes that business interests predominate and are over-represented while diffuse interests and the interests of those with few financial resources are under-represented. However, Schlozman cautions that her evidence of a significant business advantage in interest group formation and maintenance does not prove disproportionate business influence on government policy.

A pluralist interpretation correctly emphasizes that interest group politics is only one aspect of pluralist politics and that free elections are also important. If some social interests are not represented or are under-represented by organized groups, the individuals with those interests can still exert political pressure on behalf of those interests through elections since the vote is the minimal political resource possessed by every citizen in a pluralist political system. However, those individuals whose interests are least likely to be represented in interest group politics are also those who are least likely to vote. In selection 3.4, G. Bingham Powell emphasizes that non-voting is exceptionally high in the United States and is essentially caused by institutional variables, not individual attributes.

Examining one of those institutional variables cited by Bingham Powell as explaining why non-voting is so much higher in the United States than in the other Western pluralist or capitalist democracies, Howard Reiter's article (3.5) documents and explains the differences between the Republican and Democratic parties. Although emphasizing that the differences between Democrats and Republicans are not as great as those between the British Labour and Conservative parties, Reiter argues that those differences are significant.

While omitting the federal judiciary headed by the Supreme Court, the following four selections focus on the three other major institutions of the national government: the president, Congress, and the bureaucracy. In accordance with a pluralist interpretation, these four articles taken together emphasize the fragmentation of government power in the United States and consequently the numerous loci of governmental power where interest groups can bring pressure to bear. The dispersal of governmental power described in these contributions creates obstacles which any president must overcome in order to realize his policy objectives.

In selection 3.6, Morris Fiorina begins with two related facts: increasing numbers of incumbent members of the House of Representatives not only win re-election but also are re-elected by safe margins. Motivated primarily by the re-election motive, many Representatives have become mere errand boys or girls for their electoral and financial constituents. Providing their constituents with particularized benefits while avoiding controversial issues, incumbents serve as ombudsmen with the federal bureaucracy and legislate distributive policies. Although Madison as 'Publius' had expected different social interests to cancel and negate one another, Fiorina describes a process of mutual accommodation and particularized interest aggregation which neglects any broader national or public interest. Yet, as shown by the House of Representatives strengthening the civil rights bill submitted by President John F. Kennedy in June 1963, this usual congressional preference for 'pork barrel' legislation occasionally yields to more general national concerns.

Hugh Heclo's account (in 3.7) of the diffuse issue networks surrounding the executive branch emphasizes the broad array of interests and groups which frequently participate in executive decision-making. Yet, such a multitude of interested participants makes it difficult both to formulate coherent policy and to construct legislative majorities. Consequently, like the fragmentation and dispersion of power within Congress, issue networks can easily obstruct presidential initiatives.

Using the presidency of Ronald Reagan as a case study of presidential power, the next two selections explain why presidents possess greater power over foreign than domestic policy. Fragmentation of power within Congress often obstructs a president in domestic policy because a president frequently requires positive congressional action to enact his domestic agenda. Yet in foreign policy this same fragmentation can empower a president, since congressional inaction due to fragmentation of power within Congress often leaves a president free to act unilaterally.

Contrasting the Reagan presidency with the 'imperilled' presidencies of Gerald Ford and Jimmy Carter, Lester Salamon and Alan Abramson (3.8) analyze Reagan's success in getting so much of his domestic programme through Congress in his first year and his far more limited success in dealing with Congress in later years. Significantly, Reagan achieved his domestic successes not just through legislation but also via an administrative strategy at whose core lay the president's appointment power. Hence, Reagan frequently overcame later congressional opposition, not by winning majority support in both chambers of Congress, but by using administrative means to bypass Congress. Yet Reagan's successful administrative strategy required him to subordinate the bureaucracy to his purposes; therefore he had to overcome the blockages generated by the issue networks described by Heclo. Finally, this selection points to different criteria for judging whether Reagan was a successful president; furthermore, success on one dimension does not ensure success on another.

The penultimate essay on United States politics by Kenneth Sharpe (3.9) describes the checks which Congress imposed upon the foreign policy powers of presidents in the aftermath of the Vietnam war in order to prevent the recurrence of the abuses of the 'imperial presidency', and documents how President Reagan's militarized foreign policy for Central America overcame the constraints of the 'post-Vietnam formula'. Sharpe identifies various reasons why the post-Vietnam formula was ultimately unable to check Reagan's Central American policy: congressional delegation of excessive discretion to presidents in foreign policy, executive and presidential secrecy and misinformation, the president's continued ability to create an antecedent state of affairs, and ideological homogeneity – a frequently neglected source of the imperial presidency.

In the final selection on United States politics (3.10), Benjamin Page concludes that despite the difficulty, if not the impossibility, of determining exactly who gets what from the United States government it is clear that government policy has not reduced economic inequality. Page's examination of the alternative explanations of the government's failure to increase equality returns the reader to the arguments of the nine preceding selections, as well as to those found in the earlier theoretical section.

Doug Jaenicke

3.1   A pluralist defence of the US Constitution

James Madison

The Federalist No. 10

Among the numerous advantages promised by a well-constructed Union, none deserves to be more accurately developed than its tendency to break and control the violence of faction. The friend of popular governments will not fail to set a due value on any plan which, without violating the principles to which he is attached, provides a proper cure for it. The instability, injustice, and confusion introduced into the public councils, have been the mortal diseases under which popular governments have perished. The valuable improvements made by the American state constitutions on the popular models, both ancient and modern, cannot certainly be too much admired; but they have not as effectually obviated the danger on this side, as was wished and expected. Complaints are everywhere heard from our most considerate and virtuous citizens, equally the friends of public and private faith, and of public and personal liberty, that our governments are too unstable, that the public good is disregarded in the conflicts of rival parties, and that measures are too often decided, not according to the rules of justice and the rights of the minor party, but by the superior force of an interested and overbearing majority. The prevailing and increasing distrust of public engagements, and alarm for private rights, are echoed from one end of the continent to the other. These must be chiefly, if not wholly, effects of the unsteadiness and injustice with which a factious spirit has tainted our public administrations.

By a faction, I understand a number of citizens, whether amounting to a majority or minority of the whole, who are united and actuated by some common impulse of passion, or of interest, adverse to the rights of other citizens, or to the permanent and aggregate interests of the community.

There are two methods of curing the mischiefs of faction: the one, by removing its causes; the other, by controlling its effects.

There are again two methods of removing the causes of faction: the one, by destroying the liberty which is essential to its existence; the other, by giving to every citizen the same opinions, the same passions, and the same interests.

The first remedy [is] worse than the disease. Liberty is to faction what air is to fire, an aliment without which it instantly expires.

The second expedient is as impracticable as the first would be unwise. As long as the reason of man continues fallible, and he is at liberty to exercise it, different opinions will be formed. As long as the connection subsists between his reason and his self-love, his opinions and his passions will have a reciprocal influence on each other; and the former will be objects to which the latter will attach themselves. The diversity in the faculties of men, from which the rights of property originate, is not less an insuperable obstacle to a uniformity of interests. The protection of these faculties is the first object of government. From the protection of different and unequal faculties of acquiring property, the possession of different degrees and kinds of property immediately results; and from the influence of these on the sentiments and views of the respective proprietors, ensues a division of the society into different interests and parties.

The latent causes of faction are thus sown in the nature of man. A zeal for different opinions concerning religion, concerning government, and many other points, as well of speculation as of practice; an attachment of different leaders ambitiously contending for pre-eminence and power; or to persons of other descriptions whose fortunes have been interesting to the human passions, have, in turn, divided mankind into parties, inflamed them with mutual animosity, and rendered them much more disposed to vex and oppress each other than to co-operate for their common good. But the most common and durable source of factions has been the various and unequal distribution of property. Those who hold and those who are without property have ever formed distinct interests in society. Those who are creditors, and those who are debtors, fall under a like discrimination. A landed interest, a manufacturing interest, a mercantile interest, a moneyed interest, with many lesser interests, grow up of necessity in civilised nations, and divide them into different classes, actuated by different sentiments and views. The regulation of these various and interfering interests forms the principal task of modern legislation, and involves the spirit of party and faction in the necessary and ordinary operations of the government.

No man is allowed to be a judge in his own cause, because his interest would certainly bias his judgment, and, not improbably, corrupt his integrity. With greater reason, a body of men are unfit to be both judges and parties at the same time; yet what are many of the most important acts of legislation but so many judicial determinations, not indeed concerning the rights of single persons, but concerning the rights of large bodies of citizens? And what are the different classes of legislators but advocates and parties to the causes which they determine? Is a law proposed concerning private debts? The creditors are parties on one side and the debtors on the other. Justice ought to hold the balance between them. Yet the parties are, and must be, themselves the judges; and the most numerous party, or in other words, the most powerful faction must be expected to prevail. Shall domestic manufactures be encouraged, and in what degree, by restrictions on foreign manufactures? are questions which would be differently decided by the landed and the manufacturing classes, and probably by neither with a sole regard to justice and the public good. The apportionment of taxes on the various descriptions of property is an act which seems to require the most exact impartiality; yet there is, perhaps, no legislative act in which greater opportunity and temptation are given to a predominant party to trample on the rules of justice.

It is in vain to say that enlightened statesmen will be able to adjust these clashing interests, and render them all subservient to the public good. Enlightened statesmen will not always be at the helm. Nor, in many cases, can such an adjustment be made at all without taking into view indirect and remote considerations, which will rarely prevail over the immediate interest which one party may find in disregarding the rights of another or the good of the whole.

The *causes* of faction cannot be removed, and relief is only to be sought in the means of controlling its *effects*.

If a faction consists of less than a majority, relief is supplied by the republican principle, which enables the majority to defeat its sinister views by regular vote. When a majority is included in a faction, the form of popular government, on the other hand, enables it to sacrifice to its ruling passion or interest both the public good and the rights of other citizens. To secure the public good and private rights against the danger of such a faction, and at the same time to preserve the spirit and the form of popular government, is then the great object to which our inquiries are directed.

By what means is this object obtainable? Either the existence of the same passion or interest in a majority at the same time must be prevented, or the majority, having such co-existent passion or interest, must be rendered, by their number and local situation, unable to concert and carry into effect schemes of oppression. If the impulse and the opportunity be suffered to coincide, neither moral nor religious motives can be relied on as an adequate control.

A pure democracy, by which I mean a society consisting of a small number of citizens, who assemble and administer the government in person, can admit of no cure for the mischiefs of faction. A common passion or interest will, in almost every case, be felt by a majority of the whole; a communication and concert result from the form of government itself; and there is nothing to check the inducements to sacrifice the weaker party or an obnoxious individual. Hence such democracies have ever been spectacles of turbulence and contention; have ever been found incompatible with personal security or the rights of property; and have in general been as short in their lives as they have been violent in their deaths. Theoretic politicians, who have patronised this species of government, have erroneously supposed that by reducing mankind to a perfect equality in their political rights, they would, at the same time, be perfectly equalised and assimilated in their possessions, their opinions, and their passions.

A republic, by which I mean a government in which the scheme of representation takes place, opens a different prospect, and promises the cure for which we are seeking.

The two great points of difference between a democracy and a republic are: first, the delegation of the government, in the latter, to a small number of citizens elected by the rest; secondly, the greater number of citizens, and greater sphere of country, over which the latter may be extended.

The effect of the first difference is, on the one hand, to refine and enlarge the public views, by passing them through the medium of a chosen body of citizens, whose wisdom may best discern the true interest of their country, and whose partiotism and love of justice will be least likely to sacrifice it to temporary or partial considerations. Under such a regulation, it may well happen that the public voice, pronounced by the representatives of the people, will be more consonant to the public good than if pronounced by the people themselves, convened for the purpose. On the other hand, the effect may be inverted. Men of factious tempers, of local prejudices, or of sinister designs, may, by intrigue, by corruption, or by other means, first obtain the suffrages, and then betray the interests, of the people. The question resulting is, whether small or extensive republics are more favourable to the election of proper guardians of the public weal; and it is clearly decided in favour of the latter by two obvious considerations:

In the first place, however small the republic may be, the representatives must be raised to a certain number, in order to guard against the cabals of a few; and however large it may be, they must be limited to a certain number, in order to guard against the confusion of a multitude. Hence the number of representatives in the two cases not being in proportion to that of the two constituents, and being proportionally greater in the small republic, it follows that, if the proportion of fit characters be not less in the large than in the small republic, the former will present a greater option, and consequently a greater probability of a fit choice.

In the next place, as each representative will be chosen by a greater number of citizens in the large than in the small republic, it will be more difficult for unworthy candidates to practise with success the vicious arts by which elections are too often carried; and, the suffrages of the people being more free, will be more likely to centre in men who possess the most attractive merit and the most diffusive and established character.

There is a mean, on both sides of which inconveniences will be found to lie. By enlarging too much the number of electors, you render the representative too little acquainted with all their local circumstances and lesser interests; as by reducing it too much, you render him unduly attached to these, and too little fit to comprehend and pursue great and national objects. The federal Constitution forms a happy combination in this respect; the great and aggregate interests being referred to the national, the local and particular to the State legislatures.

The greater number of citizens and extent of territory which may be brought within the compass of republican than of democratic government renders factious combinations less to be dreaded in the former than in the latter. The smaller the society, the fewer probably will be the distinct parties and interests composing it; the fewer the distinct parties and interests, the more frequently will a majority be found of the same party; and the smaller the number of individuals composing a majority, and the smaller the compass within which they are placed, the more easily will they concert and execute their plans of oppression. Extend the sphere, and you take in a greater variety of parties and interests; you make it less probable that a majority of the whole will have a common motive to invade the rights of other citizens; or if such a common motive exists, it will be more difficult for all who feel it to discover their own strength, and to act in unison with each other.

The same advantage which a republic has over a democracy, in controlling the effects of faction, is enjoyed by a large over a small republic – is enjoyed by the Union over the States composing it.

The influence of factious leaders may kindle a flame within their particular States, but will be unable to spread a general conflagration through the other States. A religious sect may degenerate into a political faction in a part of the Confederacy; but the variety of sects dispersed over the entire face of it must secure the national councils against any danger from that source. A rage for paper money, for an abolition of debts, for an equal division of property, or for any other improper or wicked project, will be less apt to pervade the whole body of the Union than a particular member of it.

In the extent and proper structure of the Union, therefore, we behold a republican remedy for the diseases most incident to republican government.

The Federalist No. 51

To what expedient, then, shall we finally resort, for maintaining in practice the necessary partition of power among the several departments, as laid down in the Constitution?

In order to lay a due foundation for that separate and distinct exercise of the different powers of government, which is essential to the preservation of liberty, each department should have a will of its own; and consequently should be so constituted that the members of each should have as little agency as possible in the appointment of the members of the others.

The members of each department should be as little dependent as possible on those of the others, for the emoluments annexed to their offices. Were the executive magistrate, or the judges, not independent of the legislature in this particular, their independence in every other would be merely nominal.

But the great security against a gradual concentration of the several powers in the same department, consists in giving to those who administer each department the necessary constitutional means and personal motives to resist encroachments of the others. Ambition must be made to counteract ambition. The interest of the man must be connected with the constitutional rights of the place. It may be a reflection on human nature that such devices should be necessary to control the abuses of government. But what is government itself but the greatest of all reflections on human nature? If men were angels, no government would be necessary. If angles were to govern men, neither external nor internal controls on government would be necessary. In framing a government which is to be administered by men over men, the great difficulty lies in this: you must first enable the government to control the governed; and in the next place oblige it to control itself. A dependence on the people is, no doubt, the primary control on the government; but experience has taught mankind the necessity of auxiliary precautions.

This policy of supplying, by opposite and rival interests, the defect of better motives, might be traced through the whole system of human affairs. We see it particularly displayed in all the subordinate distributions of power, where the constant aim is to divide and arrange the several offices in such a manner as that each may be a check on the other – that the private interest of every individual may be a sentinel over the public rights.

But it is not possible to give to each department an equal power of self-defence. In republican government, the legislative authority necessarily predominates. The remedy for this inconveniency is to divide the legislature into different branches; and to render them, by different modes of election and different principles of action, as little connected with each other as the nature of their common functions and their common dependence on the society will admit. As the weight of the legislative authority requires that it should be thus divided, the weakness of the executive may require that it should be fortified. An absolute negative on the legislature appears, at first view, to be the natural defence with which the executive magistrate should be armed. But perhaps it would be neither altogether safe nor alone sufficient. May not this defect of an absolute negative be supplied by some qualified connection between this weaker department and the weaker branch of the stronger department?

There are two considerations particularly applicable to the federal system of America, which place that system in a very interesting point of view.

First. In a single republic all the power surrendered by the people is submitted to the administration of a single government. In the compound republic of America, the power surrendered by the people is first divided between two distinct governments, and then the portion allotted to each subdivided among distinct and separate departments. Hence a double security arises to the rights of the people.

Second. It is of great importance in a republic not only to guard the society against the oppression of its rulers, but to guard one part of the society against the injustice of the other part. Different interests necessarily exist in different classes of citizens. If a majority be united by a common interest, the rights of the minority will be insecure. There are but two methods of providing against this evil: the one by creating a will in the community independent of the majority – that is, of the society itself; the other, by comprehending in the society so many separate descriptions of citizens as will render an unjust combination of a majority of the whole very improbable, if not impracticable. The first method prevails in all governments possessing an hereditary or self-appointed authority. The second method will be exemplified in the federal republic of the United States. Whilst all authority in it will be derived from and dependent on the society, the society itself will be broken into so many parts, interests, and classes of citizens, that the rights of individuals, or of the minority, will be in little danger from interested combinations of the majority. In a free government the security for civil rights must be the same as that for religious rights. It consists in the one case in the multiplicity of interests, and in the other in the multiplicity of sects. The degree of security in both cases will depend on the number of interests and sects; and this may be presumed to depend on the extent of country and number of people comprehended under the same government. Justice is the end of government. It is the end of civil society. In a society under the forms of which the stronger faction can readily unite and oppress the weaker, anarchy may as truly be said to reign as in a state of nature, where the weaker individual is not secured against the violence of the stronger; and as, in the latter state, even the stronger individuals are prompted, by the uncertainty of their condition, to submit to a government which may protect the weak as well as themselves; so, in the former state, will the more powerful factions or parties be gradually induced, by a like motive, to wish for a government which will protect all parties, the weaker as well as the more powerful. In the extended republic of the United States, and among the great variety of interests, parties, and sects which it embraces, a coalition of a majority of the whole society could seldom take place on any other principles than those of justice and the general good; whilst there being thus less danger to a minor from the will of a major party, there must be less pretext, also, to provide for the security of the former, by introducing into the government a will independent of the society itself. The larger the society, provided it lie within a practical sphere, the more duly capable it will be of self-government. And happily for the *republican cause*, the practicable sphere may be carried to a very great extent by a judicious modification and mixture of the *federal principle*.

> Abridged from Numbers 10 and 51 in Alexander Hamilton, James Madison and John Jay (1787–88), *The Federalist, or the New Constitution*, with an introduction by W. J. Ashley, J. M. Dent & Sons, London, 1911, pp. 41–8, 263–7.

3.2 The civil rights movement

Frances Fox Piven and Richard A. Cloward

The black struggle was waged for two main goals. One was to secure formal political rights in the South, especially the right to the franchise; the other was to secure economic advances. In retrospect the main victory was the extension of political rights to southern blacks (together with a larger degree of black political representation in the northern cities).

Beginning in the 1940s the federal courts reversed historic doctrines and began to undercut the legality of southern state arrangements, a trend that culminated in the 1954 Supreme Court [Brown v. Board of Education of Topeka, Kansas] decision which declared racially separate schools unconstitutional because they were inherently unequal. Then, between 1957 and 1965, four civil rights bills were enacted which, taken together, finally granted a broad range of democratic political rights to blacks, and provided the mechanisms to enforce those rights. As a consequence, public accommodations were desegregated, blacks began to serve on the southern juries which had for so long provided immunity to southern whites employing terror against blacks, and the franchise was finally granted.

In the South the deepest meaning of the winning of democratic political rights is that the historical primacy of terror as a means of social control has been substantially diminished. With the winning of formal political rights, the reliance on terror – on police violence, on the lynch mob, on arbitrary imprisonment – has greatly diminished as the method of controlling blacks. Why this historic transformation came about, and the role of the civil rights movement in producing it, is the subject of this chapter.

By contrast, economic gains were limited. Many blacks entered the middle class, taking advantage of the liberal employment policies of both public and private institutions which the turbulence of the period produced. For most poor blacks, however, occupational conditions did not much improve. For many of them the main gain was the winning of liberalized welfare practices to insure their survival despite widespread unemployment and underemployment.

In the largest sense, political modernization in the South followed from economic modernization. Throughout the twentieth century industrialization had been advancing in the states of the Outer South and in some cities of the Deep South. Meanwhile, in the rural areas of the Deep South, mechanization and new agricultural technologies swept over the traditional plantation system, especially in the post-World War II period. These economic transformations rendered the semifeudal political order that prevailed in much of the South obsolete.

Our analysis focuses on the relationship between economic change, mass unrest, and the national electoral system. If political reforms throughout the South were made possible by change in the southern economy, and if economic change, by producing mass unrest, also made those reforms imperative, it was the electoral system that registered and mediated the pressures and which yielded the reforms. Political rights were finally conceded to southern blacks by a national Democratic Party whose leaders had for decades consistently refused to interfere with caste arrangements in the South.

Then, in a series of actions culminating in the mid-1960s, Democratic presidents and a Congress dominated by Democratic majorities forced political reforms on the southern wing of their party.

The civil rights movement was a vital force in this process because of the impact of its disruptive tactics on the electoral system. By defying caste domination, and by thus provoking southern whites to employ terroristic methods that were losing legitimacy, the civil rights movement succeeded in exacerbating electoral instabilities which had already been set in motion by economic modernization in the South. The national Democratic Party bore the brunt of these electoral conflicts and weakening party allegiances. The party's electoral majority had been eroding in the postwar years as polarization between southern whites on the one hand, and blacks and northern white liberals on the other, worsened. Consequently when the black assault against the caste system took form in the 1950s, polarizing northern and southern sentiments all the more, the leaders of the national Democratic Party manoeuvered to reduce their electoral losses by imposing political reforms on the South. Nor, except by enfranchising blacks and incorporating them in the southern wing of the party, could Democratic strength in the South be regained.

Economic modernization in the South

Even as caste arrangements were being consolidated in the South at the beginning of the twentieth century, large-scale economic forces were at work that would, in time, disrupt those arrangements. The most important effect of these economic forces was the dramatic shift in the character of black participation in the labor force, together with mass migration out of the South. In the course of slightly more than a half century the occupational position of blacks was transformed, and great numbers were redistributed from the agricultural South to the industrial North.

In the broadest terms, these shifts were caused by industrial expansion in the North during the first part of the twentieth century, by the decline in agricultural markets after World War I, together with federal agricultural policies originating in the 1930s, which took great masses of land out of production, and by the rapid pace of agricultural and industrial modernization in the South during and after World War II.

World War II reversed the decline in agriculture, but it also provided the impetus for a large-scale modernizing trend. The modernization of southern agriculture also stimulated increasing concentration of land ownership. Mechanization, new agricultural technologies, federal policies which removed land from production, and the enlargement of land holdings dramatically altered the labor requirements of southern agriculture.

The traditional tenant labor force of the South thus found itself increasingly obsolete, forced to search elsewhere for the means to subsist. The relative exclusion of blacks from southern industry gave many blacks little choice but to migrate northward.

Economic modernization had made the South susceptible to political modernization. In the large-scale mechanized agriculture that was developing in the rural South, market incentives were slowly substituted for the older system of serf labor. A wage labor supply – one that was somewhat more skilled (especially in the use of machinery) – was coming to be required. This transition to wage labor was greatly facilitated by the huge labor surpluses which were continually thrown up by the process of agricultural modernization itself. The constant threat of unemployment was a powerful inducement for rural workers to accept wage work on terms dictated by the planter class.

In the industrializing areas of the South a new capitalist class was emerging, especially during and following World War II. This new urban-based industrial class relied mainly on market mechanisms to insure its labor needs. To be sure, the inferior status of blacks continued to be a useful mechanism to insure maximum profits. But the deliberate exacerbation of racial competition for jobs was a strategy long used by employers to control labor both in the North and in the South, and was far from being equivalent to a system of caste. As a social system to allocate and control labor, in short, southern caste arrangements were becoming obsolete.

As economic modernization overtook the South, other changes were taking place in the North which also weakened opposition to the extension of formal rights to blacks. [And] with the rise of communism the United States was thrown into intense competition for world domination, a circumstance that demanded an ideology of 'democracy' and 'freedom'. Increasingly the circumstances prevailing in the South constituted a national embarrassment and support for these arrangements by dominant economic elites weakened.

The stakes of northern capitalism in domestic racism also weakened after World War II. By the World War II period, however, northern capitalism had largely acceded to the unionization of the industrial working class, and to that extent the exploitation of racial cleavages had begun to lose its former utility. This change, together with the growing requirement for a liberal racial ideology with which to meet the threat of Communism in international affairs, eroded support for the southern social system among economic dominants in the North.

Economic modernization and electoral instability

Economic change, by weakening the stakes of agricultural and industrial leaders in the maintenance of caste arrangements, also freed national political leaders to act against those arrangements. By the fourth and fifth decades of the twentieth century, the perpetuation of caste arrangements was being reduced to a question of public opinion. In the absence of significant opposition from economic dominants, the question was whether shifts in the alignments of broad electoral groupings would create the necessary pressures to comple national leaders to act. The Democratic Party was the main arena in which this drama of gradually intensifying electoral conflict and realignment was played out.

Since 1876 the one-party South has constituted the regional foundation of the national Democratic Party. The realignment of the Democratic Party in 1932 did not change the politics of the South, for a national coalition was formed that joined together the industrial working class in the North and the one-party agrarian South. But two sources of strain were in the making even as that alliance was formed.

For one, northern urban blacks joined that coalition in 1936. With that shift, the 'American dilemma' became a Democratic dilemma. By 1940 blacks began leaving the South in great numbers. Year by year the impact of this demographic revolution on the northern electoral system was immense, for blacks were concentrating in the northern cities of the most populous, industrialized states, the electoral strongholds of the Democratic Party. As their voting numbers swelled, leaders in the northern wing of the party began to acknowledge that concessions to blacks would have to be made.

The race issue emerged in the election of 1948 as a result of the formation of the Progressive Party led by Henry Wallace, who directed his appeals to northern liberals and to blacks. Truman's chief campaign strategist was worried about the president's strength among blacks because of Wallace and the Republicans' symbolic appeals to the black voter.

Accordingly Truman gave the appearance of championing civil rights. Thus Truman called for a broad range of civil rights measures. But having promised to issue executive orders abolishing segregation in the armed forces and discrimination in federal employment – actions which were within his immediate power – he did neither.

The nominating convention scuttled Truman's essentially rhetorical civil rights strategy. Liberal leaders intent on securing a strong civil rights plank despite Truman's opposition were joined by influential northern machine leaders who believed Truman would lose the election. They 'were less concerned with Southern diehards bolting than with solidifying the Negro vote behind their local and state candidates. Henry Wallace was making a powerful appeal to this constituency in major cities. Any spectacular demonstration of the Democrats as resolute defenders of Negro interests that would head off the Wallace threat was to be welcomed' (Cochran, 1973, 230). Consequently a strong civil rights plank was pushed through on the floor of the convention, leading Alabama and Mississippi to walk out. The Dixiecrat forces, drawing upon dissident elements throughout the South, convened two days later in Birmingham to form a States' Rights Party with Senator J. Strom Thurmond of South Carolina as its presidential nominee. With these events Truman was pushed all the more to the left on the race question, and he immediately issued the executive orders he had promised months earlier. In the ensuing election, Truman won (with the aid of the black vote) despite the loss of four Deep South states – Louisiana, South Carolina, Alabama, and Mississippi – to the States' Rights Party.

The cause of securing civil rights legislation was not immediately advanced by these events. Southern defections in the election of 1948 foreshadowed the possible dissolution of that regional base, and so concessions to the South – namely, maintaining the racial status quo – became the order of the day, as Stevenson's posture in campaigning for the Democratic nomination in 1952 revealed. Throughout the campaign Stevenson continued to appease the South, and gave relatively little attention to the black vote in the northern cities. This policy of conciliation did not stem the tide of defections in the subsequent election because an entirely different force was also at work. The Dixiecrat states, where race was the pre-eminent issue, returned to the Democratic ranks, although South Carolina and Louisiana did so by very slim majorities. But in the Outer South the Republicans made big gains; Virginia, Florida, Tennessee, and Texas delivered their electoral votes to Eisenhower. Republican strength in the Outer South was especially noticeable among the growing white middle classes in the cities.

The election of 1952 thus revealed the political effects of a second form of economic change that was sweeping the South: industrial modernization. This modernizing trend was casting up a new white middle class in the cities and suburbs (especially in the states of the Outer South) whose political sympathies inclined toward the Republican Party. In the presidential campaign of 1956 national political leaders attempted to play down the divisive race issue, particularly avoiding the inflammatory 1954 Brown decision. Although both parties avoided the school desegregation issue, the Republicans saw opportunities in the difficulties being experienced by the Democratic Party over the race question. There was the possibility of playing upon this issue to make further gains among whites in the South, or of making equally important gains among blacks in the ghettos of the North. In some measure Republican strategists were uncertain of the proper course. However, the Republicans finally cast their lot with the potential for gain among northern blacks, for the congressional Republicans were all from northern states where blacks were concentrating. Under the urging of Herbert Brownell, the attorney general, and of other party leaders, Eisenhower sent a civil rights bill to Congress in 1956 and Republicans pushed for it. In the end Lyndon B. Johnson, the Senate Majority Leader, conspired with other southern congressmen to kill the bill, and the Congress adjourned.

The election of 1956 indicated that the Democratic strategy of avoiding civil rights issues was not succeeding. The basis of the North-South Democratic coalition was inexorably weakening. On the one side, southern defections continued. When the returns were in Stevenson fared slightly worse than he had in the election of 1952. The Democrats, despite a policy of conciliation on the race question, thus suffered a net loss of one additional southern state over the election of 1952.

The election of 1956 revealed that black allegiance to the Democratic Party was also weakening. Stevenson had won about 80 percent of the black vote in 1952, but he won only about 60 percent in 1956. The upward trend of black support for the Democratic Party initiated in the election of 1936 was broken. Although the sharpest black defections occurred in the South, many northern black voters signaled their disapproval of the Democratic Party [by abstaining].

Black voting defections in 1956 were a cause for alarm among national Democratic political leaders. By the mid-fifties, migration had brought a great many blacks into the North; moreover, some 90 percent of them settled in the central cities of the ten most populous industrial states, and thus in states of crucial importance in presidential contests. In presidential contests, blacks were strategically concentrated. Moreover as southern defections developed in the elections of 1948 and 1952, the Democratic Party became all the more dependent on the northern vote.

Despite the growing importance of the black vote, Democratic leaders had continued to resist granting civil rights concessions. Democratic leaders simply did not want to further endanger electoral allegiances in the South. Nor, until 1956, did they have to take that risk, for blacks had remained steadfastly loyal. But once the black vote, like the southern white vote, also became unstable, the Democratic strategy of proceeding cautiously in order not to antagonize the South could no longer succeed. It was not the rise of a substantial black electoral bloc in the northern states that finally set the stage for civil rights concessions; it was the rise of black defections.

One of these concessions was to come in the year immediately following the election of 1956, when Congress enacted the first Civil Rights Act since 1875. Electoral instability played a significant role in the formation of the coalition in Congress which brought about passage of the bill. The Democratic party could afford southern defections, or black defections, but it could not afford both. For the Republicans, black defections confirmed the potential of their modest civil rights appeals prior to the election. Consequently the Republicans again seized the initiative and resubmitted the previously rejected civil rights bill. In doing so, they broke ranks again with southern Democrats. The cleaving of this alliance, which had previously thwarted all efforts to secure civil rights legislation, was a direct consequence of voting defections among northern blacks.

With a civil rights bill once again before Congress, Johnson engineered the necessary compromises to forestall a southern filibuster. Johnson's evolution on the civil rights question was itself a reflection of the impact of electoral dissensus on the Democratic Party, for until the mid-fifties Johnson had consistently refused to support civil rights legislation.

The chief problem confronting Johnson was the prospect of a southern filibuster. The bill contained provisions (and an amendment) which angered the South; on the other hand, Republicans and northern Democrats were prepared to press for Senate rule changes that would weaken the power of the filibuster if the South obstructed passage of the bill. With each camp fearful

162 *The American political system*

of the other's power, Johnson was able to gain support for a compromise bill that was essentially symbolic and it passed (without a filibuster) by an overwhelming margin (72 to 18, with Lyndon Johnson and four other southerners in the majority).

In other words the Democratic Party had once again weathered the deep division within its ranks. But there was this difference: it had done so *only* by enacting a civil rights measure, however weak its provisions may have been. The Civil Rights Act of 1957 was significant for that reason, for it presaged the end of an older strategy of coping with regional divisions by avoiding the civil rights issue. The growing size and instability of the black vote had forced the beginning of a new mode of adaptation to those divisions, an adaptation in which concessions would be made to blacks. Henceforth the struggle would be over the substance of those concessions.

The resurgence of black and white defiance

Just as the Democrats were to regain the presidency in 1960, defiance by blacks erupted again, and on an increasingly massive scale. It was no longer mainly the white leaders of the South who provoked confrontations with the federal government; in this period, civil rights activists began to embrace a 'strategy of using civil disobedience to force local governments into conflict with federal authority' (Killian, 63). In reaction white violence worsened, spurred by southern leaders, especially governors, and acted out by police agents and white mobs.

On February 1, 1960, four students from the Negro Agricultural and Technical College in Greensboro, North Carolina, entered a variety store and were refused service at the lunch counter where they sat in violation of caste rules. The sit-in movement swept like a brush fire from one locale to another. After a series of organizational meetings following the Montgomery boycott, Martin Lutter King formed the Southern Christian Leadership Conference (SCLC) and located its offices in Atlanta. Quick to see the significance of the student-initiated sit-in movement, SCLC officials offered moral and financial support (despite the opposition of officials in several established national civil rights organizations). In April, with SCLC aid, student delegates from dozens of universities assembled at Shaw University in Raleigh, North Carolina, to form the Student Nonviolent Coordinating Committee (SNCC).

The students who composed SNCC were animated by a belief in the efficacy of civil disobedience. Through the summer and fall of 1960 militant SNCC activities mushroomed.

None of the direct-action organizations in this struggle were either much organized or much oriented toward building formal membership. The direct-action organizations which developed during the civil rights struggle were cadre organizations.

The cadres – whether in SNCC or CORE or SCLC – at first engaged in exemplary actions. Thus 'the essence of SNCC leadership appears to be this willingness to assume personal risks, to expose oneself to imprisonment and brutality' (Clark, 260). Often in groups of just two or three or a half dozen, the cadres were the most active demonstrators. Such exemplary actions, in turn, inspired a mass mobilization.

Presidential efforts to cope with electoral instability

The arrests, the mob violence, and the police brutality that were provoked by these protest activities rapidly created major dilemmas for national political leaders. On October 25 – a few days before the presidential election of 1960 – King was arrested and convicted for violating a twelve-months' term of parole, and was sentenced to four months at hard labor in the Reidsville State Prison, a penal camp in rural Georgia. Overnight the White House was deluged with telegrams and letters.

President Eisenhower and candidate Nixon weighed the potential electoral gains and losses of intervening, deciding against taking action. Kennedy decided otherwise and that decision has since been credited with having turned the election to him. His call to King's wife, together with a call by Robert Kennedy to the judge who had committed King to prison, caused little short of delirium in black communities throughout the nation.

If any group had reason to expect presidential action on its behalf, it was blacks following the election of 1960. Without the huge black majorities in the key industrial centers of the nation, Kennedy could not have been elected. However he had won office, but narrowly, and white southern defections had been no small cause of his near defeat. A policy of conciliation toward the South still appeared to be the expedient course of action.

Moreover, Kennedy (like earlier Democratic presidents) was concerned that a confrontation with Congress over civil rights would cost him support on other domestic legislation. Instead of legislative action, therefore, the president opted for a strategy of executive action. The Justice Department thus became the chief instrument of civil rights action by the administration. Civil rights litigation was given higher priority within the department and more litigation was undertaken than had previously been the case, especially in school desegregation and on voting rights. At the same time, however, Kennedy appointed southerners to the federal bench who caused great dismay among blacks.

Defiance spreads

But the Kennedy Administration's activity on the civil rights front was both too much for southern leaders and far too little for civil rights activists.

One of the most conspicuous symbols of southern caste arrangements was the segregation of bus and train terminals – from waiting areas, to eating facilities, to restrooms. Since these public areas were under the jurisdiction of a federal agency – the Interstate Commerce Commission (ICC) – they were a logical arena in which to force confrontations over the segregation issue. In the spring of 1961 the Congress of Racial Equality, under the leadership of its new executive director, James Farmer, decided to send 'freedom riders' into the South. The freedom rides (which were subsequently joined in by SCLC, SNCC, and the Nashville Student Movement) brought on some of the worst mob violence of the era. With each outbreak of arrests and mob violence, the federal government was faced with the decision whether to intervene, for it was clear that the civil rights activists would not desist.

The Kennedy Administration was continually drawn into the conflict created by the clashing forces throughout the South. Its actions, in turn, added fuel to the fire, for when the federal government supported the goals of the movement – either symbolically or through various executive actions – the participants in the movement gained encouragement. Moreover the attorney general intervened to protect the freedom riders in Montgomery, for the events there were too violent to be ignored. Within a matter of months the federal courts and the ICC ordered the desegregation of all terminal facilities for both interstate and intrastate passengers.

Abridged from Frances Fox Piven and Richard A. Cloward (1977), *Poor People's Movements: Why They Succeed, How They Fail*, pp. 181–4, 189–201, 213–30. Reprinted by permission of Pantheon Books, New York, a division of Random House, Inc.

References

Clark, Kenneth B. (1966), 'The civil rights movement: momentum and organization', *Daedalus*, 95, Winter.
Cochran, Bert (1973), *Harry Truman and the Crisis Presidency*, Funk & Wagnalls, New York.
Killian, Lewis M. (1968), *The Impossible Revolution?* Random House, New York.

3.3   Political equality and the American pressure system

Kay Lehman Schlozman

Political scientists of an earlier era once placed pressure groups at the heart of the American political process and emphasized not only the ubiquity of

interest group activity but also the inevitability of the organizational representation of joint interests in politics. Moreover, the question of how permeable
organized pressure politics is to newly emergent issues and groups was one of
the most fundamental issues dividing the group theorists from their critics.
Antipluralists disputed the notion that the pressure system is universal, arguing
that group theorists had both underestimated the height of the barriers
to entry into the marketplace of political competition and overestimated
the inclusiveness of the interests represented. E. E. Schattschneider (1960)
observed that the representation of latent interests is not at all automatic and
that two particular kinds of interests – the interests of the poor and the
interests of broad publics – are likely to remain unorganized.

If Schattschneider's description is accurate for the 1950s – and we really do
not know if it is since his supporting evidence is illustrative rather than
systematic – there is reason to believe that important changes have occurred
since he wrote. With the mobilization of new interests over the past two
decades, the nature of the pressure system has undoubtedly been altered.
Since the 1960s, we have witnessed the mobilization of many groups and the
emergence of many new organizations – ranging from Common Cause and
the Wilderness Society to the National Urban Coalition and the Native
American Rights Fund – representing the very sorts of interests that he
observed to be underrepresented in the pressure system.

Do these developments mean that, at just the time when pluralist analysis
was being subjected to heavy criticism, its promise was being fulfilled? Surprisingly, although attention has been paid to the emergence of new organizations, there has been no systematic empirical inquiry into the contours of
the pressure system and, therefore, no systematic assessment of the meaning
of these changes for equality of representation. Because questions of equal
representation of interests are so fundamental to democracy, this paper ad-
duces systematic data to investigate the overall shape of the set of organized
private interests in Washington.

Political equality and the organizational representation of interests

It might seem that the appropriate way to investigate the shape of the pressure
system is to focus not on the organizations active in Washington but on the
individuals active in the organizations. Indeed, studies based on surveys of the
mass public indicate the strong social class bias in organizational membership. However, these studies are limited from the perspective of understanding organizational representation of collective interests. Existing surveys
are not sufficiently rich: they do not include information about either the
particular organizations to which individuals belong or the issues on behalf of
which those organizations are active; they also do not contain sufficient cases
of members of each of the various kinds of political organizations to permit
certain kinds of detailed analyses.

Even the most thorough and detailed mass surveys about membership in organizations naturally miss an important component of the pressure system; many of the private organizations active in Washington today – in particular, corporations, but also public interest law firms and institutions like universities and hospitals – have no members in the ordinary sense of the word. Other membership groups, most notably trade associations, unite member organizations which themselves have no individual members.

The data presented here are derived principally from a tally in which the nearly 7,000 organizations listed in the *Washington Representatives – 1981* directory as having a presence in Washington politics, either by maintaining an office in the capital or by hiring counsel or consultants to represent them, were enumerated and categorized.

These data provide an important supplement to evidence from existing surveys because they tell us much about the kinds of interests represented by organizations in Washington. These data do, however, have a liability: in taking the organization rather than the individual as the unit of analysis, we become unable to treat each unit as equivalent. Organizations differ in the number of members they have (if they have members at all), the number of issues on which they become involved, and the level of resources they command.

The contours of the pressure system

Table 3.3(1) presents the results of a tally of the organizations listed in *Washington Representatives*. The left-hand column shows the distribution for the 2,810 organizations (43 percent of the total) that have their own Washington offices. The right-hand column shows the distribution for the 6,601 organizations that either maintain an office in the capital to handle political matters or hire Washington-based counsel or consultants. There is one obvious difference between the distributions in the two columns. Corporations constitute 45.7 percent of all organizations having a Washington presence but only 20.6 percent of those having Washington offices.

This discrepancy should not blind us to the overall message of both columns of Table 3.3(1). Taken as a whole the pressure system is heavily weighted in favor of business organizations: 70 percent of all organizations having a Washington presence and 52 percent of those having their own offices represent business. The overrepresentation of business interests takes place at the expense of two other kinds of organizations: groups representing broad public interests and groups representing the poor (or those with few political resources). Even if we make the perhaps dubious assumption that all unions, civil rights groups, minority organizations, social welfare groups, poor people's organizations, and groups organizing the elderly, the handicapped, gays, and women represent political have-nots, less than 5 percent of all organizations having a Washington presence and less than 10 percent of those

Table 3.3(1)   *The Washington pressure system*

	Groups having their own Washington offices (%)	All groups having Washington representation (%)
Corporations	20.6%	45.7%
Trade Associations and Other Business	30.6	17.9
Foreign Commerce and Corporations	.5	6.5
Professional Associations[a]	14.8	6.9
Unions	3.3	1.7
Public Interest Groups	8.7	4.1
Civil Rights Groups/Minority Organizations	1.7	1.3
Social Welfare and the Poor	1.3	.6
New Entrants (Elderly, Gays, Women, Handicapped)	2.5	1.1
Governmental Units – U.S.	1.4	4.2
Other Foreign	1.2	2.0
Other/Unknown	13.2	8.2[b]
	99.8%	100.2%
	(N = 2,810)	(N = 6,601)

Sources: Based on information taken from Close (1981) and Akey (1981).
[a] Includes, in addition to traditional professional associations, organizations of business executives, such as the Data Processing Management Association, and organizations of professionals working in government, such as the National Conference of Bankruptcy Judges.
[b] Includes, in addition to organizations we were unable to classify (292), nine small categories. Among them are farmers' organizations (46), veterans' groups (31), and religious groups (50). Of the nine categories, only educational organizations (124, or 1.9 percent) account for more than 1 percent of the total organizations classified. Otherwise, these categories account for less than 1 percent of the total each.

having their own offices there represent those having few political resources. Similar proportions obtain for the sum total of all the various organizations – consumer groups, environmental groups, civic groups, single-issue cause groups, foreign policy groups, and so on – that represent diffuse public interests: public interest groups constitute only 4 percent of all organizations active in Washington politics and 9 percent of those having offices in the capital.[1]

Bias in the pressure system: a further probe

The pressure system, of course, includes groups organized around a vast array of dimensions – from occupation, race, age, and gender to hobbies. We can get a better idea of the degree of bias within the pressure system by considering what is probably the most important axis of political conflict in American politics: economic roles.

When we consider the substantial portion of the pressure system consisting of groups organized about economic roles, the class bias of the Washington pressure system is unambiguous. The professionals and managers who might be considered haves constitute at most 16 percent of American adults; they are represented by 88 percent of the economic organizations. Business organizations alone constitute 71 percent of the total. Had we used figures for all economic organizations involved in Washington politics – those that hire counsel or consultants as well as those that have their own offices – the data would have been even more skewed. Fully 93 percent of the economic organizations having a Washington presence represent business or professionals, and 86 percent represent business alone.

The multiple representation of business interests
We might argue that it is not the number of groups representing a particular point of view so much as the equal representation of individuals that is critical for political equality. That is, workers might be just as well represented by a few large unions as business is by a much greater number of smaller organizations if the total group-based political input were equal for all individuals represented. However, a comparison with the structure of political representation of organized labor demonstrates that the structure of business representation is such that the pressure system as presently constituted virtually guarantees the multiple representation of business interests. In terms of the level of interest aggregation, the three kinds of business organizations in politics – firms, trade associations, and peak associations – are analogous to union locals, operating unions, and the AFL-CIO. At the peak, the representation of business and labor interests is roughly equivalent: several organizations – among them the Business Roundtable, the Chamber of Commerce, and the National Association of Manufacturers – represent the most general interests of business; the AFL-CIO those of labor.

The situation is entirely reversed, however, at the most disaggregated level. While individual firms are frequently active in politics, individual union locals are not. Moreover, while each union local obviously belongs only to a single operating union, corporations – even small ones – belong to a number of trade associations, and large corporations usually belong to dozens. Of course, we cannot assume that the associations to which a corporation belongs are always active on the same issues, or that they are always allies when they are simultaneously active. Still, these many additional memberships must add considerably to the volume of a single corporation's political input. Hence, in a particular political controversy, unionized workers might be represented by their union and the AFL-CIO; stockholders or managers in the same corporation might be represented by their own firm, by other firms in the industry, by one or more trade associations, and by one or more peak business associations. It is not, then, simply a matter of equal representation of individuals being provided by a greater number of smaller organizations as opposed to a few larger ones, for the proliferation of business organizations magnifies business input into politics.

The changing pressure system

If the contemporary pressure system is biased in favor of business, what did it look like two decades ago when Schattschneider wrote? In view of the number of visible new organizations representing precisely the kinds of interests that Schattschneider predicted would remain unorganized, we would expect the pressure system of two decades ago to have been even more skewed than it is now.

Systematic data confirm the popular impression that many new public interest, civil rights, and social welfare organizations have emerged since 1960.

The overall finding is how many new groups there are on the scene. Fully 40 percent of the organizations with offices in Washington have been founded since 1960, 25 percent since 1970. Equally striking is the distribution for the various categories. Seventy-six percent of the public interest groups, 56 percent of the civil rights groups, and 79 percent of the social welfare and poor people's organizations, but only 38 percent of the trade associations and 14 percent of the corporations have been founded since 1960. In addition, 57 percent of the public interest groups, 51 percent of the social welfare and poor people's organizations, but only 23 percent of the trade and other business associations and 6 percent of the corporations have been founded since 1970. There has been an explosion in the number of groups representing the interests of broad publics and those with few political resources.

Clearly, then, the pressure system has expanded in scope, but how has the entry of all these new groups altered the bias of the pressure system? If we compare the pressure system of 1960 with the set of organizations having their own offices in the capital two decades later, we find less change than we might have expected. Although the balance between corporations and trade associations has changed, the total business presence (corporations and trade and other business associations taken together) has diminished relatively little, from 57 percent to 53 percent of all organizations. The most substantial alteration is the increase in the proportion of professional associations – and the corresponding decrease in the proportion of unions. However, it is probably more appropriate to compare the figures for 1960 with the figures for all groups having a Washington presence in 1980. This comparison leads us to a somewhat different conclusion. For all the newborn organizations representing the interests of diffuse publics, minorities, poor people, the elderly, and other disadvantaged groups, business actually is a more dominating presence in Washington now than it was two decades ago. For all organizations having representation in Washington, the proportion representing the interests of business rose from 57 percent to 72 percent since 1960. The proportion of public interest groups decreased from 9 percent to 5 percent of all organizations, and the proportion representing labor plummetted from 11 percent to 2 percent.

Movement in and out of the pressure system

The pressure system is quite fluid. Organizations vary in terms of the constancy of their political activity. Some, especially those having offices in Washington, are on the scene year in and year out. Others participate more sporadically, galvanized for politics only on those occasions when a specific issue impinges upon their vital interests. Some groups are self-consciously temporary, formed to deal with a particular policy matter.

We can get a better feel for the movement of organizations in and out of the pressure system by considering the data presented in Table 3.3(2). As Table 3.3(2) indicates, there is a remarkable amount of continuity. Sixty percent of all the organizations listed in 1960 – or 79 percent of those for which we could find information – were part of the pressure system two decades later (having been listed in the *Washington Representatives – 1981* directory).

Public interest groups are an exception to the general pattern that emerges from Table 3.3(2). Only 33 percent of the public interest groups listed in 1960 were still active in politics two decades later. Fully 27 percent (a substantially higher figure than for any other type of organization) were not around at all. Considering only those organizations for which we have information, 80 percent or more of the corporations, trade and other business associations, professional associations, unions, organizations of women, the elderly, and the handicapped, and civil rights and social welfare organizations – but only 45 percent of the public interest groups – that were active in Washington in 1960 were listed twenty years later.

Investigation of the fate of the organizations has permitted us to understand something about the relative propensities of organizations to continue to be politically involved, to become politically deactivated, or to go out of existence completely. Unfortunately, however, it is impossible to trace an additional process that affects the overall contours of the pressure system: the mobilization into national politics of existing, but previously apolitical, organizations. Many observers have remarked upon the importance of this process in recent years, especially with respect to business.

One bit of systematic evidence provides indirect confirmation of the significance of the political activation of organizations previously outside politics. Government affairs representatives in a sample of 175 organizations having offices in Washington were asked when their organizations had first established these offices. Sixty-one percent of the organizations in the survey have opened a Washington office – often a national headquarters – since 1960, 38 percent since 1970. Furthermore, 36 percent of the organizations in the

Table 3.3(2) 1980 status of organizations active in Washington politics in 1960 (%)

	Still active – still in politics	Still active – not in politics	Inactive/out of business	No information	Total	N
Corporations	63%	8	0	29	100%	(84)
Trade and Other Business Associations	61	6	10	24	101	(216)
Professional Associations	79	7	0	14	100	(28)
Unions	77	7	4	12	100	(56)
Public Interest Groups	33	13	27	27	100	(46)
Civil Rights/Social Welfare/Poor	50	12	0	38	100	(8)
Women/Elderly/Handicapped	78	11	0	11	100	(9)
Other/Unknown	46	18	3	33	100	(76)
All Organizations	60	9	7	24	100	(523)

Sources: Compiled from information contained in the following: Akey (1983); Close (1981); Craig Colgate, Jr. (ed.), *National Trade and Professional Associations of the United States.* 18th edn. (Washington, DC: Columbia Books, 1983); *Congressional Quarterly Almanac* (1960); *Directory of Corporate Affiliations – 1983* (Skokie, IL: National Register, 1983); Baldwin H. Ward (ed.), *Ward's Directory of 55,000 Largest Corporations* (Petaluma, CA: Baldwin H. Ward, 1981).

sample – including 42 percent of the corporations and 55 percent of the professional associations – existed as of 1960, but established offices in Washington since then. This indicates, presumably, the increased salience of national politics both to groups originally established for other purposes and to groups long active in politics whose political interests had become so compelling that they established a permanent beachhead in Washington.

The changing pressure system: a summary

A very large share of the civil rights and social welfare organizations and of the groups representing women, the elderly, and the handicapped are new, having been established since 1960. Although their numbers have grown substantially, there are, however, still so few of them compared with other kinds of organizations that they do not form a more significant component in the pressure system.

Many new public interests groups have also been born over this period. Like the organizations just mentioned, there are still too few of them to figure significantly in the pressure system. What is more, the public interest organizations that were part of the pressure system as of 1960 seem to be characterized by unusually high rates of attrition. This factor has had the effect of reducing public interest representation in the pressure system.

Union representation has, on the other hand, remained remarkably stable over the last two decades; the number of unions has not grown significantly. Furthermore, a large proportion of the unions active in 1980 were part of the pressure system in 1960. This stability, in a period during which many new organizations have come on the scene and many old ones have been politically mobilized, yields a situation in which the union share of the pressure system has diminished substantially. A similar, though less exaggerated, pattern is characteristic of trade associations as well. The birth rate for trade associations has been somewhat lower than for other kinds of organizations. In addition, because so many trade associations were already active in politics in 1960, the process of political activation has been less pronounced than for corporations. The net result is that trade associations, while still a crucial component of the pressure system, have lost their former unambiguous predominance. At one time the trade association was deemed the pressure group par excellence. It would be an overstatement to make such a claim today.

The pattern for corporations – and, to a lesser extent, for professional associations – is different again. The birth rate for these organizations, especially for corporations, is relatively low. However, the massive mobilization of organizations formerly outside the pressure system more than compensates for the low rate of entry of newborn organizations. Thus, in spite of their low birth rates, both professional associations and corporations have increased their share within the pressure system. Corporations alone account for 52 percent of the organizations that either maintain offices in the capital or hire counsel or consultants to represent their interests. This massive influx of corporations into the pressure system means that, in spite of the relative eclipse of trade associations, the overall business share of the pressure system has been enhanced.

Some caveats

First, we cannot treat organizations as units because the resources they command vary so substantially. There is evidence, however, to suggest that – at least in terms of subjective perceptions of resources – the distribution of material resources among organized interests further reinforces the advantage that accrues to the well-off, especially business, in terms of the number of organizations.

In addition, the claim that business is well represented within the Washington pressure community does not presuppose that the interests of business in politics are undivided. It is accurate neither to characterize business interests as always unified nor to assume that business interests active on one side of a policy controversy will necessarily be opposed by other business interests. This analysis is also not meant to suggest that business always wins in national politics. Inequalities in representation are not necessarily translated into proportional inequalities in influence.

Conclusion

The evidence indicates clearly that the pressure system is tilted heavily in favor of the well-off, especially business, at the expense of the representation of broad public interests and the interests of those with few political resources.[2] Surprisingly, in spite of the appearance of many new groups representing the previously underrepresented, the bias of the pressure system seems to have become more pronounced in recent years.

> Abridged from Kay Lehman Schlozman (1984), 'What accent the heavenly chorus? Political equality and the American pressure system', *Journal of Politics*, XLVI, pp. 1007–32. Reprinted by permission of the author and the University of Texas Press, Austin.

Notes

1 A 'public interest group' is understood here to be a group seeking a benefit whose achievement will not benefit selectively either the members or the activists of the organization. Although the supporters of public interest groups – whether they seek clean air or lower electrical rates, a more militant posture toward the Soviet Union or nuclear disarmament – seek public goods and so would not benefit selectively from the achievement of their goals, public interest groups, like other organizations active in Washington, draw their support disproportionately from the upper-middle class. Thus, while public interest groups often represent in politics positions that

would otherwise not find vigorous advocacy, their membership does not ameliorate the class bias of the pressure system.

2 The evidence here indicates that the pressure system is biased not only against groups representing broad publics but also against groups representing those with few resources. If the costs of organizational involvement are low enough, the rationality mechanism does not seem to be triggered. There seems to be a threshold level for costs, below which members do not bother to make rational calculations of economic self-interest. The point at which it becomes worthwhile to make such calculations clearly varies with the resources of the group member. Organizations representing the poor gain no extra support by virtue of the existence of a threshold level beneath which the costs of membership are so low that the rational calculations are not made. For those with few resources, the costs are never low enough.

References

Akey, Denise S., ed. (1979, 1981, 1983), *Encyclopedia of Associations*, 13th, 16th and 17th edns., Gale Research Co., Detroit, MI.

Close, Arthur C., ed. (1981), *Washington Representatives*, Columbia Books, Washington, DC.

Congressional Quarterly Almanac (1960), Congressional Quarterly, Washington, DC.

Schattschneider, E. E. (1960), *The Semisovereign People*, Holt, Rinehart and Winston, New York.

3.4 American voter turn-out: non-voting and its causes

G. Bingham Powell, Jr.

Seen in comparative perspective, American voter turn-out presents an interesting paradox. Americans seem to be more politically aware and involved than citizens in any other democracy, yet the levels of voter turn-out in the United States are consistently far below the democratic average. If citizens in other democracies possessed the American configuration of attitudes, their voter participation would on average increase. However, the American attitudinal advantage is only a marginal enhancer of voting. Its effects are limited, first, because in recent years the American attitudinal advantage has declined, and, more importantly, because voting is so powerfully shaped by institutional context. In comparative perspective, the American registration rules, electoral system, and party system inhibit voter participation, outweighing by far the attitudinal advantage.

The cultural and institutional environment for voting

Although attitudes facilitating participation declined in the United States in the late 1960s, comparison with political attitudes in the European nations still shows the American public to good advantage. Partisanship has declined, but is still equal to or above average. Eighty-three percent of Americans named a party they usually felt close to, placing the United States behind only the Netherlands and Finland in a twelve-nation comparison. On the other side of the partisanship scale, 14 percent said they felt very close to their party, a figure slightly behind only two other countries (Austria and Italy), although a drop from the America of the early 1960s.

Despite the drop in political confidence, the United States still led all countries in the number of citizens believing that they had some say in government. In general political interest, the 90 percent of Americans who reported at least some interest were comparable to their counterparts a decade earlier, and well ahead of the cross-national average. Only in the decline of political trust did the Americans drop from a leading position to one well back. But political trust, although related to voter participation in America, was the least important of the four attitude variables in the American attitude studies. Despite the decline in the period from 1960–75, American political attitudes should still facilitate more political participation than political attitudes in other democracies.

This conclusion is strongly supported by three other measures of political activity: (1) discussing politics with other people, (2) trying to convince others to vote for a party or candidate during an election campaign, and (3) working for a party or candidate during elections. Nearly 90 percent of the American public reports discussing politics at least some of the time, compared to an average of only 68 percent across the 11 European nations. Thirty percent of American citizens report having worked during a campaign at some time, more than double the average for seven European nations in which this question was asked. In reporting having tried to convince others during election campaigns, the Americans trail only the West Germans, with 40 percent affirming such activity, in comparison to an average of 27 percent in seven other countries. These American results parallel other studies of the American electorate quite closely. The strong relative position of the American public in attitudes that facilitate participation and in various measures of political activity other than voting also appears in other comparative studies.

The American participation studies, as well as the comparative studies, have demonstrated that possession of greater social and economic resources, particularly higher levels of education, is associated with attitudes and behavior that facilitate participation. The average educational level is much higher in the United States than in most of Western Europe (reflecting the much older American concern for mass education, as opposed to the European elite emphasis). The American citizen is also more likely to hold a white-collar or professional job than his European counterpart, although here the differences are not quite so marked, as all these nations are relatively economically developed.

Only in its age structure do the demographics of the American public tell against political participation. Many studies have shown that the youngest segment of the electorate, in general those under age 35, tends to participate less in most forms of political activity. At the time of the 1970 census, the proportion of young voters in the American electorate was above average, although the differences were not very great. The gap increased notably by the 1980 census, due in part to reluctance in a few European nations to lower the voting age to 18 but primarily to the 'bulge' of young people entering the American electorate in the late 1960s and the 1970s. This demographic change, as we shall discuss later, did increase the gap in turn-out between the United States and the other democracies. As late as 1970, however, the age gap was slight.

The picture of American political attitudes and demographic characteristics leads us to expect high levels of American voter participation. However, the institutional factors facing the American voters are for the most part highly inhibiting, compared with those in the other industrial nations.

The legal situation is of great importance. In some nations, legal sanctions are used to encourage voters to go to the polls. Such sanctions tend to increase voter turn-out.

Moreover, the registration laws make voting more difficult in the United States than in almost any other democracy. In 16 of the democracies examined, initiative for registering eligible voters is taken by the government in some fashion. In Australia and New Zealand the citizens must take the initiative; however, they are legally required to do so, and subject to fines or other penalties for failing to register. Of the 20 democracies outside the United States, only France leaves voter registration to voluntary initiative of citizens. In France citizens are required to register in their community and to obtain identification cards, which facilitates voter registration. In the United States registration is entirely the responsibility of the citizens and no set of require-ments brings them to the registration site. Moreover, although the residency requirement in the United States has now been limited to 30 days before a federal election, only a handful of states with small populations have day-of-voting registration. Other states vary greatly in their registration hours and places, and in the degree to which these facilitate registration, but all require the voter to re-register if he or she has changed residence since the last election. As the 1980 census showed that 47 percent of the population had moved in the past five years, it would seem that about half the eligible citizens must, in effect, make a double effort to vote in a presidential election: first the effort to register, then to vote.

A feature of the institutional context is the competitive context. Intuitively, it would seem that in elections in which the outcome was expected to be close, citizens would feel more reason to participate and, perhaps more importantly, party organizations and activists would feel more incentive to get their voters to the polls.

Two possible aspects of such competition are examined. First, considering the frequency with which control of the national chief executive, by a party or coalition of parties, changed after an election in the twenty-year period from 1961 through 1980, there is no doubt that the environment of the American presidential election was among the most competitive in any democracy. In the United States, party control of the presidency changed hands following four of the six elections between 1960 and 1980. However, there were few changes in party control of the national legislature in the United States in this period, with the Democrats maintaining control of the House and losing control of the Senate only in 1980.

The second aspect of competitiveness concerns the possible influence of the electoral constituencies on competition in different parts of a country. The electoral constituencies help determine whether parties and voters have equal incentive to get voters to the polls in all parts of the country, or whether there may be reason to neglect less evenly balanced regions in turning out the vote. Where the chief executive is chosen by simple majority or plurality vote, all regions should be equally important (e.g. France). In countries where the chief executive is chosen by the legislature, as in the various parliamentary systems, the question becomes the nature of the constituencies electing the legislators. With proportional representation from the nation as a whole or from large districts, parties have an incentive to mobilize everywhere. With single-member districts, some areas may be written off as hopeless.

Another important aspect of the partisan context is the linkage between political parties and social groups. For a variety of reasons, we expect voter turn-out to be higher in countries having sharper partisan-group differentials in support. Partisan choice should seem simpler to the less involved; cues from the personal environment of the individual (friends, family, and co-workers) should be more consistent; party organizers can more easily identify their potential supporters in making appeals and in helping voters to the polls on election day. In some countries, as in Sweden or the Netherlands, to know a voter's occupation or religion enables us to predict his or her voting preference to a very great degree. In Sweden in 1964, for example, about 84 percent of those with manual labor occupations supported the Social Democrats or the Communists, while only about 32 percent of the voters with white-collar or farm occupations did so, yielding a 'class voting' index of 52. In the United States in the same year the manual labor support for the Democrats exceeded white-collar support by only about 17 percent.

The party-group support differentials in the United States were only about half as great as those in the average democracy. In fact, the United States had one of the lowest levels of party-group support of any modern democracy. As the bases of the old Roosevelt coalition continued to crumble during the last twenty years, the vote scores on party-group differences fell even faster than these numbers, based on party identification, would indicate.

While the party-group linkage measure seems to tap an important feature of the party system for voting mobilization, it would be desirable to have explicit measures of the strength of comparative party organizations. We would expect dense, penetrative, nationally-oriented party organizations to be most effective in getting voters to the polls in national elections.

The American party system is slightly above average in the sheer magnitude and extensiveness of party organization, but highly decentralized and with very weak ties to other social organizations. The results regarding extensiveness are interesting, but most of the major parties scored close to the maximum on the measures reported. There was not much variation across nations on the variable; the slight American advantage resulted from weak scores by some of the smaller parties in multiparty systems.

The measures of centralization and organizational ties between parties and social organizations, called 'penetration' in the Janda study, differentiate the democracies more sharply. The American parties are highly decentralized, especially in the selection of legislative candidates. On a combined measure of organizational structure, funding, and candidate selection, the United States ranks lowest of the twelve modern democracies in the degree of centralization. On the 'penetration' measure, examining the ties between parties and such organizations as trade unions, religious bodies, and ethnic groups, the American parties ranked ahead of only the Irish parties. This measure seems to be the organizational counterpart of the party-group linkage measure based on partisan behavior, and empirically is closely related to it. The lesser capacity of American parties to make use of other social organizations to spread their messages and to get voters to the polls would hinder their mobilization efforts.

The institutional environment for voting in the United States in comparison with other democracies is the inverse of our description of the cultural environment. With few exceptions (age structure and political trust), the evidence on American political culture suggests that it should facilitate all kinds of individual political activity. With one exception (experience of party changes in national control of the executive), the institutional factors would seem to make the act of voting more difficult, and to impede the ability of parties and activists to mobilize supporters through appeals or through election day efforts to get them to the voting booth.

Estimating the impact of individual and institutional variables on voter turn-out

While the evidence [above] suggests reasons for America's exceptional pattern of an involved, but nonvoting citizenry, we need much more precise estimates of the relative importance of factors at the individual and system levels believed to affect voting.

Comparisons of American voter turn-out

The first step is to measure American voter turn-out in comparative perspective. In comparison with other democracies, the United States has relatively low participation of its citizens in major national elections. Average turn-out in presidential elections in the United States as a percentage of the voting-age population was 54 percent in the period from 1972 to 1980. In the other 20 industrialized democracies the average turn-out was 80 percent. American national voter participation exceeds only that of Switzerland. Among the nations that did not have compulsory voting, average voter turn-out was 77 percent of the population of voting age, nearly 50 percent higher than turn-out in the United States.

These comparisons rely on official reports of votes in the election that determines most directly the control of the chief executive. In the United States and France, these are presidential elections; in the other industrialized democracies, the most comparable elections are for the national legislature.

An important point to recognize about American voter turn-out in comparative perspective is its close relation to voter registration. The United States is unique in the low registration rate of its population of voting age. Comparisons of turn-out as percentages of either voting-age or registered populations lead to similar numbers in most countries, but radically different ones in the United States. In the United States perhaps two-thirds of eligible citizens are registered; of the other democracies, only in Switzerland are less than 90 percent of the citizens of voting age registered.

In most countries voter turn-out changed little from the 1960s to the 1970s, remaining rather stable from election to election. In the United States, however, turn-out dropped notably, for reasons various scholars have discussed elsewhere. These changes only served to widen the gap in electoral participation between the United States and the other democracies. They did not create the gap.

Aggregate-level explanations of voter turn-out

Voter turn-out in the United States is severely inhibited by its institutional context. The only feature of the institutional context where the United States seemed to enjoy a clear-cut advantage was in the frequent changes in chief executive – a variable that was insignificant in each decade in the aggregate analysis. The US was disadvantaged by voluntary registration, unevenly competitive electoral districts, and very weak linkages (perceptual and organizational) between parties and social groups. The distance of 23 points between American party-group linkages and those in the average democracy would alone have been predicted to depress turn-out by about 10 percent.

These models also work very similarly if we use turn-out as a percent of the registered electorate as the dependent variable. The major difference is a reversal in sign of the automatic registration variable. That is, the presence of automatic registration facilitates voting participation of the age-eligible population, but leads to lower turn-out among the registered. Such effects probably reflect the differing degrees of interest and partisanship required to enter the pool of the registered in the two kinds of registration situations. It is consistent with the well-known fact that turn-out of registered voters is actually very high in the United States.

While comparable education statistics were not available, I did attempt to use a measure of the percent of the labor force in white-collar occupations to get at the greater socio-economic resources and skills available in some populations. The white-collar variable was positively related to aggregate levels of political discussion. However, the percent white-collar was negatively related to voter turn-out. The effects of the white-collar variable in mobilizing awareness are not sufficient to make an impact on turn-out in the aggregate data analysis.

The variables for intranational constituencies that enhance competition, and those for party-group linkage are getting at some institutional property of the systems that affect turn-out. But these two variables are themselves related, and both are related to party organizational structure – especially party penetration of social groups. The party organization variables are not entered in the models, because of the limited number of cases and dubious nature of the data. If we do analyze those twelve countries for which we have rather doubtful data, we find that centralization and penetration of social groups are strongly associated with turn-out and with party-group linkage. In multiple regression analysis, however, party-group linkage tends to reduce the impact of centralization and penetration to insignificance. Given the measurement problems, it is unwise to be confident about which of these aspects of the party and electoral system are the ones shaping turn-out.

Individual-level explanations of voter turn-out

Our analysis of voter turn-out at the individual level relies on comparative survey studies. We would like to know two things. First, are the processes of voter involvement in the United States similar to those in other countries despite the differences in context? Second, if not, are there reasonably similar processes operating in other democracies, so that we could estimate the relative importance of various individual-level variables if the United States did have electoral and party contexts more comparable to those in other countries?

In the United States there is on average no increased probability of voting as we move from sixth grade to ninth grade education, but an increase of 10 percent as we move from ninth grade to the eleventh grade, and another 17 percent for actually completing high school. Turn-out among the college educated is 35 percent greater than among those with a primary education only. We can compare these sharp education effects with the average effects in the other eight nations: a consistent, but small, increase of 2–3 percent as we move up the comparable categories, with turn-out among the college educated only 10 percent higher than among those with a primary education. The American voter participation process is obviously far more affected by education levels than the process in other nations.

Not only education, but age, shows a different relationship to voter turn-out in the United States and the other countries. In the United States, each age increment shows increased probability of voting. In the other nations, the effects are very great going from the first to the second age group, but quite weak thereafter. On the other hand, the effect of party identification on voter turn-out, and on discussion, is about the same in the United States as in the European average. Women voted somewhat less often than men in the United States, while the average difference was very small in other countries. Political discussion showed a sex gap in all countries, but the American difference was much less than that in the other democracies.

The comparison of averages does, of course, blur differences among the non-American nations. Moreover, we need clearer evidence on the attitudinal processes involved in getting voters to the polls. In Table 3.4(1) we see individual participation models for the eight nations in the 1973–76 Political Action study plus Canada in 1974, and including measures of interest and efficacy variables used in many American studies. The top of the table shows, again, the increased amount of voting participation expected from each increment of education, controlling for interest and efficacy as well for sex, age, and party identification. Toward the bottom of the table we see the predictions for interest and efficacy. Each of the nine nations is presented separately, as we are not controlling for system-level effects.

The data in Table 3.4(1) are complex, but rich in information. The first point to note is that the individual voter participation processes in Austria and, especially, Italy (shown at the far right of the table) are rather different from those in the other countries. The attitudinal variables, particularly interest, but also efficacy, education, and even party identification, have much less effect in these two countries. It seems likely that voter participation in Austria and Italy is dominated primarily by institutional effects. Both countries have substantial compulsory voting, and Austria has an extremely well-organized and penetrative party system, so these patterns are not too surprising. Moreover, the extremely high reported turn-out levels of 95 percent leave limited room for attitudinal effects to have play.

The second point to note about Table 3.4(1) is that the six 'middle' countries, with automatic registration but without compulsory voting, manifest voter process models that seem rather similar. Naturally, we do find substantial variation – as we would expect from the measurement and language

Table 3.4(1) *Individual-level explanations of voter turn-out: Predicting the increase in probability of voting from demographic and attitudinal variables in nine nations*

Independent variables	Predicted increment in voter turn-out relative to base-line group (%)								
	USA	BRIT	WGER	NETH	SWITZ	FIN	CAN	AUST	ITALY
Education Level									
Basic	—	—	—	—	—	—	—	—	—
Lower	−5	−3	0	−1	10*	−3	1	1	0
Extended Lower	2	−2	2	2	7*	0	5	1	3
Middle	15*	1	4	7	9*	5	9*	−0	0
Post-Secondary	21*	6	3	7	15*	4	5	2	−4
Sex									
Male	—	—	—	—	—	—	—	—	—
Female	−3	1	−0	8*	−4	0	−0	1	0
Age									
20–25	—	—	—	—	—	—	—	—	—
26–29	10*	12*	14*	13*	9*	25*	3	40*	48*
30–39	19*	26*	16*	9*	16*	32*	6	39*	51*
40–49	23*	36*	15*	15*	23*	31*	15*	40*	51*
50–59	29*	34*	16*	19*	25*	35*	10*	40*	52*
60+	37*	33*	15*	21*	20*	35*	15*	40*	52*
Party Identification									
No	—	—	—	—	—	—	—	—	—
Yes	13*	24*	8*	33*	21*	9*	4*	4*	3*
Political Interest									
Not at All	—	—	—	—	—	—	—	—	—
Not Much	17*	9*	5*	8*	19*	9*	24*	2	2
Somewhat	30*	15*	7*	12*	34*	15*	34*	1	4*
Very	32*	18*	8*	8*	33*	14*	36*	2	−0
Political Efficacy									
Low	—	—	—	—	—	—	—	—	—
Mixed	6*	3	2	2	8*	1	−1	1	−3*
High	9*	6*	1	7*	6	−0	−0	1	−4*
Reported Turn-out (%)	74	79	94	85	59	90	82	96	95

*Indicates that turn-out of group was significantly above base-line group (.05). N of cases from 1030 to 2149.

differences, the rather small subgroups in some categories, and the very high reported turn-out levels (over 90 percent in Germany and Finland). But in each country we see sharp, slightly curvi-linear effects of political interest and, less consistently, efficacy.

Considering the American model in comparison with the other six nations without compulsory voting suggests both commonality and difference. On the one hand, attitudinal effects are rather similar. Party identification has an effect which falls about at the average of the other democracies. Interest is similar in strength, if on the higher side, and similar in its curvilinearity (not much impact by the increase from 'somewhat' to 'very' interested). Efficacy has an effect in the United States that is somewhat above the democratic average. Sex is insignificant in its effect on turn-out after attitudinal variables are taken into account.

On the other hand, the direct effects of age and, especially, education are much greater in the United States than in any of the other countries. The age variable is notable for its continuing impact as we move to increasingly older groups. The impact is about average as citizens age from 20 to 39, but continues in the US, while becoming weaker in the higher age categories elsewhere.

Most distinctive of all is the direct impact of education on American voter turn-out. While the effect of education is reduced somewhat with interest and efficacy in the model, the direct effects are still quite powerful, with high school graduation worth 13 percent and college work another 6 percent. Not only does the United States have the most educated citizenry, but education has much more direct impact on voter turn-out. It seems very likely, although we cannot demonstrate it directly, that the difficulty of registration in America is also responsible for this remarkable distinctiveness of American voting processes. The great weakness of the party system in its organization and linkage to social groups may also enhance the value of personal characteristics and resources.

Of course, the overwhelming point to make about individual-level explanations together with the evidence on the cultural environment is that they all lead us to expect high voter turn-out in the United States. The American electorate is highly educated, has above average levels of party identification, and is more interested and more efficacious than citizens in other democracies. The relatively low levels of trust are not as important as these other American advantages.

These individual-level modelling efforts redirect our attention to contextual factors operating largely, it would seem, at the national level. It is possible, of course, that incorporation of attitudinal and demographic variables here unmeasured would succeed in explaining the differences across nations in level of voter turn-out. But the comparisons with political discussion suggest that the present variables, at least, are being measured fairly well, and that they do not account for the relatively low levels of American voter participation.

Estimating the effects of cultural and institutional setting on relative American voter turn-out levels

Beginning with the individual-level variables, we have estimated the increment to turn-out created by increased levels of party identification, education, interest, and efficacy.

Over all, the United States is advantaged by its political culture. If the average democracy had a political culture as facilitating to voter turn-out as American education and attitudes, we would expect turn-out to increase by about 5 percent.

If the other democracies had the American levels on competition-encouraging constituencies and party-group linkages, their turn-out would be predicted to decrease by about 13 percent. The weak American linkages between parties and groups (and the associated weak party organizations) would reduce turn-out by 10 percent. The low competitiveness of some American electoral constituencies would reduce turn-out by about 3 percent. The age level increased turn-out in the 1960s by a small amount, but decreased it about 2 percent in the 1970s, with the American lowering of voting age and the age bulge among the young. The net effect of all the variables is to lower turn-out by about 10 percent, the American attitudinal advantage being outweighed by the institutional disadvantage on a 13 to 5 basis, with age adding another 2 percent disadvantage.

If we make the more heroic assumption that adopting automatic registration would create an American voting process like those in the other democracies, we would predict, then, that such registration would lead to American turn-out levels some 10 percent below those of the cross-national averages. Recalling that turn-out in the countries without compulsory voting (other than Switzerland) averaged 80 percent, we see that such changes would mean American turn-out of the age-eligible would be increased from 54 percent to 70 percent. The presence of resident aliens, ineligible to vote, would limit this by at least 2 percent, to about 68 percent. The US would still have one of the lowest turn-out levels of any democracy, but the gap would be far less.

In comparison to present American voter turn-out levels, the analysis implies that if the United States adopted automatic registration, or something similar, turn-out might be increased by 14 percent. This estimate is not inconsistent with that predicting that voter turn-out in the early 1970s would have increased by about 9 percent if all states had had registration laws as facilitating as those in the most permissive states. It also fits reasonably well with the fact that average turn-out in states with election-day registration in the 1980 election was about 66 percent, some 13 percent above the national average. None of these states, of course, had automatic or compulsory registration.

Getting most American citizens registered would lead to a major increase in American voter turn-out. However, the present analysis suggests that it would not lead the US to overtake most other democracies in voter turn-out.

The attitudinal characteristics that enhance participation in the US have declined sharply since the early 1960s. These individual characteristics are particularly important for voting in the American context. The attitudinal advantages partially compensated for the difficult US registration conditions in the 1960s, but not in the 1970s.

Abridged from G. Bingham Powell, Jr. (1986), 'American voter turnout in comparative perspective,' *American Political Science Review*, LXXX, pp. 17–35. Reprinted by permission of the author and the American Political Science Association.

3.5 Democrats and Republicans: what's the difference?

Howard Reiter

One of the most confusing aspects of American politics is the lack of apparent difference between the major parties. There is less ideological distance between the Democrats and the Republicans than there is between major parties in other industrialized capitalist states. Both parties advocate corporate capitalism (despite some farfetched conservative rhetoric about liberal Democrats being socialists), both accept the values of liberal capitalism and the decentralized American state that fits those values, and both espouse the premise that American military power should be deployed around the world to protect what the president and his advisers deem the national interests of the United States to be.

Within the bounds of a shared commitment to liberal capitalist values and corporate capitalist reality there are indeed interparty differences. They are not as fundamental as the differences between parties in other nations, but they are real nonetheless. The term 'liberal' is used to denote those who are more favorable to the use of government, and especially of the federal government, to promote certain broad goals: greater equality among the classes, among the races, and between the genders; as well as regulation of business to promote environmentalism and occupational health and safety, and to discourage job discrimination and corporate mergers. Liberals also tend to emphasize civil rights and civil liberties, from affirmative action to abortion rights, more than conservatives do. In recent years, liberals tend toward a foreign policy that emphasizes diplomacy and human rights and is less oriented toward high Pentagon budgets and military action abroad, although this is a very crude generalization. 'Conservatives' are those who want to keep the government, especially in Washington, out of the areas of public policy just mentioned, and away from the kinds of economic regulation opposed by business. They are relatively unconcerned with equalitarianism, civil rights, and civil liberties, and some are inclined to use governmental power to enforce moral values such as banning pornography and abortion and promoting school prayer. Conservatives usually favor high Pentagon budgets and are often more inclined than liberals to use military power abroad.

Perceptions of differences

Do the American people discern any significant differences between the major parties? The answer to this in itself does not prove whether or not there are any real differences; perhaps the public thinks there are real differences when there are none, or maybe the people fail to see that there are such differences in reality.

From 1952 until 1976, about half the population saw [important] differences [between the parties]. Since 1980 that proportion has risen to about 60 percent. Two out of three people who saw any differences between the parties, mentioned something related to social class. Within this category, the most frequent references were to the Democrats being the party of working people or the Republicans being the party of the wealthy or of big business. I have also included in this category references to social programs associated with class interests, such as Social Security and welfare. Although the Democrats do not serve the real interests of the working class, a sizable majority of Americans believed that there were significant class differences between the parties.

In addition, about a third of the people who thought there were differences mentioned government spending, and most of them said that the Republicans were more frugal than the Democrats. About one in four people said that the parties differed ideologically, with the Democrats usually called more liberal than the Republicans. A similar proportion cited foreign policy issues, considering the Republicans more in favor of a stronger defence. But clearly class was the major area in mind when people had to say what distinguished the parties from each other.

Almost two-thirds of the people who had something positive to say about the Democratic party included a reference to its association with average or working people, and a majority of those who made negative references to the Republican party cited its association with the privileged classes.

Ideologically, the Republicans are seen as truer to the traditional American values of liberal capitalism and limited government. The fact that many more Americans call themselves conservatives than liberals, and even many people who favor most of the liberal agenda call themselves conservatives, helps the Republicans. In the 1988 campaign both Bush and Dukakis assumed that the liberal label was a kiss of death, as Bush repeatedly tried to pin Dukakis with it, while the Democratic nominee tried to insist that the campaign was not about ideology. In 1988 the Republicans even had an edge in an area in which Democrats traditionally have shone – management of the economy.

A majority of Americans perceive that there are important differences between the parties and that each party has its strong points. The Democrats are seen as far more receptive to the needs of the common people, while the Republicans are seen as ideologically preferable and better managers of government, the economy, and foreign policy. Some political scientists believe that these comparisons help explain why the Republicans have been more successful in recent years at winning the White House, where their skills are more appropriate, while the Democrats have held on to Congress, the branch of the government which is supposed to represent the people.

Differences between the rank and file

Demographic differences
The parties differ in the social background of their [identifiers]. The Democratic party is especially attractive to Hispanics, blacks, Jews, the elderly, and those of lower socioeconomic status. Republicans attract white Protestants and the higher socioeconomic classes. Young voters are most likely to call themselves independents.

Unlike parties in other competitive capitalist regimes, American parties have more effectively divided the population along sectional, racial, and religious lines than along class lines. The extent to which American parties' coalitions are based on section, race, and religion can be illustrated by a simple comparison: in 1988, nearly half of all Republicans were northern white Protestants, while only one-fifth of Democrats were northern white Protestants. Franklin D. Roosevelt's New Deal introduced an unprecedented degree of social class to American party alignments. According to James Sundquist, Roosevelt's successor Harry Truman was the last Democratic presidential contender to use explicit class appeals. As a consequence, the upper classes have tended to divide their loyalties between the parties, and the Democratic party has since become a middle-class party like the Republican.

Even in the heyday of the New Deal, when class differences between the parties were at their apex, the Democrats were unable to represent the real interests of the working class, bound as that party was to corporate capitalism. Since that time the Democrats have been even less oriented to working-class demands. There are indeed real social differences between the parties, but less along the crucial dimension of social class than along other lines.

Ideological differences
Democrats tend to be liberal; Republicans, conservative. Nearly four times as many self-described liberals identified with the Democrats as with the Republicans, and more than twice as many self-labeled conservatives identified with the Republicans as with the Democrats.

More particularly, Democrats and Republicans have often been farthest apart on the class-oriented issues. In 1988, the widest gaps between the adherents of different parties were on the issues of government services, health care, unemployment, a government guarantee of jobs and living standards, and funding for Star Wars – all but the last class-oriented issues. On the other hand, the smallest differences between the parties were on abortion, school prayer, the environment, and drugs – none of them essentially class issues.

Table 3.5(1) *Members of Congress serving in 1987 and whether they received more contributions to their most recent campaign from corporate or labour political action committees*

	All	Republicans	Democrats	Non-Southern Democrats	Southern Democrats
Senators	69%	98%	45%	32%	76%
More from corporations	30	2	53	66	24
More from labor	1	0	2	3	0
Accepted no contributions	100	100	100	101	100
Total	100	45	55	38	17
Number of members					
Representatives					
More from corporations	65%	96%	44%	29%	78%
More from labor	34	3	54	70	21
Accepted no contributions	1	1	1	1	1
Total	100	100	99	100	100
Number of members	434	177	257	176	81

Note: Percentages do not always sum to 100 due to rounding. Data were missing for one representative.
Source: Michael Barone and Grant Ujifusa, *The Almanac of American Politics 1988* (Washington: National Journal, 1987).

Interest-group support

We can look at contributions to the campaigns of the members of Congress who were serving in 1987. A sizable majority of members received more money from corporations than from labor; Table 3.5(1) breaks down these contributions between Democrats and Republicans. Nearly every Republican in both houses received more donations from corporations than from labor, while Democrats in both houses were divided roughly in half. We can see striking sectional differences between southern and non-southern Democrats. Most southern Democrats were backed more by corporations than by labor, while most northern Democrats received more from labor than from corporations. Interparty differences on this important dimension are reduced by the presence in the Democratic party of a sizable conservative wing concentrated in the south-east.

The pro-business bias of political action committees is understated when we examine only corporate and labor PACs. Because most of the well-heeled trade association and related PACs, such as those representing doctors and realtors, also have a conservative orientation, we can add that category to corporate PACs to get a fuller picture. Because not all trade association and related PACs are conservative, this method is somewhat imprecise. Combining such PACs with corporate PACs increases the number of Democratic senators whose contributions came more from business-oriented sources than from labor, from twenty-five to thirty-four. In the House, the increase is from 284 to 338 representatives, most of that increase (fifty out of fifty-four) also being among Democrats. The net result is to put substantially more Democrats into the pro-business category, and reduce the differences between the parties still further.

Again, there appears to be some difference between the parties on a class-related dimension. Here, however, we can for the first time see the difference-blurring effect of the heterogeneity of the Democratic party, whose southern members are in this instance closer to the Republicans than to their fellow partisans outside the South.

Platforms and campaigns

By common impression, party platforms and candidates' speeches are full of empty rhetoric and meaningless promises that are ignored as soon as candidates are elected. Do the parties routinely fail to offer the electorate meaningful guides about the future during campaigns?

Platforms
Gerald Pomper[1] has analyzed both parties' platforms sentence by sentence from 1944 through 1976 and classified platform sentences into four categories:

1 *Rhetoric.* These statements, totally useless to the reader who is trying to figure out what the party wants to do, comprised about 17 percent of the average platform.
2 *General evaluations of the past.* Vague assertions about the past four years comprised another 12 percent of platforms.
3 *Specific policy statements about the past.* These more explicit remarks presumably help the voter tell what kinds of policies are likely to be maintained or changed, and they comprised 19 percent of platforms.
4 *Pledges for the future.* These are presumably the most helpful kinds of statements in a platform for a voter, and they comprised about 52 percent of all the sentences in an average platform. However, future pledges can · be general or specific.

Pomper concluded that roughly half of platform statements can help the voter reach a rational decision, but when he wanted to see if pledges were being carried out, Pomper found that fewer than a third of platform sentences were specific enough to test.

The parties differed in the issues they stressed. Democrats were more likely to discuss labor and social welfare, while Republicans concentrated more on military policy and government management. Each party stresses its areas of strength, with Democrats emphasizing class-related issues and Republicans concentrating on others. Democrats' pledges were most popular in the areas of social welfare and natural resources, while Republican pledges were closest to public opinion in the areas of civil rights and government management.[2]

Do party platforms differ? Pomper found that there were three times as many bipartisan pledges – those in which both parties took the same position – as conflicting pledges. The latter were most likely to occur on issues related to labor, followed by social welfare, economic policy, and natural resources. The area of least conflict between the parties' platforms was civil rights, followed by government management and military policy. Again, class-related issues seem disproportionately to differentiate the parties. Finally, Pomper reported that about two-thirds of platform pledges are carried out, a ratio that rises to three-quarters for the party that controls the White House. However, in recent years the proportion of pledges fulfilled has dropped, perhaps suggesting the problems of policy management during times of difficulty for corporate capitalism.

Pomper concluded that a party's platform is important 'not as an inspired gospel to which politicians resort for policy guidance. It is important because it summarizes, crystallizes, and presents to the voters the character of the party coalition'.

Table 3.5(2)   *ADA/ACU scores of members of Congress, 1990**

	All	Republicans	Democrats	Non-Southern Democrats	Southern Democrats
Senators	33	33	0	0	0
0–29 (conservative)	34	11	23	10	13
30–75 (moderate)	33	1	32	29	3
76–100 (liberal)	100	45	55	39	16
Total					
Representatives					
0–32.1 (conservative)	144	134	10	0	10
32.2–78.5 (moderate)	144	41	103	48	55
78.6–100 (liberal)	144	1	143	129	14
Total	432	176	256	177	79

*Each house is divided into three approximately equal parts based on the score, and the table shows the number of members in each third.
Note: Data are missing for three representatives due to vacancies or to the fact that the Speaker ordinarily does not vote. I am indebted to Julie McGivern Walsh for helping with this analysis.

Campaigns

There is a well-known phenomenon of political campaigns in which both parties' nominees begin to converge to the point on the policy spectrum where they think most voters are.

Worried about being perceived as too liberal and spendthrift, in the 1980s the Democrats dropped their earlier calls for such programs as national health insurance and insisted, in Dukakis's words, that the campaign [was] about competence and not ideology. Even the traditionally liberal Walter Mondale made it clear, in calling for higher taxes in 1984, that all of the funds raised would be used to reduce the deficit rather than for social spending. While Dukakis was certainly liberal on civil liberties issues, his main campaign theme was to revitalize the economy, not to create programs tailored to help the economically oppressed, as earlier Democrats had done.

Worried about being labelled warmongers and hardhearted, Republicans have down-played their ideology in campaigns. Rather than play up his often extreme views, Reagan stressed the state of the economy in 1980 and 1984. In 1988, Bush called for a 'kinder, gentler nation' and insisted that he would be 'the environmental president' and 'the education president'.

The convergence of candidates during campaigns is one of the primary reasons why American parties often seem to offer little choice to the electorate.

Congressional voting

Americans for Democratic Action (ADA) is a liberal group that selects a handful of what it considers the most important votes in each session of Congress, and rates each member of Congress on those votes. Someone who voted the ADA way on every vote gets a rating of 100, and someone who opposed ADA on every vote (or was absent) is rated zero. The American Conservative Union (ACU) does the same thing, except that it rates conservatives high and liberals low. Therefore members of Congress who get high ADA ratings are likely to get low ACU ratings, and vice versa.

For the congressional session of 1990, I have combined the ADA and ACU ratings for each member. Mathematically, the new 'ADA/ACU Score' can be represented by:

$$[ADA + (100 - ACU)]/2$$

The higher the ADA/ACU Score, the more liberal the senator or representative.

In each house the great majority of Republicans are located in the most conservative third of the spectrum and the Democrats are clustered in the liberal third. Southern Democrats occupy a centrist position and their northern counterparts are heavily concentrated at the liberal end. [See Table 3.5(2).]

In the exceptions to these generalizations, we can see some of the geographic divisions within the parties. Northeasterners comprised nearly two-

Table 3.5(3)   *Mean ADA/ACU scores, 1990, by party and section*

	All	Northeast	Southeast	Midwest	Far West
Senators					
Democrats	77	88	62	79	79
Republicans	23	39	8	21	22
Difference	54	49	54	58	57
Representatives					
Democrats	76	85	57	81	89
Republicans	23	41	14	20	17
Difference	53	44	43	61	72

Note: Data are missing for three representatives due to vacancies or to the fact that the Speaker ordinarily does not vote. I am indebted to Julie McGivern Walsh for helping with this analysis.

thirds of the moderate and liberal Republicans in the House in 1990, and almost half of those in the Senate. The most conservative House Democrats outside the South were disproportionately from the Midwest, and in the Senate they were from the great plains and Far West. Within the South, the most liberal members tended to be from the so-called rim or peripheral southern states, Arkansas, Florida, Kentucky, North Carolina, Tennessee, Texas, and Virginia, rather than the Deep South.

Table 3.5(3) shows the mean ADA/ACU Score for each party in each section of the country. In both houses, southern Democrats stand out as their party's most conservative group, and in the Senate, the northeasterners are the most liberal Democrats. Among Republicans in both houses, northeasterners are the most liberal and southerners the most conservative. The last line of each section of Table 3.5(3) also enables us to see how far apart the parties are in each region.

On what issues are the congressional parties most likely to differ? In 1981, the *National Journal* began to analyze the votes in Congress, dividing them among economic, 'social' (non-economic domestic issues such as affirmative action and gun control), and foreign policy issues. While the gap between the parties in the House tended to remain about the same regardless of issue area throughout the 1980s, in the Senate interparty differences on economic issues were almost always greater than on other types of policy.

On many issues the congressional parties often vote dissimilarly, despite the weakness of party leadership in Congress. Party leadership is not strong enough by itself to compel Democrats and Republicans to unite against each other. What then is the glue that binds the congressional parties? One factor is the different kinds of constituencies that each party represents.

There is another reason. In most parts of the country, a politically ambitious liberal will join the Democratic party, just as a politically ambitious conservative will become a Republican. There is a self-selected recruitment process going on, and it explains much of the difference between the congressional parties.

Economic policy

Even if the parties differ in their mass bases, their interest group allies, their campaign pledges, and their voting patterns in Congress, the sceptical reader might still wonder whether the parties really do produce different policies. I discuss three major economic policies: the size of the budget for social services and the management of inflation and unemployment.

We might expect from the earlier findings of this chapter that the parties will indeed handle these policies differently. Or, as Richard Rose has written, 'much of a party's record in office will be stamped upon it by forces outside its control.'[3]

Social spending, unemployment and inflation

Numerous studies have concluded that those capitalist nations that have been most often governed by parties at the left end of the spectrum have increased the public budget the most, especially in the area of social services such as health, welfare, education, housing, and so forth. Moreover, some studies have concluded that capitalist nations governed by parties of the left have a more equal distribution of income than those governed by parties of the right; if this is true, it may be a consequence of the more generous social programs.

Within the United States, have the Democrats and Republicans produced different levels of social spending? The problem for analysis is that the budget is determined by an interplay of the president with Congress. When they have been controlled by different parties, as has been the case for 28 of the 46 years from 1947 through 1992, it becomes difficult to single out the impact of each party. Another problem is that some social spending is determined by laws of eligibility established years earlier. The most conspicuous examples are Social Security and Medicare, whose steep increases in spending are due in large part to the aging of the American population and cost-of-living increases.

Table 3.5(4) shows the spending by the federal government on human services, minus Social Security and Medicare, in every presidential election year since the end of World War II. To some extent, we can see evidence of the effects of partisanship, with all of the large increases occurring in the years of undivided Democratic control of Congress from 1955 through 1980. Two of the smallest increases occurred when the Democrats lost control of at least one house, in the early 1950s and the 1980s. On the other hand, two of the declines in social spending occurred when the Democrats controlled both the White House and Congress, during the Truman and Carter administrations.

The clearest picture comes when we ignore the parties on the left side of

Table 3.5(4)   *Federal spending on human resources, minus Social Security and Medicare (in millions of 1982–1984 dollars)*

Year	Party of president, prior 4 years	Party controlling Congress, prior 4 years	Amount	Percent change
1948	Democratic	Mixed	$38,645	
1952	Democratic	Democratic	36,453	− 5.7
1956	Republican	Mixed	38,891	+ 6.7
1960	Republican	Democratic	49,185	+26.5
1964	Democratic	Democratic	60,130	+22.3
1968	Democratic	Democratic	88,695	+47.5
1972	Republican	Democratic	142,444	+60.6
1976	Republican	Democratic	200,054	+40.4
1980	Democratic	Democratic	197,725	− 1.2
1984	Republican	Mixed	188,624	− 4.6
1988	Republican	Mixed	198,967	+ 5.5

Source: *Budget of the United States Government, Fiscal Year 1992* (Washington: Government Printing Office, 1991), Part 7, pp. 31–36.

the table and just concentrate on the last two columns. Social spending shot up higher and higher until its peak in the early 1970s, and since then it has dropped and levelled off.

While it would be foolhardy to ignore, for example, the role of Reagan and the Republican Senate in the early 1980s, we should not forget the similar role played by Carter and the Democratic Congress in the late 1970s. To a great extent, we are observing long-term trends that seem to have a momentum apart from short-term partisan fluctuations.

As important as spending is as a measure of government activism, it is only one such measure. Enforcement of civil rights laws, environmental regulations, and minimum wage legislation may not cost the government much in comparison with other programs, but they too can be important parts of the liberal agenda. Second, the level of spending in itself says nothing about whether *enough* is being spent.

In Table 3.5(5) we can see the average levels of unemployment and inflation during the administrations of every president since Harry Truman. The most obvious trend in the table is that over the long run both unemployment and inflation have been rising, regardless of who was president. This is part of the increasing difficulty of managing a corporate capitalist economy. Table 3.5(5) [provides] the change in each index over the previous administration's level, because each administration could only work with the levels of unemployment and inflation that it inherited. In nearly every instance, Democrats were better at holding down unemployment and Republicans more successful at

Table 3.5(5)   *Mean levels of unemployment and inflation, 1949–88, by party of the president*

Years	Presidents and party	Unemployment	Inflation
1949–1952	Truman (Democrat)	4.4%	2.6%
1953–1960	Eisenhower (Republican)	4.9	1.4
1961–1968	Kennedy, Johnson (Democrats)	4.9	2.1
1969–1976	Nixon, Ford (Republicans)	5.7	6.4
1977–1980	Carter (Democrat)	6.4	9.7
1981–1988	Reagan (Republican)	7.4	4.7

Source: The following editions of the *Statistical Abstract of the United States*, published by the Bureau of the Census: 1960, p. 205; 1965, pp. 216, 361; 1970, p. 213; 1984, p. 405; and 1990, pp. 378, 468.

combating inflation. Under Republicans Eisenhower and Reagan, unemployment rose over their predecessors' levels while inflation fell; under the Democratic Kennedy and Johnson administrations, unemployment held steady while inflation rose. Jimmy Carter's Democratic administration saw increases in both phenomena, but, as expected, inflation rose more than unemployment did. The only exception in the table was the Republican era of Nixon and Ford, when inflation shot up more than unemployment. This was probably due to the inflation caused by the war in south-east Asia and the oil exporters' embargo.

It appears that the levels of unemployment and inflation really are affected by the party of the president, while the level of social spending is much less influenced by the party in control of the White House or Congress.

The significance of party differences

Over time, have the parties grown closer together or farther apart? In several respects, the parties seem more polarized. The proportion of people who perceive important differences has been higher since 1980 than before; some scholars have found more differences between the views of party supporters since the 1960s, and Congress has seemed more polarized between the parties since 1981. Two related trends may account for much of this change: the movement of many white conservatives, especially in the South, out of the Democratic party; and the accession of Ronald Reagan, who was probably the most self-consciously ideological candidate ever to win the White House.

The best way to think of the differences between the parties is to bear in mind the concepts of accumulation and legitimacy. Capitalism requires that business firms accumulate sufficient funds for investment, and over time the government is called upon more and more to augment the resources of the private economy, whether through its own investment (for example, in transportation facilities), its policies (tax breaks and restrictions on imports), its contracts (the military establishment), and sometimes out-and-out financial aid (most recently the savings and loans). At the same time the government must keep the rest of the population satisfied that the system is legitimate and that everyone gets an even break from the American system. In particular, the lower classes must be kept from the kind of despair that can lead to revolution. Therefore government must persuade people to accept the dominant American values and provide social services for those in need.

To a great extent, the major American political parties have differed on which of these two imperatives they choose to emphasize. The Republicans have diligently sought to provide for the needs of big business. The Reagan and Bush administrations' policies exemplify this: tax breaks for the upper classes, reductions in many social programs, a tolerant eye toward corporate mergers and anti-labor practices, and a foreign policy that both lines the pockets of military contractors and seeks to repress foreign regimes and revolutionary movements that are unsympathetic to American investment abroad. On the other hand, the demand for legitimacy has limited some of these excesses to a greater degree than if Reagan and Bush had totally free rein.

The Democrats, on the other hand, have since the 1930s laid greater emphasis on legitimizing social programs than the Republicans have. Although the rate of increase in spending on such programs seems independent of which party is in power, Democratic administrations, notably those of Franklin Roosevelt and Lyndon Johnson, were responsible for *creating* those programs. At the same time, the dominance of liberal capitalist values and the need for accumulation keep the Democrats from producing an all-out welfare state of the sort found in Western Europe.

The Democrats' rightward drift is verified by surveys. In 1972 and 1976, more than 65 percent of the people who answered the question put the Democrats on the liberal side; in the 1980s, fewer than 60 percent did so. The Democrats move right, but the parties are seen as farther and farther apart. The paradox can be resolved fairly easily: there are still differences, perhaps even greater differences, between the parties, but both have shifted to the right since the late 1970s.

While parties in much of the rest of the capitalist world present to the voters genuine ideological and class differences, with some representing socialism and the working classes and others speaking for capitalism and the upper classes, American parties offer only a pale imitation. Even so, these muted differences have become the basis of whatever distinctions exist between the Democrats and Republicans.

Abridged from Howard Reiter (1993), *Parties and Elections in Corporate America*, 2nd edition, pp. 254–73. Reprinted by permission of Longman Publishing Group, New York.

Notes

1 Gerald M. Pomper with Susan S. Lederman, *Elections in America*, 2nd edn., Longman, New York, 1980, pp. 128–78.

2 Alan D. Monroe (1983), 'American party platforms and public opinion', *American Journal of Political Science*, XXVII, p. 35.

3 Richard Rose, *Do Parties Make a Difference?* Chatham House, Chatham, NJ, 1980, p. 141.

3.6   Safe seats and the congressman as 'errand boy'

Morris P. Fiorina

Between 1940 and 1970 congressional turnover continued to decline, although the change was slight compared to what had already occurred. During this period turnover declined from about one-fourth of the members of the House [of Representatives] to about one-sixth, even slipping below 10 percent in the election of 1968. (In 1974 turnover was comparatively high, 21 percent, but this figure was lower than that recorded in nine of ten elections between 1930 and 1950. And in 1976, turnover dropped back to about 15 percent.) What accounts for this contemporary decline? Changes in the congressional context offer no clues, and the increasing congressional membership stability occurs at a time when the electorate is growing increasingly volatile at the presidential level.

'Marginal' [or 'swing'] districts [are] those congressional districts not firmly in the camp of one party or the other. 'Safe' districts are those which are not marginal. Customarily, marginal districts are identified by victory percentages of 50–55 percent. In this range a particularly strong effort by a challenger, a weak effort by the incumbent, or a national swing against the incumbent's party may be enough to swing the district from one party's camp into the other's. In the recent past marginal districts have accounted for the bulk of the change in the membership in Congress – national swings such as those occurring in 1946 and 1964 exact a high toll in congressmen from such districts.

By the 1970s fewer and fewer districts fall in the swing or marginal range. More and more fall in the range that is quite comfortable – safe – for congressional incumbents. In 1972 fewer than 25 percent of the incumbents [of the House of Representatives] who ran won by less than a 60–40 margin. Using our 55 percent rule of thumb, 90 percent of all 1972 winners would be classified as safe, whereas only 75 percent would have been similarly classified following the 1948 election.

Congressional turnover has declined in the post-war period because the kind of district that produces the lion's share of that turnover is disappearing. This partial answer, however, raises two additional questions. First, why are the marginal districts disappearing? Second, why should anyone care?

The importance of marginal districts

Popular wisdom portrays the congressman as weak and vacillating, one who sways with every political breeze. But incumbent congressmen maintain a marked stability in their positions over time.[1] If you wish to know how a congressman is voting in 1970, the chances are very good that his 1960 voting record will tell you. *As a consequence, the only reliable way to achieve policy change in Congress is to change congressmen.* And here the marginal district enters.

The existence of marginal districts builds necessary responsiveness into the electoral system. Whether coming to Washington on the coattails of a popular president (1964) or over the bodies of the congressional victims of an unpopular one (1974), the marginal district congressmen constitute the electoral mandate. *As such [marginal] districts disappear we face the possibility of a Congress composed of professional officeholders oblivious to the changing political sentiments of the country.*

Explaining the vanishing marginals

Why are some districts marginal and others not? The disappearance of the marginals suggests that we examine two factors: (1) possible changes in the socioeconomic homogeneity of congressional districts, (2) possible changes in the effectiveness of congressional incumbents. We will consider the first possibility and reject it. [Instead] we will see how incumbents have managed to structure Washington influence relationships so as to make their re-elections ever more certain.

In all likelihood, since the New Deal era the average congressman's desire for re-election has remained constant. What has changed is the set of resources he possesses to invest in his re-election effort. Today's congressmen have more productive political strategies than previously. And these strategies are an unforeseen by-product of the growth of an activist federal government.

For every voter a congressman pleases by a policy stand he will displease someone else. The consequence is a more marginal district. But if we have incumbents who de-emphasize controversial policy positions and instead place heavy emphasis on nonpartisan, nonprogrammatic constituency service (for which demand grows as government expands), the resulting blurring of political friends and enemies is sufficient to shift the district out of the marginal camp. We do not need to postulate a congressman who is more interested in re-election today than previously. All we need postulate is a congressman sufficiently interested in re-election that he would rather be re-elected as an errand boy than not be re-elected at all.

For most of the twentieth century, congressmen have engaged in a mix of three kinds of activities: lawmaking, pork barrelling, and casework. Congress is first and foremost a lawmaking body, at least according to constitutional theory. A second activity favored by congressmen consists of efforts to bring home the bacon to their districts. The [federal] pork barrel [is] a term originally applied to rivers and harbors legislation but now generalized to cover all manner of federal largesse. Congressmen consider new dams, federal buildings, sewage treatment plants, urban renewal projects, etc. as sweet plums to be plucked. Federal projects are highly visible, their economic impact is easily detected by constituents, and sometimes they even produce something of value to the district. The workers hired and supplies purchased in connection with a big federal project provide benefits that are widely appreciated. The historical importance congressmen attach to the pork barrel is reflected in the rules of the House. That body accords certain classes of legislation 'privileged' status: they may come directly to the floor without passing through the Rules Committee, a traditional graveyard for legislation. What kinds of legislation are privileged? Taxing and spending bills, for one: the government's power to raise and spend money must be kept relatively unfettered. But in addition, the omnibus rivers and harbors bills of the Public Works Committee and public lands bills from the Interior Committee share privileged status. The House will allow a civil rights or defense procurement or environmental bill to languish in the Rules Committee, but it takes special precautions to insure that nothing slows down the approval of dams and irrigation projects.

[Casework, the] third major activity, takes up perhaps as much time as the other two combined. Traditionally, constituents appeal to their congressman for myriad favors and services. Sometimes only information is needed, but often constituents request that their congressman intervene in the internal workings of federal agencies to affect a decision in a favorable way, to reverse an adverse decision, or simply to speed up the glacial bureaucratic process.

Congressmen are in an almost unique position in our system, a position shared only with high-level members of the executive branch. Congressmen possess the power to expedite and influence bureaucratic decisions. This capability flows directly from congressional control over what bureaucrats value most: higher budgets and new program authorizations. In a very real sense each congressman is a monopoly supplier of bureaucratic unsticking services for his district.

From the standpoint of capturing voters, the congressman's lawmaking activities differ in two important respects from his pork-barrel and casework activities. First, programmatic actions are inherently controversial. A congressman will find his district divided on many major issues. Some constituents may applaud the congressman's civil rights record, but others believe integration is going too fast. Some advocate economic equality, others stew over welfare cheaters. On such policy matters the congressman can expect to make friends as well as enemies. Presumably he will behave so as to maximize the excess of the former over the latter, but nevertheless a policy stand will generally make some enemies.

In contrast, the pork barrel and casework are relatively less controversial. New federal projects bring jobs, shiny new facilities, and general economic prosperity, or so people believe. Republicans and Democrats, conservatives and liberals, all generally prefer a richer district to a poorer one. Of course, in recent years the river damming and stream-bed straightening activities of the Army Corps of Engineers have aroused some opposition among environmentalists. Congressmen happily reacted by absorbing the opposition and adding environmentalism to the pork barrel: water treatment plants are currently a hot congressional item. Casework is even less controversial.

In sum, when considering the benefits of his programmatic activities, the congressman must tote up gains and losses to arrive at a net profit. Pork barreling and casework, however, are basically pure profit.

A second way in which programmatic activities differ from casework and the pork barrel is the difficulty of assigning responsibility for the former as compared with the latter. No congressman can seriously claim that he is responsible for the 1964 Civil Rights Act or the 1972 Revenue Sharing Act. Most constituents do have some vague notion that their congressman is only one of hundreds and their senator one of an even hundred. Even committee chairmen may have a difficult time claiming credit for a piece of major legislation, let alone a rank-and-file congressman. [But] in dealing with the bureaucracy, the congressman is not merely one vote of 435. Rather, he is a nonpartisan power, someone whose phone calls snap an office to attention. The constituent who receives aid believes that his congressman and his congressman alone got results. Similarly, congressmen find it easy to claim credit for federal projects awarded their districts. The congressman may have instigated the proposal for the project in the first place, issued regular progress reports, and ultimately announced the award through his office. Maybe he can't claim credit for the 1965 Voting Rights Act, but he can take credit for littletown's spanking new sewage treatment plant.

Overall then, programmatic activities are dangerous (controversial), on the one hand, and programmatic accomplishments are difficult to claim credit for, on the other. While less exciting, casework and pork barreling are both safe and profitable. For a re-election-oriented congressman the choice is obvious.

The key to the rise of the Washington establishment (and the vanishing marginals) is the following observation: *the growth of an activist federal government has stimulated a change in the mix of congressional activities.* Specifically, a lesser proportion of congressional effort is now going into programmatic activities and a greater proportion into pork-barrel and casework activities. As a result, today's congressmen make relatively fewer enemies and relatively more friends among the people of their districts.

Congressmen [do not] resist their gradual transformation from national legislators to errand boy-ombudsmen. Congressmen have buried proposals to relieve the casework burden by establishing a national ombudsman or Congressman Reuss's proposed Administrative Counsel of the Congress. One congressman stated:

> Before I came to Washington I used to think that it might be nice if the individual states had administrative arms here that would take care of necessary liaison between citizens and the national government. But a congressman running for re-election is interested in building fences by providing personal services. The system is set to re-elect incumbents regardless of party, and incumbents wouldn't dream of giving any of this service function away to any subagency . . . [2]

In addition to greatly increased casework, let us not forget that the growth of the federal role has also greatly expanded the federal pork barrel. The creative pork barreler need not limit himself to dams and post offices. Today, creative congressmen can cadge LEAA money for the local police, urban renewal and housing money for local politicians, educational program grants for the local education bureaucracy. And there are sewage treatment plants, worker training and retraining programs, health services, and programs for the elderly.

Congress is the linchpin of the Washington establishment. The bureaucracy serves as a convenient lightning rod for public frustration and a convenient whipping boy for congressmen. But so long as the bureaucracy accommodates congressmen, the latter will oblige with ever larger budgets and grants of authority. Congress does not just react to big government – it creates it. All of Washington prospers. More and more bureaucrats promulgate more and more regulations and dispense more and more money. Fewer and fewer congressmen suffer electoral defeat. Elements of the electorate benefit from government programs, and all of the electorate is eligible for ombudsman services. But the general, long-term welfare of the United States is no more than an incidental by-product of the system.

The marginals disappeared as the Washington system developed. Congressmen elected from marginal districts found it increasingly possible to base their re-election on their noncontroversial activities – their casework and success in procuring the pork – rather than on their lawmaking activities, which divided their districts.

If an increasing number of congressmen are devoting increasing resources to constituency service, then we would expect that increasing numbers of voters must think of their congressmen less as policy-makers than as ombudsmen and pork barrelers. If so, other implications are immediate. First, party identification will be less influential in determining the congressional vote, not just because of the unusual national politics of the late 1960s, but because *objectively* the congressman is no longer as policy relevant as he once was. In bureaucratic matters he is a benevolent, nonpartisan power. The basis of the incumbency effect is obvious. *Experience in Washington and congressional seniority count when dealing with the bureaucracy. This incumbency effect is not only understandable; it is rational.*

Some draw the seemingly reasonable conclusion that the incumbency effect is unrelated to the communications incumbents shower on their constituents, because the informational advantage incumbents possess did not increase between 1958 and 1974, while the incumbency advantage apparently increased during this period. But what if the *content* of the information has changed over time? What if in 1958 those voters who had heard or read something about the incumbent had heard or read about one or more of his policy stands, whereas in 1970 they had heard or read about his effectiveness in getting Vietnam veterans' checks in the mail? Thus an increasing incumbency advantage is quite consistent with a constant informational advantage if information about the incumbent has grown increasingly noncontroversial in content and correspondingly positive in its impact.

The growth of the federal role has been reasonably continuous albeit with definite take-off points such as the New Deal and World War II. The decline of congressional competition, in contrast, has been somewhat more erratic. No change was noticeable before the 1950s and the most pronounced change appears to have occurred over a relatively short period during the mid-sixties. How do we reconcile the differences in the two trends?

One would expect some lag between the onset of bureaucratic expansion and the decline of the marginals, because congressmen presumably would not grasp the new opportunities immediately. Moreover, the effects of federal expansion are cumulative. In the early part of the post-war period congressmen may have used their opportunities to the fullest, but the electoral impact might have been imperceptible. By the 1960s, however, constituency service opportunities had cumulated to a significant electoral factor.

Still, the mid-sixties decline is especially pronounced. But one possible explanation of the sixties decline lies in recent work by Professor Richard Fenno. Fenno attaches great importance to a congressman's 'homestyle', his basic patterns of interaction with his district. Homestyle includes three components: (1) the congressman's allocation of time, effort, and staff to his district, (2) his personal style, and (3) his explanation for his Washington activities. Fenno argues that congressional careers pass through two stages, expansionist and protectionist, and 'Once in the protectionist phase . . . the dominant impulse is conservative. Keep the support you had "last time"; do what you did "last time". The tendency to follow established patterns, to observe stylistic constraints, is strong.'[53] Now when one considers that between the 88th and 90th Congress (1963–67) one-third of the membership of the House changed, a plausible hypothesis emerges. The new representatives placed relatively greater emphasis on constituency service than did those whom they replaced. The average freshman in 1965 replaced a congressman elected in 1952 or 1954. The latter had formed their homestyles in a different era. Moreover, particularly in 1964, many of the freshmen were Democrats who had won election in heretofore Republican districts. They can hardly be blamed for assuming that they could not win re-election on policy grounds. They had every incentive to adopt homestyles that emphasized nonprogrammatic constituency service. The Democrat who won district A in 1964 and lost it in 1966 did not follow the good advice offered him. According to local supporters, he was seldom heard from, even during the 1966 campaign. He became totally engrossed in his Washington affairs.

Paradoxically, then, the electoral upheavals of the 1960s may have produced the electoral stability of the early 1970s. New congressmen chose homestyles best adapted to the changed congressional environment. Is it purely coincidence that these fresh Congresses have raised personal staff allotments by over 50 percent since 1967?

During the past twenty years, congressional incumbents have adopted various plans to increase the resources available for investment in their re-election efforts and to modify existing institutional arrangements to better serve their electoral ends. One highly visible change is the doubling of their personal staffs. A second is the continual increase in various congressional 'perks'. A third, more far-reaching change, is the devolution of congressional power from full committee to subcommittee level, thereby giving rank-and-file congressmen a bigger piece of the action and producing a proliferation of 'subgovernments' in Washington. Finally, the creation of formal legislative liaison offices in the bureaucracy [is] an executive innovation which incumbent congressmen have used to good advantage.

Abridged from Morris P. Fiorina (1977), *Congress: Keystone of the Washington Establishment*, pp. 7–8, 11–14, 36–7, 41–51, 54–6. Reprinted by permission of Yale University Press, New Haven.

Notes

1 Herbert Asher and Herbert Weisberg, 'Congressional voting change: a longitudinal study of voting on selected issues', paper delivered at the annual meeting of the American Political Science Association, San Francisco, 1975.
2 Charles Clapp (1963), *The Congressman: His Job as He Sees It*, Brookings Institution, Washington, DC, p. 94.
3 Richard Fenno (1977), 'US House members in their constituencies,' *American Political Science Review*, 71, pp. 883–917.

3.7 Issue networks and the executive establishment

Hugh Heclo

Unlike many other countries, the United States has never created a high level, government-wide civil service. Neither has it been favored with a political structure that automatically produces a stock of experienced political manpower for top executive positions in government. How then does political administration in Washington work? More to the point, how might the expanding role of government be changing the connection between administration and politics?

Control is said to be vested in an informal but enduring series of 'iron triangles' linking executive bureaus, congressional committees, and interest group clienteles with a stake in particular programs. A president or presidential appointee may occasionally try to muscle in, but few people doubt the capacity of these subgovernments to thwart outsiders in the long run.

Based largely on early studies of agricultural, water, and public works policies, the iron triangle concept is not so much wrong as it is disastrously incomplete. And the conventional view is especially inappropriate for understanding changes in politics and administration during recent years. Preoccupied with trying to find the few truly powerful actors, observers tend to overlook the power and influence that arise out of the configurations through which leading policy-makers move and do business with each other. Looking for the closed triangles of control, we tend to miss the fairly open networks of people that increasingly impinge upon government.

One can sketch a few of the factors that seem to be at work. The first is growth in the sheer mass of government activity and associated expectations. The second is the peculiar, loose-jointed play of influence that is accompanying this growth. Related to these two is the third: the layering and specialization that have overtaken the government work force, not least the political leadership of the bureaucracy.

All of this vastly complicates the job of presidential appointees both in controlling their own actions and in managing the bureaucracy. But there is much more at stake than the troubles faced by people in government. There is the deeper problem of connecting what politicians, officials, and their fellow travellers are doing in Washington with what the public at large can understand and accept. It is on this point that political administration registers some of the larger strains of American politics and society, much as it did in the nineteenth century. For what it shows is a dissolving of organized politics and a politicizing of organizational life throughout the nation.

Government growth in an age of improvement

Few people doubt that we live in a time of big government. During his few years in office, President Kennedy struggled to avoid becoming the first president with a $100 billion budget. Just seventeen years later, President Carter easily slipped into history as the first $500 billion president. Even in constant prices, the 1979 federal budget was about double that of 1960. The late 1950s and the entire 1960s witnessed a wave of federal initiatives in health, civil rights, education, housing, manpower, income maintenance, transportation, and urban affairs. To these, later years have added newer types of welfare concerns: consumer protection, the environment, cancer prevention, and energy, to name only a few.

However, we need to be clear concerning what it is that has gotten big in government. Our modern age of improvement has occurred with astonishingly little increase in the overall size of the federal executive establishment. The year 1955 represented a return to more normal times after the Korean conflict and may be taken as a reasonable baseline. Since that year national spending has risen sixfold in current dollars and has more than doubled in constant terms. Federal regulations have also sextupled.

Yet federal employment grew hardly at all in comparison with spending and regulations (up by less than one-fifth since 1955). Despite widespread complaints about the size of government, the federal bureaucracy is entitled to join foreign aid as one of that small band of cases where close to zero-growth has been the norm for the last twenty-five years.

The paradox of expanding government and stable bureaucracy has two explanations. In purely budgetary terms, much of the increase in federal outlays has been due to higher costs of existing policies. Such cost increases have been especially important in the area of income maintenance programs. Federal payments to individuals (social security, medical care, veterans' pensions, unemployment insurance, and public assistance) increased from $22 billion in 1960 to $167 billion in 1977, accounting for well over half of the total increase in federal domestic spending during these years. Much of this increase came not from adding new programs but from higher bills for existing programs, particularly social security.

But there is a second and at least equally important explanation for the stability of the national bureaucracy in an era of increased policy interventionism. This factor creates even more profound problems for government leadership.

In the main, Washington has not attempted to apply its policies by administering programs directly to the general population. It has therefore been able to avoid bureaucratic giantism. This is true in many programs classified as payments to individuals (for example, Medicare and Medicaid funds pass through large numbers of administrative middlemen), and it is especially true in several of the policy areas that have grown the fastest since the mid-fifties.

One such area is investment and subsidies for the physical environment. Grants for mass transit, waste treatment plants, highways, and the like have tripled in real terms since 1960. Another area rich in indirect administration falls under the heading of social investment and services; spending for education, health care, employment training, urban development, and social services has risen more than tenfold since 1960. Rather than building and staffing its own administrative facilities for these programs, the federal government has preferred to act through intermediary organizations – state governments, city halls, third party payers, consultants, contractors, and many others.

New policies associated with our modern age of improvement have tended to promote the idea of government by remote control. Political administration in Washington is heavily conditioned by an accumulation of methods for paying the bills and regulating the conduct of intermediary organizations. This pattern is consistent with a long tradition of fragmented and decentralized administration. Moreover, it offers important political and bureaucratic advantages. Spreading cash grants among various third party payers is an important way of building support for policies, translating otherwise indivisible collective goods into terms suitable for distributive politics. Rather than having to convince everyone of the value of a clean environment, government administrators can preside over a scramble for federal funds to subsidize construction of local sewage treatment plants. Likewise, in spending for health, manpower, transportation, and so on, the federal government has sidestepped the tremendously difficult task of creating a broad national consensus for its own administered activities. It has done so by counting on third parties to crave the funds which the national government makes available to serve its purposes.

In terms of using intermediaries to administer the new melioristic policies, the mushrooming of federal regulations has much in common with federal spending. Rather than having to work at building and policing its own delivery mechanisms, the Washington bureaucracy can use regulations and then rest content with telling other public and private bureaucracies what should be done. This has the added advantage of allowing federal policy-makers to distribute not only funds but also much of the blame when things go wrong.

People increasingly expect Washington to solve problems but not to get in anyone's way in the process. The result is that policy goals are piled on top of each other without generating any commitment to the administrative wherewithal to achieve them. The executive establishment in Washington tends to get the worst of both worlds – blamed for poor delivery by its public customers and besieged with bills from its middlemen.

Fraying at the centre

The strategy of responding to aspirations for improvement while maintaining a no-growth national administrative machine and relying on middlemen has saved Washington policy-makers from having to cope with what would otherwise have been an immense, nationwide bureaucracy. Yet far from simplifying operations, this 'success' has vastly complicated the connection between administration and politics in Washington. Lacking their own electoral mandates, political administrators have always been in an ambivalent position in American government. Every ambitious new program, every clever innovation in indirect administration has merely deepened this ambivalence.

What is occurring at the national level is a peculiar 'push-pull effect' on the relation between democratic politics and the executive establishment. On the one hand, government growth has pushed more and more policy concerns out of the federal government's own structure and into masses of intermediary, issue-conscious groups. On the other hand, the requirements for managing such a complex system are pulling government leadership further and further away from the non-technical, non-specialist understanding of the ordinary citizen and politician. It is both politicizing organizational life and depoliticizing democratic leadership.

All join in

As more and more puzzling, unfamiliar policy issues have been thrust on government, more and more fluid groups have been unexpectedly mobilized. As proliferating groups have claimed a stake and clamored for a place in the policy process, they have helped to diffuse the focus of political and administrative leadership.

What has happened at the subnational level of government is a striking illustration of this process. Much of the bureaucratic expansion that might otherwise have occurred nationally has taken place in state and local governments. Between 1955 and 1977 state and local public employment grew by more than two and one-half times, to 12 million people, while federal employment hovered at around 2.5 million. The increased interdependence of subnational and national bureaucracies has led to the growth of the intergovernmental lobby. Not only do governors or mayors as groups have their own specialized staffs permanently stationed in Washington, but large state governments, major units within state governments, and individual cities frequently have their own Washington offices or hired representatives.

Similarly, an even larger number of private and semi-private organizations have grown up as important extensions of the new federal policies. Virtually everyone has accepted the idea that the national government in Washington is the decisive arena and will continue to be so indefinitely.

Some groups are nurtured by the government's own need for administrative help. For example, new neighborhood associations have been asked to take a major part in Washington's urban and housing programs. Or when the Consumer Product Safety Commission sets new standards for extension cords, the National Electrical Manufacturers' Association plays a major part in drawing up the new designs. Some groups are almost spontaneously called into being by what they can gain or lose from new federal policies or – perhaps just as often – the unforeseen consequences of these policies. For example, in the early 1970s Washington launched vigorous new efforts to promote grain exports. This generated not only new borrowing by farmers to expand production but also a new, militant farmers' organization (American Agriculture) when prices later fell from their export-led highs.

A key factor in the proliferation of groups is the almost inevitable tendency of successfully enacted policies unwittingly to propagate hybrid interests. The area of health care is rich in examples. Far from solidifying the established medical interests, federal funding and regulation of health care since the mid-1960s have had diverse impacts and therefore have tended to fragment what was once a fairly monolithic system of medical representation. Public policy has not only uncovered but also helped to create diverging interests among hospital associations, insurance companies, medical schools, hospital equipment manufacturers, local health planning groups, preventive medicine advocates, non-teaching research centers, and many others. This does not necessarily mean that every group is in conflict with all of the others all of the time. The point is that even when government is not pursuing a deliberate strategy of divide and conquer, its activist policies greatly increase the incentives for groups to form around the differential effects of these policies, each refusing to allow any other group to speak in its name.

While nothing should necessarily be assumed about their political power, trade and professional associations offer a revealing pattern of growth. Since 1945 the total number has been continuously increasing, and in recent years more and more of these groups have found it useful to make their headquarters in Washington. Well over half of the nation's largest associations (those with annual budgets of over $1 million) are now located in the Washington metropolitan area. This takes no account of the large number of consumer and other public interest groups that have sprouted all over the nation's capital since the early 1960s.

Of course Americans' love affair with interest groups is hardly a new phenomenon. With more public policies, more groups are being mobilized and there are more complex relationships among them. Since very few policies ever seem to drop off the public agenda as more are added, congestion among those interested in various issues grows, the chances for accidental collisions increase, and the interaction tends to take on a distinctive group-life of its own in the Washington community.

How these changes influence the substance of public policy processes depends on what it is that the burgeoning numbers of participants want. Obviously their wants vary greatly, but to a large extent they are probably accurately reflected in the areas of greatest policy growth since the late 1950s – programs seeking social betterment in terms of civil rights, income, housing, environment, consumer protection, and so on – what I will simply refer to as 'welfare policies'. If there is a theme in the clamor of group politics and public policy, it is the idea of compensation: for past racial wrongs, for current overcharging of consumers, for future environmental damage. The idea of compensatory policy – that the federal government should put things right – fits equally well for the groups representing the disadvantaged (special treatment is required for truly equal opportunity to prevail) and for those representing the advantaged (any market-imposed loss can be defined as a special hardship). The same holds for newer public interest groups (government action is required to redress the impact of selfish private interests).

In sum, new initiatives in federal funding and regulation have infused old and new organizations with a public policy dimension, especially when such groups are used as administrative middlemen and facilitators. Moreover, the growing body of compensatory interventions by government has helped create a climate of acceptance for ever more groups to insist that things be set right on their behalf. What matters is not so much that organizations are moving to Washington as that Washington's policy problems are coming to occupy so many different facets of organizational life in the United States.

Policy as an intramural activity
A second tendency cuts in a direction opposite to the widening group participation in public policy. Expanding welfare policies and Washington's reliance on indirect administration have encouraged the development of specialized subcultures composed of highly knowledgeable policy-watchers. What they all have in common is the detailed understanding of specialized issues that comes from sustained attention to a given policy debate.

Certain of these changes are evident in the government's own work force. Employees in the field and in Washington who perform the routine chores associated with direct administration have become less prominent. More important have become those officials with the necessary technical and supervisory skills to oversee what other people are doing. Thus the surge in federal domestic activities in the 1960s and 1970s may not have increased the overall size of the bureaucracy very much, but it did markedly expand the upper and upper-middle levels of officialdom. Compared with an 18 percent rise in total civilian employment, mid-level executive positions in the federal government have increased approximately 90 percent since 1960. Most of this escalation occurring in the Washington bureaucracy could be traced to the new and expanded public programs of that decade. The general effect of these policy changes has been to require more technical skills and higher supervisory levels, overlaying routine technicians with specialist engineers, insurance claims examiners with claims administrators, and so on. Approximately two-fifths of mid-level executives in the bureaucracy are what might loosely be termed scientists, though frequently they are in fact science managers who oversee the work of other people inside and outside of the government.

For decision-makers in government – where the policy goals have been neither stable nor clear in the last twenty years – the pressures for more expert staff assistance have become immense. This is as true for legislators as it is for public executives. Congress, like the executive branch, has responded to the pressures by creating more specialists and topside staff. At the core of this blossoming congressional bureaucracy are bright, often remarkably young, technocrats who are almost indistinguishable from the analysts and subject-matter specialists in the executive branch.

The familiar nexus of less professional, economic interests can still be found linking various parts of the Washington community. But the general arrangement that is emerging is somewhat different from the conventional image of iron triangles tying together executive bureaus, interest groups, and congressional committees in all-powerful alliances. Our standard political conceptions of power and control are not very well suited to the loose-jointed play of influence that is emerging in political administration. We tend to look for one group exerting dominance over another, for subgovernments that are strongly insulated from other outside forces in the environment.

For a host of policy initiatives undertaken in the last twenty years, it is all but impossible to identify clearly who the dominant actors are. Looking for the few who are powerful, we tend to overlook the many whose webs of influence provoke and guide the exercise of power. These 'issue networks' are particularly relevant to the highly intricate and confusing welfare policies that have been undertaken in recent years.

The notion of iron triangles and subgovernments presumes small circles of participants who have succeeded in becoming largely autonomous. Issue networks, on the other hand, comprise a large number of participants with quite variable degrees of mutual commitment or of dependence on others in their environment. Iron triangles and subgovernments suggest a stable set of participants coalesced to control fairly narrow public programs which are in the direct economic interest of each party to the alliance. Issue networks are almost the reverse image in each respect. Participants move in and out of the networks constantly. Rather than groups united in dominance over a program, no one is in control of the policies and issues. Any direct material interest is often secondary to intellectual or emotional commitment. Network members reinforce each other's sense of issues as their interests, rather than (as standard political or economic models would have it) interests defining positions on issues.

The price of buying into one or another issue network is watching, reading, talking about, and trying to act on particular policy problems. The true experts in the networks are those who are issue-skilled, regardless of formal professional training. More than mere technical experts, network people are policy activists who know each other through the issues. Those who emerge to positions of wider leadership are policy politicians – experts in using experts.

In the old days – when the primary problem of government was assumed to be doing what was right, rather than knowing what was right – policy knowledge could be contained in the slim adages of public administration.

Public executives needed to know how to execute. They needed power commensurate with their responsibility. Nowadays, political administrators do not execute but are involved in making highly important decisions on society's behalf, and they must mobilize policy intermediaries to deliver the goods. Knowing what is right becomes crucial, and since no one knows that for sure, going through the process of dealing with those who are judged knowledgeable (or at least continuously concerned) becomes even more crucial. Instead of power commensurate with responsibility, issue networks seek influence commensurate with their understanding of the various, complex social choices being made.

The issue network ties together what would otherwise be the contradictory tendencies of, on the one hand, more widespread organizational participation in public policy and, on the other, more narrow technocratic specialization in complex modern policies. Such networks need to be distinguished from three other more familiar terms used in connection with political administration. An issue network is a shared-knowledge group having to do with some aspect of public policy. It is therefore more well-defined than, first, a shared-attention group or 'public'; those in the networks are likely to have a common base of information and understanding of how one knows about policy and identifies its problems. But knowledge does not necessarily produce agreement. Issue networks may or may not, therefore, be mobilized into, second, a shared-action group (creating a coalition) or, third, a shared-belief group (becoming a conventional interest organization). Increasingly, it is through networks of people who regard each other as knowledgeable, or at least as needing to be answered, that public policy issues tend to be refined, evidence debated, and alternative options worked out – though rarely in any controlled, well-organized way.

At any given time only one part of a network may be active and through time the various connections may intensify or fade among the policy intermediaries and the executive and congressional bureaucracies. For example, there is no single health policy network but various sets of people knowledgeable and concerned about cost-control mechanisms, insurance techniques, nutritional programs, prepaid plans, and so on.

The debate on energy policy is rich in examples of the kaleidoscopic interaction of changing issue networks. The Carter administration's initial proposal was worked out among experts who were closely tied in to conservation-minded networks. Soon it became clear that those concerned with macroeconomic policies had been largely bypassed in the planning, and last-minute amendments were made in the proposal presented to Congress, a fact that was not lost on the networks of leading economists and economic correspondents. Once congressional consideration began, it quickly became evident that attempts to define the energy debate in terms of a classic confrontation between big oil companies and consumer interests were doomed. More and more policy watchers joined in the debate, bringing to it their own concerns and analyses: tax reformers, nuclear power specialists, civil rights groups interested in more jobs; the list soon grew beyond the wildest dreams of the original energy policy planners. The problem was that no one could quickly turn the many networks of knowledgeable people into a shared-action coalition, much less into a single, shared-attitude group.

The clouds of issue networks have not replaced the more familiar politics of subgovernments in Washington. Rather they overlay the once stable political reference points with new forces that complicate calculations, decrease predictability, and impose considerable strains on those charged with government leadership. The overlay of networks and issue politics not only confronts but also seeps down into the formerly well-established politics of particular policies and programs. The Army Corps of Engineers, once the picturebook example of control by subgovernments, is dragged into the brawl on environmental politics. A somewhat new and difficult dynamic is being played out in the world of politics and administration. It is not what has been feared for so long: that technocrats and other people in white coats will expropriate the policy process. If there is to be any expropriation, it is likely to be by the policy activists, those who care deeply about a set of issues and are determined to shape the fabric of public policy accordingly.

Abridged from Hugh Heclo, 'Issue networks and the executive establishment' in Anthony King, ed. (1978), *The New American Political System*, American Enterprise Institute for Public Policy Research, Washington, DC, pp. 88–105. Reprinted by permission of the American Enetprise Institute for Public Policy Research.

3.8   The Reagan presidency as a case study of presidential power

Lester M. Salamon and Alan J. Abramson

The almost universal belief on the eve of Reagan's inauguration was that the presidency was in serious trouble. Far from being 'imperial', the American presidency was seriously 'imperiled', structurally incapable of meeting the expectations placed on it.

Against this backdrop, the first year of the Reagan administration appears to represent an unusual political triumph that significantly changed the terms of the national policy debate. This chapter focuses on three dimensions of presidential effectiveness in the domestic arena:

1 The president's immediate success in accomplishing his purposes.

2 His administration's longer-term impact on our nation's political processes and institutions.

3 The political viability of the substantive policy choices he makes.

Effective governance in the first sense means skill in articulating a program,
winning support for it, and putting it into effect. Effective governance in the
second sense means acting in ways that strengthen the capabilities of the
nation's political institutions to function over the long run. A president is not
simply the manager of a particular agenda; he is also the inheritor of a set
of institutions and processes which can facilitate or complicate the job of
achieving political agreement and which must in turn be handed on, in better
or worse shape, to a successor.

Finally, effective governance in the third sense involves achieving a set of
policies that are perceived as being programmatically workable over the long
run and therefore that win continued voter acceptance. No set of criteria for
evaluating presidential effectiveness can wholly ignore the substantive ends of
political action. Yet judgments here are inevitably value laden.

An immensely skillful Reagan and his political team managed to make the
most of the advantages they enjoyed and to escape temporarily the prevailing
constraints of contemporary American politics. But the long-term impact of
this administration on the nation's political institutions and processes, as well
as on its substantive policies, is likely to be far more limited and possibly
counter-productive.

The context: obstacles to presidential influence

The defining characteristic of the American political order over the past
twenty years has been its tendency to concentrate responsibility for problems
at the center while dispersing the power to deal with those problems to an
ever-expanding array of increasingly autonomous groups and institutions.
Fragmentation of power is part of the American constitutional design, institutionalized in the sharing of authority among the three branches of the
federal government, and between the federal government and the states. But
recent developments have accentuated these problems while intensifying the
need for political action to overcome them.

As the only elected official with a national constituency, the president has
become more and more the one entity in a reasonable position to bring a
societywide perspective to bear on the increasing conflicts and trade-offs
among policies. Modern presidents have been increasingly hampered in their
capacity to bring such a perspective to bear. In the first place, the ability of the
president to build the supporting coalitions needed for him to capitalize on his
unique perspective has been made more difficult by the proliferation of
interest groups, the weakening of political parties, and the dispersion of power
in Congress.

As citizens have found themselves able to express their preferences more precisely through narrow interest groups, their allegiance to political parties has fallen off. Once in office, candidates who have run personal campaigns with the aid of media consultants and citizen volunteers feel little obligation to support fellow partisans when such support conflicts with election concerns. The upshot has been a substantial weakening of the political parties, one of the most important sets of integrating institutions in the political system, and a potential unifying instrument for the president.

The diffusion of political power among an escalating number of narrow interest groups and the corresponding dilution in the power of political parties have in turn generated strong forces for diffusion of power within Congress.

Congress moved in the 1970s to exercise increased independence through a series of 'presidency-curbing' measures, such as the War Powers Act and the Congressional Budget Act. Concomitantly, presidential success in Congress declined steadily under both Democratic and Republican administrations.

Several other major trends further constrained the president's capacity to manage the government. These included the growth in judicial activism; the rise in uncontrollable spending and the emergence of a 'hidden budget' comprised of such devices as loan guarantees and tax expenditures, and the rise of 'third-party government', the use of nonfederal actors – such as state and local governments, nonprofit institutions, and banks – to carry out federal programs.

Thus, the prospects for a bold redirection of national policy in 'normal' times appeared doubtful at best, particularly in light of the further fragmentation since the mid-1960s.

Reagan's advantages and strategy of governance

A conservative president might be expected to applaud the obstacles to presidential activism. After all, through much of modern United States political history active presidencies have been associated with liberal political agendas and with the expansion of federal responsibilities, while conservatives have utilized their positions in Congress and their influence at the state and local level to resist governmental growth. By 1980, however, this situation had changed dramatically. Thanks to the policy changes of the 1960s and 1970s, the liberal-consumer-civil rights-environmental agenda had become institutionalized. Under these circumstances, the activist presidency, once the nemesis of conservatives, came to be seen as the best hope for restraining the liberal state.

But given the obstacles to presidential influence how did the Reagan administration make the headway that it did?

The Reagan advantages

Reagan's disarming manner and unusual communication skills have earned him a popularity that has helped his administration survive even major gaffes.

Beyond this advantage, two others stand out: the results of the 1980 election and the presence of a simple and straightforward ideology and program to guide the administration and its allies.]

The 1980 election. Perhaps the single most important advantage that the Reagan administration enjoyed going into its first year was the widespread impression that it had won a substantial mandate from the voters for a bold departure in national policy. In fact, of course, the results of the 1980 election were far more ambiguous than the headline snapshots. Ample evidence suggests that the election was as much a rejection of Jimmy Carter as an embrace of Ronald Reagan. Underlying the dissatisfaction with Carter was discontent with the state of the economy – notably the high rate of inflation. The 1980 vote was more a rejection of Carter than an endorsement of Reagan and his program.

The election was widely interpreted as a decisive mandate. The major reason probably was the Electoral [College] vote – 489 to 49 (81.8 percent) – the third highest of the thirteen elections since 1932. The margin of victory also was unexpected. Further strengthening the impression of a Reagan mandate were the congressional races, which produced the largest presidential-election-year increase of House Republicans since 1920 and of Senate Republicans since 1868. Perhaps most important, the election gave Republicans control of the Senate for the first time since 1954. Finally, though voters did not support the specifics of the Reagan program, they did seem to be calling for something new.

An uncomplicated program. In addition, the Reagan administration had the advantage of a relatively simple and straightforward set of ideas about government that seemed to accord reasonably well with certain popular sentiments:

- That governmental – especially federal – involvement in domestic affairs, including economic affairs, had grown much too large and needed to be pared back extensively.
- That American foreign policy had grown far too timid and that a more activist American presence backed by a military force equal to or greater than that of the Soviet Union was urgently needed.
- That 'supply-side economics' (in particular large tax cuts) would limit the further growth of the federal government and simultaneously stimulate private-sector investment and economic growth.
- That the government should strive to restore more traditional moral and religious values to American society, or at least to eliminate those government policies that impede the operation of those values.

These ideas conveniently tied together two principal concerns that pollsters had been detecting in the American population for more than a decade: (1) dissatisfaction with the performance of the economy and (2) frustration at the cost and apparent ineffectiveness of government. What Ronald Reagan did was to convert these two concerns into a program of action by identifying the growth of government as the cause of the poor performance of the economy. As a result, the administration was able to claim broad popular support for the substance of its program despite the ambiguities of the electoral result. Also, the simplicity and clarity of the ideas made executive branch management a lot easier.

Finally, the administration's political ideology enabled the Reagan administration to overcome one of the widely perceived shortcomings of the Carter presidency, its failure to articulate a clear-cut sense of purpose and direction around which to mobilize public and congressional support.

The Reagan strategy: centralization in the service of decentralization

Not content to rest on its advantages, the administration developed an active strategy for capitalizing on them that consisted of five key features: a radical narrowing of the policy agenda so far as the president was concerned; a highly centralized policy management process predicated on top-down budgeting and a tightly knit Executive Office working group to control the agenda; close attention to political liaison, especially with Congress; an 'administrative strategy' including careful personnel selection and use of administrative means to pursue policy goals; and finally, a capacity for pragmatic compromise when necessary.

Restriction of the central agenda.   At the heart of the Reagan administration's strategy was a concerted effort to limit the range of subjects in which the president was personally and publicly involved. Success in narrowing the agenda was by no means assured. A critical part of the Reagan constituency, after all, was more populist than conservative, more interested in the so-called social issues (e.g. abortion, school prayer, busing) than in economics. This constituency continued throughout the administration to push hard for a broad assault on the social issues. No such assault materialized. The new budget director, David Stockman, urged that informal agreements be reached with the key Republican committee chairmen in the Senate to defer action on some of the pet projects of the New Right, such as 'the labor policy agenda' (e.g. repeal of the minimum wage) and the 'Moral Majority agenda'. Stockman argued, 'Pursuit of these issues during the 100-day period would only unleash cross-cutting controversy and political pressures . . .'[1]

Centralization of executive decision-making.   Executive branch decision-making, at least for the major economic and budget decisions, was centralized in the Executive Office of the President and, more specifically, in a relatively small group of key advisers in the White House. This was achieved through two principal devices: first, a transformed budget process; and second, a more informal White House decision process overseen by the 'triumvirate' of chief presidential aides James Baker, Michael Deaver, and Edwin Meese.

The traditional budget process – involving submissions from the departments and agencies individually reviewed by OMB [Office of Management and Budget] 'examiners' and then assembled in the president's budget – was ill-suited to the administration's purposes and timetable. Instead, a radical centralization of executive-branch decision making occurred in OMB as an institution, and in its director David Stockman, as an individual. Stockman and his lieutenants formulated budgetary proposals from the 'top down' with only minimal involvement by agency staff and, frequently, only perfunctory input from OMB staff. Furthermore, in the drive to maintain control over the central budgetary agenda, Stockman subsequently took on many of the traditional functions of agency heads in lobbying for the administration's budget in the Congress.

Equally important, the administration came up with a plan for maintaining the integrity and momentum of its budget as it moved through the Congress. The heart of this plan was the 'reconciliation process', a complicated feature of the 1974 Congressional Budget Act intended originally to enable congressional Budget Committees to enforce spending targets in the final stages of the appropriations process. The Reagan administration, however, succeeded in moving a binding reconciliation measure to the beginning of the process, thereby wrapping the entire administration budget and program reform package into one massive piece of legislation – the Omnibus Budget and Reconciliation Act of 1981 – that could be moved through the Congress under time deadlines set by the congressional budget process and overseen by the Budget Committees, rather than having it split apart into thirteen separate appropriation bills and scattered authorizing legislation as is commonly done.

An informal working group of top White House aides monitored congressional developments and fine-tuned the proposals in order to ensure congressional passage. At the heart of this group was the trio of Baker, Meese, and Deaver. Operating through a 'legislative strategy group' involving their own key aides and representatives from the White House legislative liaison operation and OMB, the triumvirate managed to settle the intense disagreements that inevitably arose as the president's program confronted the realities of congressional pressure and come up with critical mid-course corrections.

Another element of the Reagan White House was the network of cabinet councils established under the direction of Edwin Meese. The councils ended up serving more of an information-sharing than a decision-making purpose, ensuring a common administration front on sensitive issues. The cabinet council structure [was] a way to control the cabinet rather than a way to allow the cabinet to control the administration's agenda.

The Reagan administration also made extensive use of a fourth mechanism for policy control: an elaborate procedure for regulatory clearance and review. Established by a presidential executive order in mid-February 1981, the Reagan regulatory review process built on a precedent going back to Richard Nixon and importantly expanded by both Gerald Ford and Jimmy Carter.

President Ford and President Carter elaborated procedures to review selected agency regulations with an eye to evaluating their benefits against their costs. President Reagan expanded and strengthened these procedures further, establishing a Task Force on Regulatory Relief under the chairmanship of Vice President Bush to develop regulatory policy and adjudicate regulatory disputes, and creating a more formal institutional structure within OMB to review proposed regulatory issuances of the departments and agencies before their publication in the *Federal Register* and determine whether they met more stringent cost-benefit standards. These steps significantly expanded central presidential influence over the regulatory process.

Improved political mobilization. The Reagan strategy also involved political mobilization aimed at both Congress and the public. This effort was spearheaded by the president himself. Certainly in the period following the attempted assassination, the president managed to use dramatic television appearances and other media events to solidify his hold on the electrate, putting tremendous pressure on Congress to give him what he wanted. He followed up his effective television appearances with a more old-fashioned type of political hand holding that paid handsome rewards in its own right. The courting of Congress began even before his election. These efforts continued during the transition with a series of meetings and social gatherings with members of Congress. Although the president was subsequently criticized by some for his apparent lack of substantive knowledge, his personal charm and evident enjoyment of political life earned him real popularity on the Hill despite considerable hostility to his programs.

The president's personal efforts at maintaining legislative good will were augmented by the substantive contributions of the White House legislative strategy group and by the fence tending of the formal legislative liaison operation in the White House. Unlike his predecessor, Reagan took pains to assemble an experienced legislative liaison team to maintain contact with Congress and to improve the general climate of presidential-congressional relations. The liaison office supplied invaluable intelligence in deciding strategy.

To reach beyond the halls of Congress, the administration also developed an impressive public relations operation, including an in-house pollster, a public liaison office, a political affairs staff, and a separate White House Planning and Evaluation Office to chart broad trends in public attitudes.

The administrative presidency. A fourth key element in the Reagan administration's strategy of governance has been its reliance on administrative instead of legislative changes to implement policy. Since the success of this strategy rests on the presence of reliable administration supporters in key bureaucratic positions, the administration paid close attention to the appointment process. 'The predominant characteristic of the Reagan approach to personnel selection was its emphasis on centralized, unrelenting White House control of the appointment process.' Appointees were carefully screened for policy and political background, legislative ties, ethics, and general compatibility with the core team.[2]

The early appointees at the cabinet level turned out to be more moderate, pragmatic, and politically balanced than might have been expected (David Stockman, James Watt, and Jeanne Kirkpatrick constituting the more prominent ideologues). But Reagan's second round of appointments, to subcabinet positions, exhibited 'an uncommon degree of ideological consistency and intensity'. In addition, the Reagan administration extended the reach of political appointments much further down into the operating staffs of the agencies, filling a higher proportion of allowable non-career senior executive positions than had been done in the previous administration.[3]

While moving ideologically screened appointees in, the administration also moved career federal employees out. From January 1981 to September 1983, the civilian (not including Post Office or Defense) employment of the government dropped by 92,000 – 7.4 percent – from 1,240,000 to 1,148,000. Also, the administration made generous use of the provisions of the Civil Service Reform Act of 1978 to reassign executives from one job or geographic location to another.[4]

The real heart of the administrative strategy, however, was not simply to put ideologically sympathetic personnel into sensitive administrative positions, but to encourage them to use their administrative power to advance the administration's policy objectives. This took three forms:

- The administration launched an early assault on pending regulations.
- Enforcement action diminished in many regulatory areas because of severe budget cuts, staff reductions, and a general easing of regulatory vigour.
- Reagan appointees used their administrative flexibility to reinterpret the conduct of agency business. Thus, for example, the Mine Safety and Health Administration, the EPA, and OSHA began to stress co-operation with business rather than confrontation in achieving regulatory compliance.

In short an ideologically oriented team of subcabinet officials moved into place and began implementing the Reagan agenda by administrative means, particularly in the regulatory arena.

Pragmatism Finally, in its approach to governance, the Reagan administration has exhibited an important element of pragmatism. Pragmatism has not generally characterized the president himself. Rather, pragmatism has been a characteristic of the staff system and decision apparatus the president has created, which balances those staff members whose principal concern is allegiance to a central policy agenda with others whose principal concern is maintaining a modicum of support within the other centers of political power, most notably, Congress.

The resulting tension has led the administration to some important tactical retreats that have served its strategic objectives well. Most notable, perhaps, was the endorsement of a major tax increase in mid-1982, when it began to be apparent that the hoped-for economic recovery had not materialized.

The record

In terms of success in carrying out the basic features of its programmatic goals, the Reagan administration may be one of the most effective presidencies in recent history. In its first nine months in office, the administration made a significant downpayment on its long-run objective of changing the terms of the national policy debate, putting in place a significant constraint on federal domestic spending, setting in motion a major defense build-up, and restraining the growth of federal regulation.

Legislative record

The Reagan administration's dealings with Congress have followed three more or less distinct phases that resemble all too clearly the course that previous presidencies have taken, with an initial period of achievement followed by periods of congressional dominance and legislative stalemate.

The year of the president. In its first nine months in office, the Reagan administration managed to push through Congress the central features of its Economic Recovery Program: domestic budget and tax cuts, accompanied by a massive defense build-up.

Three factors in Congress contributed most significantly to these achievements: Republican solidarity, the support of a key group of conservative southern Democrats in the House (the Boll Weevils), and a spirit of resignation among the House Democratic leaders.

Republican solidarity was particularly evident in the Senate. But the sense of responsibility for advancing the president's programs was strong among House Republicans as well. A sense of 'united we conquer' was encouraged by the common debt Republican congressmen owed to the GOP national fund-raising effort, which was able by 1980 to contribute substantial amounts of money to Republican candidates.

Republican support for the president's program was hardly automatic, however. Early on, for example, the Republican-dominated Senate Budget Committee rejected the president's FY fiscal year 1982 budget proposal out of hand because of what the committee considered (correctly, as it turned out) to be overly optimistic economic assumptions and insufficient concern for the deficit problem. Also, moderate Republicans from the midwest and northeast threatened to defect from the ranks over some of the proposed cuts in a areas of particular concern to their regions, such as mass transit, student loans, and energy conservation aid. To counter the potential defections, the administration struck some strategic bargains, moderating somewhat certain of the proposed cuts. Also, the administration's decision to keep the divisive social issues – school prayer, anti-abortion, busing – largely off the legislative agenda, went a long way toward preserving moderate support.

House Republicans were unanimous, 190-0, in their support for the president on the first budget resolution (Gramm-Latta I). On Gramm-Latta II, the endorsement of the president's reconciliation package, House Republicans voted 190-1. In the Senate, on the budget cut instructions, Republicans voted 51-1 in favor of the president's position. Overall, Republican Senators voted with Reagan 80 percent of the time in 1981, the greatest loyalty any president has commanded from members of his own party in the 30-odd years of *Congressional Quarterly* voting studies.

Equally crucial to the administration's early achievements was its success in attracting the support of conservative southern Democrats (the so-called 'Boll Weevils'). This 'conservative coalition' had its most efficacious year ever in 1981, winning 92 percent of the votes in which it was active, and providing the critical margin of 30 to 60 votes Reagan needed to carry his budget and tax proposals in the House.

The Boll Weevil alliance with Reagan does not seem to have resulted from fear of losing to a Reagan Republican in an election, since the Boll Weevils generally won in 1980 by more substantial margins than the Democratic opponents of the president in their states. The operative element, rather, seems to have been simple ideological affinity reflecting constituencies that tended to be more rural, pro-Reagan, and generally with lower proportions of blacks in their populations than the districts of southern Democrats who opposed Reagan. The president also offered not to campaign personally against the Boll Weevils (to the dismay of some House Republicans who hoped for a House majority) and offered them policy concessions beneficial to their constituents.

Finally, House Democrats chose a strategy of concession over defiance. Fearing a potential realignment in the electorate toward the Republicans and the more immediate possibility that southern House Democrats would bolt and vote with Republicans in organizing the House, Speaker Tip O'Neil quickly gave up one of his greatest powers – control of the legislative agenda. Even in their own bills, Democrats conceded a lot to Reagan.

The year of Congress. The momentum of Reagan's initial congressional victories declined abruptly in the late summer of 1981, however, as the economy refused to meet the administration's expectations and deficits began to mount. The administration's new 'fall budget offensive' met with a cool reception in Congress, which approved only half of what the administration wanted. By the time the administration submitted the FY 1983 budget in February 1982, opposition was running high even among Republicans, and the Republican-dominated Senate Budget Committee rejected the administration's budget 21-0 in early April 1982.

When the president refused to compromise with congressional moderates, congressional leaders, particularly in the Republican Senate, decided to act. The result was a budget proposal essentially drafted in Congress which denied the administration most of its proposed additional domestic budget cuts and provided for a significant tax increase hitherto adamantly opposed by the president. In the end, the administration accepted the package and worked for its passage. At the same time, the administration was stalled on many of its other legislative initiatives.

The year of stalemate. The worsening economic conditions throughout 1982 and the 1982 congressional elections, which yielded 26 additional House seats for the Democrats and eliminated a significant number of the so-called 'Reagan robots' (the class of 1980 Republican representatives who had pinned their careers to the Reagan program) intensified the president's difficulties. With the economy and the electoral results spelling trouble for the president, the Republican coalition began to splinter and Democratic unity began to grow. For the first time in the Reagan era, House Democrats managed to pass their own budget plan. Senate Republicans attempted to find some common ground between House Democrats and the administration in order to scale back growing deficits but ultimately failed. Essentially, the political system settled down to a pattern of stalemate.

Abridged from Lester M. Salamon and Alan J. Abramson, 'Governance: the politics of retrenchment' in John L. Palmer and Isobel V. Sawhill, eds. (1984), *The Reagan Record: An Assessment of America's Changing Domestic Priorities*, revised edition, Ballinger, Cambridge, MA, pp. 31–53.
Reprinted by permission of the Urban Institute, Washington DC.

Notes

1 David Stockman, 'Avoiding a GOP economic Dunkirk', mimeograph, November 1980.
2 The account of Reagan's appointment process is from G. Calvin MacKenzie, 'Personnel selection for a conservative administration: the Reagan exercise, 1980–81', mimeograph, Colby College, April 1982; the quotation is from p. 4 of MacKenzie's paper.
3 The quotation on subcabinet appointees is from MacKenzie's paper, p. 12.
4 The data on the overall drop in civilian employment are from US Office of Personnel Management, *Monthly Release: Employment and Trends as of September 1983*, Washington, DC, 1983, p. 6.

3.9 The post-Vietnam formula under siege: the imperial presidency and Central America

Kenneth E. Sharpe

The Iran-contra affair made public an abuse of executive authority that began in 1981. The deeper issues raised by the trading of arms for hostages and the diversion of profits to the contras, however, harken back to the Vietnam period. The impact of the Vietnam war on our constitutional democracy, which culminated in the Watergate scandal and Richard Nixon's resignation, served as a warning of the dangers of an imperial presidency.

Reforms that I loosely call the post-Vietnam-Watergate formula were enacted to ensure that presidential abuse of power would be less likely to again endanger constitutional democracy in the United States. Others, like Senator J. William Fulbright, supported legislative action but argued that this was not enough. The problem, they argued, was political, not legal. Congress lacked the will to enforce its constitutional authority in foreign policy. An exercise of that will required a challenge to the direction of foreign policy, and the president, drawing on his often self-proclaimed authority as commander in chief, was often able to take foreign policy steps that created a *fait accompli* and made the exercise of that will even harder. As long as a condition of permanent cold-war crisis prevailed, it would be difficult to defend the authority of Congress against usurpation by the president and the national security bureaucracy he managed.

The Reagan administration's conduct of Central American policy provided the first sustained test of the post-Vietnam-Watergate formula. It demonstrated the continued willingness of the executive branch to abuse its authority in foreign policy and suggested the limits of legislative reform when not backed by a strong congressional will.

The imperial presidency and the post-Vietnam-Watergate formula

There has been continual dispute over the balance of power in foreign policy-making. One of the major conflicts has been over efforts to reconcile the war-declaring power of Congress and the war-making power of the president. The long-term effect of such conflicts, however, has been the gradual enlargement of executive power.

The shift in the balance toward the executive began to take on alarming proportions in the cold-war decades that followed World War II. The executive developed a large independent peacetime national security apparatus whose centrepiece was the National Security Council (NSC) created in 1947. Also critical was the establishment of the Defense Department (which integrated all the services) and the giving of legislative authority to a Joint Chiefs of Staff system and to the Central Intelligence Agency (CIA).

As the security apparatus grew and cold-war tensions mounted, the executive branch became increasingly unaccountable to Congress, the press, and the public in the making of foreign policy. Congress generally acquiesced. The rough consensus over foreign policy goals and the seeming imperatives of national security muted fundamental criticism of the shift of power to the executive. The executive branch increasingly bypassed the treaty-making authority of Congress through the use of secret executive agreements. The CIA developed into an apparatus that not only gathered intelligence but secretly carried out foreign policy, often using covert operations to over-throw foreign governments and assassinate foreign leaders. The president, the Pentagon, the CIA, the NSC, and even the State Department felt less obliged to give Congress and the public information about foreign policy issues.

President Lyndon B. Johnson's commitment of half a million US troops to Vietnam under the Tonkin Gulf Resolution demonstrated how far Congress had abdicated its constitutional prerogative. In 1969 President Richard M. Nixon took the executive interpretation of war powers even further than Johnson by authorizing the bombing of Cambodia. The next year, in the face of clear congressional sentiment to terminate the war in Indochina, he authorized a US invasion of Cambodia, claiming authority as commander in chief and invoking the need to protect US troops. A few years later the Watergate revelations showed that the problem of executive secrecy and abuse of power went even further.

The reaction was growing support for impeachment and an attempt to strengthen constitutional democracy. A set of three related commitments – a post-Vietnam formula – were embodied in new laws, procedures, and insti-tutional arrangements. One commitment was to get access to information about executive activities, a necessary condition for checks and balances to work. A second was to restore congressional legislative authority in foreign policy and strengthen congressional checks on potential abuses of authority at home and abroad. A third commitment was to limit the possibilities for political repression and violations of civil liberties and civil rights. This article will focus on the first two commitments.

Access to information

The problem of the balance between secrecy and disclosure deepened during and after World War II with the development and expansion of a classification system for information, a specialized national security bureaucracy with a vested interest in secrecy, and the widespread fear of Communist agents and subversion. Only a few members of Congress were willing to take up the battle of disclosure versus secrecy during this time. But Congress was shaken out of its lethargy by Vietnam and Watergate.

One legislative response was to require certain critical information. The

1973 War Powers Resolution demanded that the president inform Congress in writing within forty-eight hours of introducing troops (in the absence of a declaration of war) into areas of hostilities or where imminent involvement in hostilities was likely. The reasons for introducing the troops, the legal authority justifying the introduction, and the scope and duration of the commitment had to be specified.

The 1974 Hughes-Ryan Amendment (amended again in 1980) required that the president report in 'a timely fashion' all CIA covert operations other than intelligence gathering to appropriate committees. And legislation in 1976 and 1977 created Select Intelligence Committees in the Senate and House respectively. This allowed some oversight and control by the Congress, and there were mechanisms under certain circumstances for public disclosure of the classified information given to the committees.

The ability of the president to make secret executive agreements was limited by the Case-Zablocki Act of 1972, which required all executive agreements to be reported to Congress. In 1974 Congress also required that arms sales be so reported.

Perhaps more important than the specific statutes was the general commitment Congress made to watch presidential actions more carefully and to use its existing powers as leverage to demand that foreign policy decisions be shared. The greater size and foreign policy expertise of staff members were also important. Such staff provided independent sources of information.

Restoring shared control

The new commitment to get access to information was aimed at allowing Congress increased participation in the making of foreign policy and a greater ability to check executive excesses. Constitutionally, much of the necessary power was already in the hands of Congress: the authority to declare war, to advise and consent on treaties and appointments, and the ultimate 'check' through its power of the purse. Of particular concern was an old problem in the struggle over foreign policy – the ability of the president to create situations that *forced congressional acquiescence* and created an antecedent, a *fait accompli*, which limited Congress's will and ability to use its existing powers.

In the cold-war years, presidents involved the United States in full-scale war by first committing troops to foreign lands (Truman in Korea, Kennedy and Johnson in Vietnam) and then arguing that the troops could not be abandoned or that commitments made had to be honored to protect American credibility. Presidents increasingly made secret executive agreements that bound the United States to certain foreign policies without congressional debate and authorization. Presidents ordered covert operations that involved the United States in policies that Congress could disown only at the risk of seeming to undermine national security. By the late 1960s the president had an unprecedented ability to create an antecedent state of things.

Congress attempted to hold the president accountable by insisting on full consultation and shared decision making *before* the policy die was cast. Some of this was handled legislatively. For example the War Powers Act aimed to 'insure that the collective judgement of both the Congress and the President will apply' to the decision to send US troops into hostilities by insisting that the president consult with Congress 'in every possible instance' *before* the troops are introduced.

Congress also established procedures by which the new access to information could be used to insist on participation or to stop the president. For example, the Senate and House Intelligence Oversight Committees could try to dissuade the CIA from continuing covert operations by using their control of authorizations for intelligence activities, or by revealing such operations, or by taking the issue to the House or Senate to pass legislation specifically forbidding or cutting appropriations for the activity. The Clark Amendment in 1976 (abolished in 1985), for example, prohibited assistance for military or paramilitary operations in Angola. Similarly, Congress could block or force the modification of executive agreements by denying funds to implement them.

The War Powers Resolution required the unauthorized use of troops to stop automatically. The War Powers Resolution required the president to terminate any unauthorized use of troops within sixty days unless Congress took affirmative action to approve it. The sixty days starts upon submission of the required report to Congress – a wrinkle that puts the starting of the clock in the hands of the president.

The new formula that emerged after Vietnam and Watergate represented concern both about the *process* of foreign-policy decision making and about the *content* of foreign policy. There was an awareness in Congress, and later in the Carter administration, that Third World turmoil was often caused by local conditions of poverty and repression, and that a 'North-South' perspective was more realistic than an 'East-West' perspective. Critics of the Vietnam policy were wary of sending US troops to fight in Third World countries where the goals were not clearly defined and the conflict was unpopular at home. Many were opposed to supporting corrupt, repressive regimes and sought instead to condition foreign military and economic aid on a regime's human rights performance.

These new commitments to both process and content allowed Congress to take a more aggressive role in shaping Central American policy than it had in shaping early Vietnam policy. But a serious and sustained test came when the Reagan adminstration took office. Its willingness to aid repressive regimes facing domestic turmoil troubled many in Congress, and its emphasis on a military strategy in Central America raised the spectre of the involvement of US troops in 'another Vietnam'. Moderates in Congress were particularly worried that the commitments being made to El Salvador (and later to Honduras and to the Nicaraguan exile army) would eventually draw in US troops. They wanted to participate from the very beginning in shaping policy.

Central America: a test case for the post-Vietnam formula

El Salvador

From 1981 until 1984, Congress attempted to participate in shaping El Salvador policy by making military aid conditional on certain requirements. The president had to certify that the Salvadoran government was 'making a concerted ... effort to comply with internationally recognized human rights,' was 'achieving substantial control over all elements of its armed forces, so as to bring an end ... to indiscriminate torture and murder,' was 'making continued progress in ... land reform,' and was 'committed to the holding of free elections.'

The conditionality requirement was weak: once the president certified, aid was automatically released. But the requirement underlined the widespread belief that real reform was the only way to stop revolution. Presidential certification every six months also forced a certain public accountability, and the congressional hearings around each certification provided for careful scrutiny of administration facts and stimulated through media coverage public debate and education.

The administration, however, provided false and misleading information in order to certify that the conditions required for aid existed, despite overwhelming evidence to the contrary. Further, it refused to put serious pressure on the Salvadoran military to end its human rights abuses. It repeatedly denied the well substantiated charges (confirmed by its own internal documents) that thousands of civilian noncombatants were being killed by government forces and 'death squads' organized or aided by top military officials. When Congress renewed the certification requirement in November 1983, Reagan pocket vetoed the bill while Congress was not in session and, therefore, had no opportunity to override it. The congressional response to such efforts to undercut or eliminate certification was weak.

Congress's ultimate leverage in the foreign policy process is the power of the purse. From 1981 until mid-1984 a majority in Congress often did seek to limit military appropriations to El Salvador. The President, however, used a number of mechanisms to increase vastly military assistance outside the regular or supplemental appropriations process. In March 1981, for example, he used his defense drawdown authority to tap special funds earmarked for military emergencies and increased congressionally authorized military aid to El Salvador by $20 million. Congress had only appropriated $5.5 million. He then used his authority to reprogram budgetary allocations to send another $5 million in military aid and $44.9 million in economic support funds. For fiscal year (FY) 1982, Congress only appropriated $27 million and turned down an administration supplemental request for another $35 million. But in February 1982, the White House, claiming that the guerrilla destruction of aircraft at the Ilopango air base created an emergency situation, used its special defense drawdown authority to dispatch $55 million to El Salvador – over twice the amount Congress had authorized.

In each case the President was obeying the letter but not the spirit of the law. The special funds he drew on for military aid were put aside by Congress for use in emergency situations at presidential discretion. Although there was no emergency in these cases, the President defined them as such in order to circumvent a congressional debate on supplemental appropriations that he was likely to lose. Similarly, reprogramming – which requires only that the appropriations committees be informed of executive budget reallocations and not object within fifteen days – was designed to give the bureaucracy flexibility in reallocating funds among budget categories, not to provide a way to circumvent congressional debate on controversial aid authorizations.

The 1984 and 1985 elections in El Salvador radically changed the character of congressional-executive relations. The election of José Napoleón Duarte, a recognized reformer, reinforced the administration's definition of the government as centrist and reformist despite evidence that the military, not Duarte, was still the real power in El Salvador. Congress approved the administration's aid requests. This aid enabled the Salvadoran military severely to limit the guerrillas' offensive capabilities. This, in turn, reassured Congress that the aid was not making US military intervention more likely. The administration continued to provide misleading and false information about the economic and political situation in El Salvador, the growing isolation of Duarte from his own supporters, and above all the repression by the military. There was some decline in politically-targeted death squad killings, but the White House denied the documented killing and forced displacement of civilians by air and ground operations. Congress made few attempts to scrutinize administration claims publicly.

Nicaragua

US policy-making toward Nicaragua illustrates graphically how emerging patterns of congressional-executive relations are undermining the intent of the post-Vietnam formula. What happened in the Nicaraguan case was the creation of an antecedent state of things that made it difficult (although not impossible) for Congress to say no by 1985. Secrecy, distortion, and circumvention were used by the executive to avoid accountability, consultation, and debate.

On 23 November 1981 President Reagan signed National Security Decision Directive 17 and a secret finding that was submitted to the House and Senate Intelligence Committees informing them that $19.95 million in CIA funds would be used to support 500 contras who would infiltrate Nicaragua to interdict purported arms flows to Salvadoran rebels. By so informing these congressional committees, the administration was carefully responding to the letter of the law. These committees did not protest, because the interdiction rationale made sense to members concerned to contain a leftist revolution supported by the Nicaraguans.

Major actors such as the exiles the CIA was funding, CIA operatives in the field, and hardliners in the administration had a very different purpose – to overthrow the Sandinista regime. This view became even more prevalent as the operation grew in 1982 and 1983.

An effort to misinform or deceive Congress was always an important element of administration policy. But as early as 4 December 1981, articles began to appear in the American press about the covert US action. As the press revealed the scope and character of contra activities, the House Intelligence Committee sought to limit American aid to its original purpose. In December 1982, Representative Edward Boland (D. Mass.), chairman of the committee, introduced language (the Boland Amendment) into the Continuing Resolution for fiscal year 1983 prohibiting the use of funds 'for the purpose of overthrowing the government of Nicaragua.'[1]

The administration's response was to *expand* contra operations to include sabotage raids on such targets as oil supplies and port facilities. While acknowledging that the aim of the contras might be to overthrow the Nicaraguan government, the administration insisted that it was within the law because *its* purpose in giving the aid was arms interdiction, not overthrow. In 1983 the House Intelligence Committee voted to cut off all funds.

The Republican-controlled Senate Intelligence Committee refused to go along with a total cut-off, and a cap of $24 million was put on contra aid for fiscal year 1984. But the administration circumvented congressional spending limits: certain expenses like the mining of Nicaragua's harbors were charged to other accounts; an airfield for the contras was built in Aguacate, Honduras, as a part of a Defense Department exercise and then made available to the contras as a logistics and transportation center; and the Defense Department donated aircraft to transport supplies to contra bases and transferred ships, planes, and guns to the CIA at little or no charge.

Some members of the House and Senate Intelligence Committees were particularly disturbed in 1984 when they discovered that the administration had violated the reporting requirements of the 1980 Intelligence Oversight Act by failing to inform the committees of the decision to mine Nicaraguan harbors. In September 1984, Congress learned of a CIA manual entitled 'Psychological Operations in Guerrilla Warfare'. Its explicit instructions underlined reports from the press and human rights organizations about contra terror. In October 1984, the House Intelligence Committee forced the Senate committee, in conference, to accept the Boland Amendment, now carefully worded to avoid administration circumvention. It was agreed that aid could only be restored by a majority vote in both houses after February 1985.

Again the administration circumvented the law. The National Security Council helped organize and advise a *private* aid network to fund the contras. Marine Lt. Col. Oliver North, a member of the National Security Council staff, was put in charge. North helped reorganize and co-ordinate operations of the two main rebel groups, gave tactical advice, helped the contras raise millions in private and secret public funds, and arranged for supplies and contributions to reach the contras.

Nothing was done to sanction North and little could be done to undo his work. The White House stonewalled, refusing, for example, to release requested documents on its management of the private network and circumvention of the Boland Amendment. It was not until the Iran-contra affair broke in late 1986 that Congress and the press began to uncover the full details of the National Security Council's involvement in circumventing Congress. Millions of dollars in profits made on secret arms sales to Iran were diverted to supply the contras; the NSC had been involved in secretly raising millions for the contras from foreign governments (Saudi Arabia, Brunei); and National Security Adviser Admiral John Poindexter and a top official at the State Department (Elliot Abrams, assistant secretary of state for Latin America) and the CIA (including Director William Casey) were also involved. The contra operation was the centerpiece of an even larger covert effort labelled 'Project Democracy' authorized by President Reagan in the January 1983 National Security Decision Directive No. 77; and North and private individuals had set up 'the enterprise', an extra-government agency to finance and carry out intelligence operations all over the world outside normal government control.

Between 1984 and 1986, as the NSC was circumventing the congressional ban, the CIA was also secretly giving the Nicaraguan rebels aid. More than $1.5 million went for 'political' operations to finance 'security', a radio station, and to seek political and financial support in Europe and Venezuela. The CIA also helped carry out the elaborate contra supply operation run by the NSC (dramatically revealed after a plane was shot down in October 1986 and American mercenary Eugene Hasenfus was captured by the Nicaraguans and put on trial) and actively tried to reorganize and strengthen contra activities in Costa Rica.

Although full details did not emerge until late 1986 and early 1987, by early 1985 there was enough information for Congress to demand that future funding of the 'covert' war be openly debated and legislated through normal channels. This debate was different from the one on El Salvador, because Congress viewed rollback much more critically than containment. US involvement in overthrowing a foreign government raised both moral issues and fears of dragging US troops into a quagmire.

When forced to fight openly for aid, the administration's strategy was to insist that there was to alternative to the contras – and that even the negotiations insisted upon by moderates needed the force of the contras to back them up. There were two elements to this strategy. One was a somewhat successful administration effort to impose its definition of reality on the situation. The internal character of the regime in Nicaragua was presented as so abhorrent and the security threat as so great that any opponent of Reagan administration efforts could be delegitimized as soft on both security and communism. The administration did not hesitate to lie and distort reality in order to create the image it wanted. The more the Democrates accepted the purpose of policy as getting the Sandinista regime out of power (as opposed to negotiating security issues), the more difficult it became to offer an alternative other than the contras.

The second element of administration strategy was systematically to scuttle all efforts at negotiated settlements that recognized the legitimacy of the Nicaraguan government. By destroying all other alternatives, the contras were made to seem the only alternative.

Important to both elements of this whole strategy, however, was the fact that the contras already existed: this *fait accompli*, brought about covertly, was what gave the administration its leverage in the important votes in 1985 and 1986.

When contra aid came before Congress in April 1985, the House narrowly defeated the administration request. But on 12 June, seventy-three Democrats abandoned the House leadership and joined 175 Republicans in supporting a compromise package that banned lethal military aid and restricted CIA involvement in disbursing the aid. A number of the Democrats were con- servative southerners who felt that voting against the aid would make them vulnerable to charges that they were 'soft on communism'.

By the time the crucial vote for $100 million in contra aid came up in the House in March 1986 (it was defeated 222–210) and in June (it passed 221–209) the hook of commitment had already been sunk. While the majority of Democrats (about 183) opposed any aid, the thirty or so crucial swing votes accepted administration arguments that the contras could not be adandoned and that they were a useful tool for pressing negotiations.

In both June 1985 and June 1986, the arguments that swayed middle-of- the-roaders would not have made sense if a huge contra army had not already been created and if other alternatives had not been undermined or defined out of existence. Administration policies had created the very 'antecedent state of things' that the post-Vietnam formula had sought to avoid. This situation had been created by the kind of circumvention, secrecy, and deception the post-Vietnam formula had sought to check.

Conclusion

We need to explain why Congress has not been more vociferous and forceful in using the institutional mechanisms and authority it has to prevent executive disregard for the commitments of the post-Vietnam formula. There are a number of explanations given in the general literature on Congress and foreign policy: the fragmentation of the foreign policy process within Congress, the president's ability to shape and present information, and the difficulty of rallying congressional opposition.

There is some truth in all of these explanations, but there is also a more fundamental problem. On the one hand, Congress faces a hard-to-control national security apparatus dedicated to maintaining US hegemony and largely unchallenged by the post-Vietnam reforms. There is no 'anti-imperial' political coalition strong enough to force Congress to check the executive and to enforce legislation against the security bureaucracy.

A coalition to reform substantively the security apparatus must challenge the foreign policy that justifies the existence of the apparatus itself. While the post-Vietnam commitment did include a reluctance to commit troops and some tolerance for leftist regimes, moderates and conservatives still shared the same underlying strategic vision – revolutionary regimes of the left were antithetical to US global interests. The US still had the right and responsibility to maintain its hegemony and to minimize the chances of leftist outbreaks and takeovers. No one argued for substantial change in the national security apparatus that planned and administered so much of foreign policy. As long as moderates and conservatives both share the assumption that the United States has the right and responsibility to keep (or get) leftist revolutionary regimes out of power, they are trapped into supporting a chronic cold war and the means necessary to carry it out – a largely unaccountable and uncontrollable imperial president and the security apparatus he manages.

> Abridged from Kenneth E. Sharpe (1987–88), 'The post-Vietnam formula under siege: the imperial presidency and Central America', *Political Science Quarterly*, CII, pp. 549–69; a revised version of this article appeared in Nora Hamilton et al., eds. (1988), *Crisis in Central America: Regional Dynamics and U.S. Policy in the 1980s*, Westview Press, Boulder. Reprinted by permission of Westview Press.

Note

1 Boland publicly introduced his amendment to block other legislation that would have cut funds off completely; the committee was not yet ready to support the cut-off of all funds.

3.10   Government and inequality

Benjamin I. Page

We do not know, and probably cannot know, exactly who gets what from government. So many government actions affect the income distribution in such complex ways that it is virtually impossible to pin down precisely to what extent the US (or any other) government contributes to – or lessens – income inequality.

Even the most straightforward sort of government action, like sending a Social Security cheque in the mail, turns out to be not so simple in its impact. We cannot just observe what the distribution of private incomes looks like (finding this out is itself a formidable task), learn how many people at each income level get what amount in Social Security cheques, add those amounts to their private incomes to compute a post-transfer income distribution, and identify the difference between pre- and post-transfer inequality as an effect of government. Beyond that, we should consider lifetime income streams and try to discover whether or not those who receive Social Security are actually poor on a lifetime basis. If not, the transfers may equalize an individual's income over his own life cycle (an important accomplishment) but not equalize the lifetime incomes of different individuals with each other, which is perhaps even more important. Lifetime incomes are not easy to measure. Moreover, we should try to figure out whether the existence of Social Security changes people's private incomes over the life cycle, perhaps leading to earlier retirements and reduced savings and thus merely replacing income that would have been generated in other ways. Even sophisticated studies cannot answer these questions with certainty.

In-kind government transfers like Medicaid or public housing raise the additional problem of figuring out how much they are actually worth to those who get them. We cannot simply divide up budget dollars and assume they are parcelled out among the recipients of services because the value to recipients may be less than what the programs cost. Furthermore, the government's purchasing of goods and services from doctors, building contractors, social workers, and the like may have indirect effects on the income distribution that offset the direct effects of the in-kind transfers. Such effects are difficult to measure with any precision.

The benefits of public goods are by their very nature hard to divide up and assign to individuals. Since few, if any, goods are purely public, different income classes tend to consume different amounts of them, and it is hard to find out how much. But even to the extent that public goods are really public and consumption by everyone is equal, the value of that consumption (i.e., its contribution either to total utility or to dollar-equivalent incomes) would ordinarily not be equal. The value of the armed forces to different groups in society, for example, depends upon who is the foreign enemy at the moment. We must rely on rough estimates that the benefits of a particular public good are, say, about the same for everybody, or proportional to income, or proportional to wealth. Which of these estimates we choose strongly affects what we will find to be government's total income-distributional impact. Moreover, we must again worry about the indirect effects of government purchases upon the private incomes of defense contractors, space engineers, and the like.

The income-distributional effects of laws and regulations are even more difficult to untangle. There are many of them, affecting every area of life, and they work in complex ways. Every one of the countless governmental-induced changes in wages or prices or quality affects the distribution of income. Merely to gauge any one rule's effect is a serious scholarly task, and to try to add them all together is mind-boggling. Further, to assess the impact of the Constitution and the legal system as a whole requires understanding what effect a capitalist economic system has upon the income distribution, which in turn necessitates both microlevel and cross-national studies of the effects of economic structure, studies that are difficult to design or execute.

It is not adequate to view government actions as tacked onto the private economy, simply adding to or subtracting from what the market does. Government actions themselves affect the 'private' behavior of individuals and firms as they make choices about work, savings, production, investments, and even living arrangements and family life. These choices, in turn, affect other 'private' choices and reverberate throughout the economy so that the net long-run impact of a government policy may be quite different from its apparent short-run effect.

Taxes provide a number of examples. The personal income tax, which on the surface looks like a relatively simple subtraction of income from individuals, actually changes people's incentives and behavior all through the economy by means of its marginal rates and its special exemptions and deductions. Capital gains rates affect savings; mortgage interest deductions encourage housing ownership and construction, municipal bond exemptions subsidize state and local governments. Each of these provisions has complex indirect effects on the income distribution as well as the direct effects of eroding progressivity and benefiting the rich.

Similarly, payroll taxes drive a significant part of the economy underground where it is not taxed or measured. The 'employer's' share of payroll taxes results in lower wages for workers and, perhaps, higher prices. Still more complicated are the effects of the corporation income tax, which is conceivably shifted forward to consumers in higher prices or backward to employees in lower wages or is borne by the owners of corporate stock or by the owners of capital generally – or some combination of these. And the property tax may be paid by the owners of land and buildings, or shifted to consumers and renters, or borne by all owners of capital. It makes a good deal of difference to the income distribution which of these things happens, but it is not easy to tell empirically what is going on.

A special difficulty in assessing the effects of government is that effects must be calculated relative to some counterfactual, some baseline model of what the world would be like without the government action. That is fairly manageable if we just want to judge the impact of a single tax or spending program: we can compare what the income distribution is like when the program is in place with what it would be like without the program, assuming everything else remains the same. But when we want to consider the impact of all programs at once, we are compelled to imagine a 'no government' counterfactual – a patent absurdity. It makes no sense to try to conceive of a modern industrial society functioning with no government at all because government is so closely interwoven with every economic activity.

For some purposes it might be useful instead to compare the status quo with a 'Lindahl equilibrium' counterfactual, in which incomes are determined by a perfect private market and public goods are paid for by each individual according to his marginal evaluation of them. But individuals' exact preferences for public goods are unknown and probably unknowable. (Nor do we know what incomes a perfect private market would produce.) To use the Lindahl equilibrium as a base for comparison also accepts as given the income-distributional consequences of its particular scheme for providing public goods, which may or may not be normatively appealing. And it ignores the important effects government has through supporting the private market itself.

For many purposes, therefore – especially when we try to assess the impact of the legal underpinnings of the capitalist system – it is desirable to compare the US or capitalist economies as a group with a socialist (or some other alternative) economic system. But since no existing economy very closely approximates ideal socialism (or, for that matter, ideal capitalism), we are forced into a speculative exercise concerning how the American reality differs from some hypothetical alternative.

The problem is twofold: (1) how to choose among different kinds of counterfactuals, and (2) how to specify the details of the chosen one so that it is not altogether unrealistic. Together with other problems of data and theory and method, this makes it essentially impossible to be sure how government affects the income distribution or even to specify precisely what we mean by 'affects'.

Still, all the uncertainty should not be taken to mean that nothing of interest can be said about connections between government and inequality. The most severe difficulties come in trying to figure out a counterfactual 'pre-government' or 'nongovernment' income distribution to compare with the actual distribution. It is more nearly feasible to calculate a '*post*-government' or actual income distribution by which we can judge how much income inequality there is *after* all government action has been taken into account – without trying to sort out precisely what part of it is due to the private market (or would be present in some other baseline model) and what part is caused by government action. Using an estimate of the post-government income distribution we can at least judge whether or not, after the government has acted, an acceptable degree of equality is achieved. And we can make comparisons over time to see whether equality has increased or not subsequent to various government initiatives.

The answers are reasonably clear. In the United States, after the government has regulated the economy, imposed taxes, and provided social welfare programs and public goods, the total distribution of income is quite unequal. Based on Reynolds and Smolensky's 'standard' incidence assumptions (but with general expenditures allocated proportionally to income rather than equally), the post-fisc Gini coefficient for 1970 was a very substantial 0.375. And, as we have seen, even this is probably too optimistic an estimate. If some public goods (e.g., defense) were apportioned partly according to property ownership rather than income and if social welfare benefits like medical care and public housing were valued at their worth to recipients rather than their cost to the government, the distribution of income would look still more unequal.

Moreover, post-government income has not, during the period studied, become more equal. Reynolds and Smolensky's Gini coefficients (under the same incidence assumptions, with general expenditures apportioned according to income) stayed at virtually identical levels for two decades: 0.384 in 1950, 0.378 in 1961, and 0.375 in 1970. The Great Society and the War on Poverty, at least in their early years, either made no difference at all in the distribution of income or only offset other factors that were tending to increase inequality. After all the government's actions are taken into account, then, income inequality in the United States is very great and has shown little or no sign of decreasing.

Because of the methodological uncertainties, we cannot be sure just how big a part government has played in causing or moderating these results, only that it has failed to overcome them. But our examination of particular government programs helps indicate how it is that government action permitted such high and stable levels of post-government inequality.

Taxes in the United States have done little or nothing to redistribute income. The federal income tax, supposedly very progressive, is undermined by exclusions and exemptions and deductions – especially the mild treatment of capital gains – that chiefly benefit the rich. Highly regressive payroll taxes have provided a larger and larger share of federal revenue. The corporate income tax, whatever its incidence, has virtually vanished. On balance, therefore, federal taxes are only moderately progressive. State taxes, on the other hand, are probably quite regressive, especially if substantial parts of the property tax are passed on to renters and consumers. State and local sales taxes, a large source of revenue, are very regressive because low-income people have to buy necessities and pay out a big part of their income in taxes on them.

 Social welfare policies, though taking up a large part of the budget, have had surprisingly little redistributive effect. The bulk of the money goes for Social Security and other retirement insurance plans that smooth out people's lifetime incomes but do not greatly increase equality across individuals. Much the same is true of the biggest health program, Medicare. Programs (like AFDC and Food Stamps) that are more sharply targeted for the poor are quite small by comparison and have been the first to lose out in budget cuts. Medicaid, which mushroomed in the 1970s, has genuinely helped the poor but not nearly as much as its cost would indicate; much of the money has gone to doctors and hospitals in the form of inflated fees.

Public goods are not particularly intended to help low-income people, and they generally don't. The biggest – defense – does provide some public service jobs for people near the bottom of the income scale; but it also subsidizes the high incomes of engineers and scientists and the owners of high-technology corporations. In its central role of backing up US foreign policy, military spending probably most greatly helps the most wealthy, owners of property, and especially owners of capital invested abroad. Many other more or less public goods probably benefit people roughly in proportion to their overall incomes. This may be true of highway programs (which help automobile drivers and the consumers of trucked merchandise), spending to clean up air and water pollution, energy production, and science and technology, including the space program. Non-military public goods spending probably tends to provide more dollars' worth of benefits to a high-income person than a low, but the amount is roughly proportional to other income and, therefore, does not (assuming a 'no-government' baseline model) much alter the income distribution.

A number of government regulations protect producers; some of these presumably increase the profits of the wealthy, but much of the excess revenue is probably competed away and results only in inefficiency not pro-rich income transfers. Regulations promoting environmental concerns are probably somewhat favorable to those of middle and upper income. Some regulations, like minimum wages and rent controls, which purport to help low-income people, are of dubious effect and, in addition to being inefficient, may actually hurt those on the very bottom of the income distribution.

Finally, the Constitution and the legal system clearly provide foundations for a capitalist economic system. Thus, the income distributional effects of that system are themselves products of government action.

Why so little redistribution

Besides trying to ascertain *how* government affects people's incomes, this book has also been concerned with *why* government has the effects (or lack of effects) it does. This is a central question for political scientists and for anyone who wants to influence policy.

I have discussed two kinds of political explanations for why government has apparently done so little to bring about income equality. [One, a type of interest group analysis which points to biased pluralism or imperfect political competition, sees corporations and organized groups with an upper-income slant as exerting political power over and above the formal one-man-one-vote standard of democracy.] The other, a structuralist view, asserts that inherent features of a capitalist economy compel rational actors, even those of low income, to accept inequality for the sake of more material goods for everyone. Either type of explanation could accommodate the fact of public acquiescence to inequality, one accounting for it in terms of ignorance or deception, the other in terms of correct calculations of self-interest.

There is some substantial evidence for each type of explanation. Both have some validity.

A capitalist system clearly imposes some bounds upon redistribution unless society as a whole is willing to sacrifice a great deal of consumption for the sake of equality. In such a system, if all the income of the wealthy is taxed away (or if incomes are somehow made equal in the first place), the formerly wealthy will presumably not save or invest as much, nor work as hard, nor innovate and produce as much. If everyone is guaranteed an equal income regardless of effort, some will undoubtedly choose not to work at all and will live off the largess of the taxpayers. There is no denying that even modest guaranteed incomes would somewhat reduce the work effort of the poor. And high taxes probably have at least a moderately negative effect on the savings, if not the work, of high-income people.

There is a trade-off between equity and efficiency. At some point, increased redistribution would so cut production that even the worst-off group would lose rather than gain from it. Particularly to the extent that the worst off are concerned with their absolute income level rather than with their relative standing, such a point can be called a 'limit' imposed by the system: further redistribution would be unanimously opposed because it would make everyone worse off. Different social welfare functions would define different degrees of equality as limits. The structure of a capitalist economic system interacts with virtually any welfare criterion to define costs that would eventually offset the benefits of increased redistribution.

The evidence from existing capitalist economies supports the argument that there are limits to redistribution. No industrialized free market economy now or in the past has come very close to complete income equality. Even the Scandinavian countries, models of social democratic capitalism with elaborate welfare state policies, retain highly unequal distributions of wealth and income. In Sweden, for example, in the early 1970s the top fifth of families got about 37 percent of all the post-tax money income while the bottom fifth got only 7 percent.

Yet we should not exaggerate the tightness of structural limits on redistribution. Other capitalist nations, including Sweden, Great Britain, Japan, the Low Countries, and (probably) Germany, have much more equal incomes than the United States has. There are several vigorous capitalist economies in which productivity has grown rapidly along with a relatively high degree of equality.

Internal evidence from the United States bolsters this point. Income maintenance experiments show that rather little production would be lost by providing a moderate guaranteed income for everyone. Taxes could be made substantially more progressive without serious disincentive effects. For those able to work, guaranteed jobs, at good wages, would cost less than guaranteed incomes and would probably increase total production as well as increasing equality.

The United States has not in fact run up against limits imposed by its economic system. With very little, if any, loss in efficiency or production, it would be possible to have considerably more income equality. *Beliefs* and rhetoric about economic structure, not just the structure itself, have been important in restricting the redistributional effects of government.

The shape of public policy is scarcely explicable in other than interest group terms, and specific policy results often correspond closely with activity by well-organized groups.

The patchwork of regressive tax loopholes, from depletion allowances to consumer interest deductions to tax shelters for Park Avenue 'farmers', hardly makes sense as a rational economic design, but it does correspond to lobbying efforts by the wealthy and well-organized. Expensive weapons systems with cost overruns and hefty profits undoubtedly have to do with the political power of defense contractors as well as with objective foreign policy needs. Large subsidies for the interstate highway system surely reflect the clout of truckers and road builders and the automobile and oil industries, just as price supports and payments to big farmers no doubt result from their political importance.

The small size and peculiar shape of programs to redistribute income to the poor reflect the lack of organization by the poor themselves and the weight of conservative groups (which block redistribution) and organized service providers (who divert government dollars to their own pockets). Why should a program to help house the poor take the form of guaranteed mortgages that led to quick foreclosures and abandonments – except that the home loan industry wanted it? Why did urban renewal for so long mean black removal unless it was that white city dwellers and construction companies had more clout than the blacks whose housing was torn down? The public housing disgrace would seem to reflect more solicitude for builders than occupants.

Similarly, Medicare's and Medicaid's pouring of money into private fee-for-service medicine can only be understood in terms of the immense power of organized doctors and hospitals. Even Food Stamps, a successful redistributive transfer program, owes its odd in-kind (rather than cash) nature to the power of agricultural interests, who thought, mistakenly, that it would increase food consumption. The low level of cash transfers or jobs for the poor and the US preference for bricks and mortar and in-kind services make sense only as a sign that corporations and the wealthy and service providers have more influence than the poor themselves.

The system of organized groups is heavily biased toward the wealthy. By any relevant measure – the number of groups, or the extent of lobbying activity, or the amount of money spent – business corporations and professional groups overwhelmingly dominate the interest group universe. This is true despite the important presence of organized labor – weaker than business, and prone to neglect the interests of the very poor in favor of its own middle-income membership – and despite the emergence of a few dedicated 'public interest' lobbies, which tend to be antibusiness but upper-middle class in orientation. Only occasionally do pro-poor social movements become significant political actors.

There are good reasons why the poor and ordinary consumers and taxpayers with diffuse interests do not usually get organized. The costs of communicating and getting together, that is, information and transaction costs, are simply too great relative to the potential gains. Each individual is tempted to act as a free rider and let someone else pay the money and do the work, so no one does it. Rational self-interest imposes a major barrier against organizing the poor into a political force whose numbers might partly counterbalance the money of business corporations.

The techniques of group influence on policy are many. Bribery may be more common than we would like to think, but it is certainly not the chief method by which groups get the public policies they want. The more important techniques are open, legal, and in themselves apparently innocuous: providing information to congressmen and regulators when little competing information is offered on the other side; using media campaigns to change the opinions of the public; cultivating personal relationships with politicians; electing friends and winning 'access' with campaign contributions; tempting politicians with the prospect of future private jobs; recruiting regulators from within industry itself.

The most important channel of group influence is probably the most legal and innocent of all: recruiting and electing friendly politicians, who are predisposed to favor a group's goals long before they get into office. Campaign money and manpower can work wonders at helping sympathetic politicians in both parties (but especially Republicans) emerge as candidates, win nominations, and prevail in general elections. The grateful winners are then open to information-providing, personal contact, and the other techniques of lobbying. But more important, their true personal convictions are in line with what the interest group wants. Bribery is quite unnecessary.

Interest group influence is greatest when political visibility is low, when the public is unaware of what is going on, and when politicians have little to fear from direct policy-related voting by ordinary citizens. On some matters of social policy, visibility tends to be high, the scope of conflict is broad, and the general public tends to prevail over organized interests – at least concerning the broad outlines of policy although the specific implementation may go awry. (The elderly get help with medical care, but doctors control the system of payment.) On other policies, especially those involving technical or apparently minor matters, the scope of conflict is narrow from the start, and

…terest groups often get their way unhindered. Examples include special tax provisions, highly sophisticated weapons systems, and Army Corps of Engineers dams. The most extreme case is regulation by little-known commissions or implementation of small programs at the local level when special interests sometimes completely capture a government agency.

Because money can influence elections and public opinion, money can influence policy. Interest group processes transmit economic inequality into political inequality, which in turn thwarts government redistribution and perpetuates economic inequality.

The United States is probably unusual in the extent to which corporations and professional groups influence policy because of the absence of leftist trade unions or a socialist party that could raise the visibility of distributive issues and mobilize the poor and the working class. The Democratic party, while somewhat more pro-redistribution than the Republican, is only a shadow of a vigorous European socialist party. In the United States there is relatively little counterweight to the influence of business and the wealthy.

In relying upon an interest group analysis to account for much of the government's failure to redistribute income, the analysis blends rather subtly back into a discussion of economic structure. It is somewhat artificial to separate the two. In *any* capitalist system with liberal democratic political institutions, interest groups with an upper-income bias will wield disproportionate political power.

Inevitably, under capitalism, a few individuals and corporations seem to hold large shares of wealth; usually they are well organized and (as a by-product of organization for other purposes) are well equipped to seek political ends. It is difficult to see how any capitalist society, so long as it permits free speech and free association, can prevent the turning of money and organization into political power. There are simply too many channels through which money can influence public opinion and policy makers. If this is so, the configuration of interest group power is itself to a substantial extent structural. Possibly, a degree of egalitarianism that would in theory be perfectly compatible with the structure of capitalist economies is ruled out by the political forces inevitably unleashed by those economies.

Part Four
The Soviet political system in perspective

Introduction

The Russian Revolution of 1917 was the greatest political upheaval in Europe since the French Revolution of 1789. It seemed to take up the challenge that the mass politics of the French Revolution had made to the absolutist monarchies of the eighteenth century and extend it in a new form to the capitalist representative democracies of the twentieth century. Lenin and the Bolsheviks did not regard their system as an alternative *to* democracy but the best possible alternative *of* democracy: the path to the classless, stateless society. During seventy years of turbulent history the Soviet Union, especially under its longest-serving ruler, Stalin, became a military superpower, challenging the hegemony of the United States by extending its own influence, through conquest and imitation, over a large part of Europe, Asia and even the Third World. Yet it appeared to have achieved this at the expense of its own model of democracy and when, in the 1980s (and at the eleventh hour), Gorbachev tried to transform the Soviet system into a more democratic form of socialism, the release of long-suppressed pressures destabilised the party-state, which suddenly disintegrated in 1991. Since then a dazed world has been trying to come to terms with the consequences of the collapse of a system which many had regarded as one of the most stable in the world.

Though the influence of the 'Soviet model' has rapidly waned since the collapse of the USSR, and though most of the former communist states have rushed headlong into *laissez-faire* capitalism and 'presidential' representative democracy, the study of the rise and fall of the Soviet system retains great theoretical and practical importance: it throws light on the problems of developing viable democratic institutions as well as on the nature of revolutionary regimes, and it also helps us to understand the problems of the successor states whose appearance has changed the political map of Europe and central Asia.

The selection of readings which follows attempts to highlight some of the most important turning-points in the evolution and ultimate decline of the Soviet Union. It cannot, of course, hope to be comprehensive and does not seek to replace standard textbooks on Soviet history and politics; rather, it seeks to supplement these by highlighting key facets of the Soviet Union's development since 1917. In this latter regard, several of the pieces have been deliberately included to illustrate the pre-Gorbachev Western debates about the nature of the Soviet system, now cast in a different light with the system's collapse. The fourteen readings are divided into five main subject areas.

We start with the *Revolutions of 1917*, which we explore through selections from the well-known study by Sheila Fitzpatrick (4.1 and 4.2). Why did the Russian autocracy collapse in 1917? Why did liberal democracy fail to develop as a result of that collapse? To help us answer these questions, Fitzpatrick first analyses the 'setting' for revolution in the disintegrating social system of late tsarism and then examines the main stages and dilemmas of the transition between the February and October revolutions and the dynamics of the Bolshevik seizure of power. It is essential to have a thorough understanding of the origins of the Soviet system if one is to gain a clear perspective on its later development and collapse.

We then move on to two pieces on the crucial historial problem of the Soviet system: *Stalinism*. Though Lenin laid the foundations of the Soviet state, it was Stalin who, during a period of dominance which extended nearly thirty years, gave it its essential character. Did he betray Lenin's ideas or simply complete Lenin's revolutionary task? How are we to understand the nature of the system which he developed? Robert Tucker (4.3) seeks the nature of Stalin's 'revolution from above' in a combination of three influences: the 'revolutionary' impulses derived from the Civil War period; the reassertion within the post-revolutionary Soviet setting of Russian political traditions; and the paranoid personality of Stalin himself. Seweryn Bialer analyses (in 4.4) the essential features and functioning of the 'mature' Stalinist system after it had become consolidated in the later 1930s.

With this background in place, it is now possible to turn to the functioning of the Soviet system at its apparent zenith in the Brezhnev era, looking at the problems of *Party control*. Bohdan Harasymiw describes (in 4.5) the working of the *nomenklatura*, the key institution by which the party controlled appointments in all important areas of state administration. Alec Nove (4.6) explores the role of these *nomenklatura* officials and asks whether they, or some other group, can be regarded within the Soviet system as a 'ruling class', a provocative question which raises fundamental issues about the character of party rule. Finally, Viktor Zaslavsky and Robert Brym discuss (in 4.7) the puzzling problem of the functions of elections to the soviets (or councils) in which there was only one candidate, who would duly receive 99.9 percent of the votes cast; Zaslavsky writes from his own direct experience as a member of a Soviet electoral commission.

Next we look at the *nationalities problem*, from the outset arguably the

'Achilles' heel' of the Soviet state. Jeremy Azrael (4.8) analyses the nationalities question from the perspective of the later 1970s. Interestingly, he sees the most intractable problems emerging from the demographic rise of Muslim Central Asia, with the numerous nationality tensions evident in the European areas of the Soviet state as being more containable; in the actual period of collapse during 1989–91, it was in fact European nationalist assertion which was to prove the most destabilizing. John Armstrong (4.9) then brings us more up to date with a survey of the development of nationality problems under Gorbachev and of key trends in the new post-Soviet republics.

We move on to a consideration of *theories and trends of social change* in the Soviet Union. David Lane (in 4.10) analyses the merits and demerits of two influential Western interpretations of Soviet politics and society during the 1950s and 1960s: theories of totalitarianism and the 'convergence' or 'industrial society' model; he finds them in the end both inadequate. However, more recently 'totalitarianism' has been brought back into vogue by post-Soviet elites as a useful intellectual framework for understanding their own past, while the 'industrial society' model, restated to exclude the 'convergence' dimension, now looks highly relevant in identifying long-term processes of change which helped bring about the collapse of the Soviet system. This theme is taken up by Moshe Lewin, who offers (in 4.11) an original and illuminating survey of the dramatic processes of urbanisation and modernisation – in part unplanned and even unnoticed by the Soviet authorities themselves – which transformed the character of Soviet society after the 1920s, and which may aid our understanding of why the pressures for democratization became so strong in the 1980s.

Finally we turn to the *dénouement*, the *Gorbachev reform programme*. Mikhail Gorbachev (4.12) presents his own analysis of his reform strategy and of the problems he faced as these appeared to him in 1987, when he wrote his book *Perestroika*. Then Stephen White (4.13) analyses the development of and constraints on Gorbachev's key political reforms (competitive elections and an 'autonomous' parliament, parties and the executive presidency independent of party control); these provide perhaps his most lasting achievements, since the resultant institutions still largely survive in the successor states. We end with White's brief summary (in 4.14) of the *coup de grâce* – the 1991 August coup and the party-state's demise, whose long-term causes, we hope, may be sought in the arguments of most of the preceding readings.

Chris Binns

4.1 Background to revolution

Sheila Fitzpatrick

At the beginning of the twentieth century, Russia was one of the great powers of Europe. But it was a great power that was universally regarded as backward by comparison with Britain, Germany and France. In economic terms, this meant that it had been late to emerge from feudalism (the peasants were freed from legal bondage to their lords or the state only in the 1860s) and late in industrializing. In political terms, it meant that until 1905 there were no legal political parties and no central elected parliament, and the autocracy survived with undiminished powers. Russia's towns had no tradition of political organization or self-government, and its nobility had similarly failed to develop a corporate sense of identity strong enough to force concessions from the throne. Legally, Russia's citizens still belonged to 'estates' (urban, peasant, clergy and noble), even though the estate system made no provision for new social groups like professionals and urban workers, and only the clergy retained anything like the characteristics of a self-contained caste.

The three decades before the 1917 Revolution saw not impoverishment but an increase in national wealth; and it was in this period that Russia experienced its first spurt of economic growth as a result of the government's industrialization policies, foreign investment, modernization of the banking and credit structure and a modest development of native entrepreneurial activity. The peasantry, which still constituted 80 percent of Russia's population at the time of the Revolution, had not experienced a marked improvement in its economic position.

As Russia's last Tsar, Nicholas II, sadly perceived, the autocracy was fighting a losing battle against insidious liberal influences from the West. The direction of political change – towards something like a Western constitutional monarchy – seemed clear, though many members of the educated classes were impatient at the slowness of change and the stubbornly obstructionist attitude of the autocracy. After the 1905 Revolution, Nicholas gave in and established a national elected parliament, the Duma, at the same time legalizing political parties and trade unions. But the old arbitrary habits of autocratic rule and the continued activity of the secret police undermined these concessions.

After the Bolshevik Revolution of October 1917, many Russian emigrés looked back on the pre-revolutionary years as a golden age of progress which had been arbitrarily interrupted (as it seemed) by the First World War, or the unruly mob, or the Bolsheviks. There was progress, but it contributed a great deal to the society's instability and the likelihood of political upheaval: the more rapidly a society changes (whether that change is perceived as progressive or regressive) the less stable it is likely to be.

[handwritten: UN-USUAL MARKED Lenin wanted stages to happen rather than allowing then.]

The society

The Russian Empire covered a vast expanse of territory, stretching from Poland in the west to the Pacific Ocean in the east, extending into the Arctic north, and reaching the Black Sea and the borders of Turkey and Afghanistan in the south. The hub of the Empire, European Russia (including some of the area that is now the Ukraine) had a population of 92 million in 1897, with the total population of the Empire recorded by that year's census at 126 million. But even European Russia and the relatively advanced western regions of the Empire remained largely rural and non-urbanized. There were a handful of big urban industrial centres, most of them the product of recent and rapid expansion: St Petersburg, the imperial capital, renamed Petrograd during the First World War and Leningrad in 1924; Moscow, the old and (from 1918) future capital; Kiev, Kharkov and Odessa, together with the new mining and metallurgical centres of the Donbass, in what is now the Ukraine; Warsaw, Lodz and Riga in the west; Rostov and the oil city of Baku in the south. But most Russian provincial towns were still sleepy backwaters at the beginning of the twentieth century.

In the villages, much of the traditional way of life remained. The peasants still held their land in communal tenure, dividing the village fields into narrow strips which were tilled separately by the various peasant households; and in many villages, the *mir* (village council) would still periodically redistribute the strips so that each household had an equal share.

Of course the Emancipation of 1861 had changed peasant life, but it had been framed with great caution so as to minimize the change and spread it over time. Before Emancipation, the peasants worked their strips on the village land, and they also worked the masters' land or paid him the equivalent of their labour in money. After the Emancipation, they continued to work their own land, and sometimes worked for hire on their former masters' land, while making 'redemption' payments to the state to offset the lump sums that had been given the landowners as immediate compensation. The redemption payments were scheduled to last for forty-nine years (although in fact the state cancelled them a few years early), and the village community was collectively responsible for the debts of all members. This meant that individual peasants were still bound to the village, though they were bound by the debt and the *mir*'s collective responsibility instead of by serfdom. The terms of the Emancipation were intended to prevent a mass influx of peasants into the towns and the creation of a landless proletariat which would represent a danger to public order. They also had the effect of reinforcing the *mir* and the old system of communal land tenure, and making it almost impossible for peasants to consolidate their strips, expand or improve their holdings, or make the transition to independent small-farming.

While permanent departure from the villages was difficult in the post-Emancipation decades, it was easy to leave the villages temporarily to work for hire in agriculture, construction, mining or in the towns. In fact such work was a necessity for many peasant families: the money was needed for taxes and redemption payments. The peasants who worked as seasonal labourers (*otkhodniki*) were often away for many months of the year, leaving their families to till their land in the villages.

With one in every two peasant households in European Russia including a family member who left the village for work – and a higher proportion in the Petersburg and Central Industrial Regions and the western provinces – the impression that old Russia survived almost unchanged in the villages may well have been deceptive. Many peasants were in fact living with one foot in the traditional village world and the other in the quite different world of the modern industrial town.

The urban working class was still very close to the peasantry. The number of permanent industrial workers (somewhat over three million in 1914) was smaller than the number of peasants who left the villages for non-agricultural seasonal work each year, and in fact it was almost impossible to make a hard-and-fast distinction between permanent urban-dwelling workers and peasants who worked most of the year in the towns. Only in St Petersburg had a large proportion of the industrial labour force severed all connection with the countryside.

The main reason for the close interconnection between the urban working class and the peasantry was that Russia's rapid industrialization was a very recent phenomenon. It was not until the 1890s – more than half a century after Britain – that Russia experienced large-scale growth of industry and expansion of towns.

Despite these characteristics of underdevelopment, Russian industry was in some respects quite advanced by the time of the First World War. The modern industrial sector was small, but unusually highly concentrated, both geographically (notably in the regions centred on Petersburg and Moscow and the Ukrainian Donbass) and in terms of the size of the industrial plants. Comparative backwardness had its own advantages: industrializing late, with the aid of large-scale foreign investment and energetic state involvement, Russia was able to skip over some of the early stages, borrow relatively advanced technology and move quickly towards large-scale modern production.

According to Marxist theory, a highly concentrated industrial proletariat in conditions of advanced capitalist production is likely to be revolutionary, whereas a pre-modern working class that retains strong ties to the peasantry is not. Yet the empirical evidence of the period from the 1890s to 1914 suggests that in fact Russia's working class, despite its close links with the peasantry, was exceptionally militant and revolutionary. Large-scale strikes were frequent, the workers showed considerable solidarity against management and state authority, and their demands were usually political as well as economic.

However, the 'modern' characteristics of Russian society, even in the urban sector and the upper educated strata, were still very incomplete. It was often said that Russia had no middle class; and indeed its business and commercial class remained comparatively weak, and the professions had only recently acquired the status normal in industrialized societies. Despite increasing professionalization of the state bureaucracy, its upper ranks remained dominated by the nobility, traditionally the state's service class. Service prerogatives were all the more important to the nobility because of its economic decline as a landowning group after the abolition of serfdom: only a minority of noble landowners had successfully made the transition to capitalist, market-oriented agriculture.

Educated Russians would often describe themselves as members of the intelligentsia. Sociologically, this was a very slippery concept, but in broad terms the word 'intelligentsia' described a Westernized educated elite, alienated from the rest of Russian society by its education and from Russia's autocratic regime by its radical ideology. However, the Russian intelligentsia did not see itself as an elite, but rather as a classless group united by moral concern for the betterment of society, the capacity for 'critical thought' and, in particular, a critical, semi-oppositionist attitude to the regime. Ideally (though not altogether in practice), intelligentsia membership and bureaucratic service were incompatible. The Russian revolutionary movement of the second half of the nineteenth century, characterized by small-scale conspiratorial organization to fight the autocracy and thus liberate the people, was largely a product of the intelligentsia's radical ideology and political disaffection.

The revolutionary tradition

The task which the Russian intelligentsia had taken on itself was the betterment of Russia – first, drawing up the social and political blue-prints for the country's future, and then, if possible, taking action to translate them into reality. The yardstick for Russia's future was Western Europe's present. In the third quarter of the nineteenth century, one of the central topics of discussion was Western European industrialization and its social and political consequences.

One view was that capitalist industrialization had produced human degradation, impoverishment of the masses and destruction of the social fabric in the West, and therefore ought to be avoided at all costs by Russia. The radical intellectuals who held this view have been retrospectively grouped under the heading of 'Populists', though the label implies a degree of coherent organization which did not in fact exist. Populism was essentially the mainstream of Russian radical thought from the 1860s to the 1880s.

The Russian intelligentsia generally accepted socialism (as understood by Europe's pre-Marxist socialists) as the most desirable form of social organization, though this was not seen as incompatible with the acceptance of liberalism as an ideology of political change. Populism combined an objection to capitalist industrialization with an idealization of the Russian peasantry.

The Populists wished to save the Russian peasants' traditional form of village organization, the commune or *mir*, from the ravages of capitalism, because they believed that the *mir* was an egalitarian institution – perhaps a survival of primitive communism – through which Russia might find a separate path to socialism.

It was in the 1880s that the Marxists emerged as a distinct group within the Russian intelligentsia, repudiating the utopian idealism, terrorist tactics and peasant orientation that had previously characterized the revolutionary movement. They argued that capitalist industrialization was inevitable in Russia, and that the peasant *mir* was already in a state of internal disintegration, propped up only by the state and its state-imposed responsibilities for the collection of taxes and redemption payments. They asserted that capitalism constituted the only possible path towards socialism, and that the industrial proletariat produced by capitalist development was the only class capable of bringing about true socialist revolution.

The Marxists made another important choice in the early controversy with the Populists over capitalism: they chose the urban working class as their base of support and Russia's main potential force for revolution. This distinguished them from the old tradition of the Russian revolutionary intelligentsia (upheld by the Populists and later, from its formation in the early 1900s, by the Socialist-Revolutionary (SR) Party), with its one-sided love affair with the peasantry. It distinguished them also from the liberals (some of them former Marxists), whose Liberation movement was to emerge as a political force shortly before 1905, since the liberals hoped for a 'bourgeois' revolution and won support from the new professional class and the liberal nobility.

The Marxists – illegally organized from 1898 as the Russian Social-Democratic Labour Party – between 1898 and 1914 ceased to be a preserve of the intelligentsia and became in the literal sense a workers' movement. Its leaders still came from the intelligentsia, and spent most of their time living outside Russia in European emigration. But in Russia, the majority of members and activists were workers (or, in the case of professional revolutionaries, former workers).

In 1903, when the Russian Social-Democratic Party held its Second Congress, the leaders fell into dispute over an apparently minor issue – the composition of the editorial board of the party newspaper *Iskra*. No real substantive questions were involved, though to the extent that the dispute revolved around Lenin it might be said that he himself was the underlying issue, and that his colleagues considered that he was too aggressively seeking a position of dominance. Lenin's manner at the congress was overbearing, and he had recently been laying down the law very decisively on various theoretical questions, notably the organization and functions of the party.

The outcome of the Second Congress was a split in the Russian Social-Democratic Labour Party between 'Bolshevik' and 'Menshevik' factions.

The Bolsheviks were those who followed Lenin's lead, and the Mensheviks constituted a larger and more diverse group of party members who thought Lenin had overreached himself. The split made little sense to Marxists inside Russia, and at the time of its occurrence was not regarded as irrevocable even by the emigrés. It proved, nevertheless, to be permanent, and as time passed the two factions acquired more clearly distinct identities than they had had in 1903.

In the years after 1903, the Mensheviks emerged as the more orthodox in their Marxism (not counting Trotsky, a Menshevik until mid-1917 but always a maverick), less inclined to force the pace of events towards revolution and less interested in creating a tightly-organized and disciplined revolutionary party. They had more success than the Bolsheviks in attracting support in the non-Russian areas of the Empire, while the Bolsheviks had the edge among Russian workers. (In both parties, however, Jews and other non-Russians were prominent in the intelligentsia-dominated leadership.) In the last pre-war years, 1910–14, the Mensheviks lost working-class support to the Bolsheviks as the workers' mood became more militant: they were perceived as a more 'respectable' party with closer links to the bourgeoisie, whereas the Bolsheviks were seen as more working class as well as more revolutionary.

The Bolsheviks, unlike the Mensheviks, had a single leader, and their identity was in large part defined by Lenin's ideas and personality. Lenin's first distinctive trait as a Marxist theoretician was his emphasis on party organization. He saw the party not only as the vanguard of proletarian revolution but also in a sense as its creator, since he argued that the proletariat alone could achieve only a trade-union consciousness and not a revolutionary one.

Lenin believed that the core of the party's membership should consist of full-time professional revolutionaries, recruited both from the intelligentsia and the working class, but concentrating on the political organization of workers rather than any other social group. In *What Is To Be Done?* (1902), he insisted on the importance of centralization, strict discipline and ideological unity within the party. These, of course, were logical prescriptions for a party operating clandestinely in a police state. Nevertheless, it seemed to many of Lenin's contemporaries (and later to many scholars) that Lenin's dislike of looser mass organizations allowing greater diversity and spontaneity was not purely expedient but reflected a natural authoritarian bent.

Lenin differed from many other Russian Marxists in seeming actively to desire a proletarian revolution rather than simply predicting that one would ultimately occur. The idea that the liberal bourgeoisie must be the natural leader of Russia's anti-autocratic revolution was never really acceptable to Lenin; and in *Two Tactics of Social Democracy*, written in the midst of the 1905 Revolution, he insisted that the proletariat – allied with Russia's rebellious peasantry – could and should play a dominant role.

The 1905 Revolution and its aftermath; the First World War

Late tsarist Russia was an expanding imperial power with the largest standing army of any of the great powers of Europe. Its strength *vis-à-vis* the outside world was a source of pride, an achievement that could be set against the country's internal political and social problems. In the words attributed to an early twentieth-century Minister of Interior, 'a small victorious war' was the best remedy for Russia's domestic unrest. Though some of Nicholas II's ministers urged caution, the prevailing sentiment in court and high bureaucratic circles was that there were easy pickings to be made in the Far East, and that Japan – an inferior, non-European power, after all – would not be a formidable adversary. Initiated by Japan, but provoked almost equally by Russian policy in the Far East, the Russo-Japanese War broke out in January 1904.

For Russia, the war turned out to be a series of disasters and humiliations on land and at sea. The early patriotic enthusiasm of respectable society quickly soured. This fuelled the liberal movement, since autocracy always seemed least tolerable when it was most clearly perceived as incompetent and inefficient.

In January 1905, Petersburg workers held a peaceful demonstration – organized not by militants and revolutionaries, but by a renegade priest with police connections, Father Gapon – to bring their economic grievances to the attention of the Tsar. On Bloody Sunday (9 January), troops fired on the demonstrators outside the Winter Palace, and the 1905 Revolution had begun.

The spirit of national solidarity against the autocracy was very strong during the first nine months of 1905. The liberals' claim to leadership of the revolutionary movement was not seriously challenged.

The culmination of the liberal revolution was Nicholas II's October Manifesto (1905), in which he conceded the principle of a constitution and promised to create a national elected parliament, the Duma. The Manifesto divided the liberals: the Octobrists accepted it, while the Constitutional Democrats (Cadets) formally withheld acceptance and hoped for further concessions. In practice, however, the liberals withdrew from revolutionary activity at this time, and concentrated their energies on organizing the new Octobrist and Cadet parties and preparing for the forthcoming Duma elections.

However, the workers remained actively revolutionary until the end of the year, achieving greater visibility than before and becoming increasingly militant. In October, the workers of Petersburg organized a 'soviet' or council of workers' representatives elected in the factories. The practical function of the Petersburg Soviet was to provide the city with a kind of emergency municipal government at a time when other institutions were paralysed and a general strike was in progress. But it also became a political forum for the workers, and to a lesser extent for socialists from the revolutionary parties (Trotsky became one of the Soviet's leaders). For a few months, the tsarist authorities handled the Soviet in a gingerly manner, but early in December it was dispersed by a successful police operation in other cities; and the news of the attack on the Petersburg Soviet led to an armed uprising by the Moscow Soviet, in which the Bolsheviks had gained considerable influence. This was put down by troops, but the workers fought back and there were many casualties.

The urban revolution of 1905 stimulated the most serious peasant uprisings since the Pugachev revolt in the late eighteenth century. But the urban and rural revolutions were not simultaneous. Peasant rioting – consisting of the sacking and burning of manor houses and attacks on landowners and officials – began in the summer of 1905 and rose to a peak in the late autumn, subsided, and then resumed on a large scale in 1906. But even in late 1905 the regime was strong enough to begin using troops in a campaign of village-by-village pacification. By the middle of 1906, all the troops were back from the Far East, and discipline had been restored in the armed forces. In the winter of 1906–07, much of rural Russia was under martial law, and summary justice (including over a thousand executions) was dispensed by field courts martial.

The political outcome of the 1905 Revolution was ambiguous, and in some ways unsatisfactory to all concerned. In the Fundamental Laws of 1906 – the closest Russia came to a constitution – Nicholas made known his belief that Russia was still an autocracy. True, the autocrat now consulted with an elected parliament, and political parties had been legalized. But the Duma had limited powers; ministers remained responsible solely to the autocrat; and, after the first two Dumas proved insubordinate and were arbitrarily dissolved, a new electoral system was introduced which virtually disfranchised some social groups and heavily over-represented the landed nobility. The Duma's main importance, perhaps, lay in providing a public forum for political debate and a training-ground for politicians.

One thing that the 1905 Revolution did *not* change was the police regime that had come to maturity in the 1880s. Due process of law was still suspended for much of the population much of the time. Of course there were understandable reasons for this: the fact that in 1908, a comparatively quiet year, 1,800 officials were killed and 2,083 were wounded in politically motivated attacks indicates how tumultuous the society remained, and how much the regime remained on the defensive. But it meant that in many respects the political reforms were only a façade. Trade unions, for example, had been made legal in principle, but individual unions were frequently closed down by the police. Political parties were legal, and even the revolutionary socialist parties could contest the Duma elections and win a few seats – yet the members of revolutionary socialist parties were no less liable to arrest than in the past, and the party leaders (most of whom returned to Russia during the

1905 Revolution) were forced back into emigration to avoid imprisonment and exile.

Neither Bolsheviks nor Mensheviks had got more than a toehold in the workers' revolution of 1905: the workers had not so much rejected as outpaced them, and this was a very sobering thought, particularly for Lenin. Revolution had come, but the regime had fought back and survived.

Among the bad news of the pre-war years was that the regime was embarking on a major programme of agrarian reform. The peasant revolts of 1905–07 had persuaded the government to abandon its earlier premiss that the *mir* was the best guarantee of rural stability. Its hopes now lay in the creation of a class of small independent farmers – a wager on 'the sober and the strong', as Nicholas's chief Minister, Petr Stolypin, described it. Peasants were now encouraged to consolidate their holdings and separate from the *mir*, and land commissions were established in the provinces to facilitate the process. The assumption was that the poor would sell up and go to the towns, while the more prosperous would improve and expand their holdings. By 1914, about 40 percent of peasant households in European Russia had formally separated from the *mir*, although, given the legal and practical complexity of the process, only a relatively small number had completed the later steps towards establishing themselves as proprietors farming their own consolidated and self-contained blocks of land. The Stolypin reforms were 'progressive' in Marxist terms, since they laid the basis for capitalist development in agriculture. But, in contrast to the development of urban capitalism, their short- and medium-range implications for Russian revolution were highly depressing. Russia's traditional peasantry was prone to revolt. If the Stolypin reforms worked (as Lenin, for one, feared that they might), the Russian proletariat would have lost an important revolutionary ally.

In 1906, the Russian economy was bolstered by an enormous loan (two and a quarter billion francs) which Witte negotiated with an international banking consortium, and both native and foreign-owned industry expanded rapidly in the pre-war years. This meant, of course, that the industrial working class also expanded. But labour unrest dropped down sharply for some years after the savage crushing of the workers' revolutionary movement in the winter of 1905–06, picking up again only around 1910. Large-scale strikes became increasingly common in the immediate pre-war years, culminating in the Petrograd general strike of the summer of 1914, which was sufficiently serious for some observers to doubt that Russia could risk mobilizing its army for war. The workers' demands were political as well as economic, and their grievances against the regime included its responsibility for foreign domination of many sectors of Russian industry as well as its use of coercion against the workers themselves. In Russia, the Mensheviks were conscious of losing support as the workers became more violent and belligerent, and the Bolsheviks were conscious of gaining it.

When war broke out in Europe in August 1914, with Russia allied with

France and England against Germany and Austria-Hungary, the political emigrés became almost completely cut off from Russia. In the European socialist movement as a whole, large numbers of former internationalists became patriots overnight when war was declared. The Russians were less inclined than others to outright patriotism, but most took the 'defensist' position of supporting Russia's war effort as long as it was in defence of Russian territory. Lenin, however, belonged to the smaller group of 'defeatists' who repudiated their country's cause entirely: it was an imperialist war, as far as Lenin was concerned, and the best prospect was a Russian defeat which might provoke civil war and revolution. This was a very controversial stand, even in the socialist movement, and the Bolsheviks found themselves very much cold-shouldered. In Russia, all known Bolsheviks – including Duma deputies – were arrested for the duration of the war.

As in 1904, Russia's declaration of war produced a public surge of patriotic enthusiasm. But once again, the mood quickly turned sour. The Russian Army suffered crushing defeats and losses (a total of five million casualties for 1914–17), and the German Army penetrated deep into the western territories of the Empire, causing a chaotic outflow of refugees into central Russia. Defeats bred suspicion of treason in high places, and one of the main targets was Nicholas's wife, Empress Alexandra, who was a German princess by birth. Scandal surrounded Alexandra's relationship with Rasputin, a shady but charismatic character whom she trusted as a true man of God who could control her son's haemophilia. When Nicholas assumed the responsibilities of Commander in Chief of the Russian Army, which took him away from the capital for long periods, Alexandra and Rasputin began to exercise a disastrous influence over ministerial appointments. Relations between the government and the Fourth Duma deteriorated drastically. Late in 1916, Rasputin was murdered by some young nobles close to the court and a right-wing Duma deputy, whose motives were to save the honour of Russia and the autocracy.

The autocracy's situation was precarious on the eve of the First World War. The society was deeply divided, and the political and bureaucratic structure was fragile and overstrained. The regime was so vulnerable to any kind of jolt or setback that it is hard to imagine that it could have survived long, even without the War, although clearly change might in other circumstances have come less violently and with less radical consequences than was the case in 1917.

The First World War both exposed and increased the vulnerability of Russia's old regime. The public applauded victories, but would not tolerate defeats. When defeats occurred, the society did not rally behind its government (a relatively normal reaction, especially if the enemy becomes an invader of the homeland, and the reaction of Russian society in 1812 and again in 1941–42) – but instead turned sharply against it, denouncing its incompetence and backwardness in tones of contempt and moral superiority. This suggests that the regime's legitimacy had become extremely shaky, and that its survival was very closely related to visible achievements or, failing that, sheer luck. The old regime had been lucky in 1904–06, an earlier occasion when war defeats had plunged it into revolution, because it got out of the war relatively quickly and honourably, and was able to obtain a very large post-war loan from Europe, which was then at peace. It was not so lucky in 1914–17. The war lasted too long, draining not only Russia but the whole of Europe. More than a year before the Armistice in Europe, Russia's old regime was dead.

Abridged from Sheila Fitzpatrick (1982), *The Russian Revolution, 1917–1932*, pp. 10–33. Reprinted by permission of Oxford University Press, Oxford.

4.2   The Russian revolutions of 1917: from February to October

Sheila Fitzpatrick

In February 1917, the autocracy collapsed in the face of popular demonstrations and the withdrawal of elite support for the regime. In the euphoria of revolution, political solutions seemed easy. Russia's future form of government would, of course, be democratic. The exact meaning of that ambiguous term and the nature of Russia's new constitution would be decided by a Constituent Assembly, to be elected by the Russian people as soon as circumstances permitted. In the meantime, the elite and popular revolutions – liberal politicians, the propertied and professional classes and the officer corps in the first category; socialist politicians, the urban working class and rank-and-file soldiers and sailors in the second – would coexist, as they had done in the glorious days of national revolutionary solidarity in 1905. In institutional terms, the new Provisional Government would represent the elite revolution, while the newly revived Petrograd Soviet would speak for the revolution of the people. Their relationship would be complementary rather than competitive, and 'dual power' (the term applied to the coexistence of the Provisional Government and the Soviet) would be a source of strength, not of weakness. Russian liberals, after all, had traditionally tended to see the socialists as allies. Most Russian socialists, similarly, were prepared to see the liberals as allies, since they accepted the Marxist view that the bourgeois liberal revolution had first place on the agenda.

Yet within eight months the hopes and expectations of February lay in ruins. 'Dual power' proved an illusion, masking something very like a power vacuum. The popular revolution became progressively more radical, while the elite revolution moved towards an anxious conservative stance in defence of property and law and order. The Provisional Government barely survived General Kornilov's attempted coup from the right before succumbing in October to the Bolsheviks' successful coup from the left, popularly associated with the slogan of 'All power to the soviets'. The long-awaited Constituent Assembly met but accomplished nothing, being unceremoniously dispersed by the Bolsheviks in January 1918. On the peripheries of Russia, officers of the old tsarist Army were mustering their forces to fight the Bolsheviks, some under the monarchist banner that had seemed banished forever in 1917. The revolution had not brought liberal democracy to Russia. Instead, it had brought anarchy and civil war.

The headlong passage from democratic February to Red October astonished victors and vanquished alike. For Russian liberals, the shock was traumatic. The revolution – *their* revolution by right, as the history of Western Europe demonstrated and even right-thinking Marxists agreed – had finally occurred, only to be snatched from their grasp by sinister and incomprehensible forces. Mensheviks and other non-Bolshevik Marxists were similarly outraged: the time was not yet ripe for proletarian socialist revolution, and it was inexcusable that a Marxist party should break the rules and seize power. Until quite recently, most historical explanations of the Bolshevik Revolution emphasized its illegitimacy in one way or the other, as if seeking to absolve the Russian people of any responsibility for the event and its consequences.

In the classic Western interpretation Lenin's pamphlet *What Is To Be Done?*, setting out the prerequisites for the successful organization of an illegal, conspiratorial party, was usually cited as the basic text; and it was argued that the ideas of *What Is To Be Done?* moulded the Bolshevik Party in its formative years and continued to determine Bolshevik behaviour even after the final emergence from underground in February 1917. The open, democratic and pluralist politics of the post-February months in Russia were thus subverted, culminating in the Bolsheviks' unlawful seizure of power by a conspiratorially organized coup in October. The Bolshevik tradition of centralized organization and strict party discipline led the new Soviet regime towards repressive authoritarianism and laid the foundations for Stalin's later totalitarian dictatorship.

Yet there have always been problems in applying this general concept of the origins of Soviet totalitarianism to the specific historical situation unfolding between February and October 1917. In the first place, the old underground Bolshevik Party was swamped by an influx of new members, outstripping all other political parties in recruitment, especially in the factories and the armed forces. By the middle of 1917, it had become an open mass party, bearing little resemblance to the disciplined elite organization of full-time revolutionaries described in *What Is To Be Done?* In the second place, neither the party as a whole nor its leadership were united on the most basic policy questions in 1917. In October, for example, disagreements within the party leadership on the desirability of insurrection were so acute that the issue was publicly debated by Bolsheviks in the daily press.

It may well be that the Bolsheviks' greatest strength in 1917 was not strict party organization and discipline (which scarcely existed at this time) but rather the party's stance of intransigent radicalism on the extreme left of the political spectrum. While other socialist and liberal groups jostled for position in the Provisional Government and Petrograd Soviet, the Bolsheviks refused to be co-opted and denounced the politics of coalition and compromise. As the 'dual power' structure disintegrated, discrediting the coalition parties represented in the Provisional Government and Petrograd Soviet leadership, only the Bolsheviks were in a position to benefit. Among the socialist parties, only the Bolsheviks had overcome Marxist scruples, caught the mood of the crowd and declared their willingness to seize power in the name of the proletarian revolution.

The 'dual power' relationship of the Provisional Government and Petrograd Soviet was conceived as an interim arrangement pending the summoning of a Constituent Assembly. But its disintegration under attack from left and right and the growing polarization of Russian politics raised disturbing questions about the future as well as the present in mid-1917. Was it still reasonable to hope that Russia's political problems could be resolved by a popularly elected Constituent Assembly and the formal institutionalization of parliamentary democracy on the Western model? The Constituent Assembly solution, like the interim 'dual power', required a degree of political consensus and agreement on the necessity of compromise. The perceived alternatives to consensus and compromise were dictatorship and civil war.

The February Revolution and 'dual power'

In the last week of February, bread shortages, strikes, lock-outs and finally a demonstration in honour of International Women's Day brought a crowd on to the streets of Petrograd that the authorities could not disperse. The Fourth Duma, which had reached the end of its term, petitioned the Emperor once again for a responsible cabinet and asked to remain in session for the duration of the crisis. Both requests were refused; but an unauthorized Duma Committee, dominated by liberals of the Cadet Party and the Progressive Bloc, did in fact remain in session. The Emperor's Ministers held one last, indecisive meeting and then took to their heels. Nicholas II himself was absent, visiting Army Headquarters in Mogilev; his response to the crisis was a laconic instruction by telegraph that the disorders should be ended immediately. But the police was disintegrating, and troops from the Petrograd garrison brought into the city to control the crowd had begun to fraternize with it. By the evening of 28 February, Petrograd's Military Commander had to report that the revolutionary crowd had taken over all railway stations, all artillery supplies and, as far as he knew, the whole city.

The Army High Command had two options, either to send in fresh troops who might or might not hold firm, or to seek a political solution with the help of the Duma politicians. It chose the latter alternative. At Pskov, on the return journey from Mogilev, Nicholas's train was met by emissaries from the High Command and the Duma who respectfully suggested that the Emperor should abdicate. After some discussion, Nicholas mildly agreed. But, having initially accepted the suggestion that he should abdicate in favour of his son, he thought further about Tsarevich Aleksei's delicate health and decided instead to abdicate on his own behalf and that of Aleksei in favour of his brother, Grand Duke Michael. Grand Duke Michael, being a prudent man, declined the invitation to succeed his brother. *De facto*, therefore, Russia was no longer a monarchy. It was decided that the country's future form of government would be determined in due course by a Constituent Assembly, and that in the meantime a self-appointed 'Provisional Government' would take over the responsibilities of the former imperial Council of Ministers. Prince Georgii Lvov, a moderate liberal, became head of the new government. His cabinet included Pavel Milyukov, Cadet Party theoretician, as Foreign Minister, two prominent industrialists as Ministers of Finance and Trade and Industry, and the socialist lawyer Aleksandr Kerensky as Minister of Justice.

The Provisional Government had no electoral mandate, deriving its authority from the now defunct Duma, the consent of the Army High Command and informal agreements with public organizations like the Zemstvo League and the War Industries Committee. The old tsarist bureaucracy provided its executive machinery but, as the result of the earlier dissolution of the Duma, it had no supporting legislative body.

From the very beginning there were reasons to doubt the effectiveness of the transfer of power. The most important reason was that the Provisional Government had a competitor: the Petrograd Soviet, formed on the pattern of the 1905 Petersburg Soviet by workers, soldiers and socialist politicians.

In the first months, the Provisional Government consisted mainly of liberals, while the Soviet's Executive Committee was dominated by socialist intellectuals, mainly Mensheviks and SRs by party affiliation. Kerensky, a Provisional Government member but also a socialist, who had been active in setting up both institutions, served as liaison between them. The socialists of the Soviet intended to act as watch-dogs over the Provisional Government, protecting the interests of the working class until such time as the bourgeois revolution had run its course.

But the workers, soldiers and sailors who made up the Soviet's rank and file were not so cautious. On 1 March, before the formal establishment of the Provisional Government or the emergence of 'responsible leadership' in the Soviet, the notorious Order No. 1 was issued in the name of the Petrograd Soviet. It called for democratization of the Army by the creation of elected soldiers' committees, reduction of officers' disciplinary powers and, most importantly, recognition of the Soviet's authority on all policy questions involving the armed forces: it stated that no governmental order to the Army was to be considered valid without the counter-signature of the Soviet. It presaged the most unworkable form of dual power, that is, a situation in which the enlisted men in the armed forces recognized only the authority of the Petrograd Soviet, while the officer corps recognized only the authority of the Provisional Government.

There were recurrent conflicts between the Soviet Executive Committee and the Provisional Government on labour policy and the problem of peasant land claims. The Provisional Government remained firmly committed to the war effort. The Soviet Executive Committee took the 'defensist' position, favouring continuation of the war as long as Russian territory was under attack but opposing annexationist war aims and the Secret Treaties. But on the floor of the Soviet – and in the streets, the factories and especially the garrisons – the attitude to the war tended to be simpler and more drastic: stop fighting, pull out of the war, bring the troops home.

The relationship that developed between the Soviet Executive Committee and the Provisional Government in the spring and summer of 1917 was intense, intimate and quarrelsome. The Executive Committee guarded its separate identity jealously, but ultimately the two institutions were too closely bound to be indifferent to each other's fate, or to dissociate themselves in the event of disaster. The link was strengthened in May, when the Provisional Government ceased to be a liberal preserve and became a coalition of liberals and socialists, drawing in representatives of the major socialist parties (Mensheviks and SRs) whose influence was predominant in the Soviet Executive Committee. The socialists were not eager to enter the government, but concluded that it was their duty to strengthen a tottering regime at a time of national crisis. They continued to regard the Soviet as their more natural sphere of political action, especially when it became clear that the new socialist Ministers of Agriculture and Labour would be unable to implement their policies because of liberal opposition. Nevertheless, a symbolic choice had been made: in associating themselves more closely with the Provisional Government, the 'responsible' socialists were separating themselves (and, by extension, the Soviet Executive Committee) from the irresponsible popular revolution.

Popular hostility to the 'bourgeois' Provisional Government mounted in the late spring, as war weariness increased and the economic situation in the towns deteriorated. During the street demonstrations that occurred in July (the July Days), demonstrators carried banners calling for 'All power to the soviets', which in effect meant the removal of power from the Provisional Government. Paradoxically – though logically in terms of its commitment to the Government – the Executive Committee of the Petrograd Soviet rejected the slogan of 'All power to the soviets'; and in fact the demonstration was directed as much against the existing Soviet leadership as against the Government itself. 'Take power, you son of a bitch, when it's given you!' shouted one demonstrator, shaking his fist at a socialist politician. But this was an appeal (or perhaps a threat?) to which those who had pledged themselves to 'dual power' could not respond.

The Bolsheviks

At the time of the February Revolution, virtually all leading Bolsheviks were in emigration abroad or in exile in remote regions of the Russian Empire, arrested *en masse* after the outbreak of war.

Before Lenin's return to Petrograd early in April, the former Siberian exiles had already begun to rebuild the Bolshevik organization and publish a newspaper. At this point the Bolsheviks, like other socialist groups, showed signs of drifting into the loose coalition around the Petrograd Soviet.

But Lenin's appraisal of the political situation, known to history as the April Theses, was belligerent, uncompromising and distinctly disconcerting to the Petrograd Bolsheviks. Scarcely pausing to acknowledge the achievements of February, Lenin was already looking forward to the second stage of revolution, the overthrow of the bourgeoisie by the proletariat. No support should be given to the Provisional Government. The present Soviet leadership, having succumbed to bourgeois influence, was useless.

Nevertheless, Lenin predicted that the soviets – under revitalized revolutionary leadership – would be the key institutions in transferring power from the bourgeoisie to the proletariat. 'All power to the soviets!', one of the slogans of Lenin's April Theses, was in effect a call for class war. 'Peace, land and bread', another of Lenin's April slogans, had similarly revolutionary implications. 'Peace', in Lenin's usage, meant not only withdrawal from the imperialist war but also recognition that such withdrawal '*is impossible* ... without the overthrow of capital'. 'Land' meant confiscation of the landowners' estates and their redistribution by the peasants themselves – something very close to spontaneous peasant land seizures.

The Bolsheviks, respectful as they were of Lenin's vision and leadership, were shocked by Lenin's April Theses. But in the following months, under Lenin's exhortations and reproaches, the Bolsheviks did move into a more intransigent position, isolating themselves from the socialist coalition.

The Bolsheviks were still in a minority at the June Congress of Soviets, and they had yet to win a major city election. But their growing strength was already evident at the grass-roots level – in the workers' factory committees, in the committees of soldiers and sailors in the armed forces, and in local district soviets in the big towns. Bolshevik Party membership was also increasing spectacularly, although the Bolsheviks never made any formal decision to launch a mass recruitment drive, and seemed almost surprised by the influx. The party's membership figures, shaky and perhaps exaggerated as they are, give some sense of its dimensions: 24,000 Bolshevik Party members at the time of the February Revolution (though this figure is particularly suspect, since the Petrograd party organization could actually identify only about 2,000 members in February, and the Moscow organization 600); more than 100,000 members by the end of April; and in October 1917 a total of 350,000 members, including 60,000 in Petrograd and the surrounding province and 70,000 in Moscow and the adjacent Central Industrial Region.

The popular revolution

Seven million men were under arms at the beginning of 1917, with two million in the reserve. The armed forces had suffered tremendous losses, and war weariness was evident in the increasing desertion rate and the soldiers' responsiveness to German fraternization at the front. To the soldiers, the February Revolution was an implicit promise that the war would soon end, and they waited impatiently for the Provisional Government to achieve this – if not on its own initiative, then under pressure from the Petrograd Soviet. By May, as the Commander-in-Chief reported with alarm, 'class antagonism' between officers and men had made deep inroads on the Army's spirit of patriotic solidarity.

The February Revolution had given birth to a formidable array of workers' organizations in all Russia's industrial centres, but especially in Petrograd and Moscow. Workers' soviets were created not only at the city level, like the Petrograd Soviet, but also at the lower level of the urban district, where the leadership usually came from the workers themselves rather than the socialist intelligentsia and the mood was often more radical. New trade unions were established; and at the plant level, workers began to set up factory committees to deal with management, which tended to be the most radical of all workers' organizations. In the factory committees of Petrograd, the Bolsheviks had assumed a dominant position by the end of May 1917.

The factory committees' original function was to be the workers' watchdog over the plant's capitalist management. The term used for this function was 'workers' control' (*rabochii kontrol'*), which implied supervision rather than control in the managerial sense. But in practice the factory committees often went further and started to take over managerial functions. The definition of 'workers' control' moved closer to something like workers' self-management.

This change took place as the workers' political mood was becoming more militant, and as the Bolsheviks were gaining influence in the factory committees. Militancy meant hostility to the bourgeoisie and assertion of the workers' primacy in the revolution: just as the revised meaning of 'workers' control' was that workers should be masters in their own plants, so there was an emerging sense in the working class that 'soviet power' meant that the workers should be sole masters in the district, the city and perhaps the country as a whole. As political theory, this was closer to anarchism or anarcho-syndiclism than to Bolshevism, and the Bolshevik leaders did not in fact share the view that direct workers' democracy through the factory committees and the soviets was a plausible or desirable alternative to their own concept of a party-led 'proletarian dictatorship'. Nevertheless, the Bolsheviks were realists, and the political reality in Petrograd in the summer of 1917 was that their party had strong support in the factory committees and did not want to lose it. Accordingliy, the Bolsheviks were in favour of 'workers' control', without defining too closely what they meant by it.

The villages were quiet in February, and many of the young peasant men were absent because of conscription for military service. But by May, it was clear that the countryside was sliding into turmoil as it had done in 1905 in response to urban revolution. As in 1905–06, manor houses were being sacked and burned. In addition, the peasants were seizing private and state land for their own use. During the summer, as the disturbances mounted, many landowners abandoned their estates and fled from the countryside. It seems to have been assumed throughout peasant Russia that this new revolution meant – or should be made to mean – that the nobles' old illegitimate title to the land was revoked. Land should belong to those who tilled it.

When unauthorized land seizures began on a large scale in the summer of 1917, the seizures were conducted on behalf of village communities, not individual peasant households, and the general pattern was that the *mir* subsequently divided up the new lands among the villagers as it had traditionally divided up the old ones.

Despite the seriousness of the land problem and the reports of land seizures from the early summer of 1917, the Provisional Government procrastinated on the issue of land reform. The liberals were not on principle against expropriation of private lands, and generally seem to have regarded the peasants' demands as just. But any radical land reform would clearly pose formidable problems. In the first place, the Government would have to set up a complicated official mechanism of expropriation and transfer of lands, which was almost certainly beyond its current administrative capacities. In the second place, it could not afford to pay the large compensation to the landowners that most liberals considered necessary. The Provisional Government's conclusion was that it would be best to shelve the problems until they could be properly resolved by the Constituent Assembly.

The political crises of the summer

In mid-June, Kerensky, now the Provisional Government's Minister of War, encouraged the Russian Army to mount a major offensive on the Galician Front. This offensive, conducted in June and early July, failed with an estimated 200,000 casualties. It was a disaster in every sense. Morale in the armed forces disintegrated further, and the Germans began a successful counter-attack that continued throughout the summer and autumn. Russian desertions, already rising as peasant soldiers responded to news of the land seizures, grew to epidemic proportions. The Provisional Government's credit was undermined, and tension between government and military leaders increased. At the beginning of July, a governmental crisis was precipitated by the withdrawal of all the Cadet (liberal) ministers and the resignation of the head of the Provisional Government, Prince Lvov.

In the midst of this crisis, Petrograd erupted once again with the mass demonstrations, street violence and popular disorder of 3–5 July known as the July Days. To the Provisional Government, it looked like a Bolshevik attempt at insurrection. Yet Lenin did not encourage them to take violent action against the Provisional Government or the present Soviet leadership. Confused and lacking leadership and specific plans, the demonstrators finally dispersed.

The July Days were a disaster for the Bolsheviks. Clearly Lenin and the Bolshevik Central Committee had been caught off balance. They had talked insurrection, in a general way, but not planned it. The Kronstadt Bolsheviks, responding to the sailors' revolutionary mood, had taken an initiative which, in effect, the Bolshevik Central Committee had disowned. The whole affair damaged Bolshevik morale and Lenin's credibility as a revolutionary leader.

The damage was all the greater because the Bolsheviks, despite the leaders' hesitant and uncertain response, were blamed for the July Days by the Provisional Government and the moderate socialists of the Soviet. Several prominent Bolsheviks were arrested, along with Trotsky, who had taken a position close to Lenin's on the extreme left since his return to Russia in May and was to become an official Bolshevik Party member in August. Orders were issued for the arrest of Lenin. During the July Days, moreover, the Provisional Government had intimated that it had evidence to support the rumours that Lenin was a German agent, and the Bolsheviks were battered by a wave of patriotic denunciations in the press that temporarily eroded their popularity in the armed forces and the factories. The Bolshevik Central Committee (and no doubt Lenin himself) feared for Lenin's life. Early in August, disguised as a workman, he crossed the border and took refuge in Finland.

If the Bolsheviks were in trouble, however, this was also true of the Provisional Government, headed from early July by Kerensky. The liberal-socialist coalition was in constant turmoil, with the socialists pushed to the left by their Soviet constituency and the liberals moving to the right under pressure from the industrialists, landowners and military commanders. The threat from the left was a popular uprising in Petrograd and/or Bolshevik coup. The other threat was the possibility of a coup from the right to establish a law-and-order dictatorship.

The coup from the right was finally attempted by General Lavr Kornilov, whom Kerensky had recently appointed Commander-in-Chief with a mandate to restore order and discipline in the Russian Army. In the last week of August General Kornilov dispatched troops from the front to Petrograd, ostensibly to quell disorders in the capital and save the Republic. But the attempted coup failed largely because of the unreliability of the troops and the energetic actions of the Petrograd workers. The troops' morale disintegrated, and the coup was aborted outside Petrograd without any serious military engagement.

In Petrograd, politicians of the centre and right rushed to reaffirm their loyalty to the Provisional Government, which Kerensky continued to head. But Kerensky's standing had been further damaged by his handling of the Kornilov affair, and the government weakened. The Executive Committee of the Petrograd Soviet also emerged with little credit, since the resistance to Kornilov had been organized largely at the local union and factory level; and this contributed to an upsurge of support for the Bolsheviks which almost immediately enabled them to displace the Soviet's old Menshevik-SR leadership. Relations between officers and men deteriorated sharply; and, as if this were not enough, the German advance was continuing.

The left gained most from the Kornilov affair, since it gave substance to the previously abstract notion of a counter-revolutionary threat from the right, demonstrated working-class strength, and at the same time convinced many workers that only their armed vigilance could save the revolution from its enemies. The Bolsheviks, with many of their leaders still gaoled or in hiding, played no special role in the actual resistance to Kornilov. But the new swing of popular opinion towards them, already discernible early in August, greatly accelerated after Kornilov's aborted coup; and in a practical sense they were to reap future benefit from the creation of workers' militia units or 'Red Guards' which began in response to the Kornilov threat. The Bolsheviks' strength was that they were the only party uncompromised by association with the bourgeoisie and the February regime, and the party most firmly identified with ideas of workers' power and armed uprising.

The October Revolution

From April to August, the Bolsheviks' solgan 'All power to the soviets' was a taunt directed at the moderates who controlled the Petrograd Soviet and did not want to take all power. But the situation changed after the Kornilov affair, when the moderates lost control. The Bolsheviks gained a majority in the Petrograd Soviet on 31 August and a majority in the Moscow Soviet on 5 September. If the second national Congress of Soviets, scheduled to meet in October, followed the same political trend as the capitals, what were the implications? Did the Bolsheviks want a quasi-legal transfer of power to the soviets, based on a decision by the Congress that the Provisional Government had no further mandate to rule? Or was their old slogan really a call for insurrection, or an affirmation that the Bolsheviks (unlike the rest) had the courage to take power?

In September, Lenin wrote from his hiding-place in Finland urging the Bolshevik Party to prepare for an armed insurrection. The Bolsheviks must act *before* the meeting of the Second Congress of Soviets, pre-empting any decision that the Congress might make.

The insurrection began on 24 October, the eve of the meeting of the Second Congress of Soviets, when the forces of the Soviet's Military-Revolutionary Committee began to occupy key governmental institutions. On the night of 24–25 October, Lenin came out of hiding. By the afternoon of the 25th, the coup was all but accomplished; the Palace fell late in the evening. The February regime had been overthrown, and power had passed to the victors of October.

Of course, this did leave one question unanswered. Who *were* the victors of October? In urging the Bolsheviks towards insurrection before the Congress of Soviets, Lenin had evidently wanted this title to go to the Bolsheviks. But the Bolsheviks had in fact organized the uprising through the Military-Revolutionary Committee of the Petrograd Soviet; and, by accident or design, the Committee had procrastinated until the eve of the meeting of the national Congress of Soviets. As the news went out to the provinces, the most common version was that the soviets had taken power.

The question was not wholly clarified at the Congress of Soviets which opened in Petrograd on 25 October. As it turned out, a clear majority of the Congress delegates had come with a mandate to support transfer of all power to the soviets. But this was not an exclusively Bolshevik group (300 of the 670 delegates were Bolsheviks, which gave the party a dominant position but not a majority), and such a mandate did not necessarily imply approval of the Bolsheviks' pre-emptive action. That action was violently criticized at the first session by a large group of Mensheviks and SRs, who then quit the Congress in protest.

At the Congress, the Bolsheviks called for the transfer of power to workers', soldiers' and peasants' soviets throughout the country. As far as central power was concerned, the logical implication was surely that the place of the old Provisional Government would be taken by the standing Central Executive Committee of the soviets, elected by the Congress and including representatives from a number of political parties. But this was not so. To the surprise of many delegates, it was announced that central governmental functions would be assumed by a new Council of People's Commissars, whose all-Bolshevik membership was read out to the Congress on 26 October by a spokesman for the Bolshevik Party. The head of the new government was Lenin, and Trotsky was People's Commissar (Minister) of Foreign Affairs.

Some historians have recently suggested that the Bolsheviks did not mean to take power for themselves alone. But if the intention in question is Lenin's, the argument seems dubious, and Lenin overrode the objections of other leading members of the party. In September and October, Lenin seems clearly to have wanted the Bolsheviks tõ take power, not the multi-party soviets. He did not even want to use the soviets as camouflage, but would apparently have preferred to stage an unambiguous Bolshevik coup. In the provinces, certainly, the immediate result of the October Revolution was that the soviets took power, and the local soviets were not always dominated by Bolsheviks. It is perhaps fair to say that they had no objection in principle to the soviets exercising power at a local level, as long as the soviets were reliably Bolshevik. But this requirement was difficult to square with democratic elections contested by other political parties.

Certainly Lenin was quite firm on the issue of coalition in the new central government, the Council of People's Commissars. In November 1917, when the Bolshevik Central Committee discussed the possibility of moving from an all-Bolshevik government to a broader socialist coalition, Lenin was adamantly against it, even though several Bolsheviks resigned from the government in protest. Later a few 'left SRs' (members of a splinter group of the SR Party that had accepted the October coup) were admitted to the Council of People's Commissars, but they were politicians without a strong party base. They were dropped from the government in mid-1918, when the left SRs staged an uprising in protest against the peace treaty recently signed with Germany. The Bolsheviks made no further effort to form a coalition government with other parties.

Had the Bolsheviks a popular mandate to rule alone, or did they believe that they had one? In the elections for the Constituent Assembly (held, as scheduled before the October coup, in November 1917), the Bolsheviks won 25 percent of the popular vote. This put them second to the SRs, who won 40 percent of the vote (left SRs, who supported the Bolsheviks on the issue of the coup, were not differentiated in the voting lists). The Bolsheviks took Petrograd and Moscow, and probably won in urban Russia as a whole. In the armed forces, whose five million votes were counted separately, the Bolsheviks had an absolute majority in the Armies of the Northern and Western Fronts and the Baltic Fleet – the constituencies they knew best, and where they were best known. On the southern fronts and in the Black Sea Fleet, they lost to the SRs and Ukrainian parties. The SRs' overall victory was the result of winning the peasant vote in the villages. But there was a certain ambiguity in this. The peasants were probably single-issue voters, and the SR and Bolshevik programmes on the land were virtually identical. The SRs, however, were much better known to the peasantry, their traditional constituency. Where the peasants knew the Bolshevik programme (usually as a result of proximity to towns, garrisons or railways, where the Bolsheviks had done more campaigning), their votes were split between the Bolsheviks and the SRs.

In democratic electoral politics, nevertheless, a loss is a loss. The Bolsheviks did not take that view of the elections to the Constituent Assembly: they did not abdicate because they had failed to win (and, when the Assembly met and proved hostile, they unceremoniously dispersed it). However, in terms of the mandate to rule, they could and did argue that it was not the population as a whole that they claimed to represent. They had taken power in the name of the working class. The conclusion to be drawn from the elections to the Second Congress of Soviets and the Constituent Assembly was that, as of October–November 1917, they were drawing more working-class votes than any other party.

But what if at some later time the workers should withdraw their support? The Bolsheviks' claim to represent the will of the proletariat was based on faith as well as observation: it was quite possible, in Lenin's terms, that at some time in the future the workers' proletarian consciousness might prove inferior to that of the Bolshevik Party, without necessarily removing the party's mandate to rule. Probably the Bolsheviks did not expect this to happen. But many of their opponents of 1917 did, and they assumed that Lenin's party would not give up power even if it lost working-class support. Engels had warned that a socialist party taking power prematurely might find itself isolated and forced into repressive dictatorship. Clearly the Bolshevik leaders, and Lenin in particular, were willing to take that risk.

> Abridged from Sheila Fitzpatrick (1982), *The Russian Revolution, 1917–1932*, pp. 34–60. Reprinted by permission of Oxford University Press, Oxford.

4.3   Stalinism as revolution from above

Robert C. Tucker

To many, 'Russian Revolution' means the events of 1917 culminating in the Bolsheviks' seizure of power toward the end of that year. From a broader and historically more adequate standpoint, the Russian Revolution was a social epoch comprising the manifold social, political, economic, and cultural transformations during the period of Civil War and War Communism that ensued after 1917 and lasted until the initiation of the New Economic Policy in 1921. And on the still more comprehensive view that is being advocated here, the Revolution extended over slightly more than two decades. Otherwise expressing it, NEP society was an interval of relative quiescence between two phases of the Russian revolutionary process: the 1917–21 phase and the Stalinist phase that ensued in 1929–39.

The NEP Russia that emerged from the Bolshevik Revolution of 1917–21 could be described as a society with two uneasily coexisting cultures. There was an officially dominant Soviet culture comprising the Revolution's myriad innovations. Side by side with it was a scarcely sovietized Russian culture that lived on from the pre-1917 past as well as in the small-scale rural and urban private enterprise that flourished under the NEP. It was the declared objective of the new one to transform the old one.

Doubts of this existed in some quarters, including the émigré Russian intellectuals associated with the symposium *Smena vekh* (Change of Landmarks). For Ustrialov and his fellow *smenavekhovtsy*, the NEP was the beginning of the end of Russian Communism as a revolutionary culture-transforming movement, its incipient deradicalization, and Russia's imminent return to national foundations. On the Bolsheviks' behalf, Lenin anathematized that perspective. And replying to those Menshevik-minded Marxists ('our European philistines') who argued, like Sukhanov, that it had been a mistake for socialists to seize power in so culturally backward a country as Russia. Lenin defiantly replied in one of his last articles, 'Why could we not first create such prerequisites of civilization in our country as the expulsion of the landowners and the Russian capitalists, and then start moving toward socialism?' If a definite level of culture was needed, as they said, for the building of socialism, 'Why cannot we begin by first achieving the prerequisites for that definite level of culture in a revolutionary way, and *then*, with the aid of the workers' and peasants' government and the Soviet system, proceed to overtake the other nations?'[1]

While upholding the historical correctness of the Bolshevik decision to take power in 1917 and to pursue the revolutionary political course that it did subsequently, Lenin in 1921 and after redefined the movement's objective and strategy in the new situation marked by retreat at home and delay of other Marxist revolutions abroad. The transcending of the NEP was to take place within the framework of the NEP, by evolution not revolution. Lenin could not have been more explicit on this point. War Communism, with its forcible food requisitioning, had represented a 'revolutionary approach' to the building of a socialist society; it had sought to break up the old social-economic system completely at one stroke and substitute for it a new one. The NEP signified an abandonment of that in favor of a 'reformist approach' whose method was 'not to *break up* the old social-economic system – trade, petty production, petty proprietorship, capitalism – but to *revive* trade, petty proprietorship, capitalism, while cautiously and gradually getting the upper hand over them. . . .'[2]

The transfer culture, as Lenin now envisaged it, was the 'co-operating of Russia' along with the development of a popularly administered, non-bureaucratized society with a large-scale, advanced machine industry based heavily on electrification and operating according to plan. The co-operating of Russia meant the involvement of the entire population in co-operative forms of work. This would realize the utopian dreams of the 'old co-operators' like Robert Owen, whose error had been not the vision of a co-operative socialism but the belief that it could be put into practice without a political revolution such as the one that the Bolsheviks had carried out. To achieve the co-operated Russia through the NEP, by the reformist methods that now defined the transfer culture in Lenin's mind, would be the work of 'a whole historical epoch' comprising one or two decades at a minimum. The methods themselves would consist very largely of 'culturalizing', the remaking of the popular mentality and ethos by educative means starting with the overcoming of illiteracy. Only through such a gradual, long-range 'cultural revolution' would it be possible to gain the population's voluntary acceptance of co-operative socialism.

History, as we know, did not go the way that Lenin charted; it went the Stalinist way. This was radically different from the path delineated in those Lenin articles of the final period that Bukharin, in the essay that he published in *Pravda* in January 1929 for the fifth anniversary of Lenin's death, described as 'Lenin's Political Testament'. Stalinism in its time of self-assertion and triumph, the 1930s, was a revolution in exactly the sense that Lenin had defined it in warning against a revolutionary approach to the further building of Soviet socialism: 'a change which breaks the old order to its very foundations, and not one that cautiously, slowly, and gradually remodels it, taking care to break as little as possible'. Instead of transcending the NEP evolutionarily, Stalinism abolished it revolutionarily, by decree and force. Instead of proceeding gradually and by means of persuasion, it proceeded at breakneck speed and wielded state power coercively to smash popular resistance by terrorizing the population. Instead of taking care to break as little as possible, it broke the spirit along with the bodies of a great proportion of the generation that had come of age during the first phase of the Revolution a decade before. It also consumed a very heavy proportion of those party leaders and members who had, in the 1920s, been Stalinists in the simple sense of supporters of the general secretary and his 'general line' in the fight with the oppositions.

The rural revolution called 'mass collectivization' illustrates these points. In the space of a few years and at the cost of untold suffering and a famine whose toll of lives ran into many millions, a countryside with about twenty-five million peasant farmsteads functioning on nationalized land was transformed into one in which the great majority of those peasants were organized into some 200,000 collective farms (*kolkhozy*), while many more were employed as hired workers on state farms (*sovkhozy*). In the *Short Course* of party history (1938), which Stalin edited personally, the collectivization is described as 'a profound revolution, a leap from an old qualitative state of society to a new qualitative stae, equivalent in its consequences to the revolution of October 1917'. The *Short Course* goes on: 'The distinguishing feature of this revolution is that it was accomplished *from above*, on the initiative of the state, and directly supported *from below* by the millions of peasants, who were fighting to throw off kulak bondage and to live in freedom in the collective farms.'[3]

It was indeed a state-initiated, state-directed, and state-enforced revolution from above – as was the Stalinist revolution as a whole – but the *Short Course* lied when it spoke of mass peasant support from below. Historical evidence available to us now in great abundance attests that not alone the ones classified as kulaks, whose 'liquidation as a class' was proclaimed as the banner of the collectivization drive, but the mass of middle peasants and even some of the rural poor were sullenly opposed to the rural revolution and joined the *kolkhozy* only under duress or because of fear. The claim in Soviet publicity of Stalin's time and after that the collectivization was Lenin's 'co-operative plan' in action is groundless. Not only was there no patient, long-drawn-out educational effort ('cultural revolution') to prepare the peasantry's mind for voluntary acceptance of co-operative farming, and no antecedent industrialization sufficient to produce the hundred thousand tractors that Lenin had foreseen as a powerful inducement to the peasants to farm co-operatively; still more important, the *kolkhozy* were (and are) socialist co-operatives only in their formal façade.

The rural revolution from above of 1929–33 proceeded simultaneously with the heroic phase of the Stalinist industrial revolution from above: that state-directed, frantic, military-oriented industrialization drive whose very slogan, 'Fulfill the Five-Year Plan in Four', reflected the gap between what actually happened and the Plan as officially adopted in 1929. The relationship between these two processes presents a highly complex problem. It was at one time widely believed that the forcible mass collectivization was a necessity for the desired high-speed superindustrialization, in that the *kolkhoz* system enabled the Soviet state to extract otherwise unobtainable (or uncertainly obtainable) agricultural surpluses. Such, indeed, appears to have been the underlying conception on which Stalin acted at the time; collectivization was envisaged as the presupposition of a form of industrialization geared to the priority of heavy industry and war industry over the consumer-goods industries whose greater development would have been a *sine qua non* of a Soviet industrialization within the frame of a continued rural NEP. In the event, however, the economic consequences of collectivization were so catastrophic that recent researches have reached the conclusions that (1) 'mass collectivization of Soviet agriculture must be reckoned as an unmitigated economic policy disaster', and (2) 'the oppressive state agricultural procurement system, rather than serving to extract a net contribution from agriculture as a whole, should be credited with preventing the collectivization disaster from disrupting the industrialization drive'.[4]

Concentrating for the present on collectivization and industrialization, I want to ask why they took place in the Stalinist way.

According to a view which draws part of its inspiration from Trotsky's thinking and which achieved wide influence owing to its espousal by Isaac

Deutscher, Stalinist industrialization-cum-collectivization (which Deutscher calls 'the second revolution') was a necessitated response to a 'grave social crisis' of the later 1920s. Citing Stalin's statistics, Deutscher states that in January 1928, in particular, government grain purchases fell short by two million tons of the minimum needed to feed the urban population.[5] Emergency measures were applied by the government to extract grain that was being withheld from the market. The peasants were not, for the most part, politically motivated against the Soviet regime, but were driven by economic circumstances, in that the small farms produced only enough to meet the peasants' own food needs while the 'big farmers' with surpluses were charging prices beyond the ability of the town population to pay and also were demanding concessions to capitalist farming. In this dilemma, yielding to the peasants would antagonize the urban working class, and refusal to yield would also bring a threat of famine and urban unrest. A 'radical solution' was demanded, and Stalin, having until the very last moment shrunk from an upheaval, acted 'under the overwhelming pressure of events' and embarked upon the second revolution in an 'unpremeditated, pragmatic manner'. He was 'precipitated into collectivization by the chronic danger of famine in 1928 and 1929'.[6]

Such, in Deutscher's classic version, is the 'circumstantial explanation' of the initial phase of the Stalinist revolution from above. It is a central thesis of the present essay that the circumstantial explanation is flawed, first, in the utterly unproven nature of its assumption that collectivization in the terroristic form that it took was the only realistic alternative for the Soviet regime in 1929. It hardly squares with the now demonstrated conclusion that this course proved in practice an 'unmitigated economic policy disaster', nor is it cogent that a policy which directly and indirectly produced the worst famine in Russia's famine-plagued history, that of 1932–34, which cost a conservatively estimated five million lives, was necessitated by the need to avert a famine. The insistently emerging conclusion from scholarly researches based on the more abundant data now available from Soviet sources is that 'a continuation of the New Economic Policy of the 1920s would have permitted at least as rapid a rate of industrialization with less cost to the urban as well as to the rural population of the Soviet Union'. In effect, informed and thoughtful historical hindsight is confirming the basic economic realism of the program for a balanced industrialization policy within the frame of a continuing NEP that Bukharin presented in his *Pravda* article of September 30, 1928, 'Notes of an Economist'.[7] The Bukharinist non-revolutionary alternative for Soviet industrialization policy at the close of the twenties, an alternative inspired in large part by the Leninist thinking of 1921–23 discussed earlier here, was real. Had it been adopted, it could well have worked; had it worked poorly, the cost to the Soviet economy could not have compared with that which had to be paid for the Stalinist solution.

At this point, a modification of the circumstantial explanation might suggest itself: if Stalinism was not the necessary or sole practicable course that it once seemed to be, it was nevertheless so *perceived* at the time by the decision-makers, who after all had to act without foreknowledge of the whole sequence of effects, including catastrophic consequences, which their decisions would bring about. The difficulty with such a hypothetical fallback position is that numerous Bolshevik minds in Moscow and around the country, including some and possibly even a majority in the Politburo, *did not perceive the Stalinist course as the only possible action to take in the circumstances then obtaining.* Bukharin clearly foresaw the catastrophic consequences of Stalin's contemplated rural revolution from above.

An influential section of Soviet political opinion opted for a course in agrarian policy and industrialization that would have been evolutionary. The inevitable next question – why did the evolutionists go down in defeat in the party struggle, or why did Stalinism win? – cannot be answered by reference to the socioeconomic circumstances over which the quarrel raged in Bolshevik circles. It can be answered only by reference to the factors that determined the *Stalinist response* to the circumstances and its political victory.

One of the forces conducive to a Stalinist revolutionary response among Bolshevik politicians was the other Lenin – the still very influential revolutionary Lenin of the War Communism period and the heritage of Bolshevik revolutionism that the other Lenin symbolized. It is understandable that Bukharin, involved as he was in a political struggle against Stalin and the policies he was advocating in 1928–29, treated Lenin's last writings as his 'political testament', and that is certainly what Lenin himself intended them to be. But for the Bolshevik movement and party, Lenin's political testament was the entire corpus of his thought and writing, the whole record of his revolutionary leadership of the movement up to, during, and after the October Revolution; and Lenin's political testament in this more comprehensive sense, contained much that Stalin and Stalinism had good claim to as an authoritative text and warrant for the policies followed in the revolution from above.

The very idea of a process of 'revolution from above', taken in the most general terms, has a Leninist pedigree. When he contended in *The State and Revolution* in 1917, and in such subsequent works as *The Proletarian Revolution and the Renegade Kautsky*, that the doctrine of proletarian dictatorship was the core idea of Marxism and that Marxism called for a seizure of power followed by dictatorial rule by violence against the internal bourgeoisie and associated social forces, he was saying: The revolution does not end with the party's taking of power; that is only a momentous point of historical transition beyond which the party continues its revolutionary destruction of the old order from above, i.e. by wielding the coercive instruments of state power against the revolution's class enemies. Leninist revolution from above meant the use of state power for the continuation of class war *after* the revolutionary party has achieved such power and formed its government under the title of 'proletarian dictatorship'. Whether Lenin ever used the phrase 'from above' in arguing this notion of the proletarian dictatorship as a continuing revolutionary struggle from the vantage-point of state power is of no consequence; the idea was unmistakably present in his thought.

When Stalin in December 1926 rhetorically asked the Comintern Executive what the building of socialism meant in class terms and answered that 'building socialism in the USSR means overcoming our own Soviet bourgeoisie by our own forces in the course of a struggle', he was simply drawing upon the Lenin and Leninism of the Civil War period and earlier. To this Leninism he did subsequently add one proposition that was original with him: that the internal class struggle intensifies with the society's advance toward socialism. He was drawing upon the Leninism that had stood during 1918–21 for forcible food requisitioning from the peasants, for stirring up of class war in the villages by means of the committees of the poor, for the belief (to cite Lenin) that the proletarian dictatorship should mean 'iron rule' and not a 'jellyfish proletarian government'. *This was Stalinist Leninism,* and the authenticity of Stalinism's claim to it is not seriously diminished by the important fact that what Leninism stood for in Lenin's own mind, as a conception of how to build socialism in Russia, underwent great modification in 1921–23.

Nor was this Stalinist Leninism Stalin's only. A considerable proportion of his generation, men who had become Bolsheviks when Bolshevism was still an anti-regime revolutionary movement and who politically came of age, as Stalin himself did, during the era of War Communism, shared his outlook to one or another degree. I am not speaking here about general ideas alone or about Leninism simply as a system of political belief, but likewise about the ingrained habits of mind, ways of defining and responding to situations, styles of action, common memories, mystique, etc., that collectively constitute the culture of a political movement insofar as a given age cohort of its member-ship (and leadership) is concerned. As its name indicates, War Communism had militarized the revolutionary political culture of the Bolshevik movement. The heritage of that formative time in the Soviet culture's history was martial zeal, revolutionary voluntarism and *élan,* readiness to resort to coercion, rule by administrative fiat, centralized administration, summary justice, and no small dose of that Communist arrogance that Lenin later inveighed against.

In seeking to refute the 'circumstantial explanation' of the initial phase of the Stalinist revolution, it is not the intent of this essay to deny historical significance to the circumstances facing the Soviet regime in 1927–29, most notably the grain-collection difficulties. The point is that these circumstances did not carry a single unmistakable definition of the situation and implicit prescription for policy. That widely different definitions of the situation and widely different policy prescriptions were possible is proved by the fierce debates and deep policy differences that emerged at the time. Our argument is that the Stalinist definition of the situation in terms of class war with the kulak forces and the Stalinist policy response of forcible grain requisitioning and then mass collectivization represented, in part, an appeal to the Bolshevik mores of War Communism, and that this orientation proved potently persuasive largely because of the surviving strength of those mores among the Bolsheviks and not by any means only, as some have thought, because of Stalin's formidable organizational power as General Secretary.

But if the surviving spirit of War Communism influenced the way in which the drives for collectivization and industrialization were conceived and carried out, it does not follow that the Stalinist revolution repeated 1917–21 or that the new Stalinist order which took shape in the 1930s was a revival of the system of War Communism. To be sure, the start of the new decade saw such reminders of the heroic period as food rationing, and other resemblances appeared. However, the early Stalinist process showed many distinctive traits that differentiated it from its pre-NEP predecessor: the feverish industrial expansion, the emergence of anti-egalitarian tendencies in contrast to the egalitarianism of the Civil War period, the rise of new elites combined with the loss of the relatively independent political role of the lesser leadership ranks at the earlier time, and the political muzzling of the party rank-and-file in relation to the leadership itself. Still other, major differences call for mention: the *kolkhoz* system itself, which bore small resemblance to the agricultural communes initiated during the Civil War period; the use of police terror as a prime instrument of government in a manner sharply differentiated from the Red terror sponsored by Lenin via the original Cheka; and the inter-relationship between internal and external policy.

It has been argued here that the idea of revolution from above had a Leninist pedigree. While that is important for an interpretation of Stalinism, it must now be stressed that the phenomenon of revolution from above has a range of forms, and that the Leninist form – revolution from above as a victorious revolutionary party's violent use of the 'cudgel' of state power to repress its internal class enemies – represented only one element in Stalinism as a complex and many-sided revolution from above. Where the Stalinist phenomenon went far beyond the Lenin heritage lay in its constructive aspect. Leninist revolution from above was essentially a destructive process, a tearing down of the old order from the vantage-point of state power; Stalinist revolution from above used destructive or repressive means, among others, for what was, both in intent and in reality, a constructive (as well as destructive) process. Its slogan or ideological banner was the building of a socialist society. But in substance, Stalinism as revolution from above was a state-building process, the construction of a powerful, highly centalized, bureaucratic, military-industrial Soviet Russian state. Although it was proclaimed 'socialist' in the mid-1930s, it differed in various vital ways from what most social thinkers – Marx, Engels, and Lenin among them – had understood socialism to mean. Stalinist 'socialism' was a socialism of mass poverty rather than plenty; of sharp social stratification rather than relative equality; of universal, constant fear rather than emancipation of personality; of national chauvinism rather than brotherhood of man; and of a monstrously hypertrophied state power rather than the decreasingly statified commune-state delineated by Marx in *The Civil War in France* and by Lenin in *The State and Revolution*.

It was not, however, by mere caprice or accident that this happened. Stalinist revolutionism from above had a prehistory in the political culture of Russian tsarism; it existed as a pattern in the Russian past and hence *could* be seen by a twentieth-century statesman as both a precedent and legitimation of a political course that would, in essentials, recapitulate the historical pattern.

Confronted in the aftermath of the two-century-long Mongol domination with hostile and in some cases more advanced neighbor-states in possession of portions of the extensive territories that had made up the loosely confederated Kievan *Rus'*, the princes – later tsars – of Muscovy undertook the building of a powerful 'military-national state' capable 'of gathering the Russian lands under its aegis. Given the primacy of the concern for external defense and expansion and the country's relative economic backwardness, the government proceeded by remodelling the social structure, at times by forcible means, in such a way that all classes of the population were bound in one or another form of compulsory service to the state.

A salient expression of the tsarist pattern of revolutionism from above was the legalized imposition of serfdom upon the Russian peasantry in the sixteenth and seventeenth centuries, the peasant's attachment by law to the soil, together with the system of *barshchina* (the *corvée*) under which the peasant was bound to contribute a certain number of days work on the landowner's (or state's) land during the agricultural year. It is a highly significant fact that the *kolkhoz* was actually perceived by many Russian peasants as a revival of serfdom.

The culminating phase of tsarism as a dynamic political superstructure engaged in the transformation of Russian society and development of its economic base for state-ordained purposes came in the long reign of Peter I. Now the pattern of revolution from above emerged most distinctly, one of its prominent aspects being an industrial revolution from above aimed at building a powerful Russian war-industrial base. Intensifying serfdom, Peter employed state-owned serfs along with prisoners of war and others for industrial projects as well as the construction of canals and on occasion moved entire townships of people to the construction sites of the new enterprises. Again, the parallel with the Stalinist industrial revolution from above is striking, the major difference being the greatly expanded scale of the use of forced labour in the Stalinist case.

Here a brief comment is called for on the view, sometimes encountered in Western thought, that sees the Stalinist revolution from above under the aspect of 'modernization'. The difficulty with this position – apart from the nebulous character of the very concept of modernization – is its obliviousness of the strong element of 'archaization' in Stalinism, its resurrection of the historic tsarist pattern of building a powerful military-national state by revolutionary means involving the extension of direct coercive controls over the population and the growth of state power in the process. Unless 'modernization' is reduced in meaning mainly to industrialization and increase of the urban population (in which case the term becomes superfluous), the use of it to characterize Stalinism is misleading. If a formula for the state-building process is needed, it might best be the one that Kliuchevsky provided in his summation of modern Russian history from the sixteenth to the nineteenth century: 'The state swelled up; the people grew lean'.

The Russian historical perspective can contribute in still a further important way to our understanding of Stalinism: it helps to make intelligible the relationship between the first and second phases of the Stalinist revolution. Following the phase that took place from 1928–29 to 1933, there was a kind of pause in 1934, after which the revolution from above moved into its second phase. Signalized by the murder of the party leader Sergei Kirov in Leningrad in December 1934 – an event conceived and organized from the center of power in Moscow as a pretext for what followed – the mass terror of the Great Purge enveloped the party and country in the later 1930s. The Great Purge destroyed a generation not simply of Old Bolshevik veterans of the anti-tsarist struggle but of very many of their juniors who had joined the movement after 1917 and served as active implementers of Stalinism in its first phase. It virtually transformed the composition of the Soviet regime and the managerial elite in all fields. This in turn was accompanied by still other manifestations of the revolution from above in its second phase, such as the destruction of the Pokrovsky school of Bolshevik historiography, the concomitant reappropriation of major elements of the Russian past as part of the official Soviet cultural heritage, the restoration of pre-1917 patterns in art, education, law and the family. In these aspects, which extended into the 1940s, there were distinctly reactionary or counter-revolutionary overtones in the revolution from above.

It has been said, rightly in my view, that 'Stalin's revolution in agriculture and industry and his assault on the party which consummated this revolution must be seen as integrated parts of one and the same process'.[8] But it remains to explicate the nexus between the two phases. It is not a persuasive argument that terror on the scale of the Stalinist holocaust of 1934–39 was necessary either to perpetuate collectivization or to prevent Stalin from losing power. Yet, the point about the two phases being 'integrated parts of one and the same process' carries conviction.

A partial explanation of this linkage can be derived from the thesis that the Stalinist revolution from above recapitulated in essentials its tsarist predecessor's pattern. The latter involved the binding of all classes of the population, from the lowest serf to the highest noble, in compulsory service to the state. As the Muscovite autocracy grew in power, the hereditary land-owning nobility was transformed into a serving class whose title to the land was made conditional upon rendering military service to the state. The Petrine revolution from above reinforced this situation by instituting an aristocracy of rank based upon the table of fourteen military and corresponding civilian ranks, under which nobility became a function of rank rather than vice versa. In one of its phases, moreover, the reduction of the boyar ruling class of Kievan and early Muscovite Russia to a serving class during the reign of Ivan IV in the sixteenth century, the chief instrument of the process was the anti-boyar terror carried out under Ivan's personal supervision of his private retinue and security police, the *oprichnina*. Ivan himself was the first of the Muscovite rulers to assume the title of tsar. Tsarism as a system of absolute autocracy was itself in part a product of this sixteenth-century purge, which, from evidence at our disposal, we know that Stalin consciously took as a model for emulation during the Great Purge of the 1930s.

The pertinence of this to the problem of the nexus between the two phases is clear. The Great Purge was at once the crucible of the restoration of an absolute autocracy in Russia – under Stalin now – and concomitantly a continuation of the process of formation of Stalin's neo-tsarist version of the compulsory-service state, an entity that may properly be called 'totalitarian'. The first phase of the revolution from above had seen the binding of the peasantry and working class in servitude to the ever swelling, ever more centralized, ever more bureaucratized, ever more police-dominated Stalinist state. The second phase brought the party itself and the intelligentsia in that greatly expanded Soviet sense of the term (which embraces managers, officials, specialists, technicians, and professionals of all sorts) into line with the rest of society. They too became a serving class whose status as such was made tangible and visible with the introduction in the later 1930s and 1940s of a Stalinist table of ranks that bore a distinct resemblance – as did the uniforms and insignia – to the corresponding tsarist set-up. Completing the process ideologically, the Stalinist order developed its own ideology of Soviet Russian statism.

To what extent was the Stalinist revolution 'from below' as well as from above? Perhaps it would be useful, as a setting for analysis and discussion, to observe two distinctions. First, the distinction between the two phases (1929–33 and 1934–39). Second, the distinction between two different possible meanings of 'below': persons in low-level roles in the regime or closely associated with it, notably the membership of the Communist Party and the Komsomol; and the population at large. Using Soviet terminology, we may call them respectively the *aktiv* and the *narod*. Although numerically substantial, the former was no more than a relatively small minority of the latter.

The *aktiv*, or large elements of it, including contingents of Soviet youth, was a vitally important instrumentality of the regime in the first phase of the Stalinist revolution. Many participated in the collectivization and industrialization drives not only actively but enthusiastically and self-sacrificingly.

But it is not clear whether any considerable portion of the *narod* gave the regime its voluntary support during this phase. As in the time of War Communism, the regime attempted to foment class war in the countryside by making the poor peasant (*bedniaki*) its allies in mass collectivization. To what extent this policy was a success is not entirely plain, as there is evidence that mass collectivization was not only opposed by the well-off and middle peasants in their great majority, but unpopular as well among no few of the *bedniaki*. As for worker participation in collectivization, we have the case of the twenty-five thousand industrial workers who were enrolled by the party to go into the villages as collectivizers. But evidence also exists that at least some portion of the 'twenty-five-thousanders' joined this movement under pressure of dire family need combined with material incentives to assist in the collectivizing.

In the second phase, the social picture changed significantly. While the *narod* remained basically passive – indeed more passive than in the early 1930s – large elements of the first-phase *aktiv* exchanged the role of implementers of the revolution for that of its victims. Very many of these people died or went to camps during the Great Purge. To a far greater extent than the first phase, the second was a police operation, and the supreme collective victim was the Communist Party itself as constituted in the early 1930s. By this very token, however, a great many who did not actively participate in the second phase, whether they belonged to the *aktiv* or the *narod*, nevertheless became its beneficiaries. For the decimation of the pre-1934 regime, party, and intelligentsia in the Great Purge opened career opportunities on a vast scale to those from below who showed ability combined with the acquiescent, state-oriented, and Stalin-centred attitudes that were hallmarks of the *chinovnik* under full Stalinism. This influx was largely an influx of the peasant-born or of those who had been children of peasants. Nicholas Vakar has argued that the Stalinist revolution, by filling the Soviet hierarchy with persons of peasant stock and infusing age-old peasant mores and values into the Soviet way, marked the complete *peasantization* of the Russian Revolution.

The question inevitably arises, why did history recapitulate itself so in this instance? Cultural patterns out of a nation's past do not repeat themselves in the present simply because they were there. Nor can we explain the phenomenon by reference to like circumstances, such as NEP Russia's relative international isolation and economic backwardness, for we have argued that circumstances do not carry their own self-evident meaning, that what people and political leaders *act upon* is always the circumstances *as perceived and defined by them*, which in turn is influenced by culture. But also, we must now add, by personality. And so we come at the end to what was mentioned at the start as a third important explanatory factor underlying the revolution from above – the mind and personality of Stalin.

To a certain extent the personal factor is covered by the culturalist explanation itself. A leader-personality becomes politically acculturated through his life-experience both in early years and during manhood. Thus, 1917 and the Civil War were a formative acculturating life-experience for Stalin and many others of his party generation, leaving a deep residue of the revolutionary political culture of War Communism within them. On this level of explanation, Stalin's historical role in the late 1920s was to make himself, as effectively as he did, the leader and spokesman of an outlook that he shared with numerous others in the party leadership and not alone the men of his own faction.

The recapitulation of the tsarist pattern of revolutionism from above presents a more difficult problem of explanation in culturalist *or* personality terms, if only because Russian tsarism, in all its manifestations, was what the Bolshevik revolutionary movement had taken originally as its mortal sociopolitical enemy. However, the Russian nationalist feeling aroused in a section of the party during the Civil War years was an element in the culture that *could* predispose a Bolshevik to perceive certain patterns of the heritage of old Russia as relevant to the circumstances of the present. On the other hand, it did not do so in the generality of instances of which we know. Hence, in this problem the explanatory emphasis must fall more on 'personality' than on 'culture'. Stalin, the commissar for nationality affairs and as such the presumable protector of the rights of the minority nations in the Soviet federation, was in fact, as Lenin discovered to his horror shortly before dying, one of those Bolsheviks most infected by 'Russian Red patriotism'. Lenin showed his realization of this in the notes on the nationality question which he dictated on December 30–31 1922 and in which he characterized Stalin as foremost among those Russified minority representatives in the party who tended to err on the side of 'true-Russianism' and 'Great Russian chauvinism'. Unbeknown to Lenin, Stalin's sense of Russian nationality, if not his true-Russianism, had dated from his youthful conversion to Lenin's leadership and to Bolshevism, which he saw as the 'Russian faction' in the Empire's Marxist Party, Menshevism being the 'Jewish faction'. It was on this foundation that Stalin, during the 1920s, went forward in his thinking and appropriative self-acculturation, as the generality of his Russian-nationalist-oriented party comrades did not, to envisage the tsarist state-building process as a model for the Soviet Russian state in its 'building of socialism.' And it was the great personal power that he acquired by 1929, with the ouster of the oppositions from the party leadership, that made it possible for him to proceed to carry out his design.

If the thesis concerning the recapitulation of the state-building process places heavy emphasis upon personality even in the context of a culturalist approach, a final explanatory consideration concerning the Stalinist phenomenon narrows the focus onto personality to a still greater degree. Unlike any other Bolshevik, to my knowledge, Stalin defined the Soviet situation in 1925 and 1926 in eve-of-October terms, implicitly presaging thereby a revolutionary assault against the existing order, i.e. the NEP, in the drive to build socialism.

Then, looking back in the *Short Course* of 1938 on the accomplishments of the Stalinist decade, he described them, and collectivization in particular, as equivalent in consequence to the October Revolution of 1917. Underlying both the definition of the situation in the mid-1920s and the retrospective satisfaction expressed in the late 1930s was Stalin's compulsive psychological need, born of neurosis, to prove himself a revolutionary hero of Lenin-like proportions, to match or surpass what all Bolsheviks considered Lenin's supreme historical exploit, the leadership of the party in the world-historic revolutionary success of October 1917. The great revolutionary drive to change Russia in the early 1930s was intended as Stalin's October.

In practice it achieved certain successes, notably in industrialization, but at a cost of such havoc and misery in Russia that Stalin, as the regime's supreme leader, aroused condemnation among many. This helps to explain, in psychological terms, the lethal vindictiveness that he visited upon millions of his party comrades, fellow countrymen, and others in the ensuing years. It was his way of trying to come to terms with the repressed fact that he, Djugashvili, had failed to prove himself the charismatically Lenin-like Stalin that it was his lifelong goal to be. If this interpretation is well founded, he was hardly the most impersonal of great historical figures.

> Abridged from Robert C. Tucker, 'Stalinism as revolution from above', in Robert C. Tucker, ed. (1977), *Stalinism, essays in historical interpretation*, pp. 79–104. Reprinted by permission of W. W. Norton & Company, Inc., New York.

Notes

1 'Our revolution (apropos of N. Sukhanov's notes)' in Robert C. Tucker, ed. (1975), *The Lenin Anthology*, New York, pp. 705–6.

2 'The importance of gold now and after the complete victory of socialism' in *The Lenin Anthology*, p. 512.

3 *History of the Communist Party of the Soviet Union (Bolsheviks), Short Course*, Moscow, 1945, p. 305.

4 J. R. Miller (1974), 'Mass collectivization and the contribution of Soviet agriculture to the first five-year plan: a review article', *The Slavic Review*, XXXIII, pp. 764, 765.

5 Isaac Deutscher (1967), *Stalin: A Political Biography*, 2nd edn., Oxford University Press, New York, p. 313.

6 Deutscher, *Stalin*, pp. 318, 322.

7 For recent arguments to this effect, see S. F. Cohen (1973), *Bukharin and the Bolshevik Revolution: A Political Biography*, A. A. Knopf, New York, Ch. 9 and Epilogue; and M. Lewin (1974), *Political Undercurrents in Soviet Economic Debates: From Bukharin to the Modern Reformers*, Princeton University Press, Princeton, NJ, pp. 52–61.

8 Leonard Schapiro (1959), *The Communist Party of the Soviet Union*, Random House, New York, p. 430.

4.4   The mature Stalinist system

Seweryn Bialer

The evolution of Stalinism in Soviet post-revolutionary history went through three major stages, each of which can be associated with a different key role played by Stalin. The first stage included the period of the consolidation of Bolshevik rule, the shaping of its basic political, administrative, and economic institutions, and the formulation in practical terms of its key long-range policies and the methods of their implementation; that is to say, the NEP period of the 1920s. It was a stage in which the principal role played by Stalin was that of a *politician* who fought for power within the Communist party, adjusted his views and policies to the needs of this power stuggle, and built an organizational base.

The second stage encompasses the period of the revolution, or rather revolutions, 'from above,'[1] roughly the years 1929–38. In this period a fundamental transformation of Soviet society took place in all areas of endeavor, and the social, economic, political, and cultural institutions of Bolshevism in power were radically reshaped. It was a stage in which the principal role played by Stalin was that of a revolutionary *transformer and restorer.*

The third stage was that of mature Stalinism, when the revolutions from above were over, the political institutions established, and the long-range social, economic, and cultural policies settled. It was a period when the key goal of the regime was the reproduction of the existing relations and the proper functioning and effectiveness of the system.[2] The principal role played by Stalin at this stage was that of a *dictator-administrator.* Only this stage of Stalinism concerns me.

The mature Stalinist system displayed some key characteristics which in their interaction and combined effect made it a distinctive system, different from both the system prevailing in the early formative stage of Soviet development and the system that evolved in the post-Stalinist era. Some of its most important characteristics were:

the system of mass terror;

the extinction of the party as a movement;

the shapelessness of the macro-political organization;

an extreme mobilizational model of economic growth, tied to goals of achieving military power, and the political consequences thereof;

a heterogeneous value system which favored economic, status, and power stratification, fostered extraordinary cultural uniformity, and was tied to extreme nationalism;

the end of the revolutionary impulse to change society and the persistence of a conservative status quo attitude toward existing institutions;

the system of personal dictatorship.

Mature Stalinism rested on the foundation of an all-pervasive political terror: 'the arbitrary use, by organs of political authority, of severe coercion against individuals or groups, the credible threat of such use, or the arbitrary extermination of such individuals or groups.'[3] The arbitrariness made impossible the calculation of behavior which would provide a reasonable chance of survival. The terror was all-pervasive in that no group or individual was exempt from being a target. As a matter of fact, it appears that the effectiveness of the terror 'has been most telling... among the bureaucracy – those who most directly depend on the regime for success and status.'[4]

Participation in the rule of terror was not confined to its direct administrators, nor was it restricted to obeying direct commands from above. The members of the political bureaucracy were actively engaged, if not physically involved, in the terror; they were guilty en masse of initiating terroristic acts. They displayed what can be described as 'preemptive obedience', the anticipation of what they considered to be their bosses' wishes and whims. It was an anticipatory obedience encouraged by their superiors and characterized favorably as 'vigilance.' The rule of terror led to the existence of a countless army of informers. The working assumption in the society and bureaucracy was that everybody was spying and informing on everybody else. Society at large, and especially its upper strata, became the victims of terror, morally if not physically. It was not an exaggeration to state, directly after Stalin's death, that 'the tragedy of contemporary Russia is that the whole elite of the nation, its intelligentsia, its civil service, and all its politically minded elements share in one degree or another in Stalin's guilt. ... Stalin made of the whole nation, at any rate of all its educated and active elements, his accomplices.'[5]

Crucial to our understanding of mature Stalinism is the proposition that terror functioned principally not as a tool of social *change*, but as a normal method of rule and *governance*. The development and continuation of terror as a method of rule and governance established an enormous bureaucratic structure devoted to its administration: the police state. This bureaucracy performed tasks that went far beyond traditional police functions; it amassed direct influence over wide areas of Soviet life and participated routinely in the political process.

The police commanded a major military force composed of internal security units (many divisions with their own armor and air force) and border troops. It administered the entire extensive prison, camp, exile, and forced-labor system.[6] It incorporated for all practical purposes the judiciary branch of the government, both the procuracy and the courts.[7] It controlled openly, directly, and exclusively the armed forces' counter-intelligence. It placed official representatives in the machine-tractor stations, the key agricultural units, and small cells in major industrial enterprises. It was directly in charge of the elite communications system, through which all high level intraparty, state, and military communications were conducted, and controlled the Ministry of

Communications. It controlled directly or indirectly the ministries in charge of producing lumber, nonferrous metals, and heavy construction. It exercised powerful and direct administrative influence over a number of non-Russian republics, especially the Transcaucasian republics of Georgia, Azerbaidjan, and Armenia. In addition to control over a number of scientific research prison establishments, it was apparently charged with supervising atomic research. In addition to directing external intelligence, it exerted direct and strong influence on the foreign service and foreign trade establishments.

Far from acting as an anonymous, discreet, and secret force, the 'secret' police was an open and recognized political force, glorified and praised in the media, highly visible at all official ceremonies and political assemblies, and extolled by Soviet propaganda as a prime example for emulation. All in all, under mature Stalinism, one deals not with an outburst of terror, a 'siege' of terror, but a generalized persistent regime of terror. Rule by terror as a method of governance for the foreseeable future rather than as an emergency measure received ideological underpinning and justification from Stalin's thesis on the 'intensification of class struggle with the advancement and success of socialist construction.' This formula not only proclaimed terror a justifiable method of rule, but also, by a reverse logic, made terror the indicator of the successes of the socialist system.

Under mature Stalinism the Communist party became extinct as a political movement. The term 'party' came to be used either as a legitimizing mantle for Stalin's rule, reflecting his continuing need, public and probably personal, to relate the roots of Soviet authority to its revolutionary origins, or as a depiction of an important part of the Stalinist administrative edifice (the party bureaucracy, the party 'apparatus'). Even in its 'dignified,' legitimizing function, the role of the party as the carrier of ideological 'truth' – while still invoked – declined visibly. It was largely replaced by the cult of Stalin and by undisguised, explicit nationalism. It is indicative of the atrophy of the party as a genuine, voluntary mass organization and 'an association of people united by an ideology' that it played a secondary role as a legitimizing institution (and, incidentally, as an organization) in the only *authentic* mass mobilization effort of the mature Stalinist era, the war effort. The mobilizing impetus came from the 'truths' of the state, not of the party; from patriotism and nationalism, not from ideology in a communist sense.

As a mass and an elite organization, the party ceased to perform a meaning-ful role in the political process. It still served as a vehicle for the political education of its members, but the key role of political socialization was performed primarily by schools and mass media on the basic level, and by the various bureaucracies for their own members, including the party bureaucracy, on the higher level. All politically powerful individuals belonged to the party; party membership became an accoutrement of power.[8] But very few party members were politically powerful. Party membership did not assure participation in the political process, beyond the privilege of receiving some additional information and beyond the duty of implementing decisions adopted *at all levels* outside the party.

The ideal of mature Stalinism was to politicize all spheres of social and often even private endeavors and to depoliticize political processes. All forms of activity, whether economic, scientific, or cultural, were imbued with political meaning; but attempts were made forcibly to reduce the political process to questions of 'pure' administration. The mass and the elite party became the key victim of this tendency. The party in its 'efficient' rather than 'dignified' function became identical with the party bureaucracy, the paid, full-time staff of its professional 'apparatus.'[9]

The prime function of this apparatus was not to administer the affairs of the mass party but to participate in the administration of the state. Its 'clients' were not the party itself, but primarily other bureaucracies. In the pre-Stalinist period the party apparatus played a lesser role in state affairs, but the party played a much more prominent role. Even so despite the fact that the party apparatus was expanded and more deeply and directly involved in state-administration, it became just *one* of the bureaucracies, albeit a very powerful one.

The popular image of Stalinism depicts extreme rigidity of procedures and policies and the petrification of the entire enormous bureaucratic edifice. This image is largely valid when applied to the micro-processes and internal procedures of each separate bureaucratic hierarchy of Stalinist Russia. The macro-dimension, however, presents, first of all, a picture of vastly over-lapping lines of control, rights, and responsibilities among the diverse bureau-cratic hierarchies; and, second, of shifting lines of responsibility and control.

The ideal of Stalinism was monocratic rule and administration. Within separate bureaucratic hierarchies, this ideal was to a large extent achieved by pursuing a course of extreme vertical centralization. On the macro-level, however, the monocratic principle was applied consistently and deliberately to only one facet of the political organization of the society – that which concerned the relations of the various bureaucracies with Stalin. The re-lations among the various enormous bureaucracies bore scant resemblance to an organizational chart with clear lines of authority, responsibilities, and prerogatives.

Even the picture of parallel party and state bureaucracies is misleading insofar as the parallelism was multiple not merely dual. The proper picture would encompass a number of major and lesser bureaucracies encroaching on each other's territory, fighting for their share of the bureaucratic empire, and duplicating each other's efforts. If the party apparatus was empowered to organize and supervise political indoctrination, it competed not only with the military's separate political department but even the Ministry of Railroads. The prerogatives of the planners were constantly challenged by the ambitions of the police to expand their own economic empire. The rights of local party secretaries to control local enterprises were effectively countered by the managers' recourse to the influence of their respective ministries, and so on.

No existing bureaucracy was delegated the exclusive authority to serve primarily as co-ordinator of the competing bureaucracies. The party apparatus was best suited for this role, due to the fact that its internal structure duplicated the structure of the state administration. Instead it performed the function of external pusher-mobilizer (and controller) rather than co-ordinator.

The reasons behind this shapelessness were varied, partly deliberate and partly the result of the difficulty of administering everything and everywhere in a vast country under conditions of constant emergency. The multiple lines of administrative responsibility reflected the center's need to compensate for the low quality and unreliability of information flowing to it through a multiplicity of sources and channels, as well as the always-suspicious dictator's need to secure validation and confirmation of routine communications. The ascendancy or decline of particular bureaucracies or their functional components partly reflected and partly determined the ascendancy or decline of their leaders at Stalin's court. The bureaucratic shapelessness reflected the dictator's need to keep the bureaucracies off balance, to prevent their and their leaders' solidification into well-established empires, to preclude any of their component parts from growing too strong without the countervailing power of competition. A secure, stable bureaucracy could only diminish the dictator's security. A divided and fluid bureaucracy provided an important margin of security for his own position.

The chief goal of the Soviet political leadership throughout its history has been economic – especially industrial – growth at the most rapid attainable rate and regardless of the social cost. The issues of economic growth permeated the entire Soviet political decision-making process. Economic growth and the military power that was to proceed from it constituted the chief indicator of the success and failure of political leadership. The economic development desired and later achieved constituted the historical justification of both the social transformation decreed by the leadership and the political order established by it.

The creation and rapid expansion of Soviet industrial might was based on a particular pattern of organization, stimuli, and policies. What has come to be called the Stalinist model of economic growth exhibits the following central characteristics:

Planning for economic growth is goal-oriented. While economic growth is a decisive goal, economic criteria for deciding what, how fast, and at what cost it should develop are a tertiary consideration.

The specific goals of economic development are highly selective. The aim is not an overall balanced growth but a relatively narrow range of high-priority tasks.

A particularly important dimension of the unbalanced strategy of growth is the place it assigns to personal consumption, which, as one economic historian has observed, is treated not as 'the ultimate goal ... but as the inevitable cost to be incurred grudgingly in the process of continued growth.'[10]

The setting of ambitious goals and the planning – or rather the command – that they be attained in the shortest possible (and impossible) time are calculated to bring forth the maximum expenditure of effort and energy.

A major feature has been the stress on ever-increasing quantities of output, achieved with massive infusions of inputs of labour and capital.

With the exception of the initial industrialization drive which relied heavily on imports of foreign technology, the Stalinist model of growth was designed as a closed market, virtually isolated from the outside world.

The key characteristic of the Stalinist model of economic growth was its lack of *economic* self-generating, self-regulating, and adjusting features. To run at all, let alone to perform well, it required an enormous political edifice to provide the decision making and the push, the regulation, supervision, and co-ordination. In fact, the Soviet political system was developed largely to run the economy and was shaped by running the economy in line with the chosen growth strategy.

The economic goals of the political elite and the strategy through which they were being pursued were either a direct primary cause of certain features of the political regime or else they reinforced or exaggerated other features to which the political elite was already committed. Of these features, four are especially notable; they concern societal controls, organizational structure, the type of regulation, and the style of leadership.

The reliance of the political elite on the three major means of societal control – material, symbolic, and physical – was highly asymmetrical. The achievement of the exorbitant planned targets of growth, the successful stretching of available resources, depended on the establishment of an extremely high level of discipline in the labor force, in the managerial strata, in the party. At the same time, the high rate of forced savings, [and] the low priority assigned to consumer goals in the growth strategy, precluded the reliance on material incentives, on controls through remunerative power, as the primary method of achieving the required discipline.

A revolutionary regime which poses ambitious goals before society in a situation of pronounced economic scarcity may and often does rely heavily on normative powers to build compliance. Indeed, if one were to judge by the extraordinary size and budget of the Stalinist propaganda machine and its saturating activity, the stress on this form of societal control would appear very substantial. One should point out, however, that despite the visible stress by the Soviet leadership under Stalin (and later) on this type of control, its importance has been secondary and its impact limited.

While it would be foolish to neglect the role of economic inducements, or especially to underestimate the role of manipulation as the basis of Soviet societal controls, nevertheless the foundation stone on which the Stalinist leadership was able to base its economic growth strategy, the real driving force, was coercion. Actual coercion or the threat or fear of its application provided within all strata of Soviet society the most important source of compliance to the regime's goals. The idiosyncratic element of Stalin's personality aside, without an inordinate reliance on coercion, the combination contained in the Soviet economic growth strategy – extremely unbalanced growth, scarcity of resources, and taut planning – could hardly have been pursued for a prolonged period with any chance of success. Of all the societal controls employed by the regime, coercion was the most instrumental, rational, and systemic; the most institutionalized and most lasting; the most deeply implanted in the system's fabric. Coercion as an underlying driving force, a method of management, pervaded all institutions of Soviet society.

The Soviet Union under Stalin became a society of organization, to which every social task of importance is entrusted at a much earlier stage and to a much greater degree than in Western industrial nations. The main peculiarity of Soviet development, associated with the growth strategy adopted by its leadership, is not that formal organizations (that is, bureaucracies) constitute the basic building blocks of the socioeconomic and political structures, but that relations among those structural units are extremely centralized. The two basic features of this centralization are: first, that decision making is reserved for the system's leadership in a degree directly related to the importance of the decisions, and second, that the link between units at various levels is direct, without an intermediary, and takes the form of commands, orders, and directives.

The Soviet model of economic growth with its ideal of total mobilization and allocation of resources, with its selectivity of high growth areas, with its pressure on the tempo of growth, has infused an extreme level of hierarchical relations, a supercentralization into the macro-economic organization, and has required an equally centralized shape in the macro-political organizations which were to mobilize resources, supervise their allocation and control, and co-ordinate their use.

The growth strategy pursued under Stalinism not only reinforced the traditional inclination of the Communist party for tight centralization but, more importantly, infused it with an intrinsic instrumental value. That is to say, it removed the question of centralization from the field of politics alone, and beyond the rationale of preserving the power of a political elite whose claim to legitimacy was narrow, and made it into the natural *modus operandi* of the system, the way considered most effective in running the society.

The economic system of planning and management was characterized by stress on detailed output targets and by proliferation of instructions not only on details of what should be done and when, but also how it should be done and according to what sequence of procedures, and following what detailed timetables. Similarly, the relations of the political bureaucracy with the economic sector (and for that matter with other sectors) were characterized not simply by the right of the former to determine key economic decisions and by its veto power but by its attempt at detailed supervision of, and intervention in, each phase and aspect of management.

One last feature of the system, of which the Stalinist growth strategy was a major co-determinant, concerns the style of leadership. The Soviet style of leadership is most commonly referred to as bureaucratic; but this identification tells very little beyond the fact that it is a leadership exercised within and through hierarchical organizations, that it is performed on a full-time basis by professionals, and that it leads to the development of standardized, routinized procedures for dealing with everyday situations. Bureaucracies, however, exhibit different types, possess diverse functions, and, consequently, display divergent styles of leadership. The style of leadership prevalent within and displayed by Soviet bureaucracies under Stalin, and especially the way in which economic management ran the economy and was in turn run by the political elite, was geared to conditions that were rightly described as those of simulated combat. The Soviet economic and political organization in terms of its power structure, its modes of operation and means of communication, its mood, began to resemble most closely a combat army in a not-too-popular war. The simulated combat conditions and the style of leadership appropriate to it, found a fitting expression even in the terminology and language of official Russia, which was most closely based on military imagery.

In Stalinist Russia one did not solve a problem, one 'attacked' it; one 'retreated,' 'regrouped', organized a 'campaign'; one was at 'war' and organized one's own 'camp' against the 'enemy'. One acted on various 'fronts' – ideological, industrial, agricultural – and one had a 'strategy' and 'tactic' for each 'sector'. The most striking imagery was of the Communist party as an 'army', which Stalin described thus:

If we have in mind its leading strata, there are about 3,000 to 4,000 first rank leaders whom I would call our Party's corps of generals.
Then there are about 30,000 to 40,000 middle rank leaders who are our Party corps of officers.
Then there are about 100,000 to 150,000 of the lower rank Party command staff who are, so to speak, our Party's non-commissioned officers.[11]

In discussing the value system of mature Stalinism, I am primarily interested in the political culture, broadly understood. But the first thing to understand is that virtually all culture became the domain of the political in a society where all aspects of life were shaped and dominated by political power. The official value system of mature Stalinism presents a bizarre amalgam compounded of old Russian values, deeply rooted among the new elite and the population and deeply detested by the revolutionary Bolsheviks, and the modernizing Soviet zeal and commitment – all cloaked in Marxist-Leninist ideology or (at the very least) Marxist-Leninist terminology. The 'dignified' dimension of this official value system was provided by the party in the political structure and by Marxism-Leninism in the political culture. From the old ideology came the sense of historical 'inevitability', the self-righteousness, and the semireligious ardor, which were curiously blended and reinforced by the propagation of nationalism and the 'Russian mission', by the cult of the leader as the carrier of ultimate truth. The new ideology chose its doctrinal references selectively, in a self-serving and mechanistic manner; it reduced them to a few slogans, incessantly repeated. Stalinism, as Isaac Deutscher remarked, was the 'Marxism of the illiterate'.[12] It sought to dominate a people and an elite just emerging from illiteracy.

Stalinism elevated Soviet nationalism in general and Russian nationalism in particular to a core, systemic value. It became *the* core value at least in terms of its effectiveness as a norm of compliance to the system's goals. It put at the center of attention the old conservative theme – the cult of national unity at any price – and the unreserved condemnation of individuals and groups who not only in fact, in thought, or in practice threatened to impair it, but who could potentially impair it. In its last phase this nationalism degenerated into extreme chauvinism and xenophobia, closing the circle from 'socialism in one country' to 'imperial socialism'. In an ironic twist, it proclaimed the essence of internationalism to be the willingness to defend the Soviet Union, an unconditional allegiance to the Soviet Union.

Under mature Stalinism economic stratification and inequalities of status were not simply tolerated; they were encouraged in actions and glorified in symbols. The multiplication of ranks, titles, uniforms, and visible accoutrements of status and power was unending. The economic distance between the haves and the have-nots was ratified: one-half of the nation, the peasantry, was virtually excluded from economic and cultural citizenship.[13] The *real* urban pay-scale was differentiated to a degree similar to or higher than in developed capitalist societies (which in a country with a low standard of living hit the lower rungs of the income ladder very hard).[14] A whole series of specific measures assured the continuous advantage of the advantaged, such as the introduction of substantial payments for middle and higher education, the substitution of vocational schools for the general education of children from lower classes, the primary reliance in taxation on such nonprogressive devices as the sales tax and the taxation of basic income alone. Social services were introduced which differentiated according to rank the extent and quality of services (medicine, vacations, and the like) and generally favored the white-collar over the blue-collar employee; the same principle was extended to pensions in an even more glaring manner.

Stalinism reinstated with a vengeance the principle of authority and social discipline in the workplace, the school, and even the family. The discipline that Stalinism tried to foster was to be ideally a conscious discipline based on the recognition and acceptance of its need. Yet in effect it was a discipline which had to rely on the fear of and the application of extreme coercive measures.

Stalinist labor laws were draconic by any standard, the Soviet Union being the only European country where absenteeism became a criminal offense, punishable by imprisonment. The broad statutory authority of the *nachal'stvo* – 'the bosses' – over the urban working class was still reinforced by the internal passport system, which prescribed the domicile, and by the labor-book system, which prescribed the workplace and recorded the worker's entire labor record; thus a convenient national blacklist was compiled.

The pluralism and creative freedom that existed before Stalin's revolutions from above were replaced by uniformity and conformity in the arts and social sciences. The tastes and predilections of the leader and his entourage became not only the measure of artistic achievement, but they prescribed the very scale of artistic expression. Literature, film, and theater were reduced to schematic morality plays of what should exist, should be emulated, and should be believed. A mixture of rococo and the nouveau riche taste of old commercial Russia reigned in architecture. Neoclassicism joined with folksongs and pop tunes as the principal expressions of musical taste. Victorian behavior was officially commended to Soviet citizens as the standard for everyday life. A traditionalism grounded in the Russian nineteenth century provided a confining condition for the arts and served at the same time in some measure to salvage the country's cultural life. It was a great but dead culture, propagated in the interests of national pride and patriotic mobilization, but a culture arrested in its development. Sociology, political science, political economy, and even the administrative and managerial sciences became virtually extinct. History was reduced to providing changing illustrations for changing political theses to serve the here and now.

What has been said about the values and culture of mature Stalinism attests to the system's conservatism in the strictest sense of the word. Its focus was not to change social relations but to preserve and enshrine those that existed. An end had come to the revolutions from above through which the system was created. Its ultimate form – the 'good society' – had arrived. Lenin once said, 'Our system is socialist because it is moving to socialism'. Stalin's system moved away from socialism, as it was understood by both traditional Marxists and Bolsheviks. The chief architect did not consider the emergent system a transitional phase, a temporary state of emergency, or a set of provisional arrangements imposed by circumstance. He considered it the proper model of the long-range political organization of *any* socialist society, that is to say, the only proper institutional embodiment of the idea of socialism.

One characteristic of the last, mature stage of Stalinism provides the focal point for understanding the phenomenon of Stalinism as a whole. It is personal dictatorship. This characteristic binds and conditions most of the system's other characteristics. In particular, it provides in my opinion the only feasible explanation for the mass terror which was directed against the elite and the population. Neither the survival of the system twenty years after the revolution nor the effectiveness of the system in mobilizing resources after virtual completion of the revolutions from above required the unleashing and persistence of terror. However, the establishment and continuation of Stalin's absolute dictatorship would have been impossible without it.

Abridged from Seweryn Bialer (1980), *Stalin's Successors: Leadership, Stability and Change in the Soviet Union*, pp. 9–27. Reprinted by permission of Cambridge University Press, Cambridge.

Notes

1 The term 'revolution from above' was used by Stalin himself to describe the collectivization of agriculture. It connotes a revolutionary change initiated and executed *by* and *not against* an existing political authority (*The History of the Communist Party of the Soviet Union (Bolsheviks), Short Course*, edited by Stalin himself, International Publishers, New York, 1939, p. 305).

2 Despite the many valuable insights into the nature of the Stalinist system provided by the totalitarian model, in my opinion its creators make the crucial mistake of failing to distinguish between the early revolutionary and the late, highly conservative nature of the system. They suggest that the 'totalitarian' impulse to reshape society is a continuous one, and they do not recognize the key characteristic of the late Stalinist and post-Stalinist Russia – its deeply conservative nature, domestically oriented to the status quo (see, for example, Carl J. Friedrich and Zbigniew Brzezinski (1961), *Totalitarian Dictatorship and Autocracy*, Praeger, New York, p. 9 and especially Ch. 27).

3 A. Dallin and G. W. Breslauer (1970), *Political Terror in Communist Systems*, Stanford University Press, Stanford, CA, p. 1.

4 *Ibid.*, p. 128.

5 Isaac Deutscher (1966), *Ironies of History: Essays on Contemporary Communism*, Oxford University Press, London, p. 15.

6 Estimates of the labour-camp population differ widely. One of the more conservative estimates is based on the 'State Plan for the Development of the National Economy of the USSR in 1941', captured by the Germans and available to the Western researcher. It suggests a camp population for 1941 of just under 7 million. The total number of the civilian population employed in 1940 in industry, mining, and construction was 31.2 million.

7 During the Great Purge and even after, aside from the cases of the most prominent victims, the 'normal' juridical procedures against individuals in the category of 'enemies of the people' were not conducted by civilian or by military courts but by so-called 'special courts' which performed the trial speedily and *in camera*. Their judges included one senior and two junior secret police officers.

8 Party membership, after a decline during the Great Purge, grew in the mature Stalinist period from 2,477,700 in 1939 to 6,882,100 in 1952. However, the purge

signified a major change in the social composition of the new enrollment. For 1929, 81.2 percent of new party members were workers, 17.1 percent peasants, and 1.7 percent white-collar workers and intelligentsia. In the November 1936–March 1939 period, workers constituted 41.0 percent of the new recruits, peasants 15.2 percent, and intelligentsia and white-collar workers 43.8 percent.

9 The size of this 'apparatus' during the Stalin era is estimated around 190,000 to 220,000.

10 A. Gershenkron (1968), 'The stability of dictatorship' in *Continuity in History and Other Essays*, Harvard University Press, Cambridge, MA, p. 317.

11 Joseph Stalin (1937), *Mastering Bolshevism*, Workers Library, New York, p. 36.

12 Deutscher, *Ironies of History*, p. 185.

13 That is to say, as long as they remained in the countryside and retained their peasant status. The only opportunity open to the peasantry was to cease being peasants, to leave the countryside and join the industrialization process in the cities or the army. The young generation of peasants in this period widely utilized this opportunity, and many of them later, through the channel of general, party, or military education, attained positions in the administrative structure.

14 Inequalities in nominal wages and salaries are not the only and the best yardstick for measuring differences in economic status. From the medium strata of officialdom upward, economic privileges of a non-monetary character increasingly affect and determine the living standard of their recipients. These privileges are hard to measure, not only because they are rarely discussed in detail in Soviet publications, but also because they are largely qualitative rather than quantitative in nature.

4.5   The *nomenklatura*: the Soviet Communist Party's personnel control system

Bohdan Harasymiw

That all important appointments in the Soviet Union are ultimately made and unmade by the CPSU is a surprise to no one. Yet very little is known about the mechanics and extent of the specific instrument of control, the *nomenklatura*, employed to support Communist hegemony in the political system, except that it exists. It is an exceedingly difficult institution to study. The reason is secrecy. The party's *nomenklatura* practices contradict Soviet democratic principles: nearly every organized body in the USSR 'elects to its leadership persons already designated for those positions by a particular party organization'. If the mythical portion of democratic centralism, that is, election, is to continue unchallenged, the machinations which go into pre-selecting these and similar leading personnel must be kept hidden from the public, foreign no less than domestic. It is, however, possible to extract some information from the general flow of discourse in the party press.

The term 'nomenklatura' literally means nothing more than 'nomenclature': it is a list of positions, arranged in order of seniority, including a description of the duties of each office. Its political importance comes from the fact that the party's *nomenklatura* – and it alone – contains the most important leading positions in all organized activities of social life. Other intermediate positions are contained in institutional *nomenklatury*, but these are subject to supervision, if not specific approval, by the party. Rank-and-file cadres are managed by institutional authorities; the party oversees this work as well. In addition, subdividing cadres into these three categories and establishing the *nomenklatury* of other institutions are exclusively party responsibilities. These structural arrangements help, incidentally, to clarify several well-known characteristics of Soviet leadership: the fact that the CPSU functions more as a simple 'transmission belt' than as a political party in the accepted sense; the ability of one man with authority over a *nomenklatura* to build a power base in the party or elsewhere and consequently the necessity for purges; and the tendency for Soviet leadership as a whole to become inbred and conservative.

For present purposes, then, *nomenklatura* means party *nomenklatura* unless otherwise specified, the same sense in which Soviet literature usually employs that term. 'The list of official positions', goes a standard description, 'which a party body takes under its permanent supervision has come to be called the *nomenklatura*'. A *nomenklatura* contains those officials directly appointed by the party committee as well as those about whom recommendations for appointment, release, or transfer may be made by other (non-party) bodies but which require the party's approval. Party committees at all levels except the lowest – the primary party organization (ppo) – have such lists. Their content, the specific posts over which the particular committee has jurisdiction, is determined by a higher party body; it varies as between similar committees and from time to time, depending on conditions. There is not, in other words, a fixed *nomenklatura*, say, for an *oblast* party committee (*obkom*), but a common complaint is that local party bodies tend to establish unnecessarily long lists.

Appointment to positions in the *nomenklatura* is not restricted to party members, although Communists are preponderant. To be a *nomenklatura* worker brings one social status and actual privileges. For example, the prosecution of a 'leading worker' on a criminal charge proceeds only with the sanction of the party. Like the whole *nomenklatura* system, its personnel are beyond the reach of the law.

A decree of the Ninth party Congress in 1920 instituted the practice under which party collectives were to report periodically to higher bodies on the performance of their personnel and to recommend future appointments for these individuals. This was apparently the embryo for today's full-blown *nomenklatura* system, which involves the maintenance not only of lists of suitable candidates but complete dossiers on them as well. Every party committee is expected to know personally each individual on its *nomenklatura* and to have accurate data on his age, education, and experience. To help improve the quality of leadership, *nomenklatura* takes two forms – the basic (*osnovnaia*) and the registered (*uchetnaia*) *nomenklatura*. The former is the effective instrument of appointment. The latter, instituted in 1951, is simply a party committee's supplementary list of likely candidates for future vacancies in its own *osnovnaia nomenklatura*. It comprises, as the Soviets say, a 'reserve' of promising, promotable young workers. These do not come under the jurisdiction of the party committee in whose *uchetnaia nomenklatura* they are found; that committee does not approve their appointments. They are in the *osnovnaia* (basic) *nomenklatura* of some lower body, and the superior party committee keeps track of their progress in the event it has an opening in its own basic list.

Nomenklatura responsibility at every level of party organization rests with the secretariat, from the Central Committee at the top of the pyramid, to the many *raion* committees (*raikomy*) at the bottom. In every secretariat there is a number of sections or departments, each concerned with the running of an aspect of the economy or of social organization and each regulating the *nomenklatura* of important jobs in its sector.

Nomenklatura of the CPSU Central Committee

The CPSU Central Committee (CC) has working for it an apparatus of twenty or more departments (*otdely*) which oversee not only their corresponding *otdely* in party committees at lower levels, but also directly supervise the central ministries and government departments. These departments of the Central Committee between them cover all the major sectors of life in the Soviet Union. They deal with enlightenment (culture, agitation, propaganda, science, and education), external affairs (cadres abroad, international affairs, and relations with ruling Communist parties), the economy (agriculture, transport and communications, every class of industry, and domestic trade), administration (of government, society, party, and CC), and the armed forces (main political administration). Technically called departments of the CC, their actual direction is implemented by the Secretariat of the Central Committee. Related *otdely* are placed in groups under one of the CC Secretaries. In a few important cases (agriculture, relations with ruling Communist parties, heavy industry, and organizational and party work) a Secretary is at the head of a single *otdel*. Each department manages a *nomenklatura* for the appropriate sector of organized life, but below the All-Union level. Appointments to the Central Committee apparatus, as well as to the highest party and government posts, are handled by the Secretariat and the CC Plenum.

It has been reported that until 1963 the following order prevailed at the highest level. In a *nomenklatura* of the first category were included: the heads of the party's highest bodies (Secretariat and Auditing and Control Commissions) as well as the whole Presidium (since renamed Politburo) and Secretariat. These cadres were to be managed, formally at least, only by the CC Plenum. More probably, the Plenum's choices were and are determined for it by the Presidium (Politburo) and the Secretariat. A *nomenklatura* of the second category, handled by the Secretariat, included a formidable array of party, government, military, press, and other public leaders. In general terms it comprised the CC departments' leading personnel (department heads and assistant heads, sector chiefs and their deputies, CC instructors); editors of the central press; government ministers and their assistants; all diplomatic officers; party secretaries down to the *obkom* level, including the capitals, their department heads and newspaper editors, and republic prime ministers; the Supreme Court; procurators and KGB chiefs down to *oblast* (province) level; leaders and leading bodies of the Supreme Soviet and its commissions; military commanders and political chiefs; *sovnarkhoz* (regional economic council, since abolished) leaders; top leaders of the trade union, youth, sport, social, and creative organisations; and, finally, heads of the central educational establishments – party, academic, and scientific. The departments of the Central Committee were to have jurisdiction over a third-category *nomenklatura*. This took care of such appointments as urban *raion* (that is, borough or ward) party secretaries, leading staff of educational and scientific establishments, directors of the country's most important factories, and posts in the central administration like inspectors and auditors. The extent, if any, to which appointment power may have been redistributed – this was believed under way in 1965 – to its departments from the Secretariat in more recent times is not exactly known.

Bohdan Harasymiw (1969), 'The *nomenklatura*: the Soviet Communist Party's leadership recruitment system', *Canadian Journal of Political Science*, II, pp. 493–512. Reprinted by permission of the Canadian Political Science Association.

4.6   Is there a ruling class in the USSR?

Alec Nove

There will probably be no major disagreement about the basic facts, though there may certainly be differences of interpretation. We are analysing a society in which almost all the means of production are owned by the state. These means of production, and also the administrative, judicial, cultural and social institutions of the USSR, are controlled, managed, dominated, by a party which is itself a centralized and disciplined body. The party selects and appoints cadres, this function being carried out by the personnel or establishment department of the central committee – for more junior appointments the republican committees. Rank-and-file party members have very limited means of influencing affairs. The ruling stratum could perhaps be formally defined as all those persons holding appointments deemed to be significant enough to figure on the central committee's establishment nomenclature of such appointments, i.e. who are on the *nomenklatura*. They are, literally, the Establishment. This covers all spheres of economic, social, cultural or political significance. It is this which distinguishes the Soviet Union from other bureaucratic or authoritarian societies: in a significant sense there is one centrally-administered hierarchy. Of course, within it there are not only gradations but differences of interest. But few will disagree that the Soviet system has evolved into a hierarchical society within which status and power depends decisively on rank.

Indeed, one could, without too much exaggeration, fit Soviet society into a 'universal civil and military service' model. Everyone (almost) is employed by the state-and-party or one of their organizations, doing the work and getting the pay laid down for the rank they occupy. The questions we will have to ask are: What are the upper strata of such a society? What should they be called? Is Marxist 'class' analysis applicable to such a system? If not, what is?

Let it be said at once that the existence of the hierarchical structure, though certainly a fact, does not imply that everyone obeys his superior passively, nor yet that there is no upward pressure exerted upon the top leadership. No student of Soviet planning can fail to notice that instructions are often ambiguous, or contradictory, or evaded, and that the content of orders received is often influenced by the recipients of the orders. Interest and pressure groups exist, as already noted. Even ordinary workers and peasants can affect plans and income schedules, e.g. by 'voting with their feet' (by leaving occupations and areas where pay is poor or by not going where the authorities wish them to go unless there are sufficient inducements). Mass terror and forced labour cannot now provide a labour force for East Siberia, for instance. However, no autonomous organizations are allowed to exist, no effective trade unions, no uncontrolled organs of the press, and the KGB is active. The structure still accords with a basically unihierarchical model.

Is the elite hereditary, or perhaps becoming such? This is certainly an important question, and one highly relevant to the issue as to whether it is becoming a class or caste. If by 'elite' is meant the apex of the state and party bureaucracy, say, the top 20,000, then one can assert with fair confidence that they are *not* hereditary. Indeed, it is hard to find a single instance of any member of the central committee, minister, party secretary or army general whose father held any of these ranks.

It is another matter if one extends one's attention to the privileged, a much larger group, defined perhaps by family income. There is indeed downward immobility, in the sense that the children not only of the elite narrowly defined but also of other privileged strata tend to receive higher education and to find jobs with reasonably good status. Statistics in this field are, however, liable to misuse because some analysts shift their attention to yet another group, much larger that the upper elite or the *nomenklatura* officials, or the privileged strata, and use figures relating to the so-called 'intelligentsia' in its Soviet definition. This 'intelligentsia' can include everyone who is not either a worker by hand or a peasant. Teachers, librarians, book-keepers, hospital nurses, shop assistants, as well as senior officials, fall within this remarkably wide and socially meaningless definition. It includes a great many badly paid persons, who could not in any circumstances be described as privileged, or influential, or elite.

This said, it must be stressed that higher education has now almost become a necessary (though not sufficient) condition to get into *nomenklatura* and into senior positions generally. Virtually every party leader or secretary of significance, nearly every industrial manager or minister, has a degree, most usually in engineering or technology. Consequently, access to higher education is vital for advancement. This is difficult for peasants, because of the persistent inadequacy of rural schooling and the low cultural level prevailing in rural areas. Talented children of workers have better opportunities, but the figures show quite clearly that a disproportionate number of places in higher education are occupied by children of the so-called intelligentsia. A few remarks are in order. The first is again to stress that many of the families of this 'intelligentsia' are not materially privileged. The majority of the group earn less than skilled workers. The second is that, owing to the very large expansion of higher education since 1928, the relative and absolute number of children of persons already educated is now much larger. The third point is that children from educated homes have a clear 'academic' advantage in competition with children from a less cultured environment. We are all familiar with the reasons. But in recent years there has been a notable increase in the intensity of the scramble for higher education places, owing to the fact that full secondary education has expanded much more rapidly than have institutions of university status. The use of backstairs methods and string-pulling via influence has therefore become more important, and here the *nomenklatura* officials and their hangers-on have evident advantages, especially as abuses they commit seldom attract publicity.

One needs more evidence before coming to any definite conclusion about recruitment of talent from below into the educational system, and ultimately co-option into the *nomenklatura* ranks, which might enable us to answer the question of whether it is an imperfect meritocracy or a closed corporation. An important point is that, while competitive entrance examinations are held for entry into higher education, recruitment to public and party office is almost always a process hidden from any public eye, and is essentially appointment from above, or co-option.

Finally, one must mention one feature of the system in its most recent evolution: the growth of job security in the *nomenklatura*. Under Stalin in the thirties there was a high death and arrest rate, though survivors of the Great Purge proved durable. Even under Khrushchev a fair number of officials were demoted. Since then, the 'civil service' habits familiar in all bureaucracies have become more firmly established, and the vast majority of *nomenklatura* officials are promoted or transferred in a routine manner, save in cases of quite outstanding failure or success. This is no more than to say that the bureaucratic machine functions in accordance with its own rules and habits, with less interference and disruption from a despotic ruler.

One objection to the use of the *nomenklatura* as a means of defining the ruling class or group is that we know little about it, apart from its existence and general function. Details and figures are unpublished in any systematic way. Consequently, even if accepting the *nomenklatura* in theoretical terms, we cannot readily translate it into concrete analysis.

Such a system is not quite the kind of thing the original revolutionaries had in mind. It is a result of a historical evolution, from the libertarian enthusiasm of 1917 to the ordered 'establishment' of today. The causes of this develop- ment have been much debated, usually in the context of explaining the rise of Stalinism. Stalin did much to create the hierarchical-bureaucratic system, true enough, but it is proving durable long after his death. I will confine myself here to a bare listing of explanatory factors.

First, there is the fact that this was Russia, with its autocratic-bureaucratic tradition and relative weakness of spontaneous social forces.

Secondly, one must mention the entire logic of change from above, inherent in a socialist-led revolution in a predominantly peasant country. A prolonged period of administered change had powerful bureaucratic implications. So did the one-party state, required to maintain Bolshevik rule in such an uncongenial environment.

Thirdly, the generally low level of education, culture, consciousness, the exhaustion after years of civil war. The few reliable and effective Bolsheviks had to be disposed in key sectors, subject to the discipline of their party superiors. Fourthly, there was Soviet Russia's isolation in a largely hostile world.

Next on the list of relevant factors must be the functional logic of a centrally planned economy. With the elimination of almost all private enterprise, and the imposition through the state planning system of centrally-determined priorities, the trends towards comprehensive bureaucratization were powerfully reinforced. The *modus operandi* of this species of centralized planning is inherently bureaucratic in nature. The replacement of the largely market economy of NEP by the directive planning of the thirties meant that decisions on resource allocation, production, investment, required to be consciously made and co-ordinated. In practice, the major part of the party-state ap- paratus, and most of the *nomenklatura* officials, have been engaged in operating some aspect of the, economy.

One other feature, particularly of Stalinism, is worth a brief mention. This is the often brutal and crude relations between superior and subordinate in all spheres of life. The attitude became known as *Borzovshchina*, after a fictional rural official, Borzov, who bulldozed his way through the pages of Ovechkin's stories. In one sense this ruthless disregard of one's subordinates' feelings and interests seems to contradict the entire spirit and purpose of the Bolshevik revolution. But in another it is one consequence of promoting men of little culture into positions of authority, a process which was an integral part of the revolution. One requires to be a starry-eyed idealist indeed to imagine that working-class origin endows individuals with virtue. The civil war brought to the fore those who could get things done in the face of appalling obstacles and much resistance. It is, indeed, an elementary social observation that first-generation promotees tend to value greatly the privileges which promotion gives them. How well Stalin knew this!

Let us now suppose that Soviet society is of the type described in the preceding pages. What should such a society be called? Does it possess a ruling *class*?

The official Soviet answer is that there are two classes, workers and peasants, and a *prosloika* (stratum) – the intelligentsia. We have noted the use-lessness of such labels as these, especially as their applicability to the Soviet economic and political structure is never discussed in Soviet publications.

A number of analysts assert the existence of a new class, or a new bour-geoisie. The most familiar argument is probably that of Milovan Djilas:

Ownership is nothing other than the right of profit and control. If one defines class benefits by this right, the communist states have seen, in the final analysis, the origin of a new form of ownership or of a new ruling and exploiting class.... The new class may be said to be made up of those who have special privileges and economic preferences because of the administrative monopoly they hold.... Membership in the new party class or political bureaucracy is reflected in larger economic and material goods and privileges than society should normally grant for such functions. In practice the ownership privilege of the new class manifests itself as an exclusive right, as a party monopoly for the political bureaucrat to distribute the national income, to set wages, direct economic development and dispose of nationalized and other property.... The so-called social ownership is a disguise for real ownership by the political bureaucracy.[1]

The essence of the case rests on the proposition that what matters is *control*, and that the upper strata are in control; they decide what should be done with nationalized means of production. This too is the basis of Bettelheim's claim that there is a 'state bourgeoisie' which runs the Soviet Union. A variant of this approach is that of Castoriadis. He argues that the productive process has a class character because 'of the effective possession of the productive apparatus by the bureaucracy, which is in full charge of it, while the proletariat is fully dispossessed'. In common with Djilas, he argues that the bureaucracy enjoys 'surplus revenue', which is unjustified by its productive contribution to society and determined by the position of any given individual in the bureaucratic pyramid. He concludes: 'It is not capitalism, it is not socialism, it is not even on its way to either of these two forms; the Soviet economy represents a historically new type, and its name matters little if its essential features are understood.'[2] Lefort also speaks of a 'collective apparatus of appropriation' exercised by a 'new class' which does not dominate through *private* appropriation. There takes place a 'fusion of all the strata of the bureaucracy in the mould of a new directing class', whose unity is linked with 'the collective appropriation of surplus'.[3]

Chinese criticisms, usually worded in very strident terms, also tend to identify a new oppressive class in the USSR, which appropriates and exploits. (In sources available to me at least, this is backed by no serious historical and social analysis, and the allegation that this class came to power after the death of Stalin is absurd.)

All this raises some awkward questions, though it is none the worse for that: we may be facing a qualitatively new phenomenon for which our customary categories may require substantial modification.

But before pursuing the argument further let us halt for a moment and consider the relationship of the *nomenklatura*-rulers to the means of production. They are in command of them. Marxists will then turn their attention to the *surplus* which they should be extracting. Do they derive an exploitation income? If so, in what does it consist? It is clear that, *qua* individuals (as Castoriadis duly noted), they do not pocket the profits.

The question of surplus in the Soviet conomy can be handled basically in two different ways. One may assert that the surplus is equal to what the Soviet leaders themselves describe as the surplus product, or 'product for society', i.e. the total profit generated by productive labour and appropriated by the state or its enterprises. It is used for a variety of purposes: hospitals, schools, investments of all kinds, administration, defence, and so on. There are those who assert both that the USSR is an autocracy which pays no attention to people's needs *and* that the masses have no means of exerting pressure. If, then, there is an increase in minimum wages and old-age pensions, this must upset these assumptions: either the leaders *are* paying attention to people's needs, or they respond to pressure from below in their own self-interest (in which case such pressure does exist). In practice, surely, both these things are true. The essential point in the present context is that the surplus is disposed of by the *nomenklatura*-apparatus; it decides what happens to it. Naturally, some part of it benefits ordinary citizens, in their capacity as pensioners, patients, students, scientists, etc. The 'collective owners' of Castoriadis's conception 'appropriate' *this* surplus in the sense of deciding on its use. They control it.

A different approach is contained in the quotation from Djilas. The 'new class' is held to divert for *its own use* 'a larger income in material goods and privileges than society should normally grant for such functions'. By this criterion, they appropriate an amount equal to the notional excess of what they earn (and receive in the form of 'perks') over what they ought to have received, an excess which control over the means of production enables them to acquire. I shall not discuss this further, but of course one must point out that *this* sense of surplus is statistically and conceptually quite different from, and much smaller than, the surplus product referred to above.

Popular among some neo-Marxists is the view that there is no ruling class in the Soviet Union, but that the USSR is a 'transitional society'. Let us examine this conception, of which Mandel is a well-known representative.

It is based on the belief that a society can be either capitalist or socialist, and that the Soviet system contains some elements of both and is neither. It has a centrally planned economy. There are no capitalists. However, it is not a workers' state, workers do not control the means of production, the plan contains many lacunae, and there is pressure to strengthen market elements, pressure which (on this interpretation) could lead to the restoration of capitalism. Alternatively, the assertion of the power of the working masses could or would lead on to socialism. Meanwhile, it is a transitional, mixed system, which must go one way or the other.

If socialism is not on the agenda, why should capitalism be restored? Why, indeed, not assume that the existing system is as durable and stable as any other in a rapidly-changing world? Mandel's answer, if I understand it correctly, is that it is in the interests of the elite, or of an important segment of the elite, to strengthen market relations. All reform proposals in Eastern Europe tend in that direction. The implication of a market system is that there will be capitalists; managers will seek the advantages and security which ownership would bring.

Is this a likely outcome? All things are possible, but I would like to question the assumption that administrators of state property have a predisposition to wish to own it. Is this so? Analysis of the interests of industrial managers can provide evidence for their desire for security and non-interference, for more autonomy (though some managers fear responsibility and like being given orders) and higher incomes. But ownership? Why is this in their interests as they conceive them? They are privileged members of the hierarchy. They see their own promotion as taking place within it. The factor of ownership is surely crucial if capitalism is to be restored by the 'Mandel' route. 'Market' type reforms are not of themselves enough.

Where has all this got us? One could go on citing other interpretations, but perhaps the heart of the matter is in the significance of *control* through a hierarchy, and the relation of this to the traditional Marxian analysis of class. Control relates to power, and power resides in ownership, so Marxists naturally look at property relations as a key to identifying a ruling class. This is a useful model for analysing capitalism. But what of other social formations?

Danilova, a Soviet anthropologist, boldly grappled with this question. Ernest Gellner should be thanked for drawing attention to her ideas.[4]

Does the ownership of the means of production constitute the determining element in all societies? Is it correct to extend the primacy of production relations to all stages of human history ... ? Contrary to the viewpoint widely diffused in Soviet science, the relations of domination-subjection conditioned by the development of the division of labour are themselves by no means relations of production. The dominant relationships in all pre-capitalist structures are non-economic ones.

In her view, 'the absolutization of the economic factor in due time became an obstacle to solving serious theoretical problems, notably the problem of socialist and pre-capitalist societies'. Gellner commented: 'The absolutization of the economic factor is applicable to the capitalist period only. Elsewhere, before and since, we must look to relations of domination-subjection'.

This, surely, means that there are circumstances in which power ('domination-subordination') determines relations of production rather than vice versa. The mention by Danilova in this connection of 'socialism' (which her readers would construe as the Soviet system) is, of course, most important.

Trotsky wrote long ago, in relation to the Soviet system, that 'the character of the economy as a whole thus depends upon the character of state power'.[5] Even longer ago Lenin wrote: 'Politics cannot but have dominance over economics. To argue otherwise is to forget the ABC of Marxism.' What, then, is the name to attach to an identifiable group which exercises state power, and achieves political and economic domination?

Let us attempt a few generalizations based upon the considerations set out above.

1 If the state owns the means of production, the nature of the state, its political processes, its power-relations, are essential determinants of production relations.

2 If such a state is in some sense a workers' state, i.e. the masses have a strong and continuous influence on public affairs and on economic policy, *and* if planning dominates in large-scale economic decision-making, I for one would accept that the system could be described as socialist.

3 If the Soviet state machine, the process of production and the producers, are directed by the party-state *nomenklatura* officials, who recruit by co-option from among the beneficiaries of higher education, and who in various ways benefit from privilege, it follows that this ruling stratum has *some* of the characteristics of a *ruling* class, though not that of ownership, except possibly in some collective sense (cf. Castoriadis). Medvedev argues, however, that 'it is evident that they are not owners of the means of production, do not possess lands and cannot bequeath their rights and their ranks to their children'. He claims that, though their power is 'very great', none the less 'the position of these men is in many ways less secure than that of high officials of a church hierarchy, for instance the Catholic one'.[6] This still leaves one perplexed about how to define the ruling stratum.

Ralf Dahrendorf distinguished 'class' and 'stratum': 'the concept class is an analytical tool that can only make sense in the context of a class theory.

"Classes" are major interest groupings emerging from specific structural circumstances, which intervene as such in social conflicts and play a part in changes of social structure.' Whereas a 'stratum' is merely an analytical category, identifying persons of a similar situation in the social hierarchy, who share some situational identities such as 'income, prestige, style of living, etc. . . .' So for him *classes* relate to groups which act together in a power context, about which one speaks in terms of 'inclusion or exclusion from positions of power'.[7] Ownership is, of course, one means of acquiring power, but Dahrendorf would certainly not confine his definition of a ruling (or any other) class to any specific property relationship: there could be ownership with little power, or more commonly, power without ownership. In these terms, the Soviet 'establishment' would seem to qualify as a 'class'. This appears to be not Marxist, but then we are trying to deal with a society unlike any that Marx described.

Is the term 'power elite', associated with C. Wright Mills, more suitable? There is no doubt that it *can* be used to describe the Soviet dominant stratum. However, the term is most usually applied to the group that exercises power within a Western class society: thus it may consist of top officials, generals, senior advisers, a few influential industrialists and bankers, even some trade union officials. The common denominator is that they all have their hands on the levers of power. Yet in this society there are a great many others who may have as much (or more) wealth or social prestige, and the power elite itself lacks social cohesion or any definite relationship to the means of production. This is not to criticize Mills's use of the term, but merely to underline that the Soviet case is different: the rulers ('power elite') are at the same time the controllers of the bulk of state property, of almost all means of production, and can determine to a great extent the status, earnings and social position of various sub-groups in society. Thus in America there is a power elite *and* a class structure, while in the USSR the power elite *is* the class structure, or rather its apex. The use of the same term for these two distinct formations may mislead.

There is another dimension to the problem of 'class' analysis of Soviet society: that of consciousness. Do *they* regard themselves as a sort of class, *sui generis*? Some would certainly argue that they do. The poet-playwright Aleksandr Galich quotes a story of a woman patient at one of the special 'government' hospitals who, eating a smoked salmon sandwich, remarked: 'I visited a school friend, not one of us (*ne iz nashikh*), who gave me tea, and it was awkward to refuse, so I ate some town sausage, and got gastritis.' The two key points are the concept of *iz nashikh*, and access to superior sausages (and smoked salmon) which are simply not on sale to ordinary townspeople. Galich speaks of a special official pass giving access to 'special buffets, smoked fish, caviare, American cigarettes, cheap dinners', and also 'dachas with paintings, Czech crystal, silver cutlery, service personnel', a separate existence with its own access to information ('the white TASS') and to politically spicy and sexy films, luxurious and cheap sanatoria and the opportunity to visit foreign countries. The beneficiaries of such privileges live in a world of their own, to which ordinary mortals are denied access. Surely they have a sense of belonging to some separate and high 'class', and their subordinates, and ordinary workers and peasants, regard them as a privileged group.

A case for the existing Soviet rulers could be made out as follows:

Whatever Marx or Lenin may have said, in the real world ordinary people pursue inconsistent objectives, do not know what is good for them, enter into conflict with competing groups. This is so everywhere, and the disarray of the Western world today is ample proof of the bankruptcy of liberal pluralist ideas, even where they have deep roots in tradition. *A fortiori*, Russia can only be ruled from above, by a disciplined party, which at least avoids the excesses of Stalin's despotic terror, and which tries – by expanding the output of goods and services and mitigating inequalities by minimum wage and social legislation – to improve the material and cultural position of the masses. We claim [says my imaginary Brezhnev-apologist] that our record is one of steady improvement. All this talk of workers' control and freedom to make demands is a recipe for confusion and anarchy, and therefore for a reduction of material standards. We plan and administer the productive process for the good of society, as best we conceive it. The elite's 'take' is small as a percentage of the national product, much smaller than that of the capitalists and landlords in the West. It is a price the people should pay for stability and order, which we ensure. There are abuses, true, but to talk of them openly would be dangerous. You say this is not socialism? Well, it is the best that we can do, and you [the critics] adopt unreal criteria.... One day we will have much greater material abundance, and then we can talk of communism.

I am unconvinced by the case put by my imaginary Brezhnevite, but it has a more solid basis than some critics (from left *and* right) are prepared to admit. It may not be socialism, but it provides stability, in an increasingly unstable world. Contrary to those who use the term 'transitional society', I am inclined to the view that this unihierarchical system can be durable. True, its leaders could commit grave errors of policy. They may fail to improve living standards, repression could cause trouble in some national republics, and if the promotion routes of able and ambitious workers are blocked this could stimulate a challenge from below. Finally, the ruling stratum can weaken itself through inner conflicts. All such things are possible. However, I take seriously the views expressed to me by several bitterly critical recent *émigrés* from the Soviet Union. They dislike the system, the *nomenklatura*, the network of controls, they also dislike their own conclusions, but none the less these conclusions pointed to stability, durability and acceptance, not instability and rebellion. One philosopher-sociologist said – I quote from memory – that 'unfortunately the system that has developed in the USSR is the one that best fits the circumstances of the second half of the twentieth century'.

If I understand him aright, the point is as follows. Our present discontents in the West arise because many people are not prepared to accept the distribution of income and property which the system of private ownership has generated and is reproducing. They make demands which the system cannot meet, which, indeed, cannot be met at all, in that they exceed productive capacity. Hence political instability, inflation, increasing disruption. The Soviet system eliminates almost totally any income from property, decides on wage and salary scales and suppresses any challenge from below, aware that no generally acceptable criteria for income distribution in fact exist. Similarly, it reconciles (more or less) the conflicting demands of all sorts of interest groups, including those which exist among the *nomenklatura* officials themselves. To operate such a system one cannot rely on coercion alone, there must be a fairly widespread acceptance. In the view of these *émigrés*, such acceptance is in fact widespread, despite the undoubted existence of grievances; all hitherto known societies contain within themselves unsatisfied aspirations, if only for higher incomes and lower prices, and a demonstration that these exist is not evidence of instability or threat to the system. Indeed, the greater ability (compared with the West) of the Soviet unihierarchy to keep demands and aspirations from below under control, ensuring some improvements in living standards the while, is part of its strength. People resent in general terms the privileges of the 'elite', and often imagine that they live like millionaires, a consequence of the secrecy surrounding this question. However, the willingness of workers and peasants to accept hierarchy and material inequalities may be greater than that of left-wing intellectuals.

The word 'accept' may be too positive, and could perhaps be replaced by 'tolerate'. Most of us 'accept', in the sense of working within, systems, which contain many things that we heartily dislike but feel powerless to change. There are indeed forces making for change, particularly those associated with the contradiction between bureaucratic centralization of the economy and the requirements of a modern industrial structure. The effort to increase expertise among the *nomenklatura* officials can only very partially resolve the problem, which will certainly continue to give trouble. So will nationalism. But enough is enough. This article is not an exercise in futurology, but an attempt to place a complex and evolving reality into some sort of conceptual framework.

Abridged from Alec Nove (1975), 'Is there a ruling class in the USSR?' *Soviet Studies*, XXVII, pp. 615–37. Reprinted by permission of Carfax Publishing Company.

Notes

1 M. Djilas (1957), *The New Class*, Thames and Hudson, London.
2 C. Castoriadis (1973), *La Société bureaucratique*, Union général d'éditions, Paris, p. 67.
3 C. Lefort (1971), *Eléments d'une critique de la bureaucratie*, Droz, Genève (Paris), pp. 148, 151.

4 *Times Literary Supplement*, 18 October 1974, citing L. V. Danilova's writings on pre-capitalist societies.
5 L. Trotsky (1937), *The Revolution Betrayed*, Faber and Faber, London, 1937, p. 237.
6 R. Medvedev (1972), *Kniga o sovetskoi demokratii*, Amsterdam, p. 347.
7 R. Dahrendorf (1957), *Soziale Klassen und Klassenkonflikt in der Industriellen Gesellschaft*, F. Enke, Stuttgart, pp. ix, 139 (translation mine).

4.7 The functions of Soviet elections

Victor Zaslavsky and Robert J. Brym

At the centre of all election campaigns in Soviet society – local, republic, judicial and Supreme Soviet – stands the *agitkollektiv*, the organization which conducts all electoral work at the 'grass roots' level by co-ordinating propaganda and related activities. It is a permanent institution which is revived in all industrial enterprises and educational establishments soon after elections are announced (i.e. about two or three months before election day). At the bottom of the *agitkollektiv*'s hierarchical structure is the *agitator*, or canvasser. Each canvasser is responsible for ensuring that about 15–20 electors register and vote. Every five canvassers are supervised by a senior; the senior canvassers are supervised by the head of the local *agitkollectiv*; and the various heads in a district (raion) are supervised by officials in the raion party apparatus (raikom). Thus, about 6–8 percent of all electors are members of *agitkollektivy*. An equal proportion are employed in district electoral commissions (which are responsible for the formal registration of voters and for counting the vote).

Well before election day the canvasser must check up on his list of electors, which is compiled by the police in co-operation with housing superintendents. After ensuring that 'his' electors reside where they are supposed to, he visits them in order to persuade them formally to register at the office of the district electoral commission. Because of genuine support for the regime; out of fear or custom; or simply in order to procure some of the scarce commodities which are distributed to electors at polling stations on election day, the elector may agree to register. He has, however, two other alternatives. First, he may refuse, either on the grounds of some specific local grievance to which the authorities have not attended (e.g. his apartment's state of disrepair) or, less commonly, as an indication of opposition to the regime. Second, a person may claim that he expects to be absent from his voting district on election day and obtain a certificate enabling him to vote elsewhere from the district electoral commission office. And when election day comes the recipient of an absentee certificate normally does not vote. Of course, members of the district electoral commissions know perfectly well why most people request such certificates:

many electors do not wish to waste time taking part in a senseless activity on election day, particularly if the election is being held in the summer when the weather is fine, while a minority view their request for a certificate as a means of expressing dissatisfaction with the regime, or at least with the electoral system.

The claim, frequently made by both Western and Soviet writers, that over 99 percent of the Soviet electorate turn out to vote, must therefore be interpreted as follows: actually, 99 percent of those who a) register *and* b) do *not* receive absentee certificates, turn out on election day. A much closer approximation to reality is that about three-quarters of Soviet electors vote.

In any event, the work of the canvasser comes to an end on election day. His final task is to ensure that everyone on his list who has registered and has not received an absentee certificate actually votes.

It appears that elections are losing their effectiveness as instruments for legitimizing the regime. One might venture to speculate that the authorities themselves have realized this and have considered the possibility of reorganizing election procedures or even of not holding elections at all. Such innovations have not, however, been made for at least two reasons. First, *any* change in the political order is perceived by contemporary Soviet leaders, who seek to maintain the *status quo* at all costs, as a threat. Second, elections are not done away with because they perform definite functions, in the sense that they serve the interests of particular groups in Soviet society – either non-ruling groups or ruling cadres:

a) Some functions of Soviet elections have grown considerably in importance over the past two decades. Foremost among these is the degree to which elections permit the population to bargain with the authorities over minor matters. Various municipal repair services are, during election campaigns, at the disposal of raikoms – the local party committees which, as noted above, supervise the activities of *agitkollektivy*. Increasingly, electors refuse to register when visited by a canvasser in the hope of having him report to his superiors dissatisfaction with unpaved roads, leaky roofs and the like. These reports are usually acted upon by the raikom, which instructs the appropriate repair services to take care of the problems.

b) Elections enable authorities to screen candidates for the party and reward them for faithful state service. These functions are most clearly operative in the universities, one of the major reservoirs from which ruling cadres are recruited. It is not widely known that one of the important causes of expulsion from university is the refusal of students to register for elections. Young persons are more likely than others to refuse paying even lip service to the regime, partly because they are in a critical period of the socialization process, partly because they are relatively free of those responsibilities – family, job and so forth – which may act as constraints on political radicalism. Labelling such potentially disruptive elements as deviants, and blocking their entry into positions of influence, enables the regime to avoid problems which might otherwise emerge at later (and therefore more sensitive) stages in their careers. At the same time, authorities can spot the future party faithful in the student who diligently serves as a canvasser or in some other capacity related to the election campaign.

c) Elections serve the interests of the canvassers themselves. Virtually all canvassers are 'activists' – a group which includes young party members (for whom such work is obligatory), party candidates, those who wish to become party candidates, and some persons who consider themselves to be in politically sensitive positions. The work of the canvasser is much more often dull than pleasant. But there are at least two advantages which accrue to those who perform this role. First, since some form of 'public service' must be undertaken by those who wish to enter and rise in the ranks of the party or the upper reaches of the occupational hierarchy; and since many other forms of public service are particularly odious, working in an *agitkollektiv* is one of the most widely traversed avenues leading to upward social mobility. Second, canvassers have access to confidential information in the form of special lectures and abstracts of the foreign press.

d) Elections perform important social control functions for the authorities. The efficiency of the internal passport system may, for example, be regularly assessed by means of election procedures. First, the police and housing superintendents provide canvassers with the addresses of 'their' voters so that the latter may be visited and persuaded to come to the district electoral commission for registration. If, after the canvasser pays the voter's address several visits, he finds that the voter does not reside where his passport says he does, a report to this effect is submitted to the senior canvasser and eventually finds its way to the party department responsible for supervising the police.

e) Elections also provide training grounds for the implementation of Soviet development policy. Officials must be trained to mobilize the population around slogans and the population must be trained to react properly if, say, a decision to treble chemical production in seven years is to bear fruit. Elections provide the necessary training for the process of actually implementing these large economic and political goals.

f) Finally, let us mention the function of Soviet elections which, more than any other, belies discussion of their legitimizing effect. It has often been remarked that the dominant ideology in the USSR – Marxism-Leninism – cannot, without considerable distortion serve to legitimize the existing regime. Professed belief in the tenets of Marxism-Leninism is actively encouraged; action in terms of these principles is negatively sanctioned because such action would undermine the power of the state. Stated otherwise, the stability of the regime is assured to the extent that the dominant ideology is viewed by the population as invalid, fictitious or – to come right out and say it – illegitimate. What S. V. Utechin said of Stalin remains true of Soviet leaders today:

Stalin intended people to be aware of the fictitious nature of the theory, for an attempt on the part of the people to treat it as truthful (e.g. to believe that they enjoyed freedom of the press) would undermine the whole of his system of rule. Therefore any action based on belief (genuine or pretended) in the truthfulness of the official theory was treated as a most serious political offence.[1]

From this point of view, Soviet leaders are faced with an exceedingly difficult task which requires special mechanisms to adjust the population to the system's irrationality, to resolve for them the blatant contradiction between official ideology and prescribed political practice. The set of procedures by which persons are elected to office ranks as one of the most important of these mechanisms. For elections encourage citizens to demonstrate that they have adjusted to the fiction of democracy in the Soviet Union. Elections buttress the regime – not by legitimizing it, but by prompting the population to show that the *illegitimacy* of its 'democratic' practice has been accepted and that no action to undermine it will be forthcoming.

> Abridged from Victor Zaslavsky and Robert J. Brym (1978), 'The functions of Soviet elections,' *Soviet Studies*, XXX, pp. 362–71. Reprinted by permission of Carfax Publishing Company, Abingdon, Oxon.

Notes

1 S. V. Utechin (1963), *Russian Political Thought: A Concise History*, Praeger, New York, p. 242.

4.8 Soviet nationality problems in the 1970s

Jeremy R. Azrael

This essay examines some of the policy problems that will confront the Soviet leadership in the 1980s and 1990s as a result of the rapidly changing ethnodemographic composition and ethnopolitical orientation of the Soviet population. The most elemental of the ethnodemographic problems confronting the regime is the large and persistent disparity in the growth rates of the country's 'European' (Slavic and Baltic) nationalities and its 'non-European' (Caucasian and Central Asian) nationalities.

The categories 'European' and 'non-European' are synthetic and each includes nationalities that differ from one another in important respects. In the case of the 'non-Europeans', the crucial internal distinction is probably between Christians (Georgians and Armenians) and Muslims (Azeri, Uzbeks, Turkmen, Tadzhiks, Kirghiz, and Kazakhs). Except for the Tadzhiks, all of the Muslim nationalities speak mutually comprehensible languages and share a common Turkic background that may be more important to them than their Soviet-sponsored national identities. Of the major 'European' nationalities, which constitute about 80 percent of the country's total population and therefore dominate its overall demographic performance, only the Moldavians have increased by more than 1.2 percent per annum in recent years. Of the major 'non-European' nationalities, on the other hand, only the Georgians and Tatars have fallen below a 2 percent increase per annum; and the Central Asian nationalities have achieved annual increases of close to 4 percent. As a result, 'non-Europeans' have increased their share in the country's total population from 11.5 percent in 1959 to a conservatively estimated 17 percent in 1977.

This disparity (the size and persistence of which the regime apparently had underestimated prior to the 1970 census) has become a source of mounting official concern. It almost certainly was a factor in Brezhnev's recent call for the formulation of an official demographic policy that would take account of 'a number of population problems which have lately become exacerbated'. For the immediate future, however, there is little that the regime can do to stimulate the growth rate among 'European' nationalities. In consequence, by the end of the century, between 20 and 25 percent of the country's total population and almost 40 percent of its teenagers and young adults will be 'non-Europeans', of whom the vast majority will be Central Asians.

That this prospect has aroused deep-seated psychological and political anxieties among members of the ruling elite is indicated, among other things, by the epithet 'yellowing' (*ozheltenie*) that is applied to it in the private conversations of many Soviet officials. These anxieties in turn are strongly reinforced by the 'jokes', which have gained currency in certain Central Asian circles, about the impending restoration of the Tatar yoke, and the fate that will befall the Russians when the Chinese 'liberate' Turkestan. Nonetheless, the current ruling elite is not discernibly racist in its outlook or composition, and it is doubtful that it feels immediately threatened by an erosion of 'white supremacy' or the emergence of a Chinese 'fifth column'. The Kremlin's concern on both these counts is almost certainly less urgent than its concern over the implications of the 'yellowing' process for the national economy. In this connection, what is most troubling is not the shift in the ethnic balance per se but the low 'European' growth rates and the fact that the Central Asian nationalities have remained outside the mainstream of the country's economic development and contain a heavy preponderance of undereducated peasants with a weak-to-nonexistent knowledge of Russian and a tenacious aversion to interregional or even intraregional migration.

Economic dilemmas

What the shortfall in the country's 'European' population means for the economy is that the latter will no longer be able to provide large-scale

Table 4.8(1)   *Changing composition of USSR population, 1959–70*

Nationality	Total population (%) 1959	Total population (%) 1970	Percent Change
Major 'European'	79.6	77.2	−2.4
Russian	54.6	53.4	−1.2
Ukrainian	17.8	16.9	−0.9
Belorussian	3.8	3.7	−0.1
Moldavian	1.1	1.1	0.0
Latvian	0.7	0.6	−0.1
Lithuanian	1.1	1.1	0.0
Estonian	0.4	0.4	0.0
Major 'non-European'	12.6	15.2	+2.6
Uzbek	2.9	3.8	+0.9
Tatar	2.4	2.4	0.0
Kazakh	1.7	2.2	+0.5
Azeri	1.4	1.8	+0.4
Armenian	1.3	1.5	+0.2
Georgian	1.3	1.3	0.0
Tadzhik	0.7	0.9	+0.2
Turkmen	0.5	0.6	+0.1
Kirghiz	0.5	0.6	+0.1
Others	7.8	7.6	−0.2
Selected national groups			
Slavs[a]	76.3	74.0	−2.3
Non-Slavic 'Europeans'[b]	3.3	3.2	−0.1
'Non-European' Christians[c]	2.6	2.8	+0.2
'Non-European' Muslims[d]	10.0	12.4	+2.4
All other	7.8	7.6	−0.2

Notes:
[a] Slavs are defined as the total of the Russian, Ukrainian, and Belorussian populations.
[b] Non-Slavic 'Europeans' are defined as the total of the Moldavian, Lithuanian, Latvian, and Estonian populations.
[c] 'Non-European' Christians are defined as the total of the Georgian and Armenian populations.
[d] 'Non-European' Muslims are defined as the total of the Uzbek, Tatar, Kazakh, Azeri, Tadzhik, Turkmen, and Kirghiz populations.

reinforcements for the industrial work-force. By the late 1980s the number of 'Europeans' reaching working age will decline from the present average of about 4 million per annum to only slightly over 2 million per annum, and the regime will be extremely hard pressed to find enough 'European' workers to replace those whose retirement can no longer be delayed. What makes this prospect particularly unsettling is the fact that the vast bulk of the increase in industrial output that has occurred in the postwar Soviet Union is attributable to increases in the 'European' work force rather than to increases in per capita labor productivity, which has grown only modestly despite the regime's frantic efforts to raise it. The only way the regime can hope to staff the many new enterprises on which it has staked so much of its prestige and credibility is either to locate the bulk of them in Central Asia or to mobilize large numbers of Central Asians for work in other regions. Unfortunately for the regime, these policies could exact a very heavy price.

Whatever its ultimate benefits, a rapid build-up of Central Asia's industrial capacity obviously would require the diversion of a great deal of scarce capital and equipment both from the already industrialized regions of the country and from underdeveloped regions such as Siberia and the Far North, which are far richer than Central Asia in essential (and hard-currency-convertible) natural resources. The chances that large numbers of Central Asians will spontaneously migrate into the labor-deficit regions of the country are virtually nil. To be sure, in the absence of accelerated industrialization of their own region, hundreds of thousands, if not millions, of natives will be unable to find full-time employment in the public sector (industrial or agricultural) of the local economy. In addition, thanks to the tenacity of early marriage and prolific childbearing practices, many of those concerned undoubtedly will have a large number of dependants to support. However, the very existence of large families will serve as a constraint on migration to cities in general and to overcrowded 'European' cities in particular. Moreover, in the absence of strong counteractions by the regime, many natives who cannot find jobs in the public sector will still be able not only to survive but also to prosper on the proceeds of the individual or familial cottage industries and private household plots that already account for a sizable share of Central Asian personal income.

A search for other policies that the regime might use to increase the supply of Central Asian *gastarbeiter* yields two basic alternatives: administrative mobilization and economic stimulation. The prospect of choosing among such unpalatable alternatives would give any leader pause, and it would not be surprising if Brezhnev continued to substitute further study for decisive action. Moreover, it is not unlikely that his successors also will try to 'muddle through'. In consequence, it would not be surprising if industrial growth rates declined substantially and if the regime found it increasingly difficult to satisfy both its own appetite for international power and the rising economic expectations of its citizens.

Military consequences

Unless there is a rise in international tensions, the size of the Soviet armed forces is likely to decrease in the 1980s (it is now estimated to be 4 to 5 million men). Even if the reduction in the draft term from three to two years were rescinded, it would be exceedingly difficult and costly to secure the requisite number of conscripts (currently estimated to number about 1.5 to 1.6 million per year) from a country in which the entire cohort of 18-year-old males will be only slightly over 2 million (as against 2.6 million today). In addition to facing a prospective cutback, moreover, the armed forces seem almost certain to undergo a very extensive 'yellowing'. This outcome is fore-shadowed by the fact that the proportion of 'non-Europeans' among prime draft-age males will rise from a low of 20 to 25 percent in the late 1980s to almost 40 percent by the turn of the century.

Indeed, if the regime were to follow the dictates of economic rationality alone, the military would become an almost entirely 'non-European' institution. In this way it would be possible not only to avoid the inordinately high civilian opportunity costs of 'European' soldiers but also to realize dispropor-tionately high civilian returns on its investments in in-service training pro-grams. Although these programs are often redundant for European trainees, they frequently provide Central Asians with new and readily transferable skills.

Even if the regime were to flout economic logic and overconscript 'Europeans', it would have to abandon what seems to be its current practice of assigning only a few Central Asians to high-priority military units, including not only units of the strategic rocket forces and anti-aircraft defense but also of the air force, the armored corps, the artillery, and even the front-line motorized infantry. Although these units could be kept preponderantly 'European', their ranks would still have to be filled with Central Asians, who now are assigned mostly to construction, supply, and rear service functions. By the late 1980s and 1990s, it is true, typical Central Asian conscripts probably will be some-what better-educated than their contemporary counterparts. However, the vast majority of them will almost certainly still be graduates of second- and third-rate rural schools. In consequence, there is little prospect that any impending decline in the quantity of Soviet military manpower could be counterbalanced by a significant increase in its quality.

The difficulties created by the low educational attainments and technical skills of typical Central Asian conscripts will be exacerbated by their rudi-mentary command of Russian, which is the only authorized medium of communication within the armed forces. If there is a significant increase in the percentage of Central Asians who are urbanized, the proportion of Central Asians who speak Russian with some fluency may rise above the current 16 percent. However, there is little prospect that it will rise sharply, and present trends suggest that it actually may decline as the proportion of 'Europeans' in Central Asia becomes progressively smaller. The language-related command, control, and communication problems that have heretofore been largely con-fined to relatively low-priority units are likely to become prevalent in other units as well, with corresponding degrading effects on the country's military capabilities. Judging by what is reported in various enterprises in Central Asia, there is good reason to believe that units in which Central Asian natives become a substantial minority will be particularly prone to demoralizing ethnic tensions and open ethnic conflicts.

Many of these difficulties could be at least partially alleviated by the reinstitution of national military formations of the sort that were the norm until 1936 and were selectively rehabilitated during World War II. Whatever discussions or experiments may be occurring, however, the regime is unlikely to sanction a return to full-fledged military federalism or to permit the 'indigenization' of local bases and garrisons to become a general policy. Rather, the fact that the constitution ratified in 1978, to replace the so-called Stalin Constitution of 1936, drops both of the latter's references to republic-level military formations suggests that the regime is eager to stifle all hopes and expectations to the contrary. Official commentators probably will continue to dwell on 'the difficulty of preparing training manuals in different national languages' and the importance of reinforcing internationalist sentiments. The underlying motive, though, will almost certainly be a fear that indigenous units might provide tacit or open military support for nationalist challenges to central authority. That such fear can be a significant factor in official thinking is indicated, for example, by Nikita Khrushchev's conduct during the riot opposing de-Stalinization that broke out in Tbilisi, Georgia, in March 1956. Although this riot clearly was beyond the control of the civil authorities, Khrushchev canceled the marching orders of a nearby military unit that happened (by a rare anomaly) to be predominantly Georgian, and allowed the rioters to rampage for 12 hours while more typical, ethnically heterogeneous troops were dispatched from outlying bases.

Political currents

Brezhnev alleged in 1972 that the past 50 years had witnessed the formation of a new 'Soviet nation' or 'Soviet people' that was now sufficiently robust to survive any ethnopolitical crisis, and eventually would encompass the entire population of the USSR. At a minimum, he could point to indisputable and massive demonstrations of all-union loyalty during World War II and to a steady, albeit slow and by no means universal, post-war growth in bilingualism, ethnic intermarriage, and interregional mobility. However, when he went on to assure his audience that the Soviet Union definitely had solved its 'historic nationality problem' – the problem of national deviationism and centrifugal nationalism – he was clearly overstating what was at best a dubious case. Indeed, the countervailing evidence is well known. A summary rundown will serve to remind the reader.

1 Many members of the country's major diaspora nationalities, including not only the Jews but also the Volga Germans, the Greeks, and the Meskhetian Turks, have become so embittered at the continued denial of

their communal rights that they have renounced their Soviet citizenship and have demanded to be 'repatriated' to their foreign 'homelands'.

2 Nearly all of the country's 'European' and Caucasian nationalities and at least one Turkic nationality (the Crimean Tatars) have produced outspoken critics of official nationality policies and practices. These critics have managed not only to replenish their own ranks in the face of hundreds, if not thousands, of arrests, but also to establish dynamic and resilient dissident organizations, ranging from clandestine parties, through underground journals, to networks for the public circulation of programs, petitions, and letters of protest, including one 1972 petition (to UN Secretary-General Kurt Waldheim) that was signed by more than 17,000 Lithuanians.

3 A number of nationalistically inspired acts of violence have included a two-day riot in Kaunas, Lithuania, in 1972 and several recent protest bombings and reported assassination attempts in Georgia.

4 There have been numerous organized protest demonstrations against centrally imposed curbs on national self-expression, including several mass gatherings by Crimean Tatars and a 1965 street vigil in Erevan that reportedly was attended by 100,000 Armenians.

5 There has been an extremely rapid increase in the membership of republic and local ethnographic societies and so-called societies for the preservation of architectural and historical monuments that were established in the 1960s to provide outlets for environmentalist and conservationist concerns. There is no doubt that the mushroom growth of these societies and their exceptional popularity reflect a more than merely antiquarian or folkloristic interest in national history and culture.

6 There have been numerous cases in which native Party and state officials, including two republic Party first secretaries with seats on the Politburo (a Georgian, V. P. Mzhavanadze, and a Ukrainian, P. Ye. Shelest), have shown a certain laxity in combating the forces of 'local nationalism' and have pursued the 'parochial' interests of their fellow nationals at the expense of their all-union responsibilities. These cases have been widely publicized in the Soviet press, and there is no reason to doubt that most of the officials concerned are at least partially 'guilty' as charged, and have in fact encouraged (or failed to discourage) the retention of local resources for local use, the curtailment of immigration by ethnic 'aliens', the preferential treatment of native cadres, the publication of 'nationally pretentious' books and articles, the 'tendentious' designation of historical monuments, the perpetuation of 'archaic' traditions and retrograde survivals of the past, and even the lenient treatment of dissident nationalist intellectuals.

Although these manifestations of national self-affirmation and self-assertiveness are a far cry from the explosive international or centre-periphery confrontations that took place in earlier periods of Soviet history, they are more than sufficient to demonstrate that the USSR has neither transcended its own history nor become immune to worldwide trends. Unless the regime undergoes an improbable re-Stalinization or an even more improbable liberal-democratic transformation, such manifestations are likely to become more frequent and more insistent over time. Although piecemeal reforms and partial crackdowns undoubtedly could have a tranquilizing effect, they would at best produce a temporary and deceptive calm.

One reason for anticipating an escalation in national self-affirmation and self-assertiveness is the accelerating 'modernization' of the Central Asian nationalities, who have been conspicuously passive since their great uprising in the early 1920s, but who are almost certain to become more militant as they are drawn into the mainstream of the country's economic development. At the same time, moreover, the 'European' nationalities are likely to become increasingly restive as they are subjected either to an 'onslaught' of Central Asian *gastarbeiter* or to an 'expropriation' of 'their' resources to speed the industrialization of distant Central Asia. In this connection, a particularly strong reaction probably can be expected from the Russians, who will soon undergo the psychological distress of losing their majority status within the country's total population. Also, increasing education and urbanization and improved communications will make it much harder for the regime to isolate the masses from dissident nationalist spokesmen or from the demonstration effects of nationalist protests within the Soviet Union or in the outside world.

Barring a breakdown of central control that might accompany a major war or the political degeneration that might accompany a prolonged and unfettered succession struggle, there is little likelihood that national protest will rise to unmanageable levels. Under more normal circumstances, centrally manipulated sanctions and incentives will almost certainly suffice to prevent large communal uprisings or national insurgencies. The most that can be readily conceived, therefore, is 'merely' more of the same – that is, more numerous acts of individual and small-group terrorism, more frequent episodes of collective violence, more massive protest demonstrations, and more extensive public or semi-public dissent. Even such manageable outcomes, however, would impose serious constraints on the regime.

At a minimum, the regime would be forced to increase its police budget and to introduce security procedures that not only would be economically counterproductive but also would demoralize citizens on whose loyalty and commitment it otherwise could rely. In the second place, the regime would find it increasingly difficult to persuade even strongly détente-oriented Western governments to authorize the volume of technology transfers, grain sales, and development credits that could significantly brighten its somewhat gloomy economic prospects. Such governments will be harder put to ignore Soviet violations of communal rights as the victims of these violations come, as they almost certainly will, from groups such as the Jews, Germans, Lithuanians, and Ukrainians whose foreign co-nationals (in the United States, West Germany, Canada, and Australia) constitute important domestic political constituencies. In the same vein, moreover, the regime could find it difficult to maintain or consolidate profitable political and economic relations with a range of non-Western countries whose native populations have strong ethnic affinities with restive nationalities in the USSR – a category of countries that includes Romania (Moldavians), Iran (Tadzhiks and Azeri), Afghanistan (Azeri and Turkmen), and Turkey (Meskhetian Turks and the entire Soviet Turkic population), and that could, by extension, include all of the countries of the Muslim world. Finally, escalating national protest would discredit the Soviet 'model' of international integration everywhere in the Third World and would undermine the regime's credibility as a spokesman for the oppressed nationalities in non-Communist countries.

> Abridged from Jeremy R. Azrael, 'Emergent nationality problems in the USSR' in Jeremy R. Azrael, ed. (1978), *Soviet Nationality Policies and Practice*, Praeger, New York, pp. 363–79. Reprinted by permission of Greenwood Publishing Group Inc., Westport, CONN.

4.9   Soviet nationalities: recent trends

John A. Armstrong

Observing the dissolution of the Soviet bloc in Eastern Europe during 1989–90, followed in 1991 by the shrinking of the USSR itself, one might regard the category 'Eastern Europe' as a transitory artefact of Leninist power. Certainly Mikhail Gorbachev's loosening of economic, ideological, and police controls was the immediate cause of centrifugal tendencies. Nevertheless, as far as the Russian power base goes, one should recall the prophecy George F. Kennan made 44 years ago:

If, consequently, anything were ever to occur to disrupt the unity and efficiency of the party as a political instrument, Soviet Russia might be changed overnight from one of the strongest to one of the weakest and most pitiable of national societies.[1]

In Eastern Europe [and European USSR] as a whole, more enduring characteristics help to explain the forms of dissolution and provide some basis for projecting the future of the independent states that are emerging. One such characteristic is the line, resembling a geologic fault, from the Caspian to the Adriatic between cultures of Islamic origin and those of Christian ancestry. The latter can, in turn, be subdivided into cultures derived from Eastern Orthodox Christianity and those of Western (Catholic and Protestant) background. Here, as subsequently, reference to cultural heritages does not necessarily imply present religious devotion, but suggests the remote, formative force of the great world religions. As cultural influences, therefore, the great 'fault lines' traversing Eastern Europe continue to influence politics, notably in Southeastern Europe and the Caucasus. A second ethno-religious characteristic is lingering antipathy of countryside to city, often manifested in antiurban ideologies that denigrate both entrepreneurial values and the minorities who exemplify them.

Both of these characteristics were confronted by the Marxist-Leninist regimes imposed throughout Eastern Europe between 1917 and 1948. These regimes asserted their intention to terminate ethno-religious conflicts and replace anti-urban ideologies with the values of urban industrialization via state socialism. From the beginning, however, subtle national biases were evident; by 1948, cynical antisemitism had become a governing principle.

The transformation of Eastern Europe after 1988 led many observers to speak of the 're-emergence of civil society'. Insofar as this concept applies to the states of East Central Europe that preserved memories of recent independence in homogeneous states, 'civil society' is appropriate. What has appeared in the Soviet Union, however, is not a single civil society, but a cluster of national civil societies. It has become evident that the USSR never constituted a single society; the interrelation of its constituent national societies has been even more complicated than in Yugoslavia.

Soviet propaganda emphasized that there were some 150 ethnic groups in the USSR; at times, indeed, official policy deliberately divided coherent ethnic units. In 1923, the Soviet Union began to impose a formal hierarchy of nationality divisions, headed by union republics. Gradually these categories shaped the consciousness of their inhabitants, until many people of diverse backgrounds identified with their republics of residence.

But implicit recognition of more subtle ethnic categories was also apparent. Russia was always in a class by itself, as were the Slavic 'younger brothers' – Ukraine and Belarus. 'Colonials' – the six union republics of Muslim background – became critical for the Soviet future as their populations multiplied; yet, the cultural distance between these populations and the Slav core made the Muslim republics' position resemble French Algeria. In contrast to the rigid centralization of cadres appointments under Stalin, Leonid Brezhnev's status quo policies led to a tacit contract between cadres of Muslim origin and central Soviet authorities. In return for verbal affirmation of Leninism and Soviet policy directives, top Muslim cadres were permitted considerable patronage power in the appointment of subordinates.

No doubt it was apparent to Soviet security agencies, as well as to outside observers, that several union-republic nations were just as firm in their ultimate attachment to independence as were the captive nations of East Central Europe. Among these union republics are the Baltic peoples forcibly incorporated by Stalin. A conspicuous minority of Latvians were Bolsheviks; their descendants included former Soviet interior minister Boris Pugo, who committed suicide after the failure of the August 1991 coup. The overwhelming majority of Latvians are, however, fervently attached to the independent state that their nation had enjoyed from 1918 to 1940. Refusal of Latvian teenagers to admit fluent knowledge of Russian during the 1960s; Latvian skill in organizing industry and consumer services; and a major naval mutiny 20 years ago all suggest that only dire threats kept Latvia in the USSR. Estonians were even more solidly anti-Soviet precisely because this nation of 1 million was threatened by massive Russian immigration. More homogeneous and stronger in religious solidarity, Lithuania has been equally opposed to the Union. Georgia, conquered by Soviet arms after only three years of independence, draws on a long history as an embattled feudal kingdom. Moldova had no experience with independence, but 'Moldavians speak Romanian, and consider themselves part of the Romanian political nation'.[2]

The clearest evidence for the state-nation status of these five nations, prior to August 1991, was their firm refusal to accept restrictions on the formal right of secession contained in the Union Treaty submitted by Mikhail Gorbachev in March 1991. All refused, as a matter of principle, to conduct a referendum on the treaty. The Armenian republic also rejected the referendum. During the Brezhnev era, Armenians appeared to be more appropriately classified as a 'mobilized diaspora' because, although united by their Gregorian Church and a tragic history longer even than Georgia's, Armenians lived scattered throughout the USSR, the Middle East, and the West as well as in their truncated homeland. As a nation, they appeared to regard Russians as allies rather than occupiers. After the coup, Armenia declared independence; but in December, it adhered to the new association, the 'Commonwealth of Independent States'.

The process of dissolution

When Gorbachev became Communist party general secretary in 1985, there was little to suggest that he would preside over a loosening of central control. In contrast to most previous general secretaries, he had had little experience with ethnic minorities. As an oblast first secretary, he supervised a territory – Stavropol – that although located on the Caucasus frontier, had just enough contact with *inorodtsy* (non-Russians) to arouse Russian ethnocentrism.

Given his background, one should not have been surprised that Gorbachev's first major move in the nationality area was to abrogate the tacit contract between Muslim leaders in Kazakhstan and Moscow that had been established under Brezhnev, who for a time had headed the Communist party there. Finding local patronage an obvious impediment to *perestroyka*, Gorbachev replaced key Kazakh cadres by imports from Russia.

Imperatives of *perestroyka* eventually produced genuine steps toward freedom of discussion (*glasnost*), including toleration of 'popular fronts' in the Baltic republics beginning in 1988. During the following year, such fronts spread rapidly, and escalated their demands. In Georgia, the stakes were raised in April 1989 through the violent repression (which Gorbachev disavowed) by KGB and military forces of mass demonstrations. Not long afterward, Armenian demands for alteration of the border with Azerbaijan to permit incorporation of the predominantly Armenian district of Nagorno-Karabakh aroused Azeri passions against their ancient enemy and caused a pogrom in a Baku suburb that led to the loss of many Armenian lives. More extensive riots at the end of 1988 produced a flight of Russians as well as Armenians. An Azerbaijan popular front temporarily gained control of large areas, including Azerbaijan's border with Iran. After brutally suppressing this uprising, the Moscow regime utilized the interethnic strife as evidence of the imprudence of relaxed central controls.

From the international standpoint, complete liberation of East Central Europe by the winter of 1989–90 was by far the most important step in the dissolution of the Soviet sphere.

In March 1990, the Lithuanian parliament reasserted Lithuania's independence. Although somewhat more restrained in their independence declarations, Latvia and Estonia also asserted the illegality of their annexations by the Soviet Union in 1940. Gorbachev denounced these 'unconstitutional secessions', but promised not to resort to violence. Nevertheless, although the Lithuanian government continued to function, public buildings were seized as state or Communist party property in January 1991. Troops from the interior ministry's Special-Purpose Police Detachment carried out violent attacks on Lithuanian customs posts, culminating in the killing of six guards on July 31, 1991. Moscow's actions up to that point strikingly resembled Soviet and Communist tactics in postwar Czechoslovakia.

The next stage ended differently. During the August coup, massive columns of troops occupied all three Baltic republics, but left precipitously when the coup failed. Thereafter, Lithuania outlawed the party, while the other two Baltic states took less sweeping measures. In rapid succession, the major European powers, followed by the United States, recognized Baltic independence; on September 6, the Soviet government formally acknowledged this fait accompli. Later, independence was sealed by admission of the Baltic states to the United Nations. Numerous practical issues remain, but return of Russia's control in the Baltic region seems as unlikely as restoration of Russia's power in East Central Europe. When, in December 1991, Boris Yel'tsin called for the formation of a 'Commonwealth of Independent States' to replace the defunct Union of Soviet Socialist Republics, the three Baltic states did not join.

The goals

Events of the last three years demonstrate that all peoples of Eastern Europe [and European USSR] advance three fundamental demands:

- For a standard of living comparable to Western Europe's.
- For return to the numerous advantages of life in stable ethno-religious communities, regarded not merely as vehicles for attaining other goals, but as intrinsically valuable.
- For responsive governments, based on popular participation through competitive elections, guaranteeing the rule of law and personal liberties.

After the attainment of national independence in most of East Central Europe and the rejection of authoritarianism in the USSR, none of these popular demands is unrealistic. But a return to some type of authoritarianism arising from overemphasis on one set of demands is always possible.

The state nations

Since recognition of their independence, the Baltic states appear to be no more worse off than the East Central European states like Poland or Czechoslovakia. Each Baltic state does face constraints inherent in a small society and market along with the legacy of closer integration into the bankrupt Soviet economy. In the absence of significant friction among the three states, however, development of a mini-confederation should pose no insurmountable difficulties. The three economies are partially complementary, and joint foreign representation and commercial ventures would reduce expenses. The biggest problem is the Russian minority in Latvia and Estonia. After intransigent early steps, Baltic governments have wisely made concessions to Russian culture. Nevertheless, restrictions on immigration and enforcing of length-of-residence requirements for voting appear to be essential for preserving the cultural integrity of such small nations. Many Russians in Latvia (especially in the old settlement in Riga) and Estonia voted for the independence of these two states.

The Ottoman invasions of Christian Europe in the 16th–18th centuries are the remote cause of population intermingling[3] and the heritage of ethnic strife in Southeastern Europe. Across the Black Sea, this Muslim-Christian fault line continues in the Caucasus region, geographically compartmentalized by a mountain range grander than the Balkans. Effects in Georgia and the North Caucasus (presently within the Russian republic) may be equally deleterious. Direct clashes between Abkhazians (predominantly Muslim) and Georgians, who make up an overwhelming majority in the Abkhaz autonomous republic as well as in Georgia as a whole, are unlikely to end in secession, but they undermine the credibility of the strongly nationalist Georgian government.

Harder to understand is Georgian harassment of the small Ossetian autonomous oblast, separated from the larger Ossetian autonomous *republic* in the RSFSR by the main Caucasus range. Ossetians by heritage are Christian like the Georgians, but the latter people's intransigent nationalism has turned them from a natural ally into an adversary.

More serious than these pathetic quarrels is the Georgians' incipient conflict with their urban minorities. As the administrative center of the Transcaucasus, Tbilisi long ago acquired a large Russian settlement. Under an independent Georgia, it would probably become vestigial. The position of the Armenian minority is quite different. In effect, Armenians constitute the indigenous core of modern Tbilisi. Having numerous talents in viniculture, arts, war, and politics, Georgians depended on Armenians for entrepreneurial and commercial skills. This situation made Georgians, like Serbs and Russians, susceptible to imported anti-urban ideologies.

Yet, in many respects, the two nations are suited to a mini-confederation like that which appears feasible for the Baltic region. Although now of different denominations, Armenians and Georgians descend from the same Christian heritage. In contrast to adamantly 'Asian' Azeris, Armenians and Georgians insist they are 'Europeans'. Precisely because their history is so intertwined, however, rivalry over accomplishments and priorities has divided these nations. Without a seacoast and situated between hereditary Turkic foes, Armenia at the moment needs Georgia more than Georgia needs Armenia. As its attachment to the new Commonwealth shows, Armenia is more open to reconciliation to Russia than is Georgia, which favors complete independence.

The Muslim nations

During the August coup, leaders in several republics of Muslim heritage voiced support for the effort. As in Kazakhstan, however, some prominent leaders supported Yel'tsin throughout, and eventually all six Muslim republics rallied to his plan for a new Commonwealth. Quite possibly the Soviet regime's insistence on maintaining existing union-republic borders by force – directed primarily against the Armenians – was a critical reassurance that it had opted to favor Muslim interests generally.

The Kazakh SSR president, Nursultan Nazarbaev, was able to claim that more than 94 percent supported continued membership in the Union. Similar overwhelming majorities in favor of continued membership in the Union were recorded in the other Muslim union republics, including Azerbaijan.

In Central Asia, Muslim cadres have been firmly quashing the turmoil and dissent that had been rife in their regions during 1988–90. Draft evasion in Central Asia has been reduced by enlisting official Muslim clergy to urge compliance, while acclaiming authorization of worship among the military. Overall, the six Muslim union republics met 80–90 percent of their draft quotas, which contrasts with most state nations, where compliance was less than 33 percent. In Tajikistan, efforts of the Sunni spiritual council to refuse religious funerals to Communists were opposed by the union-republic president.

Probably many top officials of Muslim origin, now able to turn out the

Table 4.9(1)   *Comparative income levels, 1961 vs. 1991*

Republic	Average industrial wage as percent of RSFSR wage (1961)	Percent of republic residents having incomes under 100 rubles a month (1991)
RSFSR	100	11
Ukraine	94	11
Belarus	86	7
Estonia	97	3
Kyrgystan	90	47
Azerbaijan	71	49
Turkmenistan	101	49
Tajikistan	93	69
Uzbekistan	57	80

Muslim vote, fear the rise of an Islamic state on the model of some in the Middle East. Preservation of ties to Russia may seem the best means of avoiding such an outcome. Yet, even from the average Muslim's standpoint, for economic reasons, continued alliance with Moscow may also appear desirable in the short run. As early as the 1960s, *industrial* wages in Muslim republics were near the Soviet average, but today the per capita income is woefully below that of the European republics (see Table 4.9(1)). Only heavy subsidies from European portions of the USSR have made a minimal level of consumption possible in the Muslim republics.

A lifestyle derived from Islamic practices, if not beliefs, continues to appeal to much of the population. Clearly, one factor does threaten perpetuation of this ethnoreligious lifestyle: unwillingness of a popular Moscow regime, especially if it is reduced to Slavic or even just Russian components, to maintain subsidies. Whether such republics would form a united state of 'Turkestan' or other possible combinations cannot be predicted; in all probability, the region would resemble some Middle Eastern areas with strong community solidarity and religious life but a low resource base.

Ukraine

Soviet observers realized that without Ukraine the USSR or its successor would cease to be a superpower. Moreover, as the days following the abortive coup demonstrated, the much smaller Belarus is likely to follow Ukraine's lead. The internal situation of Ukraine is, however, more complicated than that of any other union republic. Although the Christian-Muslim fault line lightly touches the Ukrainian republic, the Orthodox-Catholic division is critical. This dividing line cuts across the West Ukrainian area of 10 million people. For West Ukraine, which is the bastion of the independence movement, ethno-religious factors have been fundamental. All nationally conscious Ukrainians (as well as liberal Russians) deplore Russian Orthodox Church collaboration, after 1944, with the communist regime in violently suppressing the Ukrainian Catholic Church. The Orthodox argument that it was merely redressing a wrong that is four centuries old – the transfer of numerous West Ukrainian Orthodox congregations to Roman allegiance – rings hollow when confronted by the reality of past KGB repression and manifest West Ukrainian fervor for Byzantine-rite Catholicism today.

During 1988–91, West Ukrainian enthusiasm for independence was partly offset by popular sentiments in the ethnically mixed southeastern region. This region was the power base from which many Communist party and KGB officials trained in Brezhnev's Dnepropetrovsk apparatus originated. In 1972, Petro Shelest, the Ukrainian republic first secretary, was removed for fostering a distinctive Ukrainian culture; his replacement was V. V. Shcherbyts'kyi, a hard-line member of the Dnepropetrovsk clique. He harshly repressed literary dissent, and remained a key factor in central control of Ukraine until 1989. In March 1990, the party leaders who succeeded Shcherbyts'kyi were able to obtain a large parliamentary majority in a fairly honest election; in March 1991, a 70 percent majority endorsed the Union Treaty.

However, the Ukrainian parliament had added a second question to gauge the population's views on Ukrainian sovereignty. Sovereignty was affirmed in all but one province – the Crimea – by majorities often greater than those supporting the Union Treaty. In itself, it is hard to grasp what acceptance of the elastic term 'sovereignty' implied, but voting for it was a learning experience on the road to independence. West Ukrainian provinces *rejected* both the Union Treaty and sovereignty by overwhelming majorities, voting instead for outright independence.

More important, perhaps, than formal votes were the actions of Ukrainian miners. In the ethnically mixed Donbass, coal miners followed the lead of the Western Siberia miners by striking during the late summer of 1989. The Donbass miners rejected calls by Ukrainian nationalist emissaries to turn the strike into a pro-independence movement. The miners' lukewarm reaction was a major factor pushing the Ukrainian popular front *Rukh* toward a moderate position. Its organizers, who stem disproportionately from West Ukraine, had earlier advanced programs for rapid cultural Ukrainization as well as church freedom and imminent independence. Events in the Donbass enabled the large contingent of literary dissidents from the 'Dnieper' lands (central Ukraine) to assume the leading role in *Rukh*. To them, it was evident that a program for economic gains and gradual movement toward independence would attract the greatest support. They also endorsed equal rights for all cultural groups, including use of Russian in parliament.

During 1990–91, deputies and ministers elected with the help of Communist party endorsements began to advance measures for Ukrainian economic autonomy. Restrictions were placed on the export of the bountiful Ukrainian harvests. In April 1991, the republic's Council of Ministers decreed that 'With the aim of carrying out the Declaration of the State Sovereignty of Ukraine..., it is stipulated that conscripts shall be sent to perform their service in military units located on the republic's territory.'

Immediately after the failure of the August coup, the Ukrainian parliament declared independence. Strong cultural and religious ties connect a high proportion of residents of Ukraine to Russia, but disgust over failure of economic reform and fear of a new authoritarian centralism tipped the balance. A week later, however, Ukraine and the Russian republic signed a treaty pledging economic and military co-operation, while reserving the right to conduct separate foreign policies.

Ukraine's relatively compact territory and absence of climatic extremes makes transportation far easier than in the Russian republic. Although energy reserves are much smaller than Russia's, such minerals as manganese are plentiful. Above all, Ukraine has demonstrated that it can feed its population. The biggest problem is development of a stable, orderly civil society to complement traditional Ukrainian love of liberty. By far the strongest support for Ukrainian civil society would be membership in the European Community. Ukraine is, however, larger in population than any present member except Germany, Britain, Italy, and France. The EC, which apparently intends to delay membership for Poland, Czechoslovakia, and Hungary (all historical participants in the European international order) until the end of this decade, will be cautious about extending full membership to such a large, untried unit as Ukraine.

Russia

Small Muslim autonomous republics in the North Caucasus ought to have the right to leave the Russian republic, perhaps entering some form of union with Azerbaijan. It is practically impossible to grant independence to the larger Tartar and Bashkir autonomous republics, which are ethnically intermixed with Russians and separated from other Muslim regions by extensive Slavic areas, but they deserve guarantees of complete cultural autonomy. In very exceptional cases, the principle of border adjustment (broached by Yel'tsin but renounced in favor of maintaining existing union-republic borders) might be extended to some anomalous border districts, although certainly not to Russian migrants in the urban centers of other republics.

Russia would still stretch from St Petersburg to Vladivostok, but it would confront greater problems than most other East European nations. Although Russians did not invent them, anti-urban ideologies have repeatedly hindered employment of skilled foreigners and members of diasporas in Russia. Such thinking merges with remnants of communist populism, which 'rises up like a wall, blocking the way. "They'll make a fortune" – that is its chief objection to nonstate trade.' Like Ukrainians, although to a lesser extent, Russian civil administration can profit from a temporary injection of administrative experts from Western Europe (which originally inspired the Russian administrative practice).

Although the tradition of individual farming is weaker in Russia than in Ukraine, the North Caucasus steppe and the Volga-Kursk black-earth zone can eventually produce an abundant grain supply. The grey-earth region from Smolensk to Nizhniy Novgorod with adequate drainage and fertilization could produce large potato crops. Perhaps Russia and Belarus could follow the example set when Germany leased extensive eastern tracts with similar drainage and soil problems to an experienced Dutch firm. Industrial renovation depends, as elsewhere, on plant modernization and speedy introduction of the market economy. Fortunately, Russia's huge oil and gas reserves, if exploited with the aid of foreign technology, could provide much of the capital required.

Overall prospects

Earlier in this essay, three kinds of popular demands were listed. Attainment of adequate living standards appears to be most likely in the Baltic states and Ukraine. Russia's prospects for sufficiently rapid economic growth are endangered by a combination of geographic limitations and the intensity and duration of communist rule. The demand for stable ethno-religious communities and the spiritual values they foster that appears so strong among Muslims is somewhat less strong among Orthodox groups like Georgians. Predictably, the demand appears somewhat weaker overall in nations of mixed religious background – Ukraine, Russia, and Belarus.

Marginal trade-offs may be feasible among demands for material improvement, ethno-religious community, and the third goal of responsive government, popular participation and the rule of law. But abandonment of these prerequisites of democracy would mean a return to oppression, with no guarantee that the first two sets of demands would be met. For most East European nations, experience with democracy's complexities is too limited to make one confident that it will be retained in periods of economic stagnation or ethnic strife. Exceptions are the Baltic states and possibly Armenia. At the opposite pole are the formerly Soviet Muslim nations, which embody many democratic elements in their ethno-religious lifestyle, but consider significant aspects of Western democracy to be dispensable. Georgians also tend to treat democracy as secondary. If this analysis is correct, efforts to support recent democratic trends should be concentrated on the large Slavic nations – Poland, Ukraine, Russia – whose decisions for or against democracy are apt to determine the future of Eastern Europe.

Abridged from John A. Armstrong (1992), 'Nationalism in the former Soviet empire,' *Problems of Communism*, XLI, pp. 121–33 (where recent Soviet nationality trends are discussed in the comparative context of Eastern Europe). Reprinted by permission of the author.

Notes

1 George F. Kennan (1951), 'The sources of Soviet conduct', *American Diplomacy, 1900–1950*, University of Chicago Press, Chicago, p. 125.
2 Commission on Security and Co-operation in Europe (1990), *Elections in the Baltic States and the Soviet Republics*, US Government Printing Office, Washington, DC, p. 75; the report was quoting a senior US official.
3 Populations were uprooted as a result of these invasions, during which the Ottoman Empire swept as far as Vienna and then slowly retreated to the southern part of the Balkan peninsula. Some Slavs converted to Islam; others became refugees and border guards in regions with different cultures and religions.

4.10   Totalitarianism and industralism

David Lane

Totalitarianism as an explanation of state-socialist society

In the Western world, 'totalitarianism' is by far the most pervasive and politically important interpretation of the USSR and other states modelled on her. It is considered here to be a meta-theory, that is, a set of orientating statements to society. Its role, especially during the Cold War, has often been as a kind of 'counter ideology' to that of Soviet Marxism. It has provided a legitimation of the foreign policies of Western capitalist states in their confrontation with the Soviet Union and her allies. But totalitarianism purports to be more than a description of Soviet-type societies. It is held by some writers to be a phenomenon of the development of urban industrial society applicable in an extreme form to Nazi Germany and to states of the Soviet type. This viewpoint, adopted by C. J. Friedrich and Leonard Schapiro, by definition puts liberal democratic states (such as Britain and the USA) at the opposite end of a continuum from state-socialist states (such as the USSR). In the former the individual has certain 'private' areas of autonomy which are absent in the latter.

A totalitarian social system has been defined by Friedrich (Friedrich, Curtis and Barber, 1969: 136) as 'a system of autocratic rule for realising totalist intentions under modern technical and political conditions'. Friedrich's definition emphasises control by the ruling elite. Arendt draws our attention to the other side of the coin by discussing the state of the masses. For her, totalitarianism is 'the permanent domination of each single individual in each and every sphere of life' (Arendt, 1966: 326). Literature on utopias such as

Brave New World and *1984* vividly brings out the fact that only the technological conditions of modern society allow totalitarianism to occur through three major forms of control; in Friedrich's words – 'a totalist ideology, a party reinforced by a secret police, and monopoly control of the three major forms of inter-personal confrontation in an industrial society [weapons, communications, and work]' (Friedrich, 1972: 251). Unlike Marxism, which attributes political power to the owners of the means of production, totalitarianism is a theory which gives to politics (in the shape of Party/state control of the means of manipulation and coercion) a place of supremacy in the social system. So much has the study of politics dominated the study of totalitarianism, that there has been little sociological study of the concept. As it was generally held that in totalitarian countries there was by definition scarcely any influence on 'the state' by society, it followed that there could in theory be no such thing as a political sociology of Soviet-type societies.

In analysing the concept of totalitarianism we may distinguish between scope and values. The *scope* of activity of the polity involves its penetration into all areas of social life and the breakdown of the boundaries between them and the polity. The scope of activity is predicated on the *values* held by the rulers which in totalitarian theory are essentially malevolent and involve the exploitation of the masses. In a totalitarian state, the ends of the dominant ruling class or elite require for their realisation the total subservence of the population and the complete subordination of other goals, such as individual freedom, and values (such as found in law or religion).

Hence totalitarianism is not only concerned with the totality of political penetration but implies a form of 'false consciousness' on the part of the masses who may accept the totalitarian state and a form of exploitation on the part of the rulers. This distinction enables us to differentiate between statism and totalitarianism. In the former, there is much state activity which furthers human development, whereas under totalitarianism all-inclusive state activity denies the goal of human liberation, and the values of the political rulers are malevolent. Hence totalitarian theorists overcome the apparent differences in ideology and form of ownership between Fascist and state-socialist regimes by pointing to the similarities of wide state control linked to a common manipulation of the masses to the benefit of the rulers. Given this common feature, the institutional arrangements and legitimating ideologies between types of totalitarian society may differ. Applied to the Soviet Union, totalitarianism is said to be furthered by one dominant political party under the command of the leader, more or less complete state control of the productive forces, means of violence and communication and an 'official' ideology (Marxism-Leninism) which promises, in an unspecified future, a society of human perfection. Implicit in the writing of theorists of totalitarianism is the view that the process of politics excludes interest groups but involves a conscious 'massification' of the population, either through coercion and terror or by manipulation. This massification, however, is not complete and certain 'islands of separateness' (the family, churches, universities, the arts) continue which are not fully penetrated by the political elites.

Criticisms of the totalitarian syndrome

The discussion so far has been relatively theoretical. Let us now indicate in the light of empirical knowledge some of the deficiencies of totalitarian theory as applied to the six 'basic' features of totalitarianism spelled out by Friedrich and Brzezinski (1956: 9–10). These are: an official ideology embracing 'all vital aspects of man's existence'; a single mass Party typically led by one man; a system of terroristic police control; a technologically conditioned monopoly of all means of effective mass communication; a similar monopoly of effective armed combat; and central direction and control of the entire economy. Firstly, it is doubtful whether ideology in fact does embrace 'all vital aspects of man's existence'. Marxism-Leninism, for instance, has been shown to be largely redundant when it comes to explanation in the natural sciences and the actual structure and process of social institutions, such as the family or industrial enterprises, cannot be understood solely by reference to the 'official ideology'. Secondly, the 'dictator' is no longer a supreme ruler in the USSR. In fact, one might suggest that the British Prime Minister has greater capabilities for political leadership (though a narrower scope) than has the present General Secretary of the Communist Party of the Soviet Union, who is limited in his ability of select the membership of the Politbureau. Thirdly, the notion of 'terroristic police control' utilised against 'arbitrarily selected classes of the population' is not a feature of contemporary state socialism. While terror has been a political process in such societies it has not been institutionalised. Fourthly, the control of communication is not absolute; the 'underground' press, oral communication and foreign sources of news are important alternatives to the officially sponsored agencies. Fifthly, the monopoly of the 'means of effective armed combat' would appear to be nothing special to the USSR but a characteristic of all modern states – except perhaps the USA where the persistence of a 'frontier mentality' gives to individuals the right to own firearms. Sixthly, central control and direction of the 'entire economy' would appear to be a major distinction, though in practice this is limited by the existence of a labour market, a 'free market' in certain agricultural products and by a gradual introduction of 'market' elements in the economy to complement centralised planning.

Criticisms of a more general nature may also be made. The assumption that political elites are malevolent in intention is not universally true. It might be argued that the principal aim of the Soviet political elite has been to industrialise the USSR; Party hegemony and state control have been means to this end, rather than simply being used to further the interests of the political elites. The wider extent of government activity and control is a major distinction compared to capitalist countries. Here this difference is considered to be a form of statism rather than totalitarianism. The notion of total domination by technology is overdrawn. Technology itself is controlled by men and may be utilised not only to enslave but also to create conditions of freedom. The orientation of the totalitarian viewpoint is one of unchangeability in the political and social system. But there are types of change not allowed for by the model: first, those in the political system involving a movement from a dictatorship to collective leadership; second, the decline of terror as an instrument of compliance; third, changes in the economic system from a centralised command economy to 'market socialism'. Totalitarian theory postulates a static form of society, whereas state-socialist societies have been characterised by rapid social and economic change. Structural differentiation in an advanced society creates a group structure and the individuation of interests not only among the population but also among the elite. The notion that the USSR is ruled by an omnipotent and omniscient leader or a unitary party elite is unrealistic.

The view of the author is that no modern society is totalitarian in the sense of the state exercising total control as discussed above. State power has never been all-inclusive as totalitarian theorists have assumed. Even under Stalin, the state had insufficient resources to penetrate widely to all areas of Soviet society. In the countryside and particularly in the non-Russian republics where the Party was relatively weak, traditional ways of life were less disturbed and less subject to political control. With the maturation of the Soviet Union as an industrial state, social differentiation of the population has developed to such an extent that 'political penetration' cannot be considered total. Perhaps most important of all, the *institutionalisation* of the kind of political power wielded by Stalin cannot be taken for granted as assumed by writers advocating the totalitarian syndrome. The substantive difference between the Soviet Union under Stalin and today is that in the earlier period political activity was subordinated to the goals of economic development and the maintenance of Soviet power. Since the fall of Stalin, the Soviet Union has become more institutionally differentiated, the number of goals which are pursued by the government has increased and the political system has moved from ruthlessly pursuing a limited number of goals to aggregating many interests. The political style has moved from a reliance on terror and ideology to methods involving manipulation and material incentives as under capitalism.

The Soviet political apparatus, like that of other state-socialist societies, has mobilised the population to a greater extent than is the case in parliamentary democracies even in times of war. Historically, the Soviet Union and other communist states are distinguished by the pursuit of the goal of industrial development to the exclusion of other competing goals. The mobilisation of the population is closely linked to industrial growth: the ends which the elites seek to achieve are associated with the development of an advanced industrial society. Thus it is not true to assert that the relationship between mass and elite is predominantly exploitive. State power in the USSR has been concerned with a form of *developmental mobilisation*; it has been used to change the rural character of the population to an urban one, to enforce a high level of saving, to raise the level of industrialisation, to induce values of work discipline and to introduce both mass literacy and a comprehensive system of education. Such mobilisation has geared the population to the demands of social change. While these tasks are to some extent shared by other non-communist developing societies, they differ in that the Communist rulers nationalised much of industry and farming is collectivised. It is not denied that oppression of individuals and groups has taken place (and has occurred illegitimately) but it is contended that force is an intrinsic element of revolutionary change, and is utilised in an attempt (which has not been completely successful) to ensure societal integration and the kind of social and economic change desired by the political elites. Also, central control has been employed to break down traditional privileges and to create greater opportunities and equality for groups traditionally underprivileged. Rather than placing the USSR among the states who deny welfare to the population, the effects of the activity of the political rulers have increased welfare: compared to the situation under pre-communist rulers there is greater economic and educational equality, a longer life expectancy and far greater social and political stability. One other major political difference which has to be brought out when comparing the communist form of modernisation process to other forms of directed social change is the saliency of its belief system: comparatively, communist beliefs are held more seriously by the political elites and a conscious effort is made to indoctrinate the population.

Convergence to a common type of industrial society

One variant of totalitarianism (that of Marcuse) is a type of convergence thesis: it is postulated that with the attrition of democratic participation and with the demise of the market in the economy, the United Sates becomes more like the USSR; at the same time, the rise of technology in the USSR with its attendant growth of bureaucracy and the ideology of technical rationality entails this country becoming more like the USA. There is a double convergence towards totalitarianism. Yet another and perhaps more widely recognised convergence thesis is that which posits the view that there is an evolutionary tendency for societies to converge to a single type of *industrial* society, in which the homogenisation of the social structure is brought out. One implication of this theory is that Marxist-type analyses as discussed above are irrelevant to the understanding of the structure and dynamics of industrial societies.

The convergence thesis is much more than a cataloguing of similarities. We may define convergence as a process by which heterogeneous cultures, characterising different societies, develop and change in the direction of greater likeness one to another until eventually they adopt similar arrangements for the performance of important social functions. This definition involves three major assumptions. First, that there is a 'process of change': convergence is concerned with the social dynamics of change, not with the description of a static state. Second, that societies remain relatively independent and autonomous as behavioural entities; they do not merge into a common single behavioural unit – socialist and capitalist states retain distinct personalities. Third, that with the passage of time they become in important ways more alike; it is not a necessary condition that the converging societies become identical in all respects.

It would be misleading to assume that convergence is a simple concept and much of the criticism of it is misplaced because the implications of the notion are not understood. Discussion of convergence, then, must distinguish which institutions or processes are becoming alike and the respects in which each society is changing. For it is possible that there may be divergence and convergence occurring simultaneously.

The theory which underpins the views of many convergence writers is evolutionism. The clearest recent statement of this position has been put by Talcott Parsons. His thesis is that world history has moved through three stages: primitive, intermediate and modern. Parsons explicitly, and other 'convergence' writers often implicitly, assume that world history is moving different societies to copy the structural and functional features of American society. 'The United States' new type of societal community, more than any other single factor, justifies our assigning it the lead in the latest phase of modernisation. ... American society has gone farther than any comparable large-scale society in its dissociation from the older ascriptive inequalities and [towards] the institutionalisation of a basically egalitarian pattern' (1971: 114). The United States as the most advanced industrial society becomes a model for the rest of the world. Parsons seems clear that the possibilities of creating an essentially different kind of society are limited. One of the most important consequences of the increasing division of labour is the necessary development of social and political differentiation which are not compatible with totalitarianism. Parsons argues that communist societies are likely to become more like those of the western world because of the 'centrifugal' effect on the social system of differentiation in the economy, science and the arts.

Industrialism

The idea of an 'industrial society', though not new, was articulated most forcefully in the 1960s and became counterposed to the dominant Soviet interpretation of Marxism, which analysed the world in terms of a rather rigid kind of economic determinism, positing the objective class struggle and the economic crises of capitalism. Opponents of this view put forward a battery of arguments. First, it was denied that the abolition of the capitalist class in the Russian October Revolution had led to a qualitatively superior type of civilisation (socialism) and that in fact the economic, political and social characteristics of the Soviet Union had much in common with those of advanced capitalist states. Secondly, the traditional Marxian argument concerning the crash of the capitalist economic system appeared to be no longer true. The eased atmosphere of international relations created a congenial political environment for the reception of such ideas.

What, then, is the evidence to which convergence theorists refer? Parallels were perceived in the highly developed division of labour giving rise to a hierarchy of statuses and political, economic and social elites. Structural differentiation, it was argued, led to a decline of the roles of the family and to the development of specialised institutions, such as the educational system and the industrial enterprise. The value system of an industrial system puts great emphasis on the instrumentality of work, a striving for mastery of the environment, for individual advancement and status differentiation. Large-scale production required central planning, state control and greater power to technocrats at the plant level. The economy is dominated by *manufacturing* industry, the semi-skilled worker and engineer; economic growth is a major objective. The radical's conception of a utopian order, of a higher form of democracy, of a classless society, it was held, had largely met with no response from the masses, and intellectuals were becoming absorbed within the framework of their own society. Convergence theorists said that a value system linked to the exigencies of industrialism had replaced the utopianism of revolutionaries and radicals. Politics had become more an affair of 'managing' an industrial society than the expression of the class struggle.

Research on the Soviet Union suggested that many of those developments were true for that country. Even in the study of the political systems some commentators have pointed to similarities. This view has been put by Ionescu: 'No contemporary society can, on the one hand, run all the complex activities of the state, political, cultural, social and economic, exclusively, by its own ubiquitous and omniscient servants, without collaboration and bargains with, or checks by, other interest groups' (Ionescu, 1967, 3–4). Thus in state-socialist societies the process of social differentiation results in systems of exchange between interest groups.

Criticisms of convergence

These views have precipitated a reaction from some sociologists. The most notable opponent of the industrial society thesis is Goldthorpe who argued that social stratification and economic order are subject to '*political* regulation' and that totalitarianism and industrialism may coexist:

The experience of Soviet society can be taken as indicating that the structural and functional imperatives of an industrial order are not so stringent as to prevent quite wide variations in patterns of social stratification, nor to prohibit the systematic manipulation of social inequalities by a regime commanding modern administrative resources and under no constraints from an organised opposition or rule of law (Goldthorpe, 657–8).

Goldthorpe argues specifically against the convergence thesis as it applies to social stratification. He considers three major propositions: differentiation, consistency, mobility. After considering developments in these areas in Western societies, Goldthorpe concludes that empirical findings do not substantiate convergence. With regard to differentiation, he denies that there is any 'process in industrialism' which ensures a 'continuing egalitarian trend'. By 'consistency', Goldthorpe refers to the tendency for the relative position of persons and groups to be the same or similar in different industrial societies. Against this he argues that status does not automatically follow changes in economic position, and thus the achievement of 'middle incomes' does not result in ' "middle class" ways of life or of "middle class" status'. He also argues that 'occupational roles with similar economic rewards may in some instances be quite differently related to the exercise of authority'. Lastly, Goldthorpe takes issue with the proposition of convergence theory that mobility in industrial societies is high, that it is dependent on achievement rather than ascription and that educational systems are crucial in the allocation process. Goldthorpe contends that, in fact, industrial societies differ considerably when the range and frequency of mobility are taken into consideration.

Critics of the industrial society thesis are open to the charge that they knock down a theory of 'convergence' that only a simplistic 'convergence theorist' would put forward. What is at issue is not whether any two or more societies are 'the same', but whether they are becoming more alike and in what respects they are becoming alike. This does not mean to say that one may not differentiate between main types of industrial society nor does it mean that educational and cultural systems may not influence the nature of the system of stratification.

If the notion that the 'convergence' of industrial societies means that they are alike in all respects then it is clearly an untenable thesis. Such a view is a crude form of technological determinism. In fact, most theorists of convergence admit that there are important modifications and divergencies from an ideal typical model of industrial society. Two kinds of modification may be noted here. First is the fact that the diffusion of technology passes through a *cultural filter*; technology is lodged in different cultural contexts and this results in different forms of social life. Second, that capitalism works through a more or less pronounced market mechanism and is organised for private profit, whereas under state socialism, industrialism is ordered by the political institutions. A much more realistic approach is to conceive of there being limited forms of convergence in addition to cultural difference and even divergence.

Abridged from David Lane (1976), *The Socialist Industrial State: Towards a Political Sociology of State Socialism*, George Allen

& Unwin, London, pp. 44–61. Reprinted by permission of
Routledge, London.

References

Arendt, Hannah (1966), *The Origins of Totalitarianism*, Harcourt, Brace, New York.
Friedrich, Carl J. (1972), 'In defence of a concept' in L. Schapiro, ed., *Political Opposition in One-Party States*, Macmillan, London.
Friedrich, Carl J., *et al.* (1969), *Totalitarianism in Perspective: Three Views*, Praeger, New York.
Friedrich, Carl J. and Z. K. Brzezinski (1956), *Totalitarian Dictatorship and Autocracy*, Praeger, New York.
Goldthorpe, J. (1967), 'Social stratification in industrial society,' in R. Bendix and S. M. Lipset, eds., *Class, Status and Power*, 2nd edn., Routledge & Kegal Paul, London.
Ionescu, Ghita (1967), *The Politics of the European Communist States*, Weidenfeld & Nicolson.
Parsons, Talcott (1971), *The System of Modern Societies*, Prentice-Hall, Englewood Cliffs, NJ.

4.11   The urban revolution in the USSR

Moshe Lewin

Despite the vigorous economic and cultural advances that followed the emancipation of the peasants, and which continued, impressively, until World War I, tsarist Russia remained an agrarian system and state. The revolution and civil war destroyed the old system and created a different kind of state. The social composition of the leadership, the personnel of governmental institutions, together with the very character of the system changed drastically (even if specialists and professionals from the previous era were still needed for their expertise). The new revolutionary ideology was, unlike that of the previous regime, deeply committed to industrialization and economic development. But, paradoxically, postrevolutionary Russia, during Lenin's New Economic Policy (NEP), was even more rural, and equally – if not more – backward than tsarist Russia. The urban population, by official count, merely returned to its pre-war share of the total. A more exacting evaluation shows convincingly that no more than 16 percent of the people were city dwellers, leaving 84 percent in the countryside and dependent on a low-yielding agriculture.

Furthermore, during the revolution the peasants took over all lands that had belonged to landowners and to some richer peasants and thereby destroyed most of the market-oriented sectors of agriculture. The resulting ocean of small family farms was owned and organized under a complex, communal-cum-homestead system. The farmers' mediocre output – meant mainly for home consumption – left little to spare for the cities and the state, and the capitalist inroads made possible by the reforms of the tsarist Prime Minister Piotr Arkadevich Stolypin were wiped out. The peasantry thus settled into a more archaic mode of life and production that imposed on the whole country the dilemmas of what is known today as underdevelopment. Indeed, a reputable Soviet sociologist, Iu. Arutiunian, considered the USSR in the 1920s to be at almost the same level as India and Egypt, for the combined effects of the civil war and the agrarian revolution had produced a dangerous economic backslide, as evidenced by most of the vital indices of the system. If the prerevolutionary society Lenin's government took over was backward enough, its problems were aggravated by the Civil War that wiped out many of the advanced social, cultural, and economic sectors of tsarist Russia. In sum, 'archaization' seems quite suitable to characterize the postrevolutionary situation, except for the emergence of a new agency in power – the party.

Though the urban sector was expected to serve as a springboard for further advances, it still was, before and after the revolution, deeply embedded in rural society. Most cities were small, and their rural origins and connections with the country were highly visible. The occupations, ethos, and way of life of many city-dwellers bore deep similarities with the prevailing peasant models: small-scale family businesses, traditional festivals and mores, high rates of illiteracy – all quite well documented by ethnographers. Data reported by the noted Soviet demographer V. Ts. Urlanis about tsarist cities before World War I were still valid for the Soviet period under the NEP: most of the houses in the cities were built of timber; only one third had iron roofs, one third had timber roofs, and one quarter had thatched roofs. Half the cities had no library of any kind, and 95 percent had no institutions of higher education. Though this semi-urban branch of the rural world kept developing into new directions, whenever new waves of migrants arrived from the villages a considerable 'ruralization' often occurred – to which many cities easily succumbed.

Evidently, the bigger cities, especially the capitals, were better able to resist such waves. They created and kept reproducing, even spreading, models of a genuine urban civilization. Yet they were still, under the tsar as well as under Lenin, just islands in the muzhik ocean.

The next period in Soviet history was to become crucial for the future of the country and was to pose an extremely complicated problem for the national conscience. This period began in 1928 with a dramatic change of policies in reaction to old problems coupled with a crisis, one of several, in the vital flow of grain supplies. The new policy showed the state's ability to muster its institutions and whatever public support was available into a program for accelerated economic growth. The subsequent 'big drive' changed the entire country and the political system quite profoundly. It produced a new state model, some of whose features became fixed in the system, while others subsided or disappeared in later decades. A series of furious economic, educational, and military undertakings shook up and restructured society, affected all its social classes, and thereby caused havoc in the system. Sudden changes of social position, occupation, status, and location operated on such a scale as to create a 'quicksand society' characterized by flux, uncertainty, mobility, high turnover, and anomie.

The resulting chaos, especially in the early 1930s, much of it creative, much unexpected and damaging, is an important historical factor. The system was supposedly planned and administered, and much was, in fact, tightly controlled. But although the government tried to dominate the work and movement of people, there was also at play an enormous spontaneity and drift. An unprecedented, quite spontaneous influx into the cities of about 27 million people (in a decade), to mention only those who not merely visited but stayed, brought a new, awesome wave of 'ruralization' to the cities, the working class, and parts of the bureaucracy.

Bureaucratization is the other relevant phenomenon. It was growing by leaps and bounds, but this social and political product was crumbly, as one would expect from such sudden growth in the absence of an adequate and timely supply of necessary cadres. Although in due course a modernized Soviet bureaucracy would abolish the stalinist police-autocracy, at this stage the cadres were extremely disoriented (not unlike the whole social system at the time) and not yet 'modern' at all. They were most often self-made, quickly 'baked', promoted en masse to ever more complex jobs. No doubt the rapid advancement was an exhilarating novelty for them, but certainly they needed more time and instruction to learn how to handle those jobs and conduct themselves in the new environment. It is no exaggeration to see the cadres of these years, with some notable exceptions, basically as *praktiki*, that is, responsible, often top-level cadres in political, social, technological, and even cultural positions whose training was inadequate or nonexistent; they learned as they went along.

It is clear that this period of social upheaval and crisis sorely overtaxed the freshly promoted, still unstable bureaucracy, and that the struggling bureaucracy's shortcomings and lack of experience presented a particularly propitious ground for the usurpation of power at the top – by a dictator and at lower levels by despotic bosses.

While Stalin often blamed the failures of the system on 'sabotage,' the disorder among the population was a normal reaction of a hard-pressed, disoriented body social trying to defend itself and cope with everyday problems and tasks. Such predictable spontaneity, however, was deeply unsettling when seen from above. Misunderstanding the character of spontaneity and thus fearing it, the police-autocracy inflicted retribution on the masses of people.

By now we have come to realize how feverish and almost chaotic was the large-scale restructuring undertaken during those years. In particular, the process of state building has been deeply affected by the social phenomena of the 1930s. We have in mind here the resurgence, again, in a new and peculiar form, of the rural nexus. This time the poorly collectivized peasants were flanked by millions of poorly urbanized ones, and they were ruled by a mass of bureaucratic praktiki, many of whom, at least in the lower ranks, were also partly of rural or semi-rural origin. Such was the social background of the regime in those years.

The power of the state under Stalin, however harsh the controls and the dictatorship, could not thwart the force and impact of spontaneous social developments. In the social sphere a persistent and irresistible autonomy gathered its own momentum, posed reactions to state actions, and created many unpredictable results. For no matter how stern or cruel a regime, in the laboratory of history only rarely can state coercion be so powerful as to control fully the course of events. The depth and scope of spontaneous events that counter the wishes and expectations of a dictatorial government are not a lesser part of history than the deeds and misdeeds of the government and the state.

To illustrate these contentions, let us consider the main social groups during the stalinist period. Workers, for instance, reacted to the worsening conditions of life by learning and applying the techniques of self-defense: the turnover rate soared and labor discipline plummeted. Widespread connivance between managers and their labor forces proved to be ineradicable, despite official efforts to instil or coerce discipline and productivity. When authorities did achieve some success in pressuring co-operation but did not propose the improvements that workers expected, a new 'front' would open up against procedures and norms, mostly by tacit agreement, without any organizers or leaders, just an invisible wink. This was a constant battle, with victories and defeats for both sides.

The same applies to the peasants in kolkhozy. Their reactions to collectivization included a massive slaughter of cattle, the flight to cities or construction sites, and endless strategems to beat the system. Great zeal was shown in working on the private plots, little zeal displayed in working in the collectivized fields. On many points, the government finally had to yield: the granting to kolkhoz families of the right to a private plot and a cow is one well-known example. In any case, the state never got from the kolkhozy all it really wanted. The pressure of the peasants managed to transform the kolkhoz into a hybrid organization that was nothing like what state authorities had hoped for.

The bureaucracy is yet another case in point. Although the state gave orders and expected their execution, it never truly mastered this social group. For the bureaucrats, too, had their techniques of self-defense: they knew how to conceal realities and performances, how to help each other get jobs during interminable contractions of staffs (which nevertheless kept growing). In a word, the bureaucracy never became the pliable tool it was expected to be. Purges and persecutions only lowered the bureaucracy's performance, sharpened the 'creativity' of its defensive techniques, and intensified the lobbying and pressuring of superiors.

Indeed, whatever field, function, or action we study, we discover that the government's battle for its programs, plans, and objectives always encountered social reaction, drift, spontaneity, and the powerful force of inertia.

In the field of culture, for example, various social groups accepted certain values preferred and propagandized by the government, but they also created their own countercultures or subcultures. Every official slogan, song, or even speech by Stalin was immediately paraphrased and parodied, sung or recited by students, soldiers, and peasants all over the country. The camps that were supposed to isolate the population from all kinds of 'enemies of the people' produced an enormous output of texts and songs, some of them deeply gloomy and hooligan in style, some of a political character. These lampoons and scornful satires stalked the country despite the fact that no media were at their disposal other than word-of-mouth communication. Everywhere people made barbed jokes and witticisms, thousands of them, that were irreverent, uncensorable, often punishable by a minimum of five years in a labor camp – and indomitable.

Ideological indoctrination was not ineffective – far from it – but it wasn't fully effective either. People could listen attentively with one ear, and let the message pass through the other. Re-education was successful only up to a certain point, depending on the character of the social group and its filters. Some slogans were accepted, if they did not seriously contradict the listeners' perception of reality. Social, economic, and cultural developments signaled to the population, sometimes sooner than to the authorities, what life was really about. But the authorities complained constantly that people did not go where asked, found ways of doing things their own way, exploited any loophole to play or outplay the system, and helped themselves through networks of friends, acquaintances, briberies, and adventurous risks.

The idea that the Russians and the other nationalities of the USSR are unquestioningly obedient and are easy to rule is a pipe dream. I could cite many government decisions and orders, sternly worded, that no one paid any attention to. Aware that it was losing the fight, the government resorted to the ultimate tool that denotes frustration and ineptitude: terror. Sometimes even terror had no effect or produced results contrary to the perpetrators' intention. Every state measure, control system, interdiction or exhortation provoked some sort of battle, quite often a losing one. Some things worked: many, sooner or later, didn't. The internal passport system, for instance, was introduced to control the movements of, in particular, the peasant population. But it could not stop spontaneous and unwanted migrations: peasants continued to move into cities, where growth was to be controlled, and out of the kolkhozy, where they were badly needed.

The rise of the cities

The pace of Soviet urban development in the 1930s, its scope, intensity, and speed, was described by the American geographer Chauncy Harris as 'record breaking'. The urban population grew at an annual rate of 6.5 percent between 1926 and 1939, peaking at an annual rate of over 10 percent in the later thirties. Concurrently, the urban share of the USSR's population rose from 18 percent to over 32 percent. Such an increase, Harris notes, required three decades in the United States, from 1856 to 1887.[1] He might have added that in the Soviet case these percentage shifts represented far greater numbers of people: in the 1930s the Soviet urban population grew from 26.3 million to 56.1 million. Many new cities were created, and many others saw their populations double or triple in twelve years. Further, these figures include only those people who permanently settled in the cities. Millions of others arrived in towns and cities only to soon wander away or run away, according to their circumstances.

Such a degree of social flux could not but trigger crises and mutations. But let us follow the story into the post-war period, when the USSR crossed the threshold of urbanization. In 1960 the urban population accounted for 49 percent of the total; by 1972 urban dwellers outnumbered rural dwellers, 58 percent to 42 percent.[2] Between 1972 and 1985 the dominantly urban Soviet society became almost predominantly urban, accounting for 65 percent of the total population and 70 percent of the population of the RSFSR. Today over 180 million Soviet citizens live in cities – compared to 56 million just before World War II.

Urbanization has entailed both the vigorous creation of new settlements and the expansion of old ones. The most recent intercensus period, 1959 to 1980, shows an increase in all categories of towns, townships, and settlements, but of particular importance are the bigger cities:

Population	*Number of Soviet cites*	
	1959	*1980*
100,000 to 250,000	88	163
250,000 to 500,000	34	65
1,000,000 +	3	23

All in all, in 1980 some 272 Soviet cities had more than 100,000 inhabitants (compared to only 89 cities in 1939), and these cities are now home to almost half of the urban population and about one third of the total population of the country.

As these data indicate, the pace of urban formation during the post-war period, especially after 1959, has been quite remarkable. During the last three decades an average of twenty-two new cities were created every year. In this field of social development surely lies one of the most momentous achievements brought about by the Soviet period. Only about 700 cities were chartered by tsarist Russia; today there are over 2,000 formally designated cities. Since the 1930s some 400 cities, by now often big and bustling, were created from scratch, on the site of small villages or on empty terrain. This, despite the fact that much of the decade immediately after World War II was devoted to the task of restoring the hundreds of cities that had been destroyed or badly damaged during the war.

Finally, we may note that in recent years growth in the urban sector has been slowing. Since the 1960s the population of the cities has increased by 3 million a year, partly from internal growth, partly due to migration from rural areas. Between 1959 and 1970, some 1.5 million migrants a year came from villages, even 1.9 million a year in the 1970s. But this influx has tapered off, and in the past ten years it has been the migration from smaller to larger cities that has come to the fore in fashioning the character of the urban phenomenon. The overall size of the urban sector is remaining steady, giving the new complex urban system time to assimilate decades of momentous change. New cities are still being created, especially in Siberia, but everywhere the system and its institutions are, as it were, taking stock.

Thus it is evident that the post-war years, a period of Soviet history that many Western observers characterize as an era of stagnation, actually constitute a period of deep social change. Unfortunately, all too often, the Soviet urban phenomenon has escaped the attention of analysts, with the exception of several books and articles by a few pioneering scholars.

But before we consider what Soviet society has become in the wake of its urbanization, we must return again to the countryside.

In discussing the 1930s, I earlier referred to the ruralization of the cities. The flood of peasants to cities old and new was enormous: in the 1930s almost 27 million peasants migrated to towns, doubling the size of the urban population. Although the tide receded, the influx remained considerable and certainly too high for the good of either agriculture or the economy. About 24 million migrants moved to the cities between 1939 and 1959, another 8.4 million between 1959 and 1964, and 16 million between 1964 and 1970. This continual influx of peasants, most of them young people, did not effect a ruralization comparable to that of the 1930s, but the recurrent dilution of urban culture is a social phenomenon of considerable importance. At least during the earlier post-war period of rapid and extensive urbanization, up to 1959, even as the cities quickly became industrial their culture and way of life remained rural.

The problem is that the rural mind, way of life, and culture are extremely tenacious. It may take some three generations for the peasant outlook and mentality to disappear and for a true urbanite to emerge. This transformation is still in mid-process in the Soviet Union today, still an important feature of the social and cultural scene, although subject to considerable regional and national variations.

When such phenomena are reproduced massively over an entire national system that is undergoing a hectic industrialization and urbanization, we can certainly speak of a stage, transitional, specific, and exhibiting complexities and aberrations in society, culture, and politics.

That is what we observe throughout Russian history, in different forms, but occurring with particular intensity in the 1930s and again after World War II. Nowadays ruralization on any significant scale cannot happen anymore, but the sequels of the previous stages and of the last, equally traumatic one are still part of the new urban scene.

The making of a stable and more self-controlling urban culture and moral world is certainly a difficult task. Once the aftershocks of the previous shattering events begin to subside, the cities begin to reconsider their own identities, and urban problems come to the fore, becoming the subject of public awareness and of political and scholarly treatment. But some of the older tasks remain on the agenda; the diminishing but still important battle between the rural and urban worlds, or cultures, continues.

Urban society, a new labour force

In the history of Soviet cities, we may single out three large waves of growth: the recovery of the urban population in the 1920s to the pre-revolutionary levels, the feverish development during the 1930s, and the post-war boom, especially the period after 1956, when the bulk of the nation became urban.

The social consequences of this transformation unfolded in fits and starts and, quite naturally, the emergence of an urban social structure also came in stages and, as it were, in patches.

As is well known, in their earlier stage most Russian cities were quite rural. During the 1920s, in the very heart of Moscow, observers found, with disbelief, authentic villages over big areas of the capital.

The next stage may be called, though without any claim to precision, the early industrial period, characterized by the prevalence, in the composition of the labor force, of simple physical labor, with low skills and relatively little use of advanced machinery. Similar developments had marked the earlier history of Western industrial cities, but in Russia this stage of industrialization evolved and continued, in part, into the current period; it was particularly characteristic of the pre- and post-war decades. In 1939, for example, 82.5 percent of the Soviet labor force was engaged in primarily physical labor, the remaining 17.5 percent in primarily intellectual work. Astonishingly, and very significantly, by 1959 the relative sizes of these sectors changed only slightly, to 79.3 percent and 20.7 percent.

Certainly this small shift represented a considerable number of workers. Yet 'intellectual labor' (*umstvennyi trud*) is much too pompous a label for the professional reality of the Khrushchev era. Even in the cities, where by 1959 an apparently impressive 29.4 percent of the work-force was employed in the 'intellectual' sector (compared to 57 percent in physical labor), the majority of these employees were plain, low-key nonspecialists, as the sociologists call them; in other words, rather primitive paper shufflers. Which is to say that less than half of the so-called intellectual urban work-force was engaged in professional endeavors. And of this group, only some had any professional education. Many others, lacking formal education, learned on the job to be engineers and managers. This class of praktiki will be of some interest to us. They, too, symbolize an era.

A similarly low level of skill pervaded the manual labor force during this phase of Soviet industrialization. In most of the cities the composition of the manual labor force reflected the national priority to industrialize. In 222 of the 304 cities whose populations exceeded 50,000, a high proportion of the labor force – between 50 and 70 percent – was engaged in industry, transportation, and construction. In addition to the predominantly industrial cities, a considerable number, some 134 of the 304, can be characterized as diversified administrative centers. Harris, who cites these figures, observes that 'the overwhelming predominance of these two types – namely the administrative and the industrial – reflects the nature of Soviet economy as a command economy where the political administration focused its attention primarily on the industrial side of the economy'.[3]

Thus by 1959 the peasantry had been slowly replaced by a working class. However, initially, one type of predominantly physical labor was merely replacing another, although the new jobs were located in different and crucially important sectors. The earlier stages of this development deserve the epithet 'extensive', as quantity and speed were the slogans of those years.

But during the next twenty years, we see the making of a more variegated and professionally differentiated national and urban social structure. Urbanization, industrial and scientifico-technical development, mass schooling and quality schooling, communications and arts, state policies and myriad spontaneous events changed the nation's overall social, professional, and cultural profile, and the social structure underwent a significant qualitative transformation. Workers in the national economy soared from about 24 million before the war, to almost 81 million in 1983; of these, the number engaged in industry jumped from 11 million to over 31 million. Transportation, construction, and communications also grew at a rapid pace; much more modest growth of employment was registered in different services. The role of the working class in the economy is underscored by the fact that it is now the prevailing group in society and in the cities: 61.5 percent of the population, almost twice their share in 1939. In comparison, the kolkhoz peasants, once over half of the population, are now barely 12.5 percent of the nation.

A second group, presented in Soviet statistics as 'employees,' increased from 11 million in 1941 to about 35 million in 1983, a rate of growth surpassing that of workers. To understand the importance of this group, we must turn to another way of classifying them.

'Specialists' – otherwise also called in the Soviet literature 'intelligentsia' – show an even faster rate of growth than the category of 'officials.' Most notably, in 1941 only about 2.4 million of the 11 million employees had higher or specialized technical education; in 1960 only half of the 16 million employees were 'specialists'; today, an overwhelming majority of officials accede to this category, thanks to considerably improved standards of professional education. Recent figures show over 31.5 million specialists, among them 13.5 million with higher education and over 18 million with specialized secondary training.

Before we turn to those officials qua 'intelligentsia,' let us survey the educational standards of the whole population. In 1939 the overwhelming majority of the workers and peasants had only an elementary education (four years of primary school). By 1959, little had changed: 91.3 percent of workers and 98.2 percent of kolkhoz peasants still achieved only elementary standards. But by 1984 no more than 18.5 percent of manual laborers had only an elementary education – and, one would assume, a majority of the least educated were from the older generation.

In the population at large the massive educational efforts yielded significant results. Forty-six million people received a 'secondary incomplete' education (seven years of schooling). Fifty-eight million enjoyed a full secondary education, which is now legally obligatory for all children. Alumni of the 'secondary specialized' establishments that train technicians of all denominations numbered 28 million. A full higher education was received by 18.5 million people, and another 3.6 million received an incomplete higher education.

Among university and high school graduates, the numbers of men and women are substantially equal. Women constitute 54 percent of university students, 58 percent of the enrollment in secondary specialized schools, and 60 percent of all specialists with both higher and secondary education. Further, though women constitute 51 percent of the labour force as a whole, they account for about 56 percent of educated specialists, and 40 percent of scientists and scholars. This emancipation of women – for centuries the predominantly uneducated mass and the most neglected – is perhaps the most visible part of what can be called the Soviet 'cultural revolution.' (This term was improperly applied by official propaganda to the 1930s, when most citizens received barely three to four years of elementary education. Today, millions attend universities and high schools, and all children have access to at least a modicum of instruction. But by now, of course, 'cultural revolution' acquires a new meaning again.)

Thus the development of professional and educational standards that began in the 1930s only to be interrupted by the ordeal of World War II, has come to fruition on a large scale during the last three decades. In particular, we must emphasize the making and remaking of the Soviet intelligentsia.[4]

The history of the intelligentsia is tortuous, even tortured, but it has now become, in fact, a mass of people, composed of all the professionals the modern world requires and of numerous groups, subgroups, and categories: technical, managerial-administrative, scientific, artistic, educational, and political. Even if we restrict ourselves to those with a higher education, their number reaches now about 15 million, a vast pool of 'grey matter' and the fastest-growing part of the new social structure. While the employed population grew by 155 percent between 1960 and 1986, the number of specialists grew fourfold. Over 5 million students are attending institutions of higher education, taught by half a million professors.

In effect, in the past five decades the USSR has leaped into the twentieth century, although in the 1930s most of the nations of the territory still belonged to a far earlier age. The creation of the techno-scientific and intellectual class, accompanying the urbanization process, is thus a momentous development. The further advance of the economy and the survival of the political system are dependent on this layer, which has become a large, almost 'popular' mass. The new intelligentsia, members of the different categories of this stratum, have moved beyond research institutes and universities. Numbers of them are government experts, medium- and top-level executives, participants and members of the highest administrative and political apparaty. And it is a sign of the new times in Russia that this amalgam is deepening and expanding.

Two able Soviet sociologists, L. A. Gordon and V. V. Komarovskii studied three generations in the active working population: men born around 1910, who entered the labor force in the 1930s and reached their vocational peak in the 1950s; their sons, born in the 1930s, who entered the labor force in the 1950s and peaked in the 1970s; and their grandsons, born in the 1950s, who entered the labor force in the 1970s.

In the second generation, we see some results of the nation's industrialization. This generation was the first in which more workers were employed in industry than in agriculture; the first in which skilled labor predominated over unskilled physical labor; and the first in which the number of non-manual workers equaled that of unskilled manual workers. But alongside the important shift from agriculture to industry and the lower ratio of unskilled workers, this cohort's advance into the branches of information, services, and organization was modest.

In the third generation we see a substantial increase in the numbers engaged in the service and information professions, and a corresponding decrease in unskilled manual laborers and agriculturists. From the very start of their careers twice as many of this cohort are entering the intellectual labor force as the physical labor force. Herein we see the industrial era yielding to the scientific-industrial-information era. Already this youngest generation lives in a different environment and faces different pressures.

Gordon and Komarovskii calculate that in contemporary society one-fourth of each generation moves up the socioprofessional ladder, and they predict that vocational mobility will probably accelerate. Unfortunately, these authors do not indicate whether this rate of intergenerational mobility is sufficient, nor do they cite the relevant Western figures for comparison. But, as they note, this rate is high enough to create tensions among the generations. The young quickly develop different styles of life, form new approaches to life and work, and often reject, we can safely add, the methods and culture of their predecessors.

Such tensions are unavoidable and not unexpected, and they are likely to increase in the coming decade as intragenerational changes accelerate. In the 1990s, Gordon and Komarovskii project, the proportion of crude agricultural and industrial labor will drop to barely 10 percent among the third generation, as it approaches its career peak, and close to 40 percent of this cohort will be employed in intellectual professions. And the researchers predict that 30–40 percent of the work-force will be involved in sociocultural and other services and in professions related to the creation and processing of information.

Yet Gordon and Komarovskii caution that this inter- and intragenerational thrust forward into modern intellectual and professional life portends social trouble of great magnitude if it is not matched by reforms in the prevailing economic mechanism and in the 'relations of production'. The different spheres of the socioeconomic system suffer from discordances (*rassoglasovanie*) that threaten the nation's entire professional and educational endeavor. The state cannot allow 'a socioprofessional structure adequate to the needs of a scientific-industrial system to be straitjacketed into a production system that is still stuck in an earlier technical and technological age.' In the absence of reform, not only will professionalization not improve the performance of the system, it could also create widespread social crises and even pressures to return to the old patterns.

The stern warning sounded by these researchers may seem overly alarmist, but it reflects recent developments well known to readers of Soviet sociology. The list is long: widespread job dissatisfaction among educated youth and highly trained professionals; low morale – poor 'sociopsychological climate' is the Soviet term – in many workplaces; underutilized engineers and scientists who waste their time on menial jobs because of a shortage of technicians and auxiliary personnel; hordes of poorly trained people parading, easily, as engineers or scientists. These images of a wasted generation and a potentially disastrous backsliding for the whole country certainly hang over the heads of the nation's political and economic leadership.

Abridged from Moshe Lewin (1988), *The Gorbachev Phenomenon: A Historical Interpretation*, Century Hutchinson, London, pp. 13–56. Copyright © 1988 The Regents of the University of California. Reprinted by permission of the University of California Press, Berkeley, CA.

Notes

1 C. D. Harris (1970), *Cities of the Soviet Union*, Rand McNally, Chicago, pp. 239, 240.
2 In comparison, the urban sector passed the 50 percent mark in the US in 1921. France finally crossed this threshold between 1925 and 1931. Germany had already reached the 65 percent mark by 1925.
3 Harris, *Cities of the Soviet Union*, p. 61.
4 Soviet authors argue whether technicians with secondary special education should be included in the intelligentsia, a term that implies not only high professional skill but also an appropriate cultural background and the ability to use – if not create – concepts. Although this argument is of interest, it can be disregarded here. My primary point is that the creation of a layer of professionally and intellectually advanced people has long been at the centre of Russian and Soviet theoretical and ideological debates. The Soviet leadership has always dreamed of producing a broad layer of such people, who would emerge from the popular classes and become committed to the new regime.

4.12   Perestroika: the challenge of radical reform

Mikhail Gorbachev

What is perestroika? What prompted the idea of restructuring? What does it mean in the history of socialism? Let me first explain the far-from-simple situation which had developed in the country by the eighties and which made perestroika necessary and inevitable.

At some stage – this became particularly clear in the latter half of the seventies – something happened that was at first sight inexplicable. The country began to lose momentum. Economic failures became more frequent. Difficulties began to accumulate. Elements of what we call stagnation and other phenomena alien to socialism began to appear in the life of society. A kind of 'braking mechanism' affecting social and economic development formed. And all this happened at a time when scientific and technological revolution opened up new prospects for economic and social progress.

Analyzing the situation, we first discovered a slowing economic growth. In the last fifteen years the national income growth rates had declined by more than a half and by the beginning of the eighties had fallen to a level close to economic stagnation. A country that was once quickly closing on the world's advanced nations began to lose one position after another. Moreover, the gap in the efficiency of production, quality of products, scientific and technological development, the production of advanced technology and the use of advanced techniques began to widen, and not to our advantage.

The gross output drive, particularly in heavy industry, turned out to be a 'top-priority' task, just an end in itself. The same happened in capital construction, where a sizable portion of the national wealth became idle capital. There were costly projects that never lived up to the highest scientific and technological standards. The worker or the enterprise that had expended the greatest amount of labor, material and money was considered the best. It is natural for the producer to 'please' the consumer, if I may put it that way. With us, however, the consumer found himself totally at the mercy of the producer and had to make do with what the latter chose to give him. This was again a result of the gross output drive.

It became typical of many of our economic executives to think not of how to build up the national asset, but of how to put more material, labor and working time into an item to sell it at a higher price. Consequently, for all 'gross output,' there was a shortage of goods. We spent, in fact we are still spending, far more on raw materials, energy and other resources per unit of output than other developed nations. Our country's wealth in terms of natural and manpower resources has spoilt, one may even say corrupted, us. That, in fact, is chiefly the reason why it was possible for our economy to develop extensively for decades.

Accustomed to giving priority to quantitative growth in production, we tried to check the falling rates of growth, but did so mainly by continually increasing expenditures: we built up the fuel and energy industries and increased the use of natural resources in production.

As time went on, material resources became harder to get and more expensive. On the other hand, the extensive methods of fixed capital expansion resulted in an artificial shortage of manpower. In an attempt to rectify the situation somehow, large, unjustified, i.e. in fact unearned, bonuses began to be paid and all kinds of undeserved incentives introduced under the pressure of this shortage, and that led, at a later stage, to the practice of padding reports merely for gain. Parasitical attitudes were on the rise, the prestige of conscientious and high-quality labor began to diminish and a 'wage-levelling' mentality was becoming widespread. The imbalance between the measure of work and the measure of consumption, which had become something like the linchpin of the braking mechanism, not only obstructed the growth of labor productivity, but led to the distortion of the principle of social justice.

So the inertia of extensive economic development was leading to an economic deadlock and stagnation.

The economy was increasingly squeezed financially. The sale of large quantities of oil and other fuel and energy resources and raw materials on the world market did not help. It only aggravated the situation. Currency earnings thus made were predominantly used for tackling problems of the moment rather than on economic modernization or on catching up technologically.

Declining rates of growth and economic stagnation were bound to affect other aspects of the life of Soviet society. Negative trends seriously affected the social sphere. This led to the appearance of the so-called 'residual principle' in accordance with which social and cultural programs received what remained in the budget after allocations to production. A 'deaf ear' sometimes seemed to be turned to social problems. The social sphere began to lag behind other spheres in terms of technological development, personnel, know-how and, most importantly, quality of work.

Here we have more paradoxes. Our society has ensured full employment and provided fundamental social guarantees. At the same time, we failed to use to the full the potential of socialism to meet the growing requirements in housing, in quality and sometimes quantity of foodstuffs, in the proper organization of the work of transport, in health services, in education and in tackling other problems which, nautrally, arose in the course of society's development.

An absurd situation was developing. The Soviet Union, the world's biggest producer of steel, raw materials, fuel and energy, has shortfalls in them due to wasteful or inefficient use. One of the biggest producers of grain for food, it nevertheless has to buy millions of tons of grain a year for fodder. We have the largest number of doctors and hospital beds per thousand of the population and, at the same time, there are glaring shortcomings in our health services. Our rockets can find Halley's comet and fly to Venus with amazing accuracy, but side by side with these scientific and technological triumphs is an obvious lack of efficiency in using scientific achievements for economic needs, and many Soviet household appliances are of poor quality.

This, unfortunately, is not all. On the ideological plane as well, the braking mechanism brought about ever greater resistance to the attempts to constructively scrutinize the problems that were emerging and to the new ideas. Propaganda of success – real or imagined – was gaining the upper hand. Eulogizing and servility were encouraged; the needs and opinions of ordinary working people, of the public at large, were ignored. In the social sciences scholastic theorization was encouraged and developed, but creative thinking was driven out from the social sciences, and superfluous and voluntarist assessments and judgments were declared indisputable truths. Scientific, theoretical and other discussions, which are indispensable for the development of thought and for creative endeavor, were emasculated. Similar negative tendencies also affected culture, the arts and journalism, as well as the teaching process and medicine, where mediocrity, formalism and loud eulogizing surfaced, too.

The presentation of a 'problem-free' reality backfired: a breach had formed between word and deed, which bred public passivity and disbelief in the slogans being proclaimed. It was only natural that this situation resulted in a credibility gap: everything that was proclaimed from the rostrums and printed in newspapers and textbooks was put in question. Decay began in public morals; the great feeling of solidarity with each other that was forged during the heroic times of the Revolution, the first five-year plans, the Great Patriotic War and post-war rehabilitation was weakening; alcoholism, drug addiction and crime were growing; and the penetration of the stereotypes of mass culture alien to us, which bred vulgarity and low tastes and brought about ideological barrenness, increased.

Party guidance was relaxed, and initiative lost in some of the vital social processes. Everybody started noticing the stagnation among the leadership and the violation of the natural process of change there. At a certain stage this made for a poorer performance by the Politburo and the Secretariat of the CPSU Central Committee, by the government and throughout the entire Central Committee and the Party apparatus, for that matter.

Political flirtation and mass distribution of awards, titles and bonuses often replaced genuine concern for the people, for their living and working conditions, for a favorable social atmosphere. An atmosphere emerged of 'anything goes,' and fewer and fewer demands were made on discipline and responsibility. Attempts were made to cover it all up with pompous campaigns and undertakings and celebrations of numerous anniversaries centrally and locally. The world of day-to-day realities and the world of feigned prosperity were diverging more and more.

Many Party organizations in the regions were unable to uphold principles or to attack with determination bad tendencies, slack attitudes, the practice of covering up for one another and lax discipline. More often than not, the principles of equality among Party members were violated. Many Party members in leading posts stood beyond control and criticism, which led to failures in work and to serious malpractices.

At some administrative levels there emerged a disrespect for the law and encouragement of eyewash and bribery, servility and glorification. Working people were justly indignant at the behavior of people who, enjoying trust and responsibility, abused power, suppressed criticism, made fortunes and, in some cases, even became accomplices in – if not organizers of – criminal acts.

But the need for change was brewing not only in the material sphere of life but also in public consciousness. People who had practical experience, a sense of justice and commitment to the ideals of Bolshevism criticized the established practice of doing things and noted with anxiety the symptoms of moral degradation and erosion of revolutionary ideals and socialist values.

Workers, farmers and intellectuals, Party functionaries centrally and locally, came to ponder the situation in the country. There was a growing awareness that things could not go on like this much longer. Perplexity and indignation welled up that the great values born of the October Revolution and the heroic struggle for socialism were being trampled underfoot.

A carefully prepared program, rather than a pompous declaration

At the April 1985 Plenary Meeting we managed to propose a more or less well-considered, systematized program and to outline a concrete strategy for the country's further development and a plan of action. It was clear that cosmetic repairs and patching would not do; a major overhaul was required. Nor was it possible to wait, for much time had been lost as it was.

The first question to arise was one of improving the economic situation, stopping and reversing the unfavorable trends in that sphere.

The most immediate priority, which we naturally first looked to, was to put the economy into some kind of order, to tighten up discipline, to raise the level of organization and responsibility, and to catch up in areas where we were behind. A great deal of hard work was done and, for that matter, is continuing. As expected, it has produced its first results. The rates of economic growth have stopped declining and are even showing some signs of improvement.

To be sure, we saw that these means alone would not impart a great dynamism to the economy. The principal priorities are known to lie elsewhere – in a profound structural reorganization of the economy, in reconstruction of its material base, in new technologies, in investment policy changes, and in high standards in management. All that adds up to one thing – acceleration of scientific and technological progress. Substantial comprehensive programs were worked out in major areas of science and technology. They are aimed at achieving a major breakthrough and reaching the world level by the end of this century.

In effect, we have here a new investment and structural policy. The emphasis has been shifted from new construction to the technical retooling of enterprises, to saving the resources, and sharply raising the quality of output. A special program has been developed for modernizing the engineering industry, which has been neglected. And, sure enough, the program includes a radical transformation of the economic mechanism, which, as we now know well, is essential for a breakthrough in technological progress and for increasing economic efficiency.

The economy has, of course, been and remains our main concern. But at the same time we have set about changing the moral and psychological situation in society. Back in the 1970s many people realized that we could not do without drastic changes in thinking and psychology, in the organization, style and methods of work everywhere – in the Party, the state machinery, and upper echelons. And this has happened, in the Party's Central Committee, in the government, as well as elsewhere. Certain personnel changes at all levels were needed. New people took over leadership positions, people who understood the situation well and had ideas as to what should be done and how.

An uncompromising struggle was launched against violations of the principles of socialist justice with no account being taken of who committed these violations. A policy of openness was proclaimed. Those who spoke in favor of Party, government and economic bodies and public organizations conducting their activities openly were allowed to have their say and unwaranted restrictions and bans were removed.

We have come to the conclusion that unless we activate the human factor, that is, unless we take into consideration the diverse interests of people, work collectives, public bodies, and various social groups, unless we rely on them, and draw them into active, constructive endeavor, it will be impossible for us to accomplish any of the tasks set, or to change the situation in the country.

I have long appreciated a remarkable formula advanced by Lenin: socialism is the living creativity of the masses. Socialism is not an *a priori* theoretical scheme.

Today our main job is to lift the individual spiritually, respecting his inner world and giving him moral strength. We are seeking to make the whole intellectual potential of society and all the potentialities of culture work to mold a socially active person, spiritually rich, just and conscientious. An individual must know and feel that his contribution is needed, that his dignity is not being infringed upon, that he is being treated with trust and respect. When an individual sees all this, he is capable of accomplishing much.

Of course, perestroika somehow affects everybody; it jolts many out of their customary state of calm and satisfaction at the existing way of life. Here I think it is appropriate to draw your attention to one specific feature of socialism. I have in mind the high degree of social protection in our society. On the one hand, it is, doubtless, a benefit and a major achievement of ours. On the other, it makes some people spongers.

There is virtually no unemployment. The state has assumed concern for ensuring employment. Even a person dismissed for laziness or a breach of labor discipline must be given another job. Also, wage-levelling has become a regular feature of our everyday life: even if a person is a bad worker, he gets enough to live fairly comfortably. The children of an outright parasite will not be left to the mercy of fate. We have enormous sums of money concentrated in the social funds from which people receive financial assistance. The same funds provide subsidies for the upkeep of kindergartens, orphanages, Young Pioneer houses and other institutions related to children's creativity and sport. Health care is free, and so is education. People are protected from the vicissitudes of life, and we are proud of this.

But we also see that dishonest people try to exploit these advantages of socialism; they know only their rights, but they do not want to know their duties: they work poorly, shirk and drink hard. There are quite a few people who have adapted the existing laws and practices to their own selfish interests.

They give little to society, but nevertheless managed to get from it all that is possible and what even seems impossible; they have lived on unearned incomes.

The policy of restructuring puts everything in its place. We are fully restoring the principle of socialism: 'From each according to his ability, to each according to his work,' and we seek to affirm social justice for all, equal rights for all, one law for all, one kind of discipline for all, and high responsibilities for each. Perestroika raises the level of social responsibility and expectation.

We need wholesome, fullblooded functioning by all public organisations, all production teams and creative unions, new forms of activity by citizens, and the revival of those which have been forgotten. In short, *we need broad democratization of all aspects of society.* That democratization is also the main guarantee that the current processes are irreversible.

We know today that we would have been able to avoid many of these difficulties if the democratic process had developed normally in our country. We have learned this lesson of our history well and will never forget it. We will now firmly stick to the line that only through the consistent development of the democratic forms inherent in socialism and through the expansion of self-government can we make progress in production, science and technology, culture and art, and in all social spheres. This is the only way we can ensure conscious discipline. Perestroika itself can only come through democracy. Since we see our task as unfolding and utilizing the potential of socialism through the intensification of the human factor, there can be no other way but democratization, including reform of the economic mechanism and management, a reform whose main element is promotion of the role of work collectives.

The January 1987 Plenary Meeting of the CPSU Central Committee encouraged extensive efforts to strengthen the democratic basis of Soviet society, to develop self-government and extend glasnost, that is openness, in the entire management network. We see now how stimulating that impulse was for the nation. Democratic changes have been taking place at every work collective, at every state and public organization, and within the Party. More glasnost, genuine control from 'below,' and greater initiative and enterprise at work are now part and parcel of our life.

The democratic process allowed us to take a wider view of economic issues, and put forward a program for radical economic reforms. The economic mechanism now well fits the overall system of social management which is based on renewed democratic principles.

The June 1987 Plenary Meeting of the CPSU Central Committee adopted 'Fundamentals of Radical Restructuring of Economic Management.' Perhaps this is the most important and most radical program for economic reform our country has had since Lenin introduced his New Economic Policy in 1921. The present economic reform envisages that the emphasis will be shifted from primarily administrative to primarily economic management methods at every

level, and calls for extensive democratization of management, and the overall
activization of the human factor.

The reform is based on dramatically increased independence of enterprises
and associations, their transition to full self-accounting and self-financing, and
granting all appropriate rights to work collectives. They will now be fully
responsible for efficient management and end results. A collective's profits
will be directly proportionate to its efficiency.

In this connection, a radical reorganization of centralized economic man-
agemet is envisaged in the interests of enterprises. We will free the central
management of operational functions in the running of enterprises and this
will enable it to concentrate on key processes determining the strategy of
economic growth. To make this a reality we launched a serious radical reform
in planning, price formation, the financial and crediting mechanism, the
network of material and technological production supplies, and management
of scientific and technological progress, labor and the social sphere. The aim
of this reform is to ensure – within the next two or three years – the transition
from an excessively centralized management system relying on orders, to a
democratic one, based on the combination of democratic centralism and self-
management.

The adoption of fundamental principles for a radical change in economic
management was a big step forward in the program of perestroika. Now
perestroika concerns virtually every main aspect of public life.

We are often asked what we want of perestroika. What are our final goals?
We can hardly give a detailed, exact answer. It's not our way to engage in
prophesying and trying to predestinate all the architectural elements of the
public building we will erect in the process of perestroika.

But in principle I can say that the end result of perestroika is clear to us. It
is a thorough renewal of every aspect of Soviet life; it is giving socialism the
most progressive forms of social organization; it is the fullest exposure of the
humanist nature of our social system in its crucial aspects – economic, social,
political and moral.

I stress once again: perestroika is not some kind of illumination or revelation.
To restructure our life means to understand the objective necessity for
renovation and acceleration. And that necessity emerged in the heart of our
society. The essence of perestroika lies in the fact that *it unites socialism with
democracy* and revives the Leninist concept of socialist construction both in
theory and in practice. Such is the essence of perestroika, which accounts for
its genuine revolutionary spirit and its all-embracing scope.

Does perestroika mean that we are giving up socialism or at least some of
its foundations? Some ask this question with hope, others with misgiving.

There are people in the West who would like to tell us that socialism is in a
deep crisis and has brought our society to a dead end. That's how they
interpret our critical analysis of the situation at the end of the seventies and
beginning of the eighties. We have only one way out, they say: to adopt

capitalist methods of economic management and social patterns, to drift toward capitalism.

They tell us that nothing will come of perestroika within the framework of our system. They say we should change this system and borrow from the experience of another socio-political system. To this they add that, if the Soviet Union takes this path and gives up its socialist choice, close links with the West will supposedly become possible. They go so far as to claim that the October 1917 Revolution was a mistake which almost completely cut off our country from world social progress.

To put an end to all the rumors and speculations that abound in the West about this, I would like to point out once again that we are conducting all our reforms in accordance with the socialist choice. We are looking within socialism, rather than outside it, for the answers to all the questions that arise. We assess our successes and errors alike by socialist standards. Those who hope that we shall move away from the socialist path will be greatly disappointed. Every part of our program of perestroika – and the program as a whole, for that matter – is fully based on the principle of more socialism and more democracy.

As we understand it, the difficulties and problems of the seventies and eighties did not signify some kind of crisis for socialism as a social and political system, but rather were the result of insufficient consistency in applying the principles of socialism.

Perestroika is a revolution

Perestroika is a word with many meanings. But if we are to choose from its many possible synonyms the key one which expresses its essence most accurately, then we can say thus: perestroika is a revolution. A decisive acceleration of the socioeconomic and cultural development of Soviet society which involves radical changes on the way to a qualitatively new state is undoubtedly a revolutionary task.

And yet, why in the seventieth year of the October Revolution do we speak of a new revolution? Historical analogy may be helpful in answering this question. Lenin once noted that in the country of the classical bourgeois revolution, France, after its Great Revolution of 1789–93, it took another three revolutions (1830, 1848 and 1871) to carry through its aims. The same applies to Britain where, after the Cromwellian Revolution of 1649, came the 'glorious' Revolution of 1688–89, and then the 1832 reform was necessary to finally establish the new class in power – the bourgeoisie. In Germany there were two bourgeois-democratic revolutions (1848 and 1918), and in between them the drastic reforms of the 1860s, which Bismarck carried out by 'iron and blood.'

'Never in history,' wrote Lenin, 'has there been a revolution in which it was

possible to lay down one's arms and rest on one's laurels after the victory.'
Why then should not socialism, called upon to carry out even more profound
socio-political and cultural changes in society's development than capitalism,
go through several revolutionary stages in order to reveal its full potential and
finally crystallize as a radically new formation?

[Perestroika is a revolutionary process for it is a jump forward in the
development of socialism, in the realization of its essential characteristics.]
From the outset we realized that we had no time to lose. It is very important
not to stay too long on the starting line, to overcome the lag, to get out of the
quagmire of conservatism, and to break the inertia of stagnation. This cannot
be done in a evolutionary way, by timid, creeping reforms. We simply have no
right to relax, even for a day.]

One of the signs of a revolutionary period is a more or less pronounced
discrepancy between vital interests of society whose front ranks are ready for
major changes, and the immediate, day-to-day interests of people. Perestroika
hits hardest those who are used to working in the old way. We have no
political opposition, but this does not mean there is no confrontation with
those who, for various reasons, do not accept perestroika. Everyone will
probably have to make sacrifices at the first stage of perestroika, but some will
have to give up for good the privileges and prerogatives which they do not
deserve and which they have acquired illegitimately, and the rights which have
impeded our progress. Conservatism does not want to give way, but all this
can and must be overcome if we want to meet the long-term interests of
society and every individual.

We actually faced the issue of the relationship between immediate and
long-term interests when we began introducing state quality inspection. To
improve the quality of products we instituted an independent body for ensuring
that products met existing standards. At first many workers' earnings dropped,
but the improved quality was needed by society and workers regarded the new
measure with understanding. There were no protests from them. On the
contrary, workers now say: 'It is shameful to get what you have not earned.' At
the same time, they want managers, engineers and technical personnel to
assume the same attitude. So state quality inspection has become a good
testing ground for perstroika. It revealed people's attitudes to work and
human reserves which could be utilized for perestroika. State quality inspection has become a litmus test confirming once again that the Soviet working
class as a whole totally supports the restructuring, and is ready to promote it,
fulfilling in practice its role as the vanguard class of the socialist society.

It may seem that our current perestroika could be called a 'revolution
from above.' True, the perestroika drive started on the Communist Party's
initiative, and the Party leads it. We began from the top of the pyramid and
went down to its base, as it were. Still, the concept of 'revolution from above'
doesn't quite apply to our perestroika, at least it requires some qualifications.
[Yes, the Party leadership started it. The highest Party and state bodies]

elaborated and adopted the program. True, perestroika is not a spontaneous, but a governed process. But that's only one side of the matter.⌉

Perestroika would not have been a truly revolutionary undertaking, it would not have acquired its present scope, nor would it have had any firm chance of success if it had not merged the initiative from 'above' with the grass-roots movement; if it had not expressed the fundamental, long-term interests of all the working people; if the masses had not regarded it as their program, a response to their own thoughts and a recognition of their own demands; and if the people had not supported it so vehemently and effectively.

It is a distinctive feature and strength of perestroika that it is simultaneously a revolution 'from above' and 'from below.' This is one of the most reliable guarantees of its success and irreversibility.

> Abridged from Mikhail Gorbachev (1988), *Perestroika: New Thinking for Our Country and the World*, revised edition, Fontana Collins, London, pp. 17–37, 49–57. Reprinted by permission of Harper Collins Publishers Ltd., New York.

4.13   Democratizing the political system

Stephen White

Political reform was not, at the outset, one of the chief priorities of the new administration. In July 1988, Gorbachev conceded that he had not, to begin with, fully appreciated the importance of political reform both for its own sake and for the contribution it could make to other social and economic objectives. At the Central Committee meeting which took place in January 1987 political reform became one of the central priorities of the new leadership. The plenum marked the beginning of a second, more broadly reformist stage in the development of the Gorbachev administration. Gorbachev made clear that economic reform was conceivable only in association with a far-reaching 'democratisation' of the political system. In his address to the 19th Party Conference, which met from 28 June to 1 July 1988, Gorbachev called for 'radical, reform' of the political system, not just 'democratisation', and went on to argue that it was crucial to the solution of all the other problems that faced Soviet society. The conference, after an extended debate remarkable for its plain speaking and lack of unanimity, duly adopted a series of resolutions calling for the further democratisation of Soviet society and reform of the political system. These proposals were carried further at Central Committee meetings in July and September, and were in turn the basis for a series of constitutional reforms which were approved in November and December 1988.

The new electoral law was adopted on 1 December 1988; the right to nominate was extended to voters' meetings of 500 or more (Art. 37), and an unlimited number of candidates could be put forward (Art. 38). Deputies were not allowed to hold governmental posts at the same time as they exercised their representative duties, and they were normally required to live or work in the area for which they had been nominated (Arts. 11 and 37). Candidates, moreover, were required to present 'programmes' to the electorate (Art. 45) and had the right to appoint up to ten campaign staff to assist them (Art. 46). Electors, for their part, were required to pass through a booth or room before casting their vote and to make a positive indication of their preference unless (exceptionally) only a single candidate was standing (Art. 53). The new law was to apply to all future elections, beginning with the national elections in March 1989. The constitutional amendments that were adopted by the Supreme Soviet, after a month of public discussion, on 1 December 1988 established that all soviets were to be elected for five rather than two and a half years at a time, and that no deputy could serve on more than two soviets at the same time (Arts. 90 and 96). Much more controversially, the Supreme Soviet accepted Gorbachev's proposal that the new supreme state body, the USSR Congress of People's Deputies containing 2250 deputies, meeting twice yearly, should be elected not only by the population at large and by national-territorial areas but also by a wide range of social organisations, including the CPSU, the trade unions and women's councils (Art. 109). The Congress would, as had been suggested, elect a new-style Supreme Soviet of 542 deputies which would meet, as a rule, for two three- or four-month sessions every year (Art. 112). A fifth of its members would stand down annually, as would a fifth of the membership of its standing committees (Arts. 111 and 122). Wide-ranging powers were given to the new Chairman of the USSR Supreme Soviet i.e. the State President, who was to exercise 'general guidance' over the work of state bodies, report on major questions of foreign and domestic affairs, make nominations to leading state positions, head the Defence Council of the USSR, and issue his own directives (Art. 121). It was also agreed, although not formally specified, that this post would normally be combined with the party leadership (and similarly at lower levels of government).

The party and its role

The Party Conference of June 1988 agreed that membership should be determined by political criteria rather than centrally-determined quotas; and meetings should be more critical and constructive. Central Committee members should be able to play a more active role in the work of the leadership; more records of party meetings should be published; and – a matter of 'prime importance' – all posts up to the Central Committee level should be filled by secret and competitive ballot for a maximum of two five-year terms. These reforms, like their counterparts in the state system, gradually began to be implemented over the months that followed. Further changes followed in the autumn of 1988 when the Central Committee approved six new commissions dealing respectively with party affairs, ideology, social and economic policy, agriculture, international affairs and law reform. Each of them was chaired by a senior member of the leadership, and taken as a whole they were intended to involve the Central Committee membership in policy formation at the highest level. The Central Committee apparatus was simplified and reduced in size: from 1988 onwards there were nine departments rather than twenty, and their total staff was reduced by about 30 percent.

Matters were taken further at a plenum in February 1990 at which the Central Committee accepted Gorbachev's proposal that the party should abandon its guaranteed leading role (in effect, that it should move the modification of Article 6 of the Constitution). Gorbachev was still concerned that the CPSU should play a 'consolidating' role in Soviet political life, indeed that it should remain a 'ruling' party and the 'political leader' of the society as a whole. Any position of this kind, however, should be won by a competitive struggle for popular support, not guaranteed in advance by the Constitution. Article 6 was modified in the Constitutional Amendment of March 1990.

The 28th Congress adopted a new set of rules later in 1990 which increased the rights of ordinary members still further. 'Platforms', if not organized factions, were approved, minority rights were strengthened, and 'horizontal' links between members and branches at the same level were specifically encouraged. All of this was designed to provide the basis, as Gorbachev saw it, for an 'updated CPSU' that would combine a parliamentary with its traditional vanguard role.

The outcome of such exhortations, by the early 1990s, was most unclear. There was little doubt, however, that the CPSU was restructuring itself much more slowly than other public organisations. More than a thousand local secretaries had been chosen on a competitive basis in the last round of party elections. This, however, was only 8.6 percent of the total. No fewer than 74 percent of the members of the new Congress of People's Deputies, by contrast, had been elected from a choice of candidate.

Still more important the party began to lose members, particularly among the working class. The rate of increase in party membership, first of all, slowed down, and then in 1989 it recorded its first decline for more than thirty years. In 1990 and 1991 the decline was precipitous: over 4 million members left the party in a period of eighteen months, about a quarter of the total, and the great majority of them 'of their own volition'. More than 300 Communist deputies to the Russian and Soviet parliaments left the party, and even members of the party's own Central Committee. The Komsomol, the party's youth wing, fell more sharply still, losing about a quarter of its members in 1990 alone (in 1991, after the coup, it disappeared entirely). The circulation of the party press fell dramatically (most party publications lost between two-thirds and three-quarters of their subscribers), and over a million members fell behind with their dues (a phenomenon that had earlier been almost unknown). The party organisation as a whole began to run at a loss, and a regime of 'severe economy' had to be instituted; Gorbachev, speaking in July 1991, himself called it the most serious crisis in the party's history.

Lacking clear agreement on fundamentals, and hardly successful in terms of its performance, the party began to lose the 'monolithic unity' on which it had earlier insisted. Several organised groupings made their appearance in the months before the 28th Party Congress: a liberal 'Democratic Platform' and a more orthodox 'Marxist Platform' among others. By the early 1990s, according to party officials, there were 'at least a dozen' currents of this kind within the party's ranks. They ranged from a 'social democratic' wing at one extreme, to a hard-line 'Unity' grouping at the other, who planned a return to the Communist Party as it had existed in late Stalinist times. There were open revolts against local party leaderships. A few republican party organisations, in turn, fragmented or seceded from the CPSU altogether: the Lithuanian party was the first to leave, in December 1989, followed by the Georgian party a year later and by the Moldavian party early in 1991. More generally, throughout the USSR increasing numbers of party members elected to the soviets refused to accept any direction of their activities. The party's public standing declined sharply. By July 1990 only 14 percent 'completely trusted' the CPSU, as compared with 38 percent who had 'absolutely no confidence' in it. It was this mistrust, strengthened by the apparent complicity of its leadership in the coup, that later allowed Boris Yel'tsin first to suspend and then to ban the party altogether (by September 1991, following the coup, only 2.3 percent were still prepared to give the party their 'full support').

An entirely new concept, the 'socialist law-based state' became the centrepiece of a resolution adopted at the conference of June 1988. This called for 'large-scale legal reform' over the coming years, including a review of existing codes of law, greater safeguards for the independence of judges, and an extensive programme of legal education for the population as a whole. The process of reform was carried further in the constitutional amendments that were adopted by the Supreme Soviet on 1 December 1988. In perhaps the most notable of these changes, a twenty-three member Committee of Constitutional Supervision was established, elected by the Congress from 'specialists in politics and law', with responsibility for ensuring the constitutionality of governmental decisions and draft legislation (Art. 125). Judges, in addition, were to be elected by soviets at the level immediately above them, and for ten, rather than five, years at a time (Art. 152). All of this, in Gorbachev's view, represented a distinctive 'socialist system of checks and balances'.

A greater emphasis upon the rule of law helped equally to encourage the growth of a more autonomous citizen-based politics, reflecting what Gorbachev described, from 1988 onwards, as a 'socialist pluralism of opinions'.

Of great significance, in terms of the development of a Soviet 'civil society', was the formation from 1987 onwards of a range of 'informal' movements, so called because of their distrust of organisational structures and their ambiguous status under Soviet law. Although it was difficult to establish the number and, still more, the membership of such groups, it was estimated in 1990 that there were between two and three thousand of them with a national membership of at least two million. Ecological movements had much more support than those that had directly political objectives; but among those that came into this last category at least four broad tendencies could be identified.

First of all, there were a number of liberal-socialist associations which, supported the main principles of *perestroika* but wished to accelerate it in various directions. Memorial, for instance, established in August 1988, sought to reconstitute the historical record of Stalinism by collecting oral and other forms of testimony. The Federation of Socialist Clubs sought to revive the democratic principles that were, in their view, inherent in socialism. 'Moscow Tribune', founded in 1988, sought to democratise the election law, to extend the rights of nationalities and to reduce administrative control over the economy; its membership was largely confined to academics and professionals. Most of these concerns overlapped with those of a second group, the popular fronts, which came into existence in the Baltic and other republics from 1987 onwards. Although they naturally attached a much higher priority to the national question, the fronts also emphasised issues such as an honest historiography, economic decentralisation and the environment, and they drew upon a very much wider base of public support.

Less easy to reconcile with official policy were two other trends in the 'informal' movement. The Democratic Union, founded in 1988, took the view that Gorbachev's *perestroika* was too limited in its objectives and argued that the sociopolitical order established in October 1917 was a 'system of stagnant totalitarianism in conditions of the omnipotence of the *nomenklatura*', and it openly adopted the role of an oppositional political party dedicated to the overthrow of the CPSU and the socialist order it represented. *Pamyat'* also rejected Soviet socialism, but held it to be Jewish and not simply a Marxist conspiracy. In its early stages a movement in defence of the Russian cultural heritage *Pamyat'*, from 1986 onwards, became increasingly chauvinist and antisemitic in character. The official media, in a succession of warnings, emphasised that there could be no room in the USSR for 'open attacks' on the Soviet order or for 'pluralism on the Western model'.

The 1989 elections to the Congress of People's Deputies

The first real test of political reform was the elections which took place in March 1989 to the USSR Congress of People's Deputies. Under the new law the campaign was to proceed in two stages. In the first, nominations were to be made and then approved by a selection conference in the constituency or social organisation for which the candidate was seeking election. In the second, the candidates who had been 'registered' in this way were to compete for the support of their respective electorates: in the ordinary constituencies up to polling day, which was fixed for 26 March 1989, or in the social organisations up to an election meeting at some point during the previous fortnight. This was a new, elaborate and largely unfamiliar set of procedures; it was also one to which many citizens had strong objections. The representation that had been given to social organisations, in particular, appeared to violate the principle of 'one person, one vote', and the holding of selection conferences to approve a final list of candidates was also unpopular. In any case this stage in the proceedings was bypassed in Estonia, most of Lithuania and some districts of Moscow precisely in order to leave such choices to the electorate.

The selection of candidates in the social organisations took a variety of forms. The Communist Party itself caused some controversy by nominating no more than 100 names for the 100 seats it had been allocated under the constitution. The selection of candidates in the constituencies took a still wider variety of forms. A selection conference at Melitopol in the Ukraine, for instance, was packed out by officials to such an extent that it reminded one participant of a conference of party activists. The party secretary was duly registered by an overwhelming majority. In other constituencies, however, a rather more open atmosphere prevailed. In Moscow's Lenin territorial constituency no. 1, for instance, a 'long and heated struggle' took place to determine which of the thirteen nominations should be placed upon the ballot paper.

An overall turnout of 89.8 percent must be accounted a considerable success, modest though it was compared with the artificially inflated totals of previous years. The results, constituency by constituency, were still more remarkable. Some 2,884 candidates had been selected to contest the 1,500 constituencies; in 384 of them, despite the intentions of the new law, there was just a single nomination, but elsewhere there was a choice and in one Moscow constituency as many as twelve candidates were competing for the support of voters. In the event, in seventy-six of the constituencies where three or more candidates had been nominated none secured more than half the votes and a run-off between the two most successful candidates had to be announced, to be held within the following two weeks. Under the election law the result would be determined by a relative majority, not an absolute one. Unexpectedly, however, in 195 constituencies where only one or two candidates were standing none of them secured more than half the vote and no result could be declared. This meant that in these constituencies the whole exercise would have to be repeated, beginning with the nomination of new and normally different candidates, within a two-month period. In a further three constituencies there would have to be a repeat ballot because fewer than half of the registered electors had voted.

Still more unexpected was the number of defeats suffered by leading party and state officials. A whole series of local leaders, admittedly, were successfully returned. But the defeats that were suffered by local party and state leaders were remarkable. The prime minister of Latvia was defeated, and the prime minister and president of Lithuania; so too were some thirty-eight regional and district party secretaries throughout the country. The mayors of Moscow and Kiev were defeated. The runaway success of Yel'tsin in Moscow (with 89.4 percent of the vote) was a particular snub to the party authorities, given the attempts that had been made to frustrate his campaign. The most spectacular defeats of all, however, were in Leningrad, where the list of casualties included the regional first secretary (a candidate member of the Politburo) and the second secretary, the chairman of the city soviet and his deputy, the chairman of the regional soviet and the city party secretary.

The Congress of People's Deputies and Supreme Soviet

The representative institutions that emerged from this new-style electoral process were very different from the 'supreme state organs' that had preceded them. There were, in fact, more party members than ever before, despite the setbacks that some of its leading officials had suffered: 87.6 percent of the new deputies were CPSU members or candidates. The scientific and cultural intelligentsia was much more fully represented in the new Congress than in the old Supreme Soviet. There were five religious leaders, the first ever elected to Soviet legislative body; rural leaseholders and commercial cooperators were also represented for the first time. The Congress was also less representative in a sociological sense of the population that had elected it. The proportion of women deputies, most notably, was down by about half, from 32.8 to 17.1 percent, and would have been lower still but for the seventy-five seats specifically reserved for women's councils. The proportion of workers and collective farmers, equally, was down by about half: workers from 34.3 percent in the outgoing Supreme Soviet to 17.9 percent in the new Congress, and collective farmers from 10.6 to 4.9 percent.

The Congress of People's Deputies, which held its first session on 25 May 1989, made a number of further innovations in Soviet political and constitutional practice. Gorbachev, as expected, was elected to the newly-established post of Chairman of the Supreme Soviet; what could hardly have been predicted was that two candidates were nominated to stand against him and that he secured election, after a series of searching questions from the deputies, by a less than unanimous vote (2,123 in favour, but 87 against). The Congress established a constitutional commission to prepare a replacement for the document adopted in the Brezhnev era; it also set up a commission to investigate the 1939 Nazi-Soviet pact.

One of the Congress's first acts was to set up the new-style Supreme Soviet, a much smaller body which was expected to remain in session for most of the year. The elections were based in part on a regional quota system; Boris Yel'tsin, nominated for the Russian Republic, failed at first to secure election but then obtained a place when another deputy stood down in his favour. The new Supreme Soviet when it met for the first time on 3 June soon showed that it would be a very different institution from its unlamented predecessor. One sign of this was the elaborate committee system that was set up, including committees of the Supreme Soviet as a whole and commissions attached to each of its two chambers. One of the Supreme Soviet's new committees dealt with defence and state security; another with *glasnost'* and the rights of citizens. Some 928 deputies, about half of whom were members of the Supreme Soviet itself, were elected to serve on the new committees and commissions; and at least two-thirds of the work of the new parliament was expected to take place under their auspices. Potentially much more important was the formation of an inter-regional deputies' group, in effect a radical caucus, under the effective leadership of Boris Yel'tsin. Nearly 400 deputies attended its inaugural meeting at the end of July 1989 and some 260 agreed to join it. The group, which had its own funds and newspaper, was at least potentially the beginning of a form of parliamentary politics unprecedented in the Soviet period.

The structure of government was also revised. There were to be no more than fifty-seven ministries and state committees altogether, twenty-five existing ministries were to be wound up; and those that remained were to be 'ministries of a new type', exercising general rather than detailed guidance within their sphere of competence. What was certainly new was the attention with which these nominees were received: both in committee and later in the Supreme Soviet itself the candidates were intensively questioned, and about a third of Ryzhkov's original nominations were rejected.

Republican elections and party formation

At the Second Congress of People's Deputies in December 1989 it was made clear that Congresses of People's Deputies would not be obligatory at the republican level (Art. 91); in the event only the Russian Republic introduced the complicated two-level parliamentary institution that remained in existence at the national level. It was decided to make no reference at all to the representation of social organisations in the USSR Constitution; the Congress of People's Deputies would continue to be composed in the same way, but republics would be free to make their own arrangements. In the event, two of them – Kazakhstan and Belorussia decided to retain such representation in their republican parliaments. The reference to selection conferences, equally, was dropped from the Constitution, allowing republics to make their own decisions. The number of candidates that were to be nominated remained as before: there could be any number, leaving the decision (at least in principle) to the electorate.

The republican and local elections that took place upon the basis of this amended law were held over a period of months and often on different dates. The elections in the Baltic were among the first: in Estonia, for instance, elections to local soviets took place in December 1989 and to the republican Supreme Soviet in March 1990. More than twenty organised groups took place in the elections to the republican parliament; the Communist Party took 55 of the 105 seats, but it was the Popular Front, with 46 seats and allies in other groups, that headed the largest group of deputies and provided the new prime minister. The outcomes in the other Baltic states were broadly similar, with sweeping successes for nationalist candidates. This was particularly true of Lithuania, where 90 of the 141 seats in the elections of February 1990 went to supporters of Sajudis; the Communist Party's leading role had been removed from the republican constitution the previous December and these were, in effect, the first genuinely competitive elections in Soviet history.

The Slavic republics voted in early March 1990. Over 6,700 candidates competed for the 1,068 seats that were available in the Russian Republic, with up to 28 nominations for a single seat. The 'Democratic Russia' bloc of candidates enjoyed considerable success, taking 20–23 percent of the vote in the republic as a whole and a considerably larger share in the cities and after several inconclusive votes its candidate, the former Moscow party secretary Boris Yel'tsin, was elected to the chairmanship of the republican Supreme Soviet on 29 May. Another radical, the economist Gavriil Popov, became mayor of Moscow, and Anatolii Sobchak, up to this point a law professor, became head of the city administration in Leningrad. All three announced their resignation from the Communist Party later in the year.

In the Ukraine large numbers of seats were won by candidates associated with the nationalist movement 'Rukh' and the Greens; Rukh, for instance, took control of Kiev and of much of the west of the republic (a nationalist heartland). In Georgia, the elections which finally took place at the end of October led to the clear victory of a nationalist coalition, Round Table/Free Georgia, which took 54 percent of the vote as compared with the Communists' 29.6 percent. Shortly afterwards the veteran dissident Zviad Gamsakhurdia was elected republican president on a programme of transition to full independence. As before, there was least competition in Central Asia. In Uzbekistan, for instance, about a third of seats in the February 1990 elections had only one candidate, and a 'good half' of all the candidates were managers or executives.

The republican elections in the spring and autumn of 1990 had a number of common characteristics. In the first place, turnout levels were down on those that had been recorded a year earlier, particularly in the later rounds of voting and in the towns as compared with the countryside. Turnout levels, as in March 1989, were higher in Central Asia than in the other republics; Armenia, on both occasions, recorded the lowest figures. Secondly, there was a greater degree of electoral choice than in the elections to the Congress of

People's Deputies, although the level of competition remained much lower in Central Asia and in the elections to local rather than republican levels of government. As a result, larger numbers of seats remained unfilled after the first round of balloting than ever before; the whole exercise became a lengthier and, inevitably, a more expensive one (Estonia, the only republic to employ the single transferable vote system, was able to avoid most of these difficulties). The candidates, in the third place, remained overwhelmingly CPSU members, but a greater share of seats than ever before went to managers, executives, academics and clerics, and the representation of workers, collective farmers, women and young people declined even further. And finally, there was a significantly higher level of party or organised group activity, with the beginnings of co-ordinated platforms across or within republics. This was particularly true of the Baltic and the major cities.

Party formation, in the early 1990s, was still at a rudimentary level, with no clear association between a candidate's programme, his organisational affiliation and his subsequent behaviour in the legislature. There were, however, at least 20 parties in operation on an all-union basis by this time, with a membership ranging from a few dozen to some tens of thousands. In addition, about 500 parties were active at the republican level. Membership figures were difficult to establish. The new parties fell into two main types: 'vanguard parties' (which had adopted some of the organisational forms of the CPSU and were in some cases successors to it), and 'movement parties' (which were similar to the broadly-based popular coalitions that had been formed in Eastern Europe in the late 1980s). The Democratic Party, an example of the first of these, based itself on democratic centralism and exercised strict discipline over the activities of its members; the Democratic Union, which fell into the second category, did not impose the decisions of its leadership upon the mass membership and allowed the formation of organised factions (even of communists) within its ranks. All of these parties operated within the framework of a Law on Public Associations, approved in October 1990, which laid the formal basis of a multiparty system.

There was certainly no shortage of parties, with or without the law that gave them a legal basis: a reference guide published in late 1991 listed over 300 of them, including nine anarchist parties, 17 different monarchist groupings and no fewer than 53 'national-patriotic' parties. Some restored the names of pre-revolutionary parties, like the Constitutional Democrats or Kadets; other took more obvious labels, such as the Liberal Democratic or Social Democratic Party; and others still were more inventive. There was a Humour Party, founded in Odessa, and an Idiots' Party of Russia, certain of victory in a 'land of fools', with its persuasive slogan 'Give the people beer and sausage!' By August 1991, however, only two parties had completed all the necessary formalities: the Liberal Democratic Party and the Communist Party, whose registration had obviously no practical effect after its suspension. As late as November 1991 only twelve parties had been formally registered under

Soviet and Russian law, although the deadline for doing so was the end of December, a new and multiparty system had, nonetheless, clearly come into being, and it represented a recognisable spectrum of opinion.

On the 'right' (in the sense that it sought generally to return to the pre-Soviet order) there were a number of business parties including one that openly entitled itself the Bourgeois Democratic Party, representing the interests of small and medium enterpreneurs. There was an Order of Orthodox Monarchists, and several Christian Democratic parties. More significant, among the new parties, were the Liberal Democratic Party and the grouping collectively known as 'Democratic Russia'. The Liberal Democratic Party, established in 1990, was formally dedicated to the idea of a state based on law and a market economy. In practice, however, it became identified with the extravagant views of its leader, Vladimir Zhirinovsky, who came third in the Russian presidential elections in the summer of 1991 with over six million votes. Zhirinovsky called for the re-establishment of the Russian state within the boundaries of the USSR, or if possible those of January 1917, or 'ideally' those of 1865; after the coup, which he openly supported, he suggested that the LDP might form part of a 'bloc of patriotic parties' in opposition to democrats and radicals. 'Democratic Russia', whose founding congress was held in Moscow in October 1990, was a more loosely structured coalition of political forces originally formed to contest the republican elections of that year in opposition to the CPSU, it was able to mobilise enormous numbers of demonstrators in support of Boris Yel'tsin in early 1991, but its effectiveness was seriously damaged when three member parties withdrew at its second congress in November 1991.

About twenty different parties and movements constituted the 'centre' of the political spectrum, including the Russian Popular Front, the Democratic Reform Movement and the Democratic Party of Russia. This, according to most estimates, was the largest of the new parties, with about 50,000 members in the early 1990s. Founded in May 1990, the Democratic Pary declared its aim to be the restoration of an independent Russian democratic state within a voluntary union of republics. State power was to be decentralised, and a 'society of equal opportunities' was to be created on the basis of market relations and equality of all forms of property. Travkin, a national and Russian people's deputy, was the party's most prominent public spokesman. The Democratic Reform Movement, formally established in December 1991, saw itself as a 'third force' between authoritarianism and anarchy; its leaders included many former members of the Gorbachev administration, including Alexander Yakovlev and Eduard Shevardnadze, and its membership was disproportionately drawn from scientific staff, academics and professionals.

Finally, there was a 'left' grouping based upon the Socialist and Social Democratic parties, the Greens and an anarcho-syndicalist confederation. These groups were joined in November 1990 by the Republican Party of the Russian Federation, a 'left centrist party of the parliamentary type', which occupied an intermediate position between the CPSU and the Democratic Party. The Republican Party consisted largely of former members of the CPSU who had been members of the Democratic Platform, a group that had been active in pressing for party democratisation before the 28th Congress. Estimates suggested that this was, by the early 1990s, the second largest of the new parties, with about 20,000 members; the Social Democrats and Christian Democrats had about 10,000 members each, and other parties 'significantly less'. Further to the left were the political groupings that claimed the political legacy – and often the property – of the former CPSU. These included the Soviet Communist Party of Bolsheviks, which accused Gorbachev of 'betrayal of the cause of Lenin'; the Russian Communist Workers' Party; the Russian Communist Party, which was based on the former Marxist Platform within the CPSU; the Socialist Workers' Party, which included the historian and deputy Roy Medvedev; and a re-established Menshevik Party. Rather more influential was the People's Party of Free Russia, originally a 'Communists for democracy' grouping in the Ruissian parliament, led by Vice-President Alexander Rutskoi; on some counts this was the largest of the new parties, with an estimated 100,000 members.

There were clearly weaknesses in the new party system that had developed beside and (later) in the place of the CPSU. One of these was their limited membership. Another was a recurrent tendency to divide. More serious than this, perhaps, was a general failure to articulate a clear and distinctive political position apart from opposition to the CPSU, and a related failure to establish a social base.

The executive Presidency

The converse of this process of pluralisation, party formation and republican assertiveness was a strengthening of central authority, above all through the establishment of an executive Presidency in 1990.

Any citizen aged between 35 and 65 could be elected to the Presidency for a maximum of two five-year terms. The President was normally to be elected by universal, equal and direct suffrage, although in the difficult circumstances that obtained it was agreed that Gorbachev – exceptionally – would be elected by the Congress itself. Gorbachev was duly elected to the new post on 15 March, although he received no more than 59 percent of the votes of all the members of the Congress (or 71 percent of those who took part) in an uncontested ballot. The President, under the terms of the legislation, was to report annually to the Congress of People's Deputies and would brief the Supreme Soviet on the 'most important questions of the USSR's domestic and foreign policy'. He would propose candidates for the premiership and other leading state positions; he had a suspensory veto over legislation; and he could dissolve the government and suspend its directives. He could also declare a state of emergency, and introduce direct presidential rule.

The President headed a new Council of the Federation, consisting of the presidents of the fifteen union republics, with responsibility for inter-ethnic and inter-republican issues; he also headed a new Presidential Council, which was responsible for the 'main directions of the USSR's foreign and domestic policy'.

In September 1990 these already impressive powers were extended by parliamentary vote, giving Gorbachev the right to institute emergency measures to 'stabilise the country's sociopolitical life' for a period of 18 months. Several further changes were made by the Fourth Congress of People's Deputies in December 1990, completing the move to a fully presidential administration. The Council of Ministers was replaced by a more limited 'Cabinet', headed by a prime minister who – together with his colleagues – would be nominated by the President and accountable to him (the former finance minister, Valentin Pavlov, was elected to this position in January 1991). The President became head of a new Security Council with overall responsibility for defence and public order (he himself appointed its other members). He also appointed a new Vice-President, responsible for carrying out the functions that were entrusted to him (Gennadii Yanaev, a member of the Secretariat who had formerly worked in the trade union movement and Komsomol, was elected to this position on 27 December). The Presidential Council, formed the previous March, disappeared entirely, and a reconstituted Council of the Federation headed by the President became, in effect, the supreme state decision-making body.

There was some concern among Soviet liberals that these extensive powers, greater even than Stalin had commanded, could open the way to a new dictatorship. There were, in fact, considerable limitations upon the powers of the new President, extensive though they undoubtedly were. He could be impeached by a two-thirds vote of the Congress of People's Deputies; his ministerial nominations required the approval of the Supreme Soviet, which could force the resignation of the Cabinet as a whole if it voted accordingly; and he had himself to report annually to the Congress of People's Deputies upon the exercise of his responsibilities.

Gorbachev's real power, in any case, was far less than his formal pre-rogatives might have suggested. Indeed by the early 1990s he was, politically, the least powerful leader the Soviet Union had yet experienced. He was, for instance, the first Soviet leader to face an open call for his resignation, not only as President but also as General Secretary. His presidential decrees, moreover, were ignored or even rejected by the bodies that were responsible for implementing them. Most fundamentally of all, the authority of the central government, for so long unchallengeable, was undermined by the decision (during 1990) of all fifteen union republics to declare their laws sovereign over those of the USSR as a whole. The Soviet Constitution, adopted in 1977, insisted upon the opposite; but its effective force had by the early 1990s become so limited that the illegality of the republics' action was not even a subject of public discussion.

Political change and the Soviet public

It was none the less far from clear, by the early 1990s, that this new-style Soviet political system represented a stable and workable combination of centralised direction 'from above' with democratic control 'from below'. There was considerable opposition, in the first place, to the shortcomings that still remained in the new electoral system. The early experience of 'democratisation' was also a somewhat disillusioning one. The new-style soviets, it emerged, had rather limited powers, and often made little use of them in any case.

The system of linkage that had been established between Soviet voters and the making of public policy was an unsatisfactory one in several other respects. Deputies, for example, had relatively few opportunities to press the popular demands on the basis of which they had been elected, as only a small minority of them could serve as full-time legislators at any time. The others, people's deputies but not members of the Supreme Soviet, were able to attend meetings of the Congress of People's Deputies once or twice a year, and perhaps an occasional committee meeting, but had otherwise little more to do than members of the discredited Supreme Soviet of old. There was, in any case, no obvious mechanism to connect public concerns with the conduct of government. Candidates at the election put forward individual programmes, and could hardly offer a co-ordinated programme of action for the country as a whole. Nor could they, as isolated legislators, put forward a list of deputies who might form an alternative administration. For purposes of this kind the experience of Western nations has devised an effective instrument: the political party, which sponsors candidates in all or most constituencies and presents a coherent and notionally workable programme of government for the forthcoming period. If Soviet elections were to provide a meaningful choice it was likely to be difficult to resist the logic of a choice of parties, not just of individuals; and it was this that appeared to have inspired the growth of electoral blocs and the rapid, even chaotic growth of new parties in the early 1990s. The logic of an organised choice of political alternatives, however, left no obvious role for the Communist Party, supposedly the instrument uniquely capable of articulating the real interests of all working people.

Political reform, by the early 1990s, had certainly succeeded in dismantling a largely Stalinist inheritance; but it had not yet succeeded in replacing it with a viable combination of Leninism and democracy, of central party control which yet allowed the voters to be sovereign. Voters could reject party officials, but not, at least nationally, effect a change of regime. The new representative system, with its inclusion of a range of organised interests, lent itself to the articulation of grievances rather than solutions. Most fundamentally of all, there was an unresolved tension between the 'will of the people', expressed through open and competitive elections, and the 'will of the party', based ultimately on the doctrine of Marxism – Leninism.

If there was to be a reconciliation of these two principles, at least for a limited and transitional period, the only possible basis in the early 1990s appeared to be a form of power sharing. In April 1991 the heads of state of nine republics – meeting at Novo-Ogarevo, a government house near Moscow – agreed a joint declaration on measures to deal with the crisis that had developed in every sphere, but particularly in the Soviet economy. The agreement, similar in some respects to the 'round tables' that had been convened in Eastern Europe during the transition from communist rule, became known as the '9 + 1'; it was to be followed by the adoption of a new constitution and fresh elections at all levels of government.

The agreement made it clear that 'Leninism' no longer provided a sufficient basis on which to exercise political authority. Indeed it acknowledged that not even an indirectly elected President and a partly elected parliament had the authority that was necessary to address a deepening political as well as economic crisis. Only a properly representative government, it appeared, would have the legitimacy that was needed to make unpopular decisions and then ensure their implementation; and at least in the short term, this meant a 'government of national unity' bringing together the CPSU and other parties and movements that had demonstrated their popular support of and commitment to constitutional politics. This was certainly the end of the CPSU as a party uniquely qualified to articulate the national interest; it was not, perhaps, necessarily the end of the CPSU as a party that could at least contribute to the formation of national policy. Communist parties had of course lost power elsewhere in Eastern Europe in 1989 and 1990, but in these countries communist rule had generally been an external imposition. The end of communist rule in the USSR stemmed much more directly from the party's failure to articulate a convincing vision of the Soviet future and to democratise its own manner of operation; its leaders committed the party's support to the attempted coup of August 1991, and its members – who had never exercised much influence in the party that spoke in their name – were left to pay the price. This certainly resolved the tension between Leninism and popular sovereignty; it did not, by itself, provide a basis for stable government in the divided and recessionary society of the later 1990s.

Abridged from Stephen White (1992), *Gorbachev and After*, revised edition, pp. 28–30, 34–41, 252–6, 42–75. Reprinted by permission of Cambridge University Press, Cambridge.

4.14   The August 1991 coup

Stephen White

The attempted coup of August 1991, which led to Gorbachev's resignation, was itself a demonstration of the limits of a leadership style that placed its main emphasis upon personal rather than institutional change. Many of the conspirators had been Gorbachev's own appointees, even friends. The coup, in fact, had not come without warning. Foreign minister Eduard Shevardnadze, tendering his resignation in December 1990, warned the Soviet parliament that a 'dictatorship' was approaching although no one yet knew what form it would take.

Nevertheless, the attempted coup of August 1991 was a shock as well as a surprise to the Soviet leader and to the outside world. August was the month in which the Soviet President normally took his family holidays in the Crimea. He was working on the text of a speech on 18 August when four emissaries arrived unexpectedly from Moscow. All his telephones had been disconnected. Gorbachev refused either to resign or to sign a decree instituting a state of emergency, and was thereupon placed under house arrest and isolated from the outside world. In the early hours of 19 August a self-styled State Emergency Committee informed a startled world that Gorbachev was 'unwell' and unable to perform his duties; his responsibilities would be assumed under these circumstances by his Vice-President, Gennadii Yanaev. The Emergency Committee, it later emerged, had eight members. Apart from Yanaev himself there was the KGB chairman, Vladimir Kryuchkov; the Defence Minister, Dmitri Yazov; the Interior Minister, Boris Pugo; the Prime Minister, Valentin Pavlov; and three other members of less prominence. Yanaev, and four other members of the Committee, addressed a hastily convened press conference later the same day; Gorbachev, they promised, would return to his position as soon as his health had improved.

The Committee, in a series of decrees, meanwhile suspended the activities of all parties (other than those that supported the emergency), banned the publication of all but a small number of newspapers (including *Pravda*), ordered the surrender of firearms, and prohibited meetings, strikes and demonstrations. It also promised to cut prices and increase wages, and to place food supplies under strict control with priority being given to schools, hospitals, pensioners and the disabled. In a 'message to the Soviet people', broadcast on the morning of 19 August, the Committee offered a more extended justification of its action. The Soviet people, it explained, were in 'mortal danger'. *Perestroika* had reached an 'impasse'. The country had become 'ungovernable'. Not only this: 'extremist forces' had emerged that were seeking to break up the Soviet state and to seize power for themselves.

The economy was in crisis, with the breakdown of central planning, a 'chaotic, ungoverned slide towards a market', and famine a real possibility. Crime and immorality were rampant. The Committee, it promised, would reverse these trends, strengthen public order, arrest the fall in living standards and restore the Soviet Union's international standing; it appealed, in turn, for the support of 'all true patriots and people of goodwill', making no reference at all to socialism.

The coup, it soon became clear, had been poorly planned – two of its principal members, Yanaev and Pavlov, appear to have been drunk for most of its duration – and it was opposed from the outset by Boris Yel'tsin, now Russian President, who made a dramatic call for resistance on 19 August standing on one of the tanks stationed outside the Russian parliament building. Yel'tsin denounced the Committee's action as a 'right-wing, reactionary, unconstitutional coup' and declared all its decisions illegal. Gorbachev, he insisted, must be restored immediately to his position, and he called for an indefinite strike until the Soviet parliament had met and constitutional propriety had been reestablished. Huge demonstrations in front of the Russian parliament the following day were addressed by Shevardnadze, Yakovlev, Andrei Sakharov's widow Yelena Bonner and other democrats. The critical moment was the evening of 20 August when about 70,000 Muscovites defied the curfew and assembled in front of the 'White House' to defend it against an expected attack by pro-coup forces. That night, three men were killed – one shot and two crushed by tanks on the Moscow ring road – but the attack on the Russian parliament itself did not materialise. It later emerged that substantial sections of the armed forces had declared against the coup, and that the elite KGB 'Alpha' anti-terrorist group had rejected the order they had been given to storm the building.

On Wednesday 21 August the coup began to collapse. The Russian parliament met in emergency session and gave Yel'tsin their unqualified support. Media restrictions were lifted, and the Ministry of Defence ordered troops to return to their barracks. The USSR Supreme Soviet Presidium declared the actions of the Emergency Committee illegal, and the Procurator General's office announced that criminal proceedings for high treason had been instigated against its members.

Gorbachev was flown back to Moscow in the early hours of 22 August, where he later addressed a crowded press conference. There was some surprise that the Soviet leader continued to defend the Communist Party, whose role in the attempted coup had been obscure. Later, however, when the complicity of the party leadership became clear, Gorbachev resigned the general secretaryship and called upon the Central Committee to take the 'difficult but honourable decision to dissolve itself'. Yel'tsin had signed a decree suspending the activity of the Communist Party throughout the Russian Federation on 23 August, at a meeting of the Russian parliament that Gorbachev himself attended, and a few days later the USSR Supreme Soviet suspended the activities of the party throughout the Soviet Union; its bank accounts and financial operations had meantime been frozen, and its buildings placed under the control of local soviets.

The Soviet Union itself was a still greater casualty of the coup. Launched to block the signature of a new union treaty, the conspirators – in the end – accelerated the collapse of the state they had sought to preserve. Lithuania had already declared its independence, in the spring of 1990; the other Baltic republics followed immediately; and by the end of the year all of the republics, apart from Russia, had adopted declarations of a similar kind. Several of them had in addition begun to establish their own armies, and had applied to join the United Nations. Finally, in December 1991, the three Slavic republics – Russia, the Ukraine and Belorussia – established a new Commonwealth of Independent States, which was later joined by almost all of the other former Soviet republics. The new Commonwealth was not a state, it had no common parliament, and in particular it had no presidency; the states concerned also agreed that its establishment brought an end to the political union that had originally been established in 1922. With the disappearance of the USSR and of its Presidency Gorbachev's position became untenable and he resigned his last remaining public office on 25 December 1991. The post-Soviet era had begun.

Abridged from Stephen White (1992), *Gorbachev and After*, revised edition, pp. 23–7. Reprinted by permission of Cambridge University Press, Cambridge.

Index